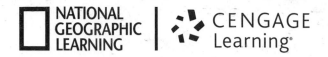
NATIONAL
GEOGRAPHIC
LEARNING

CENGAGE
Learning

Life

UPPER INTERMEDIATE

TEACHER'S BOOK

David A. Hill

Life Upper Intermediate Teacher's book
David A. Hill

Publisher: Jason Mann

Commissioning Editor: Alistair Baxter

Editorial Project Manager: Karen Spiller

Development Editor: Clare Shaw

Marketing Manager: Michelle Cresswell

Project Editor: Amy Smith

Production Controller: Elaine Willis

National Geographic Liaison: Leila Hishmeh

Art Director: Natasa Arsenidou

Cover design: Vasiliki Christoforidou

Text design: Vasiliki Christoforidou

Compositor: MPS Limited

Audio: Prolingua Productions

ISBN: 978-1-133-31547-6

National Geographic Learning
Cheriton House, North Way, Andover, Hampshire, SP10 5BE
United Kingdom

Cengage Learning is a leading provider of customised learning solutions with office locations around the globe, including Singapore, the United Kingdom, Australia, Mexico, Brazil and Japan. Locate our local office at **international.cengage.com/region**

Cengage Learning products are represented in Canada by Nelson Education Ltd.

Visit National Geographic Learning at **ngl.cengage.com**
Visit our corporate website at **www.cengage.com**

CREDITS

Although every effort has been made to contact copyright holders before publication, this has not always been possible. If notified, the publisher will undertake to rectify any errors or omissions at the earliest opportunity.

Photos

The publisher would like to thank the following sources for permission to reproduce their copyright protected photographs.
Cover: Paul Cheung/My Shot/National Geographic Image Collection
Inside: 12 (Randy Olson/National Geographic Image Collection), 15 (ShelterBox), 16 (Shutterstock).

Printed in China by RR Donnelley
1 2 3 4 5 6 7 8 9 10 – 16 15 14 13 12

Contents

Contents

4   Contents

Listening	Reading	Critical thinking	Speaking	Writing
three people talking about important relationships in their lives a radio extract about animal friendships	an article about changing attitudes in China an article about immigrant families in New York	identifying the main aspect	your friends the generation gap family influences	text type: an informal email (1) writing skill: greetings and endings
a conversation about different accounts of Ayrton Senna's life an interview with a film critic	a true story about dangerous animals an article about the brothers Grimm	close reading	the film of the book a famous writer or filmmaker narrow escapes storytelling	text type: a story writing skill: using descriptive words
three people making predictions about the future a presentation about overpopulation	an article about augmented reality an article about appropriate technology	balancing arguments	global problems overpopulation information age predictions technological solutions	text type: short email requests writing skill: being polite
a conversation about two people who do artistic things in their free time an extract from a radio programme about what's on in Melbourne an artist's opinion about what art is	an article about unusual street art an article about the origins of rap	analysing contrasts	participation in the arts an art competition music and values	text type: an online review writing skill: personalising your writing
three speakers talking about different types of development someone talking about redevelopment in their city an interview with a journalist talking about social development in southern India	an article about urban development in Dubai an article about a hydropower dam project in Laos	fact or opinion	changes in your town a happy society sensitive development evaluating a development project	text type: an opinion essay writing skill: linking words
someone describing their stay at an ice hotel an interview about volunteer vacations	a blog about holidays at home an extract from a travel magazine about historical hotels	claims and justifications	local knowledge planning a staycation opinions about travel ideas for an unusual hotel	text type: a letter of complaint writing skill: formal language

Contents

Contents

Introduction

National Geographic

National Geographic was founded in 1888 and defines its mission as 'to inspire people to care about the planet'. The *National Geographic Society* is one of the world's largest non-profit scientific and educational organisations. It reaches more than 325 million people in more than thirty languages through its magazines, books, TV channels, interactive media, maps, films, and music. Proceeds from these activities have funded more than 9,000 scientific, conservation, and educational projects around the world. *LIFE* is published in partnership with *National Geographic*, using *National Geographic*'s content and values to 'inspire people to learn English'.

National Geographic topics

The topics are paramount and are the starting point for the lessons. These topics have been selected for their intrinsic interest and ability to fascinate students – and teachers. Once the material has been gathered from the *National Geographic* archives, the language objectives have been matched to the content, and then organised into a tried and tested syllabus. The richness of the listening and reading texts and video means that students are so engaged in learning about the content, and expressing their own opinions, that language learning has to take place in order for students to satisfy their curiosity and then react personally to what they have learnt. This element of transfer from the topics to students' own realities and experiences converts the input into a vehicle for language practice and production which fits the recognised frameworks for language learning and can be mapped to the CEFR scales. (Full mapping documents are available separately.)

People and places

LIFE takes students around the globe, investigating the origins of ancient civilisations, showing the drama of natural forces at work, and exploring some of the world's most beautiful places. These uplifting tales of adventure and discovery are told through eye witness accounts and first-class reportage, with superb photos, maps and videos. For example Unit 8 of the Upper Intermediate level tells the true story behind the famous 'Afghan girl' photograph and Unit 10 includes a radio feature about a tribe who have never seen or eaten meat.

Science and technology

Students learn about significant scientific discoveries and breakthroughs, both historic and current. These stories are related by journalists or told by the scientists and explorers themselves through interviews or first person accounts. Students see the impact of the discoveries on our lifestyles and cultures. Because the material comes from a huge archive that has been developed and designed to appeal to the millions of individuals who make up *National Geographic*'s audience, it reflects the broadest possible range of topics. For example Unit 3 of the Upper Intermediate level examines the risks and benefits of 'appropriate technology', and the possible applications of augmented reality.

History

History can be a dry topic, especially if it's overloaded with facts and dates. However, the *National Geographic* treatment of historical events brings them to life and there is often a human dimension and universal themes that keep the events relevant to students and to our time. History – or the re-telling of historical events – can also be influenced by a culture or nation's perception of the events. *National Geographic*'s non-judgemental and culture-neutral accounts allow students to look behind the superficial events and gain a deeper understanding of our ancestors. For example Unit 6 of the Upper Intermediate level looks at how the hotel industry is capitalising on historic buildings to offer guests an unusual experience, and Unit 9 examines the legacy of the controversial Hatshepsut, a 15th-century pharaoh who ruled as 'king'.

Animals

The animal kingdom is exceptionally generative in terms of interesting topics. *LIFE* provides astonishing photos that give a unique insight into the hidden lives of known and lesser-known animals, offering rare glimpses of mammals, birds, bugs and reptiles in their daily struggle for survival. It also informs and surprises with accounts of animals now extinct, species still evolving, and endangered species which are literally fighting for their existence. For example Unit 1 of the Upper Intermediate level presents some unlikely friendships between members of the animal kingdom.

Environment

It isn't always possible to find clarity in texts on the environment and climate change, or trust that they are true and not driven by a political agenda. *National Geographic*'s objective journalism, supported by easy-to-understand visuals, presents the issues in an accessible way. The articles are written by experts in their fields. It's often true that those who have the deepest understanding of issues are also able to express the ideas in the simplest way. High quality thinking and expertise are not synonymous with complicated concepts expressed through complicated language – usually quite the reverse is true. For example Unit 4 of the Upper Intermediate is based around an article about an environmentally-friendly form of graffiti.

National Geographic photography

We live in a world where images are used more than ever to reinforce, and at times replace, the spoken and written word. To present discourse without them is both unrealistic and unhelpful. Our memories work in pictures, our experiences and the things we learn about the world are stored using them. Raising awareness of this can help students to remember language more easily. All too often photos in books are cosmetic and without impact. *National Geographic* has great photography and powerful images at its core, so it seems natural that photographs in *LIFE* should serve as the starting point for each unit. The photographs in each spread are also integral to the written and recorded content and every opportunity has been taken to use photographs to stimulate learning.

There are photographs which:

- tell a story by themselves
- support understanding of a text and make it memorable
- provoke debate
- stimulate critical thinking by asking you to examine detail OR think about what is NOT shown OR by questioning the photographer's motives
- mean little without a caption or accompanying explanation
- raise questions about the ethics of journalism and photojournalism
- are accompanied by a memorable quotation
- help to remember a lexical set
- help to learn functional language (e.g. how something works)
- lend themselves to practice of a specific grammar point (e.g. significant historical events)

As a first exercise when handing out the new book to your students, why not ask them to flick through the book, select their favourite photograph, and then explain to the class what it is they like about it. You will find specific suggestions in the teacher's notes for using the photographs featured within each unit, but two important things to note are:

- pictures of people or animals capture a moment, so ask students to speculate on the events that led up to this moment and those that followed it
- pictures of places aim to capture their essence, so feed students the vocabulary they need to describe the details that together convey this (the light, the colours, the landscape, the buildings)

National Geographic video

At the back of the Student's Book is a DVD with twelve different National Geographic videos on a whole range of subjects. Each video is connected with the topic of a corresponding unit and can be used in conjunction with the video lesson pages in the unit. Typically, a video lesson is divided into three parts:

Before you watch

This section leads students in to the topic of the video and engages them in a pre-watching task.

While you watch

These exercises provide detailed comprehension of the video itself, both in terms of what a student sees and what they hear.

After you watch

This section allows students to respond to the video as a whole and take part in a productive speaking task using language and contexts from the video.

The videos are designed to form part of your lessons. However, if you don't have time in class to watch

them all, you can ask students to watch the videos and complete many of the exercises on the page in the Student's Book. This can form a useful part of their self-study. Students can also watch the videos again after seeing them in class. This is useful for review and students can focus on parts of the audio that particularly interest them.

For further variation with the videos, here are some more ideas you can use and develop:

- Play the video with the sound down. Students predict what the narrator or people are saying. Then play with the sound up and compare.
- Play the sound only with no video. Students predict where the video takes place and what is happening on the screen. Then play with the screen on and compare.
- Show the first part of the video, pause it, and then ask students what they think happens next.
- Give students a copy of the audioscript for the video and ask them to imagine they are the director. What will they need to film and show on the screen? Afterwards, they present their 'screen play' and finally watch the original.
- Write a short text on the same topic as the one in the video. However, don't include the same amount of information and leave some facts out. Students read the text and then watch the video. They make notes on any new information and rewrite the text so it includes the new details.
- With monolingual groups, choose part of the video with someone talking. Ask students to listen and write down what they say. Then, in groups, ask them to create subtitles in their own language for that part of the video. Each group present their subtitles and the class compares how similar they are.

National Geographic and critical thinking

There is a graded critical thinking syllabus in LIFE that starts with the Elementary level and runs through all the later levels. The critical thinking activities appear in the c spreads in each unit. The syllabus covers areas such as reading between the lines, differentiating between opinion and fact, evaluating the reliability of source material, assessing the relevance of information, identifying the techniques used by an author to persuade the reader, weighing up evidence, etc. These activities require students to engage with the reading texts at a deeper level, and to show real understanding – not just reading comprehension. This training – in evaluating texts, assessing the validity and strength of arguments and developing an awareness of authorial techniques – is clearly a valuable skill for those students learning English for academic purposes (EAP), where reflective learning is essential. However, it is also very much part of the National Geographic spirit which encourages people to question assumptions, and develop their own well-informed and reasoned opinions. In this sense it adds another dimension to the experience of learning English through National Geographic material.

LIFE methodology

Treatment of grammar

Target grammar is presented through texts in the first two spreads of each unit. These texts are authentic reading and listening texts, adapted for level as necessary, which use the target language in natural and appropriate linguistic contexts. Such texts not only aid comprehension, but present good models for the learner's own language production through a variety of 'voices' and genres. The main input alternates between reading and listening on these first two spreads. Where a presentation is a listening text, written examples of the grammar structures are given on the page, for example in content comprehension tasks, so that visual support is also provided.

The primary focus is on the topic content before the learner's attention is drawn to the target grammar structures. Learners are first directed to *notice* this language by various means, such as using highlighting within the text, extracting sample sentences or having learners locate examples themselves.

A variety of task formats are used to lead learners to *analyse* the form, meaning and use of the grammar structures, as appropriate. Such an approach can be highly motivational by actively engaging learners in the lesson and allowing them to share and discuss their interpretation of the new language. After this stage, clear paradigms or examples of form and use are given on the page in a simple *summary* box. This supports the learners and is a 'check point' for the teacher and learners alike as it summarises the information learners will have arrived at through completing the discovery tasks. A cross-reference is provided to more detailed information and additional exercises at the back of the book. These are suitable for use both in class and for self-study, according to the needs of the learners.

The grammar *practice* tasks within the unit are linked to the presentation text and topic and are thus content-rich in the same way. They move from more supported exercises through to more challenging tasks. Depending on the level, they have a differing emphasis on form and use. The practice tasks give learners an opportunity to *personalise* the structures and practise them in the context of their own experiences and situations. This *anchors* the new language in existing frameworks and leads to a clearer understanding of the usage of this new or revised language. Equally, the practice exercises incorporate a real reason to use the target structure whether by devices such as quizzes, games etc or by genuine exchange of information between students.

A final task on each spread allows the learners to create their own output and is structured so that learners have the opportunity to use the target grammar as well as other target language, for example vocabulary, in a meaningful context. This final task has a variety of formats such as discussions, personal narratives, task-based activities (ranking, etc) and the emphasis from the learner's perspective is on *content and fluency* rather than grammatical accuracy.

Aside from the two main grammar input spreads, the target grammar is also recycled in the subsequent spreads of each unit and beyond.

Treatment of vocabulary

LIFE teaches vocabulary in a range of different ways. This eclectic approach takes account of recent research, but doesn't abandon tried and tested methods. There is further practice of all of this vocabulary input (apart from words occurring in glossaries) in the Workbook.

1 Lexical sets

Some of the benefits generally associated with teaching words in lexical sets are:

- learning words in a set requires less effort
- retrieving related words from memory is easier
- seeing how knowledge can be organised can be helpful to learners
- it mirrors how such information is stored in the brain
- the meaning of words can be made clearer by comparing and contrasting them to similar words in the set

Each unit usually has two or more lexical sets. The lexical sets also cover commonly-confused words. There is evidence to suggest that once students have learnt one or more of the words that belong to a group of commonly-confused words (eg *job* and *work*), it is useful to compare and contrast these words directly to clarify the differences (or similarities) in meaning. *LIFE* focuses on these groups of words as and when they come up.

2 Word focus

The *Word focus* sections take high-frequency words and give examples of the different meanings they can have according to the contexts in which they appear and the different words they collocate with. At higher levels there is increased exposure to idioms and colloquial usage. The Workbook expands the range of phrases and expressions generated by these key words, and provides further practice.

3 Wordbuilding

The independent wordbuilding syllabus offers students another opportunity to expand their vocabulary. The *Wordbuilding* boxes in the units focus on areas such as prefixes, suffixes, collocations, parts of speech (e.g. noun→adjective), compound nouns, phrasal verbs, and highlight examples from the reading or listening texts. The box gives a brief explanation and some examples. There is an activity for further practice and a reference to an activity in the Workbook which introduces more words that belong to the same morphological area.

4 Glossaries

Where certain words are important to the meaning of a text, but are above the level of the student, they are glossed. Students aren't expected to learn these words, but the short and simple definition prevents them from being a barrier to understanding.

Learning skills

There is a comprehensive learning skills syllabus in the Workbook. This covers traditional learning skills, such as recording new vocabulary, using a dictionary, remembering new vocabulary, planning study time, assessing your own progress, etc.

Assessment

Students and teachers can assess progress in the following ways:

- Each unit in the Student's Book finishes with a one-page review where students do the exercises and complete a number of 'can-do' statements linked to the objectives of the unit.
- There are photocopiable tests in the Teacher's Book.
- There is a *Check!* section at the end of each unit in the Workbook for students to check what they have learnt (general knowledge as well as language).
- There are IELTs practice tests at the end of the Workbooks. These have been graded to the level of the course, but follow the format of the test. These allow students to benchmark their progress against the course objectives, whilst becoming familiar with a global test format.

Components

- Student's Book + DVD
- Workbook + audio
- Teacher's Book and class audio

Overview of a Student's Book unit

Opener: a one-page introduction to the unit that gets students interested in the topic

a and b: double-page lessons that teach grammar and vocabulary through reading and listening texts

c: a double-page lesson that focuses on reading comprehension and critical thinking

d: a one-page lesson that teaches functional/situational language

e: a one-page lesson that teaches a writing skill and the features of a text type

f: a double-page lesson of video comprehension exercises

Review: a one-page lesson of practice activities and 'can-do' check statements

Lesson type a

Grammar and vocabulary

This double-page spread is a grammar and vocabulary lesson: Lesson 3a Is technology the answer?

Target grammar is presented through texts in the first two spreads of each unit. These texts are authentic reading and listening texts, adapted for level as necessary, which use the target language in natural and appropriate linguistic contexts. Such texts not only aid comprehension, but present good models for the learner's own language production through a variety of 'voices' and genres. The main input alternates between reading and listening on these first two spreads.

The primary focus is on the topic content before the learner's attention is drawn to the target grammar structures.

speaking **global problems** • a scientist's view • /r/ and /t/ in American English •
future forms review • overpopulation

Is technology the answer?

Kolkata's streets crammed with vendors, pedestrians and taxis.

Speaking

1 Work in groups. Look at the photo. Which of these following problems does it illustrate?

congestion   epidemic
overpopulation   pollution
poverty   starvation

2 Which of these problems could have a technological solution?

Listening

3 1.17 Read the opinions (1–4). Then listen to the presentation about overpopulation. Match the opinion with the people (a–c).

1 Whenever the population is too big, a disaster happens and reduces it.
2 Many people will die because there is not enough food for the growing population.
3 Science and technology will find a solution to the problem of overpopulation.

a the speaker
b Thomas Malthus
c Paul Ehrlich

4 1.17 Listen again. Are the sentences true (T) or false (F)?

1 The speaker has some ideas for action which can immediately solve the problem of overpopulation.
2 Paul Ehrlich thought that we should control the number of babies being born.
3 There will be seven billion people in the world by the middle of the century.
4 Nanotechnology has saved the world from mass starvation.
5 There is not enough space on the Earth for nine billion people.
6 The growth in the 'global middle class' will put big pressure on resources.
7 According to the speaker, people are basically lazy. They will only act when they have to.

5 What is the meaning of each underlined prefix in these words from the passage? Match the prefix (1–6) to the meaning (a–f).

1 biofuels   a very small
2 nanotechnology   b very big
3 megacities   c extremely
4 microphone   d of life or living things
5 semi-retired   e half
6 ultra-cautious   f x10⁻⁹

▶ **WORDBUILDING prefixes**

There are many prefixes in English taken from Latin and Greek, each of which have a particular meaning.
microphone, megacity

For further information and practice, see Workbook page 27.

6 Do you share the speaker's faith in science and technology? Why? / Why not?

34

The independent wordbuilding syllabus offers students another opportunity to expand their vocabulary. The *Wordbuilding* boxes in the units focus on areas such as prefixes, suffixes, collocations, parts of speech (eg noun > adjective), compound nouns, phrasal verbs, and highlight examples from the reading or listening texts. The box gives a brief explanation and some examples. There is an activity for further practice and a reference to an activity in the Workbook which introduces more words that belong to the same morphological area.

The grammar practice tasks within the unit are linked to the presentation text and topic and are thus content-rich in the same way. They move from more supported exercises through to more challenging tasks.

7 Pronunciation /r/ and /t/ in American English

a 🔊 1.18 The speaker of the passage is American. Listen to these words from the passage. What can you say about how she pronounces the letter *r*? And the letter *t*?

answer	better	birth	eating	first
heart	megacities	part	rate	world

b 🔊 1.19 Now listen to these phrases said by an American speaker. Write in the missing words. How do you think a British speaker would pronounce /r/ and /t/ in these phrases?

1 _____ metres   4 a _____ letter
2 an _____ site   5 a _____ birthday
3 a _____ bar   6 a _____ beater

c 🔊 1.20 Listen and check.

Grammar future forms review

> ▶ **FUTURE FORMS REVIEW**
>
> **will**
> *One moment, I'll just adjust my microphone.*
> *It will be a bad thing for the planet if all those people start eating meat and driving big cars.*
> *The population will probably peak at around 9 billion by the middle of the century.*
> **going to**
> *I'm not going to speak for too long.*
> *Those of you who have come here looking for answers are going to be disappointed.*
> **about to**
> *Science is about to step in again with nanotechnology solutions.*
> **Present continuous**
> *I'm speaking to a government committee tomorrow.*
> **Present simple**
> *Oh, by the way, one more thing: the necessity train arrives in half an hour.*
>
> For further information and practice, see page 159.

8 Look at the grammar box. Match the verb forms (1–5) with their uses (a–i). Some verb forms have more than one use.

1 *will*   4 present continuous
2 *going to*   5 present simple
3 *about to*

a a scheduled or timetabled event
b a future event in an *if* or *when* clause
c a prediction
d a confident prediction based on present information
e a decision made at the time of speaking
f an intention or previously made decision
g a formal arrangement
h a simple statement of fact
i an event in the immediate future

9 Underline the correct future forms in this presentation. Sometimes there is more than one possibility.

I think ¹ *we wait / we'll wait* a few moments until everyone ² *arrives / will arrive* ... OK, ³ *I am beginning / I'll begin* now. Hello everyone and thank you for coming to hear my presentation about appropriate technology. I am ⁴ *about to / going to* speak for about 30 minutes and then I ⁵ *will take / am taking* your questions. If there ⁶ *is / is going to be* anything that you don't understand, please ask me then rather than during the presentation. My colleague, Liesel Babel, ⁷ *talks / is talking* this afternoon in the green seminar room, if people would like to learn more about appropriate technology. I think her session ⁸ *starts / is starting* at two o'clock. She ⁹ *is speaking / will speak* about her experience in the field, working on various development projects in Africa. OK ¹⁰ *I am going to show / I'll show* you a short film now so could someone at the back please turn the lights down?

10 🔊 1.21 Complete the radio news headlines about overpopulation using an appropriate future form. Then listen and check.

1 World leaders _____ (meet) in Geneva tomorrow to discuss the issue of overpopulation.
2 In the next few weeks, the government _____ (introduce) a fee for each child that couples have after their first two children.
3 Scientists say that space colonies _____ (be) the only solution for overpopulation in the medium term.
4 Doctors have said that in future they _____ (not / spend) so much effort keeping the old alive.
5 The government _____ (launch) a new education programme later today to encourage women to have fewer children.
6 People _____ (have to) change their lifestyles if they _____ (want) the world's resources to support the growing population in the coming years.

11 Work in pairs. Underline all the time expressions in the sentences in Exercise 10. Then put them in order of the nearest to the most distant future. Compare your answers with another pair.

Speaking

12 Work in groups. Decide which of the ideas in Exercise 10, or one of your own, are the best course of action for dealing with overpopulation. Then explain your plan and the reasons for it to the rest of the class.

Clear paradigms or examples of form and use are given on the page in a simple *summary* box. This supports the learners and is a 'check point' for the teacher and learners alike as it summarises the information learners will have arrived at through completing the discovery tasks. A cross-reference is provided to more detailed information and additional exercises at the back of the book. These are suitable both for use in class and self-study, according to the needs of the learners.

A variety of task formats are used to lead learners to *analyse* the form, meaning and use of the grammar structures, as appropriate.

A final task on each spread allows the learners to create their own output and is structured so that learners have the opportunity to use the target grammar as well as other target language, for example vocabulary, in a meaningful context. This final task has a variety of formats such as discussions, personal narratives, task-based activities (ranking, etc) and the emphasis from the learner's perspective is on content and fluency rather than grammatical accuracy.

Lesson type c

Reading

This page is the first page of a double-page reading lesson. The reading text is always on the right-hand page, and the activities on the left.

The mini contents section at the beginning of every lesson sets clear targets.

Critical thinking activities require students to engage with the reading texts at a deeper level, and require them to show real understanding – not just reading comprehension. This training – in evaluating texts, assessing the validity and strength of arguments and developing an awareness of authorial techniques – is clearly a valuable skill for those students learning English for academic purposes (EAP) where reflective learning is essential. However, it is also very much part of the *National Geographic* spirit which encourages people to question assumptions, and develop their own well-informed and reasoned opinions.

The *Word focus* sections take high-frequency words and give examples of the different meanings they can have according to the contexts in which they appear and the different words they collocate with.

---

reading **the power of the press** • critical thinking **different perspectives** • word focus **word** • speaking **reputations**

8c From hero to zero

Reading

1 Work in pairs. Look at the headlines below, in the order they appeared in the newspapers over several months. Discuss what you think happened.

HERO BA PILOT PETER BURKILL SPEAKS: I THOUGHT WE'D DIE IN HEATHROW CRASH

'I AM NOT A HERO'
SAYS BA CRASH PILOT CAPTAIN PETER BURKILL

REAL HERO OF BA FLIGHT 38 **IS CO-PILOT JOHN COWARD**

HERO PILOT 'FORCED OUT OF BA'

FALLEN HERO: THAT DAY CHANGED MY LIFE FOREVER

OFFICIAL REPORT SAYS ICE FAULT CAUSED BA AIRPORT CRASH

2 Read the story quickly. Then check the sequence of key events with your partner. How did the story differ from your answer in Exercise 1?

3 Read the article again. Are the statements true (T) or false (F)?

1 Burkill's co-pilot was at the controls when the engines failed.
2 Some passengers were badly hurt during evacuation.
3 At the time of the accident, Burkill was a single man who liked to enjoy himself.
4 Burkill's crew read BA's internal report.
5 Burkill was praised in the AAIB report.
6 He was too loyal to BA to work for another airline.

4 Complete the sentences with words from the article.

1 Burkill went from being a hero to being a (opposite of *hero*) _villain_ . (para 1)
2 When the plane crash landed, (incredibly) _____ it stayed upright and no one was hurt. (para 2)
3 Perhaps his colleagues believed he was (no good at his job) _____ . (para 3)
4 The press portrayed Burkill as irresponsible: he (failed) _____ the people he was supposed to be responsible for. (para 4)
5 Burkill felt (completely unsupported) _____ by his colleagues and the company. (para 5)
6 After the official report was published, Burkill was (given as a prize) _____ a medal for his actions. (para 7)

Critical thinking **different perspectives**

6 Each participant has a different perspective and a different motivation for acting as they did after the accident. Make notes to complete the table.

People involved	Their view of Burkill's role	Motivations for their actions
Peter Burkill	*he did what any pilot would have done*	*to clear his name and keep his job*
BA staff		
BA management		
AAIB*		
the newspapers		

*Air Accidents Investigation Branch

7 Which of the people do you believe? Who do you think the newspaper's readers believed?

Word focus *word*

8 Find four expressions in the article with *word*. Match each one with the definitions below.

1 to be the one who is able to make the final point in an argument and win it
2 news or a rumour starts to circulate
3 there is no evidence other than what two people claim to be true
4 there is no news about something

9 Work in pairs. What do these other expressions with *word* mean?

1 'The new gallery is amazing. But **don't take my word for it**: go and see for yourself.'
2 'When my husband handed me the keys to a new car for my birthday, I was **lost for words**.'
3 'The hotel doesn't advertise at all. It just relies on **word of mouth** to get new customers.'
4 'I can't believe the council are closing the library. They **gave their word** that they wouldn't.'

Speaking

10 Work in groups. Discuss the media in your country.
1 How respectful are journalists towards politicians?
2 How balanced is the reporting of public scandals?
3 Are people interested in reading about the private lives of famous people?

98

Lesson type d

Real life

This page is the one-page functional lesson from Unit 9.

---

real life **describing skills, talents and experience** • pronunciation **difficult words**

9d Right for the job

Real life describing skills, talents and experience

> The d lessons have clear 'Real life' functional aims.

Shelterbox
is a charity which sends boxes of essential items needed in an emergency – a tent, tools, cooking utensils, a water purification kit – to places where disasters, such as earthquakes and floods, have struck. Boxes are prepared in the USA and delivered immediately by Shelterbox employees to anywhere in the world where they will help to save lives.

1 Read the description of Shelterbox. What kind of organisation is it and what service do they offer?

2 🔊 2.17 Listen to someone being interviewed for a job at Shelterbox. Answer the questions.

1 What aspect of their work is the candidate interested in?
2 What is the interviewer concerned about?

3 🔊 2.17 Look at these phrases from the interview describing the candidate's suitability for a job. Note the prepositions used in each case. Then listen to the interview again and complete each one.

> **DESCRIBING SKILLS, TALENTS AND EXPERIENCE**
> I'm familiar with your work because I have a friend who ¹_____.
> I'm very keen on the idea of ²_____.
> I specialised in ³_____.
> I think I would be suited to ⁴_____.
> I'm good at coping with ⁵_____.
> I have quite a lot of experience of ⁶_____.
> I'm quite good with ⁷_____.
> I'm comfortable with all ⁸_____.
> I'm serious about wanting to ⁹_____.
> I need to become more knowledgeable about ¹⁰_____.

4 Work in pairs. Discuss if the candidate did a good job of selling himself to the interviewer?

5 Pronunciation difficult words

a 🔊 2.18 The spelling of a word in English is not always a clear indication of its pronunciation. How confident are you that you can pronounce these words from the interview? For very confident put a (✓), quite confident put a (?) and unconfident put a (✗). Then listen and check.

> although   business   comfortable
> environment   foreign   knowledgeable
> months   specialised   suited   world

b 🔊 2.19 Listen to eight more words and try to spell them.

6 Work in pairs.

Student A: choose one of the jobs below that interests you and think about the skills, talents and experience you have that would help you do it. Try to convince Student B why this would be a good job for you.
Student B: ask Student A questions. Then swap roles.

- a travel guide for a tour operator taking groups on walking holidays in Italy
- a sales assistant in a children's bookshop
- a fund-raiser for a charity that helps the homeless
- an assistant to a cameraman who makes films about plants and wildlife

> The pronunciation syllabus covers sounds and spelling; connected speech; stress and intonation.

> The key expressions are made memorable through an activation activity.

TALK ABOUT ▸ A CAREER PATH ▸ PERSONAL QUALITIES ▸ WOMEN AT WORK ▸ SKILLS, TALENTS AND EXPERIENCE
WRITE ▸ AN ONLINE PROFILE

Lesson type e

Writing

This page is the one-page writing lesson from Unit 9.

Every e lesson has a specific text type.

Every writing lesson includes a model.

A different writing skill is presented and practised in every e lesson.

9e Professional networking

Writing an online profile

1 Do you use any professional networking sites (e.g. Biznik, LinkedIn, Ecademy, Xing)? Why? / Why not?

2 Read the profile and summarise in no more than nine words what this person's main skills and qualities are. How effective was his profile in putting across the key points?

3 Read the tips on how to write a profile on a professional networking site. Put a tick (✓) next to each tip that has been followed, a cross (✗) next to those which have not and a question mark (?) if the tip has only been partly followed.

> **Tips:**
> 1 Include a personal photo and recommendations from others to show you really exist!
> 2 Give a heading and summary so that readers can get the main idea quickly.
> 3 Include your current status i.e. what you're doing now.
> 4 List all the places you have worked or studied at – someone from the same organisation or school may be looking at your profile!
> 5 Job titles may mean nothing to others so always describe what you did in each job.

4 Writing skill writing in note form

a Look at these four extracts from the profile. Which are proper sentences? Which are written in note or shortened form? Why is this?

1 responsible for new products
2 Learning is my passion.
3 published *Learning in the 21st Century*
4 Developing innovative e-learning programme for the car industry

b Insert the necessary words (pronouns, articles, auxiliary verbs) to show what the extracts in note form would look like as full sentences.

Profile

Barton McCready
Managing Director of Evercready Learning

Location: York, UK
Industry: Online learning
Current: Developing innovative e-learning programme for the car industry

Past
- Head of development, Faheys Educational – responsible for new products
- Commissioning Editor, York Books – published *Learning in the 21st Century*
- Director of Business Studies, Carston University

Education: Cardiff University

Summary
Learning is my passion. I specialise in the design and management of online learning programmes for industry, but I am also a writer, editor, blogger, educator and business consultant. My work has brought me into contact with many companies and I am now skilled at identifying and responding to the learning needs of any business sector, from cosmetics to car-making. If this experience has taught me one thing, it's that learning is the key to improvement for all of us.

---

c Convert these statements from other profiles into a shorter, more concise form by deleting the unnecessary words.

1 I worked as a personal assistant to the Marketing Director.
2 I am currently writing an article for *National Geographic* magazine.
3 I was in charge of organising corporate social events.
4 I took the official photos for the National Basketball Championships.
5 I am working for various charities.
6 I was employed by a local college to raise money for them.

5 Write your own short professional profile, similar to the one in Exercise 2. Think about the message you would most like the reader to be left with. When you have finished exchange profiles with another member of the class. Read the profile once quickly and tell each other what your main impression was.

6 Read your partner's profile again. Check the following points:

- Has the profile been laid out correctly?
- Have the tips in Exercise 3 been followed?
- Has note form been used in places to make the profile more concise?

TALK ABOUT ▸ A CAREER PATH ▸ PERSONAL QUALITIES ▸ WOMEN AT WORK ▸ SKILLS, TALENTS AND EXPERIENCE
WRITE ▸ AN ONLINE PROFILE

113

Students always finish with a productive task.

Students are encouraged to take part in peer correction.

Unit 1 Relationships

Lead-in

Personal Response

Ask students to say what they know about camels. Try to elicit the two kinds (Dromedary, with one hump, and Bactrian with two humps), and ask what they are used for (transporting things and people), where (in hot dry countries) and why (because they are able to travel long distances without water). Ask students if they have any experience of camels, and how (in zoos, in the countries where they live).

1 Ask students to work in pairs to choose the best phrase to describe the photo. They may need to use dictionaries to find out the meaning of the words. When they have discussed their ideas with another pair, elicit ideas from the class, and open up the discussion to everyone.

Extra activity

Practise saying the phrases with the class chorally and individually. Take care with the words which do not have the stress on the first syllable:

re*spect*
ac*quain*tance
com*pan*ion

2 Ask the class to read the four sayings, and elicit the meanings (see Vocabulary notes below). If you are teaching a monolingual class, ask them to discuss if there are any equivalent sayings in their language, or how they might translate the English, and then get them to back-translate the phrases to you if you don't understand the language. Discuss how similar their versions are to the English.

If you are teaching a multilingual class, have them translate and back-translate, and compare all the different versions.

Vocabulary notes

Blood is thicker than water = people in your family are more important than others

A friend in need is a friend indeed = a friend who helps you when you are in trouble shows they are really a good friend

Like father, like son = children tend to do and say similar things to their parents

No man is an island = we all need other people – we cannot exist in isolation

3 [1.1] Ask students to read who the possible people are to focus their listening. Play the recording once and ask students to answer. They can then check with a partner. Play the recording once more to check, correct and complete. Elicit the answers.

ANSWERS

1 A husband
2 an old friend
3 a colleague

Audioscript [1.1]

Speaker 1

It's a bit odd because I see him almost every day at work. He has a job in the marketing department on the 4th floor and my office is on the 5th floor and occasionally, just occasionally, we are asked to attend the same meetings. Umm … it's strange seeing someone you're so close to in a different context. We've been married for seven years, and colleagues for longer than that, but we try not to discuss work when we're at home with the rest of the family …

Speaker 2

We were such good mates at school and then we went travelling together, but we see each other very rarely now, because John lives in Birmingham with his wife and I still live in London. The funny thing is, it doesn't matter how little we see each other – we're still great friends. Actually, he never calls me – and every time I call him he says, 'Oh, I've been meaning to call you for ages,' but I don't mind …

Speaker 3

We get on very well as colleagues, but I never see him outside work. He's one of those people that can always make you laugh, which is really important in a stressful work environment. He's very good at his job too and I'm always asking for help for things.

Extra activity

Ask students to choose one of the people listed in Exercise 3 who is particularly important in their life, and tell a partner all about them. The partner should ask questions to elicit more information.

4 Read through the instructions with the class. Students should then think about people they know who fit the situations, and ask and answer questions with a partner. Ask each student to talk about the most interesting person they heard about from their partner.

1a Unlikely friends

Lead-in

Personal Response

Ask the class if they have had any interesting or unusual relationships with animals, e.g. a pet that was like a member of the family. Ask questions to elicit further information, e.g. *Did it do anything unusual? Were you very sad when it died?*

Listening

1 Ask students to work in pairs to answer the questions about the photo. Elicit answers from the whole class, and discuss their ideas further.

> SAMPLE ANSWERS
>
> 1 an orang-utan and a dog
> 2 An orang-utan is normally a wild animal, a dog might be a pet or a working animal.
> 3 They look friendly and affectionate.

2 [1.2] Read through the rubric with the class to focus their listening. Play the recording once, and ask students to discuss what they heard. Then play the recording again for them to check, complete and correct their answers. Elicit answers from the class.

> ANSWER
>
> They wrestle, hug and play together. The orang-utan shares his food with the dog.

Audioscript [1.2]

It's known that animals often co-operate in their own social groups, helping each other to hunt or raise their young. Some highly intelligent animals, like elephants, go even further than this, and help other animals who are not in their own family group. But co-operation between animals of different species is unusual, so that's why the story of Suriya, the orang-utan, has attracted a lot of interest.

Suriya lives with his keepers at the Institute of Greatly Endangered and Rare Species in Myrtle Beach, South Carolina, which is a kind of sanctuary for rare animals. Recently this orang-utan has made an unlikely friend in a local hound dog. Now most dogs avoid apes, because they are scared of them basically, but these two have formed a strong bond. Each day the dog comes into the compound and searches out Suriya.

When he finds him, they carry on like long lost friends, wrestling and hugging and playing together. They've been doing this every day since they first met and their friendship has attracted the curiosity of millions of viewers on the *National Geographic Channel*. The founder of the institute, Dr Antle, explains: 'It's clear they are having the time of their life. What is more striking is that Suriya has also understood that the hound dog is very hungry and so he regularly shares his monkey biscuits with him. Orang-utans are very generous creatures. If you give one a piece of candy, often they will break it in half and hand one piece back to you.'

So how does he explain the fact that their relationship has a lot of the characteristics of what we call 'friendship'? Antle says that the two animals are fulfilling a basic social need in each other that perhaps we don't normally associate with animals. 'It's a relationship with attributes of fun and interaction that they are not getting from anyone else.'

3 [1.2] Ask students to read through all six multiple choice questions; suggest that they might already be able to mark some answers in pencil. Play the recording once, then allow students to check their answers with a partner; play the recording again for them to check their answers. Elicit answers from the class.

> ANSWERS
>
> 1 c   2 b   3 a   4 a   5 c   6 c

4 Read through the rubric with the class and make sure they understand the questions. Ask them to discuss the issues in pairs. Take feedback from the class.

Grammar present tenses review

5 Read through the examples in the grammar box with the class. To check students' understanding, ask them to think of further examples for each tense. Then ask them to do the matching activity as a class, and correct the answers as they go.

> ANSWERS
>
> 1 c   2 b   3 d   4 a

6 Ask students to choose the correct verb forms individually, then check with a partner. Elicit answers as complete sentences from the whole class.

> ANSWERS
>
> 1 have started
> 2 have been discussing
> 3 show
> 4 has recovered
> 5 are asking
> 6 have been living
> 7 has provided
> 8 live

7 Read the example with the class and make sure students understand what to do. Suggest that they refer back to the grammar box if they are unsure about the use of the verbs.

> ANSWERS
>
> 2 permanent / usual situation
> 3 present result of past action
> 4 present result of past action
> 5 permanent / usual situation
> 6 permanent / usual situation
> 7 present result of past action, permanent situation
> 8 recent activity, permanent / usual situation
> 9 present result of past action
> 10 situation happening around now

Extra activity

Ask students to write two sentences using each tense to describe relationship situations which are true for them. They should then work with a partner and take it in turns to read the sentences and talk about the situations.

Vocabulary friends: nouns and phrasal verbs

8 Read through the types of friends with the class and make sure that they understand the meaning of each one. Ask them to do the exercise individually, and then discuss the answers with a partner. Then elicit the answers from the whole class. In feedback, point out some of the alternative phrases, e.g. *fellow student* or *classmate*.

Vocabulary notes

mate (as in *workmate*, *flatmate*, *classmate*): *mate* can mean *friend*, but in this situation it means somebody who you do something with (e.g. work, share a flat).

fair-weather friend = a friend who uses you when it is convenient for them

companion = somebody who *accompanies* you (in this case they are on the same holiday together, but didn't know each other before).

mutual friend = someone who happens to be a friend to both people in a pair (*we met through a mutual friend*)

acquaintance = somebody you have met a few times and maybe talked to a little, but do not know properly

fellow (student) = someone who is doing the same thing as you (*a fellow worker* means a *workmate*).

ANSWERS

1 a fellow student (*classmate* is an alternative for this term)
2 a flatmate
3 a travel companion (*fellow traveller* is an alternative)
4 an acquaintance
5 a mutual friend
6 a fair-weather friend
7 a true friend
8 a workmate
9 an old friend
10 a girlfriend

9 Ask students to do this in pairs; they may need dictionaries. Elicit the answers from the whole class.

SAMPLE ANSWERS

to get on (with): to enjoy being with another person

to stand by (someone): to be loyal to someone

to hang out with: to spend time with a group of people

to hang around: to be there when you are not wanted, or to not do anything much

to come round: to visit

to go round to: to visit

to keep up with: to continue to see someone

to meet up (with): to meet, to get together (with)

to pick up: to continue

10 Ask students to complete the sentences individually and then check with a partner.

Elicit answers from the class as complete sentences.

ANSWERS

1 get on
2 hang out
3 kept up
4 come round
5 stand by
6 meet up

Grammar note

Note that many of these verb + preposition constructions have at least two meanings; a literal one (sometimes known as a prepositional verb) and a figurative one (sometimes known as a phrasal verb), like those in Exercise 10. Phrasal verbs often have several completely different meanings, depending on the context. These are the literal meanings of the verbs which have a figurative meaning in Exercise 10:

get on = to move onto something
He got on the bus and waved goodbye.

hang out = to put something to hang outside somewhere
We hung out our wet clothes on the tree.

keep up = to support something
I use a belt to keep up my trousers.

come round = to move from one side of something to another
A met her as I came round the corner.

stand by = to stand close to something
I stood by the fire to get warm again.

meet up = when two or more things come to the same point
You can take either road; they meet up by the station.

Speaking

11 Ask students to discuss their friendships in pairs.

1b   A confused generation

Lead-in

Personal response

Ask the class to talk about their upbringing. Ask: *Was your upbringing formal, strict, informal, relaxed, traditional or modern? What did you like about it? What didn't you like about it? What would you have liked that you didn't have?*

Reading

1 Ask the class to look at the picture and discuss the questions together. Elicit ideas and comments.

> **ANSWERS**
>
> 1 It shows a teenage girl with her head in her hands, looking unhappy or cross.
> 2 She is unhappy about something; maybe she doesn't like the food that she has been given.

Extra activity

Ask the class what they know about China. Elicit whatever information you can. If students mention changes in society, encourage them to expand on this area; if not, then try to elicit it by asking questions, e.g. *What changes have there been in China in the last ten or twenty years? Do you think these changes will have had an effect on Chinese society?*

2 Ask students to work with a partner to discuss the effects of China's economic boom on attitudes. Elicit answers from the whole class, and open up the discussion.

3 Students read the article and compare it with their own ideas.

> **SAMPLE ANSWERS**
>
> The younger generation don't listen to their parents; they have different attitudes; they are influenced by western culture and want different things.
>
> For the older generation money is becoming more important; traditional values, like respect for family and for older people, are being replaced by more materialistic values.

4 Ask students to look for the examples of changes individually. Then elicit answers from the whole class.

> **ANSWERS**
>
> Language use: young people use slang and speak English; their parents don't.
> Caring for the old: it is normal for people to put their elderly parents into care homes now – in the past everyone cared for the older members of the family.
> The relationship between parents and children: parents do what children want – in the past it was the other way round.
> Shopping: children want to buy modern, western things.
> Knowledge of the world: the young are more tuned in to what is happening in the world than their parents.

5 Ask the class to discuss these questions in pairs. Elicit answers from the whole class.

Ask students to read the information about forming adjectives in the *Wordbuilding* box on page 13 of the Student's Book. Refer them also to page 11 in the Workbook, if you feel they need extra practice in this area.

> **SAMPLE ANSWERS**
>
> Bella's parents seem resigned to the changes, but they are sad about their daughter's attitude and they feel that they have failed.

Grammar the passive

6 Ask students to work with a partner to decide if the statements are true or false. Then elicit the answers from the whole class.

> **ANSWERS**
>
> a true   b false (we use *by*)   c true   d true

7 [1.3] Ask students to do this exercise with a partner. Elicit answers from the whole class as complete sentences.

> **ANSWERS**
>
> 1 better as active   4 change to passive
> 2 change to passive   5 change to passive
> 3 better as active   6 change to passive

Audioscript [1.3]

There are many children like Bella in China. They admire western brands. They have been spoiled a little perhaps by their parents. Often these children receive a better education than their parents. They are sent to private schools and are encouraged to go to university. In China everyone's hopes and aspirations are being raised by the new economy.

Pronunciation

8a [1.3] Write the four passive verbs from the text on the board and ask students to copy them down. Ask them to listen and decide which parts of the passive verbs are stressed, then check with a partner. Ask different students to come and underline the stressed syllable in each verb.

> **ANSWERS**
>
> have been <u>spoi</u>led
> are <u>sent</u>
> are en<u>cou</u>raged
> are being <u>raised</u>

8b Before students do this activity, check that they know where the stress falls in the main verbs where it is not on the first syllable: intro<u>duc</u>ed, all<u>ow</u>ed, in<u>ves</u>ted, dis<u>cuss</u>ed, con<u>cern</u>ed. Then say the sentences and have students repeat them chorally and individually. Ask them to work in pairs and help each other with their stress. Circulate and monitor their pronunciation.

Pronunciation note

Note that we often use contractions in the passive (e.g. *I'm given, we're being given, they've been given*). When we use full forms (*I am, we are, they have*), the auxiliaries are always unstressed and therefore pronounced as the weak form.

I am given	am = /əm/
We are being given	are = /ə/
Have they been given …?	have = /həv/

9 Ask students to complete the sentences with the correct form of the verbs.

> **ANSWERS**
>
> 1 are growing, dress
> 2 have been left / are being left
> 3 probably work / don't have
> 4 are living / are expected
> 5 listen
> 6 have been replaced
> 7 are expected
> 8 are often criticised, have been spoilt

Speaking

10 Ask students to work in groups of four to discuss who is most likely to have said the sentences from Exercise 9, and which statements they agree with. Elicit ideas from the whole class, and open up the discussion.

> **SAMPLE ANSWERS**
>
> 1, 2, 6 and 7 were probably said by an older person
> 3, 4, 5 and 8 were probably said by a younger person

11 Once students have discussed the issues relating to generation gaps in pairs, elicit ideas from the whole class and get a fuller discussion going.

Homework

Ask students to write 150 words on the differences between their generation and either their parents' generation, or the younger generation. They can use ideas and language from the previous few exercises.

1c Bloodlines

Lead-in

Personal response

Ask the class to say what they know about emigration from and to their country, e.g. *Do many people emigrate to your country? Which countries or parts of the world do they come from? Which countries did they come from in the past, e.g. 50 years ago, or 100 years ago?*

Reading

1 Ask students to work in pairs to discuss the questions. They should then share their ideas with another pair, then report back to the class.

2 Ask students to read the questions to focus their reading, then read the article individually and find the answers, then check with a partner. Elicit answers from the whole class and check students' understanding of the key words (see Vocabulary notes below).

> **ANSWERS**
>
> 1 It is an area with immigrants from many countries living side-by-side.
> 2 Their families emigrated to the USA.
> 3 Tanja's parents came as a couple, with a profession, and went on to study. Richard's great-grandfather came with nothing and no skills. Richard's family has been there longer than Tanja's.

Vocabulary notes

diversity = difference

to be curious about = to want to find out about something

to trace = to follow and look for something

to intrigue = to make you interested, to fascinate

to board a ship = to get onto a ship

an announcement = a public notice, e.g. in a newspaper

subsequently = after that, next

to settle (in) = to move and live in a place

a strong work ethic = to believe that hard work is necessary and important

3 Ask students to answer the questions individually, then check with a partner. Elicit answers from the class.

> **ANSWERS**
>
> 1 T   2 F   3 F   4 T   5 F   6 T

4 Ask students to work in pairs to decide on the meaning of the words from the context. Elicit answers from the whole class.

> **ANSWERS**
>
> 1 b   2 a   3 b   4 c   5 c

Critical thinking identifying the main aspect

5 Ask students to read the article again and decide what is the most important aspect of immigration in each paragraph. Elicit answers from the whole class.

ANSWERS

Paragraph 1: Immigrants from all over the world mix in New York; they are proud to be Americans.
Paragraph 2: People are also interested in their roots, particularly their immediate ancestors.
Paragraph 3: People had to work hard when they first arrived, and their descendants work hard in their honour.

6 Ask students to see which aspects from the first paragraph are discussed in the personal accounts.

ANSWERS

Both mention hard work and the struggle to succeed; both are proud of the achievements of their parents and great-grandparents. Both talk a lot about how their ancestors arrived in America and where they came from. Neither really mention pride in their American identity.

7 Ask students to discuss the main message of the article, and elicit answers from the whole class.

ANSWERS

The immigrants had to be strong and work hard to succeed. Their descendants have a strong sense of family and pride in their roots.

Speaking

8 Discuss the meaning of the phrases with the whole class, eliciting suggestions and discussing them.

ANSWERS

1 He was independent, doing what he wanted to and not always following the rules.
2 They believe it is important to work hard.
3 They want to succeed and improve themselves.

9 Ask students to complete the questionnaire, then compare their answers with a partner. Elicit some answers from the whole class. They could then use the answers to write a continuous text about their relationship with their family for homework.

Vocabulary notes

a consideration = something you think about and that influences what you do
a trait = a characteristic (usually behaviour or personality)
approval = having something accepted
influenced = had a strong effect on what you did

1d A face from the past

Lead-in
Personal response
Ask students to think about people they used to know well and meet on a regular basis (e.g. at school, college or in previous jobs) but whom they haven't seen since. Are any of those people they would really like to meet again? Ask them to work in pairs and talk about the person / people.

Real life meeting people you know

1 Make sure students understand the phrase *to bump into someone* in both its literal sense (i.e. you actually knocked into another person accidentally) and, as here, in the figurative sense of meeting someone you know by chance. Then ask them to discuss the questions with a partner.

2 [1.4] Read the two questions with the class to focus their listening, then play the recording and ask if they heard the answers. If not, then play it again.

ANSWERS

1 Tim has been doing teacher training for the British Council in India. Greta has being setting up her online shoe shop business.
2 They will meet up in two months' time, with another friend, Amanda, when Tim gets back from his next trip to India.

Audioscript [1.4]

G = Greta; T = Tim

G: Tim, hello. Fancy bumping into you here. How are you?

T: Oh hi Greta. Yeah, I'm doing fine, thanks. Wow, what a surprise …

G: It's been ages. What have you been up to?

T: I know. It's been far too long. Umm … I've been working abroad for the last 18 months.

G: Anywhere exciting?

T: Yes, in India, actually. I had a contract with the British Council, doing some teacher training.

G: Well, it obviously suits you: you're looking very tanned and relaxed.

T: Oh, thanks, it's been a lot of fun. And you? You're looking well too. How are things?

G: Oh you know, busy as ever. I've been completely snowed under with work the last few months, trying to get my online shoe shop business off the ground.

T: Is it going OK?

G: Well, you know. It has its ups and downs. But we're getting there.

T: And what about Amanda? Do you see much of her?

G: Yeah, we still get together now and then. She was asking after you just the other day, actually.

T: Oh. Well I probably won't have time to look her up this time. I'm only back for a week. But do give her my regards.

G: I will.

T: And the next time I'm back, perhaps we can all meet and catch up.

G: Yeah, that'd be great. How long will you be gone for?

T: I've just got to do another two months over there. Then I'll be back in the UK for a while, I hope.

G: OK. Well give me a call when you're back. You've got my number, haven't you?

T: Yes, if it's still the same one.

G: Yeah, it is. I'll look forward to that. Is Sarah going out there with you?

T: She has been with me, but umm … she's staying back this time.

G: Oh. Well, say hello to her from me … er … Look, I don't mean to be rude, but I need to get back to work – but it was really nice to see you. Hope the trip goes well.

T: Thanks. Yeah I've got to rush too. Anyway, great to see you too, Greta. Take care … and see you soon. Good luck with the business.

3 🎵 [1.4] Read through the phrases in the box with the class. Make sure that they are familiar with them all, especially the use of *Fancy…!* to start an exclamation of surprise, and the phrase *to be snowed under* meaning having lots of work to do.

Ask them to listen to the recording and tick the phrases used. You may need to play it through twice.

ANSWERS

Fancy bumping into you here!
What a surprise!
How are things?
What have you been up to?
Busy as ever.
I've been completely snowed under.
It has its ups and downs.
You're looking well.
It obviously suits you.
Do you see much of …?
She was asking after you the other day.
Do give her my regards.
Say hello to her from me.
I've got to rush.
I don't mean to be rude, but I need to …
It was really nice to see you.
Great to see you.
Good luck with …

4 Ask students to find the expressions that match the sentences.

ANSWERS

1 Fancy bumping into you here!
2 What have you been up to?
3 You're looking well too.
4 It has its ups and downs.
5 She was asking after you just the other day, actually.
6 I don't mean to be rude, but I need to get back to work.

Pronunciation expressive intonation

5a 🎵 [1.5] Ask students to listen to the phrases and decide if the intonation is flat or expressive. Play the recording twice for them to answer.

ANSWERS

1 E   2 F   3 F   4 F   5 E   6 E

Extra activity

Play the recording again, pausing after each sentence for students to repeat chorally and individually, with the correct expressive / flat intonation.

5b Ask students to work in groups of four to practise varying their intonation. Circulate and monitor their speaking.

6 Find or create a suitable space to do this mingle activity. Ask students to walk around, then when you clap, turn to the person nearest to them and have a conversation; give them enough time to talk. When you clap again they walk around, and at a third clap they turn to someone new.

1e News from home

Lead-in

Personal response

Ask each student to tell the class what the last piece of personal 'snail mail' they got through the post was, e.g. bank statement, bill (for what?), personal letter, postcard, catalogue, documents; *junk mail* is not included.

Writing an informal email

1 Ask students to talk to their partner about the two questions. Elicit some responses from the whole class by asking students to talk about their partner's ways of communicating.

2 Ask students to read the email individually and answer the questions. They can then check with a partner before you elicit answers from the class.

> ANSWERS
>
> Ben is in Sri Lanka, writing articles about people who work in the tea plantations.
> Paragraph 1: apologising and explaining silence
> Paragraph 2: saying what he is doing now
> Paragraph 3: future plans

Vocabulary notes

Check that students are familiar with these words and phrases, or use the opportunity for a dictionary exercise:

a journal = a personal diary

to feel homesick = to miss the people and places and way of life where you come from

to get established = to become known and have a position and name that people recognise

freelance = working for yourself, not employed by anyone

tea plantations = a 'farm' where tea is grown

lush = green and healthy (of plants)

a feature for a magazine = a main article

3 Ask students to identify the informal language features. Elicit answers from the whole class.

> ANSWERS
>
> contractions: *I hope all's well*,
> exclamations: *Fingers crossed!*
> colloquial language: *some of this stuff, all the best, do give them all my love, you wouldn't believe it*
> phrasal verbs: *get together with*
> use of *get*: *getting homesick, get established, get an interview, get a plane,*
> personal comments: *that horrible estate agent*

Writing skill greetings and endings

4 Elicit from the whole class which phrases from the box are informal.

> ANSWERS
>
> All my love, Best wishes, Hello, Hi John, Love, Regards, Yours

Word focus get

5a Ask students to find the phrases with *get* individually, then check with a partner. Elicit answers from the whole class.

> ANSWERS
>
> 1 *I'm getting quite homesick* = I am becoming homesick
> 2 *to get established* = to become known in a business or profession
> 3 *to get an interview* = to obtain an interview
> 4 *to get a plane* = to catch / take a plane
> 5 *to get together* = to meet up

5b Ask students to match the uses of *get* individually, then check with a partner. Elicit answers from the whole class, having them read the original sentence and then say the sentence with the new verb in it.

> ANSWERS
>
> 1 receive
> 2 do / manage
> 3 catch
> 4 be
> 5 persuade
> 6 reach

5c Ask students to write their sentences individually, then get into groups of four to read them to each other.

6 Ask students to write the email individually. This would be a good homework exercise.

7 Ask students to exchange letters and check the style using the questions given. Ask them to talk about each other's letters in pairs.

Homework

Students could write the email in Exercise 6 for homework, or if they have done this in class, they could write a reply to their partner's email. They can then discuss their replies using the same criteria as in Exercise 7.

1f Immigration

Before you watch

1 Students work in groups. Ask them to look at the photo and discuss the questions. Take feedback from the class.

> **ANSWERS**
> 1 on a ship about to arrive in New York
> 2 They are waiting to see what the place is like.
> 3 That they are leaving their homes to come to America.

2 Before watching the video, ask students to predict five images that they think they will see.

While you watch

3 Give students time to read through the words in the glossary. Play the whole of the video for students to check their answers to Exercise 2.

4 Give students time to read the text. Then play the first part of the video (to 02.30). Ask students to find the errors and write the correct information.

> **ANSWERS**
> 1 since the early **19th** century
> 2 Europeans settled mainly in the **eastern** half.
> 3 Immigrants from Asia and from Mexico tended to settle in the **west** and **southwest**.
> 4 between 1892 and **1924**
> 5 Ellis Island in **New York** harbour
> 6 11,000 people a **day** were processed.
> 7 Four out of every **ten** Americans can trace their family history to Ellis Island.
> 8 They settled on the **Lower** East side.
> 9 The apartments had **three** rooms.
> 10 On the west coast people arrived at **Angel Island**.
> 11 Immigration laws were **especially strict** for Asians.

5 Give students time to read the questions, then play the second part of the video (02.31 to the end) for them to answer.

> **ANSWERS**
> 1 about 1 million
> 2 illegal immigrants
> 3 education, technical skills, a great desire to work and succeed and personal connections to other countries
> 4 It has an ever-growing force of immigrant labourers and professionals.
> 5 similar values
> 6 It helps make them successful members of American society.

After you watch

6 Students work in pairs to roleplay arriving at Ellis Island, according to the instructions.

7 Elicit ideas from the class about what the quote means and whether they agree with it.

8 Students work in groups to ask and answer the questions.

Videoscript

Part 1

00.03–00.23 Every day, a massive number of aeroplanes, cars and ships cross America's borders, bringing people from other lands.

Some 430 million passengers arrived in 2004 alone, and as has been the case for centuries, many of the people who come to the United States end up staying.

00.24–00.41 Lavinia Limon America is by its nature more diverse, more welcoming to immigrants, less discrimination, more opportunities for their children. They choose to come here and I think, you know, not only have we by policy had more immigration, but by our very nature we're more welcoming to people.

00.42–01.07 Great waves of immigration have broken on American shores since the early part of the 19th century. Fleeing economic and political hardships, many millions left their homelands in Europe and Asia in search of a better life. Europeans including Irish, Germans, Italians and others, settled in the eastern half of the United States. Immigrants from Asia and from Mexico tended to settle in the west and southwest.

01.08–01.45 During the period between 1892 to 1924, Ellis Island in New York harbour opened its doors to some 17 million immigrants. In 1907 alone, as many as 11,000 people flowed through its Great Hall on a single day. And today, four out of every ten Americans can trace part of their family history directly back to this one point of entry.

Virtually all of these immigrants faced hardships. Many of them settled on the Lower East side of Manhattan.

The Tenement Museum shows how harsh their living conditions could be.

01.46–02.11 Philip Cohen It was pretty much just three rooms, 325 square feet, partitioned into three rooms. You had the front room, which was the only room with direct access to light and air. The centre room was typically the kitchen. And then you had a smaller room in the back, which was typically, you know, from our records of this building, families as large as eleven people living. So, you know, when night fell, every room became a bedroom.

02.12–02.30 Meanwhile, on the west coast, immigrants passed through a point of entry called Angel Island in California's San Francisco Bay. Here, they had to contend with immigration laws that were especially strict for Asians.

But despite the conditions, immigrants continued to arrive by the thousands.

Part 2

02.31–02.48 The United States remains open to new settlers today with about a million new legal immigrants each year.

A large number of immigrants also enter the United States illegally. This situation presents a challenge to the nation and especially for states on the US–Mexico border.

02.48–03.12 Despite these challenges, America's long history of immigration has clearly strengthened the nation. Foreign-born citizens have brought with them education, technical skills, a great desire to work and succeed and personal connections to other countries. One reason the United States is such a dominant power in the world economy is that it has an ever-growing force of immigrant labourers and professionals.

03.13–03.18 Lavinia Limon We're in a much better position because we have maintained our immigration flows.

03.19–03.37 More than two hundred years of immigration to the United States has shown that even immigrants who keep their language, their way of dress and their own customs often share very similar values to the people already living here. Values that will eventually help make them successful members of American society.

03.38–03.58 *Lavinia Limon* The immigrants who come here, they have chosen. They have made an incredible leap to leave everything they know, everything that gives them self-identity and self-respect to come here. And they have bought into, they, you know, believe in American independence, freedom and democracy.

UNIT 1 Review
Grammar
1 Ask students to find the answers in the text individually. Elicit ideas from the whole class.

> ANSWERS
>
> 1 A nuclear family is just parents and their children; an extended family includes other relatives such as grandparents, cousins, and aunts and uncles.
> 2 Members can support one another, share care for children and elderly members, save money by eating and living together.

2 Ask students to underline the correct verb forms in the text, then check their answers with a partner. Elicit the correct sentences from the class.

> ANSWERS
>
> 1 is made
> 2 are related
> 3 has decreased
> 4 help
> 5 are looked after
> 6 are being shared
> 7 have been choosing
> 8 have been changing
> 9 are being lost
> 10 has been taken away

3 Ask students to do this in pairs, then compare with another pair. Elicit ideas from the class.

> SAMPLE ANSWERS
>
> Advantages: family members can enjoy one another's company, give moral support, share experience and knowledge, do activities together
>
> Disadvantages: if you do not share the values and interests of other members, you might not enjoy living in an extended family; you might want more independence, freedom and privacy

Vocabulary
4 Ask students to complete the words and phrases individually, then check with a partner.

> ANSWERS
>
> 1 fellow
> 2 travel
> 3 true
> 4 mutual
> 5 flatmate
> 6 acquaintance
> 7 blood

5 Ask students to talk about the people in pairs.

Real life
6 Ask students to order the conversation in pairs. Check the answers by asking students to read the lines in order.

> ANSWERS
>
> The sentences in the Student's Book should be numbered as follows: 1, 11, 9, 7, 13, 3, 5, 6, 8, 10, 12, 4, 2

7 Ask students to act out the conversation in pairs.

Speaking
8 Ask students to talk about a personal relationship in pairs. Circulate and monitor their speaking.

Unit 2 Storytelling

Lead-in

Personal response

Ask members of the class to talk about a real person, living or dead, they have recently read a biography of, seen a biopic about, read an obituary of, or read about in a newspaper or magazine. Ask them to give a few details about their life and achievements. It could also be just somebody they like and know things about, such as a sports person, or film or music star.

1 🔊 [1.6] Read the questions with the class to focus their listening. Play the recording, and ask students to answer the questions and discuss their answers with a partner. Play the recording again for them to check. Elicit answers from the class.

> **ANSWERS**
>
> 1 He was a Formula One driver; he died in a crash in 1994; he had a rivalry with Alain Prost; he did charity work; he was Brazilian.
> 2 The film is neutral; the book was very biased against Alain Prost.

Audioscript 🔊 [1.6]

A: Have you seen the film *Senna*?

B: No, I read a biography of him a few years back. I've heard the film's really good. What did you think?

A: I thought it was fantastic. It's a documentary essentially, but unlike most documentaries there's no narrator. It just tells the story of his life through archive footage. Actually, I'm not a huge fan of Formula One so I wasn't really expecting to enjoy it, but it's really gripping.

B: Oh, so it didn't really give any opinion on whether Senna really believed he was superior to every other driver or whether he acted unfairly sometimes …

A: No, not at all … it leaves you to make up your own mind about him completely. A lot of the film focuses on his driving career, from his early wins to his death in a crash in, ummm, 1994, I think it was. For much of it, he had this big rivalry with the French driver Alain Prost and they took each other off the track at critical times. But the film doesn't say who was right or wrong … although in the end you come down on Senna's side …

B: Well, you say it's objective, but of course the viewer's opinion can be manipulated by the director… just in the way he chooses to edit the film.

A: Yes, no, I suppose that's true … but it's not a sentimental film. Perhaps you feel sympathetic towards Senna, 'cos he seemed like a nice guy – ummm … he did a lot of charity work in his native Brazil – but it felt very fair and impartial …

B: Well, that's very different from the biography I read. The writer made his opinion very clear. He was very biased against Alain Prost and took every opportunity to tell you so.

A: Was it good otherwise?

B: Well, quite good but rather repetitive and not very well written. But there were a few good anecdotes in it. There are better biographies out there, I'm told.

Background notes

Ayrton Senna was born on 21 March, 1960 in São Paolo, Brazil into a wealthy family. In 1981 he moved to England and started racing in cars, with increasing success, until in 1983 he won the British Formula 3 Championship. For the next 11 years he worked his way up to become one of the top drivers of his generation. In 1988 he joined McLaren, where Alain Prost was number 1 driver, and a fierce rivalry developed between them. Controversy surrounded some of Senna's behaviour on the track, particularly in some of the intense battles with Prost. Senna often angered Prost by his aggressive driving. On one occasion, for example, Prost claimed that Senna's driving during a race went against what he had agreed in a pre-race agreement. The end came in 1994 with the third race of the season at Imola in Italy. Already in qualifying his friend and fellow Brazilian Barrichello had crashed, breaking his arm and nose. Then Austrian Ratzenberger was killed. Senna was very concerned and upset; he called a meeting of the drivers to lead them for moves for greater race safety. However, on the 6th lap of the race, Senna's car left the track at 330 kph and crashed into a concrete wall, killing him. The Brazilian government declared three days of national mourning, and 3 million people lined the streets for his funeral.

2 🔊 [1.6] Ask students to decide the opposites of the words in pairs – they may need to use a dictionary to do this. Then play the recording again for students to hear which ones were used.

> **ANSWERS**
>
> objective – subjective
> truthful – untruthful (lying)
> biased – neutral
> fair – unfair
> partial – impartial
> sympathetic – unsympathetic
> accurate – inaccurate
> The speakers use: *unfairly, objective, sympathetic, impartial, fair, biased*

3 Ask students to match the adjectives to the genres individually, then check with a partner. Elicit the answers from the whole class.

> **SAMPLE ANSWERS**
>
> 1 d   2 e   3 a   4 c   5 b

4 Ask students to describe a book or a film to a partner. Encourage them to use some of the vocabulary from the previous exercises.

2a The film of the book

Lead-in

Personal response

Ask the class to name five books which have been made into films. Try to get them name the author of the book and the star and/or director of the film.

Vocabulary books and films

1 Ask students to talk about the photo and say what sort of film the location was for.

> **ANSWER**
>
> Probably a cowboy film or western.

2 Ask students to categorise the words in the box, then discuss their ideas with a partner.

> **ANSWERS**
>
> Books only: author, best-seller, chapter, publisher, readers
> Films only: blockbuster, box office, cast, director, location, producer, screenwriter, script
> Both: audience, character, plot, portrayal, scene, setting, storyline, theme, trilogy

3 Ask students to match the words in pairs and explain the difference, and then compare their answers with another pair. Ask students to look at the example and read the information in the *Wordbuilding* box. Refer to page 19 of the Workbook if you feel students need more practice. Elicit answers from the class.

> **ANSWERS**
>
> | Books | Films |
> |---|---|
> | author | screenwriter |
> | best-seller | blockbuster |
> | chapter | scene |
> | publisher | producer |
> | readers | audience |

Vocabulary notes

Some of the words in the list can be used in relation to both films and books, though they may have a different meaning in each context.

setting: has a similar meaning in both, referring to the place where the action takes place

cast: only refers to the actors who play the characters in the film; we talk about *characters* in both novels and films

audience: refers to the people watching the film, or to the people who might watch a film (e.g. *There isn't a big audience for that kind of film in France.*)

trilogy: a sequence of three books or films about the same characters

plot: this is the storyline in a book or a film

portrayal: the way that a character is shown in a film or a book

scene: sections of a film are called scenes. In a novel, a *scene* means an interaction in a particular place (a formal section of a novel is called a chapter).

theme: this refers to what the film or book is about, e.g. human cruelty, the importance of love

Speaking and listening

4 Ask students to ask and answer the questions in pairs. Elicit some specific examples from the whole class.

5 [1.7] Ask students to discuss the question, and elicit some suggestions from the class. Then play the recording and ask students to say which answer the film critic gives.

> **ANSWER**
>
> b

Audioscript [1.7]

P = Presenter; M = Mark Mowlam

P: Take a bestselling book, a great storyline and add a great cast, an experienced director and a large filming budget. And what do you get? A box office success, you would think. Think again. There's no guarantee that a book that has enjoyed great success will make a good film. Some film adaptations have worked, others have flopped. So what's the secret? That was the question I put earlier to film critic Mark Mowlam, who has followed the progress of many book-to-film adaptations in his time and has recently reported on the making of Tolkien's *The Hobbit*.

M: Well, the goal is really to make a good film that remains true to the spirit of the book. There are many examples of adaptations which have failed because they tried to remain too faithful to the plot and the characters of the book. Probably because at the time the producers worried that they'd alienate loyal readers if they departed too much from the original text. But in fact that's a mistake: what works well on the page doesn't necessarily work well on screen: you have to give the screenwriter freedom to create a script that flows, even if that means changing the original.

So what we find is a lot of good films – *Sense and Sensibility, the Shining*, for example – that are completely unlike the original book. And readers are generally OK about this because they think of book and film as two separate works of art. But there are films that have managed to stay true to the book and still be good films. What they've done – a bit like in cooking, I suppose – is to put in all the book's good ingredients and then boil them down to a concentrated mixture that's packed with the flavour of the original work.

Probably the best example of this is the *Lord of the Rings* trilogy by Peter Jackson. The central theme of the book – which is a struggle between the forces of good and evil – perhaps wasn't so difficult to portray, but J.R. Tolkien created a very original other world and reproducing that was a much more difficult task, because each reader has their own very distinct idea of what this world was like. I think Jackson did a fantastic job, using the spectacular scenery of New Zealand for the film's location. The other thing about *The Lord of the Rings* is that it's a very substantial work – three books, each containing over twenty long chapters – so Jackson had to leave some elements of the story out. To compensate for this, he took the most important scenes and then put all the emotional force behind these. The result is that it has become one of the most successful films of all time, a blockbuster that has grossed almost $3 billion.

Background note

In 1937 J.R.R.Tolkien published *The Hobbit*, which has gone on to become the third best-selling novel of all time. From 1937 to 1949 he wrote the sequel, *The Lord of the Rings*. It is an epic fantasy story in three books, and became the second best-selling novel ever.

New Zealand film director Peter Jackson spent eight years working on a three-part film version of the novel, which came out over the years 2001–2003. The three films won 4, 2 and 11 Oscars respectively.

6 [1.7] Ask students to read through the questions to focus their listening and write any answers they remember. Play the recording again for them to check and complete their answers. Elicit answers from the class.

ANSWERS

1 a bestselling book, a great storyline, a great cast, an experienced director and a large budget
2 You have to give the screenwriter freedom to create a script that flows, even if that means changing the original.
3 good films that are completely unlike the original book
4 cooking
5 a struggle between the forces of good and evil
6 Because Tolkien created a very original other world.
7 He took the most important scenes and then put all the emotional force behind these.

7 Ask the class to discuss these questions in groups of three or four. Elicit some examples from the whole class.

Grammar past simple and present perfect

8 Elicit examples of the past simple and present perfect from the class, then ask students to match the sentences and the uses.

ANSWERS

1 b 2 a 3 c 4 d 5 e

9 Read the examples of the past simple and present perfect in the grammar box and ask students to complete the sentences with the correct form of the verb. They should do this individually, then check with a partner. Elicit answers from the class. Refer to page 158 of the Student's Book if necessary for further information and practice.

ANSWERS

1 read, have never read, has read
2 have been, was
3 Have ... written, wrote
4 Did ... see, have seen

Pronunciation note

Ensure that students are pronouncing *have* and *has* as /həv/ and /həz/ in unstressed situation, and also that they use contractions ('*ve* and '*s*) as far as possible.

Pronunciation the letter *l*

10a [1.8] Ask students to read the examples and say the words to themselves. Play the recording for students to listen, then again for them to repeat.

Audioscript [1.8]

location   film   would

10b [1.9] Ask students to read through the words first, then play the recording while they listen and write the correct number next to each word. Check the answers and play the recording again for students to practise.

ANSWERS

1 loyal (first 'l'), screenplay, plot, best-seller, trilogy
2 loyal (second 'l'), faithful, told, details, felt, child
3 calm, half, should, walk

Pronunciation: the letter 'l'

Note that the clear 'l' of *love* is often said to seem like /iː/, while the dark 'l' of *milk* is said to seem like /uː/. Note that the dark 'l' not only occurs before a consonant, but also before a pause, for example at the end of a sentence, so there is still a dark 'l' at the end of *faithful* whether the sentence is *He is faithful to his ideals* or *My dog is very faithful*.

Writing and speaking

11 Ask students to make notes about a writer or film maker, using the language they have practised in this section. You could then have some students tell the whole class what they know.

2b A close shave

Lead-in

Personal response
Elicit / Explain the meaning of *a close shave* (a near miss, a dangerous situation that nearly had serious results), then ask students if they have had any close shaves while driving, or know other friends or family who have. Ask them to describe the situation to the class.

Reading

1 Ask students to discuss the three situations with a partner. Elicit some suggestions about what would be the best thing to do from the whole class.

2 Ask students to talk about their close shaves with dangerous animals, if they have had any.

3 Read the rubric with the class to focus their attention, then ask them to read and answer individually. Elicit answers from the whole class.

> **ANSWERS**
> 1 A single rhino charged, but the guard acted quickly and fired a shot into the ground. The people were shaken.
> 2 Three young rhinos climbed onto the road in front of the jeep, then disappeared into the forest. The driver stopped the jeep quickly.
> 3 A female rhino (the mother of the three young) attacked the jeep and started biting it and pushing it; the driver managed to drive the jeep away.

4 Ask students to work in pairs to guess the meaning of the highlighted words, then check the meanings in a dictionary.

> **ANSWERS**
> *stretch their legs* = to walk around after sitting for a while
> *sprint* = run very fast
> *leap* = to make a long jump
> *veered off* = went off sharply in a different direction
> *slammed into* = ran into with full force
> *wrestle* = move by force
> *gouging* = sticking something sharp (in this case teeth) into a surface
> *skidded* = to slide out of control

5 Ask the class what the effect of these verbs is on the story.

> **ANSWER**
> They are dynamic verbs of motion, which add interest and excitement.

Grammar past tenses review

6 Read through the grammar box with the class to remind them of the four tenses under discussion. Ask students to match the tenses to the uses individually, then check with a partner. Elicit answers from the whole class.

> **ANSWERS**
> 1 c   2 a   3 b   4 d

7 Ask students to complete the summary individually, and then check with a partner.

> **ANSWERS**
> 1 were working
> 2 had
> 3 had told
> 4 hadn't been / weren't
> 5 shocked
> 6 knew / had known
> 7 hadn't been expecting / hadn't expected
> 8 didn't stop

Pronunciation contracted negative forms

8a [1.10] Ask students to listen and circle the contracted forms, then check with a partner. Elicit answers from the whole class.

> **ANSWERS**
> **weren't** (1 syllable)
> **hadn't** been expecting (2 syllables)
> **didn't** stop (2 syllables)

Audioscript [1.10]

Steve Winter and Douglas Chadwick, who **were working** in Kaziranga National Park, **had** three close encounters with rhinos all on the same day. Before entering the park, their guide **had told** them not to be afraid, so they **weren't** especially worried, but clearly the incidents **shocked** them. They **knew** that filming in the Park was dangerous work, but they **hadn't been expecting** to meet danger quite so soon or so frequently. But it **didn't stop** them carrying on!

Background notes

White Rhino: these live in Africa, and are the biggest species. They weigh over 3500 kg, are 3.5–4.6 m long, and 1.8–2 m high. They have 2 horns.

Black Rhino: these are similar to the White Rhino. There are only around 2,000 of them left in the wild in Africa.

Indian Rhino: These are usually slightly smaller than the White and Black Rhino, and only have one horn. They live in Nepal and northeastern India.

Javan Rhino: This is an endangered animal, with perhaps only 50 left in the wild in Java and Vietnam. They are a smaller species.

Sumatran Rhino: This is the smallest, with a single horn.

8b 🔘 [1.11] Ask students to work in pairs and note the syllables. Elicit answers from the whole class. Play the recording for them to check. Play the recording again and pause it after each sentence for students to repeat chorally and individually

ANSWERS

1 2 syllables	5 2 syllables
2 2 syllables	6 1 syllable
3 1 syllable	7 2 syllables
4 2 syllables	8 2 syllables

9 You might want to pre-teach the difficult vocabulary from the texts (see Vocabulary notes below), so students can concentrate on the task. Ask students to complete the reports individually, then check with a partner. Have the class read the answers back as complete sentences. Alternatively, the activity could be completed as homework.

ANSWERS

Report 1

1 was mountain-biking
2 had just finished
3 had been raining
4 was shining
5 were feeling
6 took
7 set
8 became
9 picked
10 went

Report 2

11 were driving
12 fell
13 landed
14 had escaped
15 had been grazing
16 had slipped
17 arrived

Vocabulary notes

off-road = riding across countryside, not on roads.

tarmac = mixture used for the surface of roads

bonnet = the cover of the engine at the front of a car

a breeding farm = a farm where they breed animals to produce young

to graze = to eat grass

to plunge = to fall a long way down

Grammar note

Note that we can make sentences with more than one past simple verb, to indicate a series of actions:

*He **looked** carefully around him, then he **opened** the door.*

We can have sentences with a past simple and a past continuous to indicate interrupted past action:

*I **was washing** the car when the boys **arrived** home.*

We can use to past continuous verbs to indicate simultaneous past action:

*While Paul **was cooking** lunch, Jane **was cleaning** the windows.*

10 🔘 [1.12] Ask students to complete the last sentence of each story in pairs. Play the recording and ask them to listen and compare, and check their answers to Exercise 9. Afterwards discuss their suggestions and the originals.

Audioscript 🔘 [1.12]

I was mountain-biking with a friend in Wales and we'd just finished a long off-road climb out of the Dysynni valley. It had been raining earlier but now the sun was shining and we were feeling quite warm. Since the rest of the route was downhill on tarmac roads, I took off my bike helmet and set off. Suddenly the road became very steep and the bike picked up speed quickly. There was a turn ahead in the road and I knew I was going to crash. The bike went straight into a wall, but luckily I flew over it and landed in a field of long grass.

Mr Charles Everson and his wife, Linda, were driving home from church one Sunday when a cow fell from the sky and landed on the bonnet of their van. The cow, which had escaped from a breeding farm, had been grazing too close to the edge of a cliff next to the road and had slipped and plunged 200ft. When the emergency services arrived at the scene they found the cow dead and Mr and Mrs Everson in shock.

Speaking

11 Ask students to prepare a description of a near miss, telling them that they can use a story about someone else, or invent one, if they don't have a story of their own. They should then tell their story to their partner, or to a group of students.

Homework

Students could prepare the story in Exercise 11 for homework, or write up their story after the speaking activity.

2c Once upon a time ...

Lead-in

Personal response

Ask the class to tell a fairy story – one from their country if they are a monolingual class, or an internationally known one if they are of mixed nationalities. (Try to avoid those in Exercise 2.) They should take it in turns to continue the story incident by incident around the class, correcting each other if somebody goes wrong.

Reading

1 Ask students to discuss their favourite stories in pairs, then report back to the class.

2 Ask students to discuss the questions about the fairy tales in pairs.

> **ANSWERS**
>
> 1 The Frog Prince
> 2 and 3 Students' own answers.

3 Elicit answers to the questions from the class and discuss the suggestions. Then ask them to read the text very quickly and find out if they were correct.

> **ANSWERS**
>
> They came from ordinary local people. At first the brothers just recorded them and wrote notes about them, then Wilhelm polished and reshaped them to make them more acceptable to children and parents.

Vocabulary note

to account for = be the reason for

to charm = to please

the core = the central part of

enchanting = magical

gender roles = what is expected of men and women

humble = modest, from a poor and simple background

implied = suggested something without saying it

occupied = in the control of another country

scholarly footnotes = serious academic notes

striving = fighting against difficulties

suppressed = not allowed – pushed down

thrived = continued and increased

4 Ask students to read and answer the questions individually, then check their answers with a partner.

> **ANSWERS**
>
> 1 They are popular around the world.
> 2 The brothers only sold a few copies of their books.
> 3 Germany was occupied by Napoleon and the French.
> 4 These stories were told by one woman (Marie) and she had had French nannies who told them, so they were probably not originally German.
> 5 Parents like the moral aspects, but not the violence.

5 Ask students to find the words and expressions to match the definitions, then check with a partner.

> **ANSWERS**
>
> | | |
> |---|---|
> | 1 Once upon a time | 5 moral |
> | 2 villain | 6 witch |
> | 3 wise | 7 cruel |
> | 4 faraway lands | 8 ever after |

Critical thinking close reading

6 Ask students to read the statements and decide if the information is true, false, or not given in the text. Elicit answers from the whole class.

> **ANSWERS**
>
> 1 N   2 T   3 T   4 F   5 F   6 T

Teaching note

Suggest students go through the reading passage and find the statements that are clearly supported or contradicted by information in the text. Then they should spend more time checking whether the remaining statements have any supporting information. Note that the information may be anywhere in the text. If they can't find information that supports or contradicts the statement, the answer must be 'not given'.

7 Ask students to work in pairs to summarise the Grimms' achievement.

> **SAMPLE ANSWER**
>
> They have made a set of old folk tales popular right around the world.

Word focus *keep*

8 Ask students to do this individually, then compare their answers with a partner.

> **ANSWERS**
>
> *kept each other company*: sat together as friends
> *keeping records of*: taking notes so they didn't get lost
> *keep your promises*: do what you have promised to do
>
> 1 don't forget about the time – remember to check it
> 2 stay happy, don't get depressed
> 3 not telling people something they aren't supposed to know
> 4 make sure you know about all the changes
> 5 stop you doing what you were going to do
> 6 write a diary regularly

Writing and speaking

9 Ask students to make notes about a traditional story.

10 Students tell their story to a partner.

Homework

Ask students to write up the story.

2d What a disaster!

Lead-in

Personal response

Ask the class to mention some recent disasters (natural or man-made) they have heard about in the world. Ask them to comment on their causes and effects.

Real life reacting to stories

1 Ask students to discuss things that go wrong, in pairs, and then elicit some of their comments for wider class discussion.

2 ✪ [1.13] Ask students to read the situations with a partner and discuss what they think happened next. You may need to explain some of the language used (see Vocabulary notes below). Elicit ideas from around the class. Then play the recording for them to see how close they got to the original.

> **ANSWERS**
> 1 Another bus came in 15 minutes.
> 2 He put his hands over the hole.
> 3 He had to wait for someone else to come home.
> 4 The lights went out and a person in the lift started screaming.
> 5 She fell off the bike and cut her hand.
> 6 Most of the work had been saved into a temporary file.

Audioscript ✪ [1.13]

Conversation 1

A: The bus broke down on the motorway, so we were all left stranded until help could arrive.

B: What did you do?

A: Luckily another bus came within about 15 minutes and we all transferred to that.

B: That must have been a relief.

Conversation 2

A: My trousers got caught on the door handle and as I walked away they tore.

B: Oh, that's awful.

A: Yes, I had to walk right across the restaurant back to our table with my hands over the hole.

B: How embarrassing!

Conversation 3

A: I bent the key trying to force it into the door lock and when I tried to straighten the key it snapped.

B: How did you get in?

A: I went to the neighbours', but they weren't at home. So I just had to wait 'til someone came home.

B: Yeah, a similar thing happened to me once.

Conversation 4

A: The lift got stuck between floors 25 storeys up and two of the occupants were completely panic-stricken.

B: What a nightmare!

A: It was. Then the lights in the lift went off and one of them started screaming.

B: Yeah I think I would have done the same thing.

Conversation 5

A: The tyres on my bicycle were badly worn and when I hit a bump in the road one of them burst.

B: Poor you!

A: Well, I came off and cut my hand. Thank goodness there were no cars behind me.

B: That was lucky.

Conversation 6

A: My computer froze without any reason while I was working.

B: Really? How strange.

A: Yeah, I thought I'd lost about four hours' work, but when I rebooted the computer I searched for some of the key words in my document and I found a temporary file which had most of the document in it.

B: That was good thinking.

Vocabulary notes

we were left stranded = on our own, with nobody around to help

to get caught on something = to get hooked onto something so you cannot move without tearing or breaking it

to bend something = to turn something – usually metal – at right-angles to its previous shape

to snap = to break suddenly

panic-stricken = hit by panic (*stricken* is one form of the past participle of *strike*)

badly worn = the surface has become smooth, or there is very little of it left

a bump = a raised area

3 ✪ [1.13] Read through the expressions with the class, and check that students understand them all. Ask them to work in pairs and say which ones were used in which conversations, then elicit answers from the whole class. Don't confirm or correct their answers. Finally, play the recording for them to check.

> **ANSWERS**
> 1 That must have been a relief.
> 2 Oh, that's awful. / Oh, how embarrassing!
> 3 Yeah, a similar thing happened to me once.
> 4 What a nightmare! / Yeah, I think I would have done the same thing.
> 5 Poor you! / That was lucky!
> 6 Really? How strange! / That was good thinking.

Pronunciation linking and assimilation

4a 🔊 [1.14] Read the rubric and examples with the class, and listen to the examples. Ask students to repeat them chorally and individually.

4b 🔊 [1.15] Ask students to work with a partner to underline the sounds that are linked or assimilated. Elicit suggested answers from the class and discuss them, but don't say what is correct. Play the recording a few times for them to check, then play it with pauses for them to practise chorally and individually.

> ANSWERS
>
> 1. What a nightmare!
> 2. Oh, that's awful. Poor you!
> 3. How embarrassing!
> 4. Really? That's odd.
> 5. That was good thinking.
> 6. A similar thing happened to me.

> **Pronunciation note**
>
> Make sure students have understood that **linking** takes place:
>
> – when one word ends with vowel (or is a vowel, as in *a*) and the next starts with a consonant, e.g. *It's a long way.*
>
> – when one word ends with a consonant and the next starts with a vowel, e.g. *He went away.*
>
> **Assimilation** is when one consonant gets mixed with the one that follows it, e.g. *He went with them.*
>
> *I talked to the prime minister.*

5 Ask students to choose one of the topics listed (or another if they have a more interesting story about it), and make some notes about what happened to them (or someone else they know well, if they don't have a story of their own). Ask them to get into groups of four to tell and listen to the stories. Encourage them to use the reaction comments from the box as people tell the story – and to get the intonation correct. Circulate and monitor students' speaking for later feedback.

2e A real-life drama

> **Lead-in**
>
> **Personal response**
> Ask the class to talk briefly about a recent real-life drama that has been in the news in the past few weeks or months.

Writing a story

1 Ask students to read the two questions to focus their reading, then read the paragraph and answer the questions. Elicit the answers from the class.

> ANSWERS
>
> 1 He had got his foot caught in a metal animal trap.
> 2 tired, hungry, nervous, not happy

2 Ask students to work in pairs to identify the events and put them in order. Then elicit the order from the class. Make sure they understand that they should give the order the events happened, not the order they are written in the story.

> ANSWERS
>
> 1 Rowan had been moaning about sore feet all day.
> 2 They had something to eat (more than three hours ago).
> 3 They weren't carrying many supplies.
> 4 Rowan was struggling.
> 5 Chris was tired.
> 6 He wanted to get back to the camp before dark.
> 7 'I can't move,' cried Rowan.
> 8 Chris walked back slowly.
> 9 'Reach down and try to free your foot.'
> 10 Chris could see that Rowan was caught in a trap.

3 Ask students to think about why the story starts when it does.

> ANSWER
>
> to make the story more dramatic

Writing skill using descriptive words

4a Ask students to discuss the meaning of the expressions with a partner. Then elicit and discuss ideas with the class.

> ANSWERS
>
> **Way of speaking:**
> *cried* = shouting in fear and/or pain
> *moaning* = complaining about everything
> *said encouragingly* = speaking in a happy, helpful-sounding, friendly way
> **Movement:**
> *struggling* = finding it hard to keep going
> *trudging* = walking slowly, when tired
> *walking back slowly* = returning the way he had just come

4b Ask students to work out the meaning of the words in pairs, then use a dictionary to check. Elicit answers from the whole class.

ANSWERS

1 to shout in a loud, high voice, when you are in danger or pain, or excited
2 to talk quietly to yourself, complaining about a person or a situation
3 to talk quietly so other people cannot hear, often a complaint
4 to speak in a tired way, because you have had enough of the other person
5 to speak in a confident way, even though you do not feel confident
6 to go very slowly and carefully along the edge of something
7 to jump up quickly
8 to almost fall over
9 to walk quickly and energetically
10 to turn slowly because you are afraid or worried

4c Ask the class to call out other verbs; list them on the board under *speaking* and *walking* (e.g. speaking: *whisper, shout, bawl, chatter*; walking: *trot, gallop, speed, hurry, race, crawl*) and discuss what they mean.

5 Ask students to write the ending of the story about Rowan and Chris individually. This could be done for homework.

6 Ask students to exchange their story with a partner and check their partner's story.

7 Ask students to read one another's stories in groups, or have some individuals read their ending out to the rest of the class for comment.

Homework

Ask students to write a story of their own – real or invented – in which they use different verbs of speaking and moving. They can then bring them to class to share and read.

2f History of film

Before you watch

1 Students work in groups. Ask them to look at the photo and discuss the questions. Take feedback from the class.

ANSWERS

1 It looks as if he might be sneezing.
2 in the late 19th century
3 Because it is an early piece of moving film.

2 Before watching the video, ask students to predict which things from the box they will see.

While you watch

3 Play the video for students to check their ideas for Exercise 2 and answer the question.

ANSWERS

We see all the things listed except for actors arriving at an awards ceremony, an Oscar statue, and a scene from an animated film.
Mary Pickford is the other actor mentioned.

4 Give students time to read the events. Play the first part of the video (to 01.36) for them to put them in order.

ANSWERS

1 f   2 b   3 a   4 d   5 c   6 e

5 Give students time to read the questions. Then play the second part of the video (01.37 to the end) and ask students to answer the questions.

ANSWERS

1 go to new places and see the world in a different way
2 a presidential inauguration, an earthquake or bomb, arctic explorers, Wright brothers, flights
3 a plant growing and a hawk flying
4 Documentaries use actors, set design, lighting, costume and even computer animation.

6 Ask students to read the sentences from the script. Then play the video for them to complete them.

ANSWERS

1 For over a century
2 In the 19th century
3 Before long
4 By the 1920s
5 At the turn of the 20th century
6 Since those early days

After you watch

7 Students work in pairs to roleplay an interview with an actor or actress, according to the instructions.

8 Students work in groups to discuss the questions.

Videoscript

Part 1

00.01–00.20 For over a century, film has captured the imagination of audiences all over the world. Motion pictures have allowed us to explore the unknown, bring histories to life and allow generations to dream of living like the stars of the silver screen.

00.21–01.09 In the 19th century, inventors realised they could create the illusion of motion by presenting a quick succession of pictures. In the US, inventors Thomas Edison and William Dixon exploited this idea and created the kinetoscope in 1891, bringing motion pictures to the American public.

In arcades, viewers peeped at short films in a cabinet-like machine, which played continuously in a loop. Before long, projection allowed large audiences to view the spectacle at the local cinema or nickelodeon. Audiences were captivated by this new technology. Everyday life became entrancing on the big screen.

01.10–01.44 Soon enough, images of roaring trains and vaudeville acts were replaced by the complex story lines of human melodramas. By the 1920s, the emerging film studio system was centred in Hollywood, California. The increasingly expensive productions drew crowds to fill newly-built movie palaces. And actors like Mary Pickford and Charlie Chaplin became stars. They were the new American aristocracy, a tradition that continues with Hollywood blockbusters and film stars of today.

Part 2

01.45–02.24 But outside of Tinseltown's dream factories, film has taken us to new places and allowed us to see the world in a different way.

At the turn of the 20th century, newsmen carried cameras looking for real spectacles and history in the making.

They filmed presidential inaugurations, explorers in the Arctic, and landmark events like the Wright brothers' flights.

In the hands of explorers and scientists, the camera has proven an amazing window to the world, bringing home images of distant cultures and putting the far corners of the Earth into clearer focus.

02.25–03.13 Since those early days, documentary filmmakers have trained their lenses on reality, showing life in new ways. Activities that take hours or days to occur pass by in only seconds. Likewise, film can reveal the agility of a hawk in slow motion.

In places impossible for us to visit, the camera brings us images of great beauty.

Over the years, documentary film makers have learned to borrow from the studio blockbusters. While unravelling the mysteries of distant cultures or ancient histories, documentaries employ actors, set design, lighting, costume and even computer animation to bring important moments back to life.

03.16–03.32 With these tools, we can learn, envision and experience the past in a way inconceivable only a few generations ago. Who knew that those early flickering images would have such a tremendous impact?

UNIT 2 Review

Grammar

1 Ask students to complete the text with the correct form of the verbs. Elicit answers from the class.

ANSWERS	
1 have filmed	11 had parked
2 have never had	12 ran
3 felt / have felt	13 zipped
4 wanted	14 assumed
5 was sitting	15 had gone
6 called	16 waited
7 wasn't	17 had died
8 didn't take	18 looked
9 called	19 had locked
10 were slowly approaching	20 had been playing

2 Ask students to answer the questions in pairs. Elicit answers from the class.

ANSWERS
1 He hid in his tent.
2 He thought they had made a noise in the kitchen.
3 The lions played in the kitchen and made a terrible mess.

Vocabulary

3 Ask students to choose the words to complete the sentences individually, then check with a partner. Elicit the answers from the class as complete sentences.

ANSWERS
1 impartial, accurate
2 author, characters
3 plot, gripping
4 audience, portrayal
5 blockbuster, thought-provoking

4 Ask students to talk about a film of a book in pairs.

Real life

5 Ask students to match the news and responses individually, then check with a partner. Elicit the answers from the class.

ANSWERS
1 d   2 f   3 c   4 a   5 b   6 e

6 Ask students to tell each other about their bad experience in pairs. Circulate and monitor their speaking.

Speaking

7 Ask students to work in groups of four and complete the story. They should practise it together, so that they can each tell the whole story. Give the students in each group the letter A, B, C or D, then ask all the people with the same letter to tell one another their stories.

Unit 3 Science and technology

Lead-in

Personal response

Ask students to work in groups of four to discuss this question:

What are the five most important developments in science and technology in the history of mankind?

Ask them to appoint a secretary to note their ideas, and the reasons for them. Ask the secretaries to report back to the class and open the discussion to everyone.

1 Read through the questions with the class, and invite students to discuss them. Elicit what effects these two situations might have for them or for other people, e.g. they might lose hours of work on their computer, they might not have access to documents or contact details they need for an important meeting, etc.

2 Ask students to look at the picture and read the caption. Read the first question with the class and check they understand the meaning of *breakthrough* (see Vocabulary notes below). Ask the whole class for the answer to question 1, then ask students to discuss question 2 in pairs, and give reasons for their answers.

> ANSWERS
> 1 communications
> 2 students' own answers (possible answers include: using the power of thought, more practical applications of virtual reality)

Pronunciation note

Read through the words in the box with the class, and have them repeat them chorally and individually. Check the words where the stress is not on the first syllable:

artificial, intelligence, communication, exploration

Note also the elision in *medicine*: /medsn/

Vocabulary notes

artificial = not natural, i.e. electronic or technological

benefits = advantages, positive effects

breakthrough = important new discovery that has a serious effect

interact = communicate with one another

3 🔊 [1.16] Read through the three predictions with the class. Ask the class to suggest some justifications the speakers might make for their predictions. Then listen to the recording and compare the justifications actually given by the speakers with those suggested by the class.

> ANSWERS
> 1 Because some people are already living to be 100 and numbers are likely to increase.
> 2 Because the technology already exists and will probably become more sophisticated.
> 3 Because people will soon discover how to control the weather.

Audioscript 🔊 [1.16]

1 I expect that most of my generation will live to be around 100 years old. There are already 12,000 people in the UK aged over 100 and it's predicted that by the year 2060 that number will have risen to about one million.

2 I think people will be interacting with intelligent machines even more than they do now. I read this article about things called *chatbots* which are programmes that can hold intelligent conversations with people in chat rooms on the Internet. These programmes already exist.

3 I don't think global warming is going to be the problem that everyone says it is. By the middle of this century I think humans will have discovered ways to control the weather. If you think about it, the benefits – commercial and otherwise – are so great – for agriculture, for stopping natural disasters and so on – that it's only a matter of time before someone works out a way.

4 Ask students to get into pairs to discuss which of the predictions they think will come true. Elicit some ideas from the whole class.

3a Is technology the answer?

Lead-in

Personal response

Ask the class: *What do you think are the main problems that will face mankind in the next 50 years?* Ask students to make suggestions and invite others to comment on them. Note the main problem areas they raise on the board, and when they have discussed them say: *Put the problems in order of possibility by writing an order number next to them.* Then discuss their suggested orders and reasons for them as a class.

Speaking

1 Ask students to discuss which problem the picture represents in a group of four. They could use dictionaries to check the meanings of the words for this activity. Elicit answers from the class.

> **ANSWER**
>
> Congestion, overpopulation

Pronunciation note

Read through the problems in the box with the class, and have them repeat them chorally and individually, taking care with word stress:

epi*dem*ic, overpopu*la*tion, pol*lu*tion, *pov*erty

Vocabulary notes

congestion = when there is too much traffic and vehicles or people cannot move freely

epidemic = when there is a serious illness that spreads rapidly through the population

overpopulation = when there are too many people living in an area

pollution = air, land or water that is dirty and affected by chemicals

poverty = when people don't have enough money to pay for food, clothing and a place to live

starvation = not having enough food to stay alive

2 Ask students to stay in their groups to discuss the question of technological solutions to the problems listed. Elicit some suggestions from the class.

> **SAMPLE ANSWERS**
>
> congestion: regulate traffic flow to keep traffic moving
>
> epidemic: medical technology can treat disease
>
> pollution: technological solutions can prevent factories, cars etc. from emitting pollution (but often people don't want to pay for them).
>
> starvation: pesticides, nano-technology, GM foods

Listening

3 🔊 [1.17] Ask students to read the three statements about overpopulation, and the names of the three people,

to focus their listening. Then ask students to listen and match the statements to the speakers. Play the recording once while they just listen. Play the recording again for them to answer, then check with a partner. Check any new language, particularly the key words (see Vocabulary notes below). If necessary, play it a third time for them to check, correct and complete. Elicit the answers from the whole class.

> **ANSWERS**
>
> 1 Thomas Malthus
> 2 Paul Ehrlich
> 3 the speaker

Audioscript 🔊 [1.17]

Hello everyone … one moment, I'll just adjust my microphone … OK, that's better. I can see a lot of hopeful-looking faces out there. I'm speaking to a government committee tomorrow and I hope they look as bright-eyed as you do … Let me just say that I'm afraid that those of you who have come looking for immediate answers to overpopulation are going to be disappointed, but I hope I can at least give you some cause for optimism. I'm not going to speak for too long because I'd like to hear what you have to say too, but let me tell you first how I see the situation …

In 1798 an English economist, Thomas Malthus, claimed that the population always grows faster than the food supply, until war, disease or famine arrive to reduce the number of people. A century and a half later in 1968, Paul Ehrlich wrote in his book *The Population Bomb* that medical science was keeping too many people alive and that we had failed to control the birth rate. He predicted that as a result hundreds of millions of people would soon starve to death.

But his bomb was a dud. Yes, medical science has extended life expectancy and the population carries on growing: around seven billion today and it will probably peak at around 9 billion by 2050. But mass starvation? It hasn't happened. Why? Because science stepped in with better seeds and better pesticides to boost food production and it's about to step in again with nano-technology, which will in turn help us to engineer safer and cheaper foods.

So what about overpopulation? Let me give you a fact: if in 2045 there are 9 billion people in the world, the population density will still only be half that of France today. And no-one complains about overcrowding there: France is the world's favourite holiday destination! Some of the new megacities of Asia might not be such pleasant places to live … but the problem is not just the number of people. The problem is how people consume resources.

By 2030 more than a billion people in the developing world will belong to the 'global middle class'. That's a good thing. But it will be a bad thing for the planet if those people start eating meat and driving big cars every day. Some – ultracautious – people say we should bring in wartime emergency measures to conserve resources. I don't think that's the answer, but then I'm a scientist at heart (even if I'm semi-retired now). For me the answer lies in innovations like biofuels and other alternative energy sources …

I'll talk about these specific solutions in the second part of my talk but let's just go back to Malthus for a moment.

<u>People, he argued, are basically lazy. They won't do anything unless they are forced to by necessity</u>. But what he didn't take into account is that faced with disaster people are not lazy. Mankind and science will rise to the challenge … that is my sincere belief … Oh, by the way, one more thing: the necessity train arrives in half an hour …

Vocabulary notes

bright-eyed = enthusiastic, interested

famine = a time when there is no food and everyone is hungry

to starve to death = to die of hunger

a dud = something which did not function

to step in = to enter into a situation

to boost = to increase; to give power to

to conserve = to protect

at heart = basically, deep down

to take into account = to consider, to think about

Background notes

Thomas Malthus (1766–1834) studied at Jesus College, Cambridge 1784–96, and then in 1797 became a curate at a country church. Between 1798 and 1826 he published six editions of his controversial work *An Essay on the Principle of Population*. From 1805 he was Professor of History and Political Economy at a small private college, and in 1818 he was elected a Fellow of the Royal Society.

Paul Ehrlich (born 1932) took a BSc degree at the University of Pennsylvania (1953) and an MA (1955) and PhD (1957) at the University of Kansas. From 1959 he held various lecturing posts at Stanford University. He developed the idea that sustainability is due to population, affluence and technology.

4 🔊 [1.17] Read through the sentences with the class. Check that they understand them all. Play the recording and ask students to decide if the sentences are true or false, then check with a partner. Play the recording once more for them to check. Elicit answers from the class.

ANSWERS

See also underlined phrases in the audioscript

1 F (he doesn't have immediate answers)

2 T

3 F (there will be 9 million)

4 F (it will help in the future)

5 F (the population density overall would be half that of France)

6 T

7 T

5 Ask students to say what a prefix is (a particle added to the front of a word to change its meaning). Read the information in the *Wordbuilding* box, then ask students to do the exercise individually, before checking with a partner. Elicit answers from the whole class. Refer to page 27 of the Workbook for further information and practice.

ANSWERS

1 d   2 f   3 b   4 a   5 e   6 c

Extra activity

Ask students to decide the meaning of the following words with prefixes, based on the previous exercise:

megaphone	an instrument for speaking to a crowd of people
microscope	an instrument for looking at very small objects
nanosecond	a tiny part of a second
biology	the study of living things
ultrasonic	beyond the level of sound

6 Ask students in the whole class to give their opinions on this question, with reasons, and discuss any comments made.

Pronunciation /r/ and /t/ in American English

7a 🔊 [1.18] Ask students to read through the words in the box and think about how they say them. Elicit any differences between their pronunciation and that of the speaker on the recording. Play the recording and ask the same question again.

ANSWERS

For /t/ he says /d/. The /r/ sound in the middle of the word is pronounced more than in British English.

7b 🔊 [1.19] Ask students to read the gapped phrases to focus their listening. Play the recording for them to answer, then give them time to check with a partner. Play the recording again for them to check the words and focus on the American pronunciation. Elicit the answers, and ask students how they think a British speaker would say the phrases.

Audioscript and key 🔊 [1.19]

1 eight metres

2 an Internet site

3 a metal bar

4 a short letter

5 a twenty-first birthday

6 a world beater

7c 🔊 [1.20] Play the recording for students to check the British pronunciation (see audioscript 1.19).

Grammar future forms review

8 The extra activity below could be done in preparation for Exercise 8. Ask students to match the verbs forms and uses individually, then check with a partner. Elicit the answers from the class. If you feel students need further clarification or practice, see page 159 of the Student's Book.

ANSWERS

a 5   b 5   c 1   d 2   e 1
f 2   g 4   h 1   i 3

Extra activity

Ask students to first match the sentences in the grammar box with the uses a–i in Exercise 8 (answers below). This will make it easier for them to complete Exercise 8.

a The necessity train **arrives** in half an hour.

b It **will be** a bad thing for the planet if all those people **start** eating meat and driving big cars.

c The population **will** probably **peak** at around 9 billion by the middle of the century.

d Those of you who have come here looking for answers **are going to be** disappointed.

e One moment, **I'll just adjust** my microphone.

f **I'm not going to speak** for too long.

g **I'm speaking** to a government committee tomorrow.

h It **will be** a bad thing for the planet if all those people **start** eating meat and driving big cars.

i Science **is about to step** in again with nanotechnology solutions.

9 Ask students to choose the correct future forms in the text individually, then check with a partner. Elicit answers from the whole class as complete sentences.

> ANSWERS
>
> | | | |
> |---|---|---|
> | 1 we'll wait | 5 will take | 8 starts |
> | 2 arrives | 6 is | 9 is speaking |
> | 3 I'll begin | 7 is talking | 10 I am going to show |
> | 4 going to | | |

10 🔵 [1.21] Ask students to read through the sentences and complete them with a suitable future form. Ask them to check with a partner. They should refer to the examples and the list in Exercise 8 to help them decide. Elicit some answers from the class, and note them. Then play the recording for them to note the correct answers. Afterwards, compare them with the students' answers.

Audioscript and key 🔵 [1.21]

1 World leaders **are meeting** in Geneva tomorrow to discuss the issue of overpopulation.

2 In the next few weeks, the government **is going to introduce** a fee for each child that couples have after their first two children.

3 Scientists say that space colonies **will be** the only solution for overpopulation in the medium term.

4 Doctors have said that in future they **are not going to spend** so much effort keeping the old alive.

5 The government **will launch** a new education programme later today to encourage women to have fewer children.

6 People **will have to** change their lifestyles if they **want** the world's resources to support the growing population in the coming years.

Vocabulary notes

the issue = a problem

a fee = a payment of money

colonies = groups of people living together

in the medium term = not immediate (short term) or far in the future (long term), but in a few years' time

11 Ask students to find the time expressions from Exercise 10 in pairs, and then order them as required from nearest to furthest from now. Elicit the answers from the class in that order. You may want to write them on the board as they give them.

> ANSWERS
>
> | | |
> |---|---|
> | 1 later today | 4 in the coming years |
> | 2 tomorrow | 5 in the medium term |
> | 3 in the next few weeks | 6 in future |

Speaking

12 Ask students to work in groups of four to discuss and develop their plan to deal with overpopulation. One should be a secretary who keeps a note of everything that is said. Ask the secretaries to explain their plan and reasons to the rest of the class for further comment and discussion.

Homework

Ask students to write an essay (150–200 words) explaining their plan for preventing the overpopulation of the planet. When they have written it, ask them to share it in a group of four, and rewrite it on the basis of any language or content comments made.

3b Revealed world

Lead-in

Personal response

Say to students: *Think about some recent times that you have used a paper map.* Ask: *What kind of map was it?* (e.g. a single town plan, a book of road maps, a world atlas) *Why did you use it?* Ask them to share and compare this information in a group of four. Finally elicit some details from the whole class. Build up necessary language on the board (e.g. *town plan, atlas, map book*).

Speaking

1 Ask students to work in pairs to discuss how they use printed and digital media. Elicit some details from the class. Read the information in the *Wordbuilding* box and make sure students are familiar with this type of compound noun, where the first noun works like an adjective in front of the second noun which it describes. Compare *good advice* with *travel advice,* and *a strict rule* with *a grammar rule* to clarify the point. Refer to Workbook page 27 for further examples and practice.

Reading

2 Ask students to talk about the picture and the labels on it in pairs, and answer the two questions. Elicit some responses from the whole class.

3 Ask students to look carefully at the table to focus their reading, then read the article and complete the table individually. They can then check their answers with a partner, before you elicit them from the whole class.

> ANSWERS
>
> 2 reality 2.0
> 3 information about ATMs, restaurants etc.
> 5 how busy the restaurant is
> 6 smart phone, special video glasses
> 7 projected images onto objects we are using
> 9 show transcript of what people are saying

Vocabulary notes

Ensure students understand the meaning of the expression *augmented reality* (AR). It is a term used to refer to a live view of the physical world where certain elements are *augmented* (i.e. added to) by computer-generated information which can include graphics, sound, words or video. Also check that they are familiar with the following vocabulary:

to superimpose = to put one thing on top of another

sophisticated = very intelligent and complicated

an interface = the place where two things meet

overload = too much of something to cope with

wraparound sunglasses = glasses that go around the head

etched = cut into glass

inconspicuous = not easily seen

to be absorbed in = to be occupied doing something

4 Ask the class to read and respond to each question in turn, and discuss the issues as a class.

Grammar future continuous and future perfect simple

5 Ask students to match the uses and the sentences individually, then check with a partner. Elicit the answers from the whole class. Read through the information in the grammar box with the class and check they understand the differences in use explained in sentences 1 and 2. For further examples and practice, refer students to page 160 of the Student's Book.

> ANSWERS
>
> 1 b, c, e   2 a, d

Grammar note

Ask students to look at the structure of these two future tenses:

Future continuous: *will be* + the present participle of the main verb

Future perfect: *will have* + the past participle of the main verb

We often use the future continuous with a point in time, e.g. *Next Friday I'll be swimming in the Mediterranean.* or with a period of time, e.g. *Next week I'll be staying in an Italian hotel.*

We often use the future perfect with *by* + a time expression: e.g. *I'll have finished this cleaning by four o'clock.* *He'll have finished his degree course by next May.*

6 Ask students to complete the sentences with the correct future forms of the verbs in brackets. They should do this individually, then check with a partner. Elicit the answers from the class as complete sentences.

> ANSWERS
>
> 1 will be using, will have replaced
> 2 will be sitting
> 3 will have become
> 4 will be putting
> 5 will have got
> 6 will be providing
> 7 will have disappeared, will be using
> 8 will have become, will also be using
> 9 will be using
> 10 will have found

Speaking

7 Ask students to work in groups of four to discuss the predictions. Elicit students' own predictions for the technological future and discuss them.

Homework

Ask students to write a dialogue between a person making future predictions about technological advances, and a person who disagrees with them. Back in class they can perform the dialogues with a partner.

3c One size doesn't fit all

Lead-in

Personal response

Say to students: *Think of two pieces of equipment (not computer-related) which you have at home. They should be things which you use a lot and which you really cannot do without. They should be things with moving parts, not simple objects like a knife or a pen.* Ask them to talk about their objects in a group of four. Elicit a few examples from the whole class.

Reading

1 Ask the class to explain the meaning of *one size fits all*. Explain that the phrase was originally used to refer to clothing produced in one large size only, to fit everybody. It is now used about any product which is used in a range of different situations. Ask students to suggest answers to the question.

2 Read through the three sentences with the class to focus their reading, then ask them to read quickly and find if they are true or false. Elicit the answers from the class.

ANSWERS

1 T   2 F   3 T

Vocabulary notes

to empower = to give someone the ability to act for themselves

self-reliant = able to rely upon themselves – able to cope without help

to promote = to put forward an idea

firmly = fixed, not able to move from

ethical = moral issues connected to right and wrong

to harness = to get hold of and control

to pump through = to force through by mechanical means

to deploy = to use in different places

labour-intensive = using a lot of man-hours

a fleet = a group of vehicles

gas-guzzling = to use a lot of petrol (*gas* in US English)

implications = outcomes and results

3 Ask students to find the phrase and what the author says about this. Elicit the answer from the class.

ANSWERS

the term 'appropriate technology' has come to mean not just technology which is suited to the needs and capabilities of the user, but technology that takes particular account of environmental, ethical and cultural considerations.

The author says: *that is clearly a much more difficult thing to achieve.* He gives two examples of apparently 'appropriate technology' where the technology was not in fact appropriate because it had unforeseen consequences.

Background notes

Gandhi was born in India in 1869. From 1888 to 1891 he studied law at University College, London. From 1893 to 1914 he lived in South Africa, where he became a legal and political activist for the rights of Indians; it was here during many protests that he developed the concept of non-violent resistance. Returning to India in 1915, he became involved in World War I, leading a troop of ambulance workers for the British Army. From 1918 onwards he led many national protests for the rights of the poor and the oppressed. He did much in the way of social good, building schools and hospitals in poor rural areas. He was assassinated in 1948 and is generally considered one of the greatest men to have ever lived.

Ernst Schumacher was an economist and statistician, born in Bonn, Germany in 1911. In 1930 he won a scholarship to study at Oxford University, and later went on to Columbia University in the USA. He came back to Britain before World War II and spent 20 years as the Chief Economic Adviser to the UK National Coal Board – one of the world's largest employers, with 800,000 workers.

As well as being influenced by the British economist Keynes, he was also interested in what Ghandi had to say about organisations and labour, and in Buddhist ideas.

He came to global fame with his 1973 book *Small is Beautiful* which changed many attitudes about economics.

4 Ask students to work in pairs and discuss what the devices are. Check their answers, then ask how the author uses them in the text.

ANSWERS

a central heating system: a system for heating the whole of a building from one source

a device for shelling corn: a device that removes the edible corn from the hard centre

a sewing machine: a machine that sews clothes etc.

an efficient cooking stove: a stove that cooks quicker and uses less fuel

a solar-powered lamp: a lamp that works without electricity, using the power of the sun

a water purifier: a device that makes dirty water drinkable

He uses them all as examples of appropriate technology which is suited to the needs and capabilities of the users.

5 Ask students to read the sentences and choose the correct meaning. Elicit the answers from the whole class.

ANSWERS

1 control	4 make use
2 not too complicated	5 appreciated
3 be useful	6 a lot of petrol

Pronunciation note

There are quite a lot of longer words in the text which have the syllable stress on syllables other than the first.

ab*sorbed*, ap*pro*priate, capa*bi*lities, conside*ra*tions, de*ployed*, em*pow*ered, environ*men*tal, entrepre*neur*, impli*ca*tions, in*dus*trialised, inter*me*diate, me*chan*ical, pro*mo*ted, self-re*li*ant, so*phis*ticated, techno*lo*gical

Critical thinking balancing arguments

6 Ask students to note the arguments individually.

> **ANSWERS**
>
> Risks: it's difficult to take account of environmental, ethical and cultural considerations; there is no guarantee that it will be appropriate
>
> Benefits: it can save money, save human effort, save time, protect the environment

7 Ask students to compare their answers. Then elicit answers from the class.

> **ANSWER**
>
> He is in favour of it if it is done correctly.

Vocabulary useful devices

8 Ask students to complete the expressions individually, then check with a partner. Elicit the answers from the class as complete sentences.

> **ANSWERS**
>
> 2 efficient   5 old
> 3 long-term   6 easy
> 4 useful   7 renewable

9 Ask students to tell each other about a gadget they have at home, using language from the text and Exercise 8.

Speaking

10 Ask students to work in pairs to complete the sentences and decide what the objects are. They can then tell the class, and see if everyone agrees.

> **ANSWERS**
>
> 1 6 people   5 solar power
> 2 strong nylon   6 6 hours
> 3 put up in a few minutes 7 only £1.90
> 4 only 2 kilos   8 light and a little heat
>
> Product 1 is a tent. Product 2 is a solar-powered light.

11 Read through the instructions with the class. Ask students to get into groups, and allocate each group one of the four objects at the bottom of page 38. Ask students to follow the instructions to prepare and give their presentation. The other groups should ask questions. Students should decide which was the best presentation and why.

Homework

Ask students to draw a gadget from home, and draw arrows to different parts of it explaining what they are and how it works.

3d Computer problems

Lead-in

Personal response

Ask students to tell a partner when the last time they asked someone for help was, what the situation was and why. Also, ask them to tell each other the last time someone asked them for help, what it was and why. Elicit a few situations from the whole class.

Real life asking for and offering technical help

1 Ask students to ask and answer the questions in pairs. Elicit responses from the class.

2 Ask students to answer these questions as a whole class. Find out the most common source of technical help among the students.

3 [1.22] Read through the two questions with the class to focus their listening, then play the recording and elicit the answers from the class. If necessary, play the recording again.

> **ANSWERS**
>
> 1 copy and print a map
> 2 take a screen shot or find a different map

Audioscript [1.22]

B = Ben; **S** = Sophie

B: Can you give me a hand? I'm having trouble making this map.

S: Hang on. I'm just finishing a letter. I'll be with you in a second. … OK. What do you want to do exactly?

B: I'm just making some directions for some friends who are staying in our house next week. I'm trying to paste this map into a Word document.

S: Are you going to email it to them? Because if so, you could just email them the link to the map.

B: No I'm going to print it out and give it to them when they get here, because we're going away … The trouble is it won't allow me to copy it.

S: Let me have a look. Oh, I see … Oh, it's a Google map: you can't select and copy them, I'm afraid.

B: Oh … what shall I do then?

S: Well, you've got two possibilities. You can either take a screen shot …

B: What's that?

S: Here I'll show you. Just press Alt print screen like this, then open a new Word document and paste it in. That should do the trick.

B: Oh, I see, but it's come out very small. That's going to be too difficult for them to read. What else do you suggest?

S: Have you tried looking for a different map. If you do a search, you might find one that you can copy.

B: OK … I'll give that a try. Thanks …

S: Feel free to ask me again if that doesn't work.

4 ⊚ [1.22] Ask students to read through the expressions in the box to focus their listening. Play the recording through twice while they complete the sentences. Ask them to check with a partner, and then elicit the answers from the whole class.

> **ANSWERS**
>
> 1 making this map
> 2 paste this map into a Word document
> 3 email them the link to the map
> 4 it won't allow me to copy it
> 5 take a screen shot
> 6 press Alt print screen like this, then open a new Word document and paste it in
> 7 it's come out very small
> 8 looking for a different map
> 9 find one that you can copy
> 10 ask me again if that doesn't work

Pronunciation stress in two-syllable verbs

5a ⊚ [1.23] Ask students to read the sentences to themselves and think about the stress indicated on the verbs. Then play the recording, and have them repeat each sentence chorally and individually, with the stress on the second syllable of the underlined words.

5b Ask students to think of two two-syllable verbs in pairs and then put them into a sentence to tell another pair.

> **SAMPLE ANSWERS**
>
> complete, compare, involve, direct, adjust, return, accept, provide, persuade, divide, control, expect, forget, appeal, release, patrol, enjoy, dislike, contain

6 Ask students to work in pairs, first choosing one of the tasks listed, then working out a conversation about it modelled on the one in Exercise 4. Circulate and monitor their conversations for later feedback.

Homework

Students can write up their dialogue from Exercise 6.

3e A technical problem

Lead-in

Personal response
Ask students to talk about any problems they have ever had with any kind of electrical or optical equipment, describing what the problem was and what they did about it.

Writing short email requests

1 Ask students to match the emails and replies first, and elicit the answers from the class. Then read the two questions with the class and ask them to decide the answers and check with a partner before you elicit them from the class.

> **ANSWERS**
>
> 1 D   2 B   3 C   4 A
> 1 1 customer–manufacturer
> 2 customer–shop
> 3 friends
> 4 friends
> 2 1 They can't give him a new manual, but he can download one.
> 2 They can't exchange it, but it may be just out of ink.
> 3 The friend doesn't know about it, but suggests a discussion board.
> 4 The friend is going away and suggests somewhere to take the bike.

Writing skill being polite

2a Ask students to underline the polite phrases individually, then check with a partner. Elicit answers from the whole class.

> **ANSWERS**
>
> 1 Could you please tell me …
> 2 Please can you advise me …
> 3 Do you happen to know …
> 4 Would you mind … I'd be really grateful …
> A Sorry … but
> B I am sorry, but … Please check the …
> C I'm afraid …
> D I regret to say that …

2b Ask students to answer these questions individually, then check with a partner. Elicit the answers from the whole class.

> **ANSWERS**
>
> 1 could
> 2 Could you is more formal and polite.
> 3 less direct
> 4 I regret to say
> 5 do

Word focus *out of*

3a Ask students to underline the examples of *out of* in the texts and discuss the meaning. They should compare their ideas with another pair. Elicit ideas from the whole class.

> ANSWERS
>
> 1 gone *out of* business = no longer in business
> 3 *out of* interest = I'm interested in knowing
> 4 don't go *out of* your way = don't do anything extra or make a lot of effort
> B it is *out of* the question = impossible
> C *out of* my depth = it's too complicated for me

3b Ask students to complete the sentences using *out of* plus the words in the box. Elicit answers from the class as complete sentences.

> ANSWERS
>
> 1 hands 2 blue 3 order 4 date 5 time 6 luck

4 Ask students to use the models (1–4) to help them write their email.

> MODEL ANSWER
>
> I ordered two cartridges for my printer from you. When they arrived this morning, I was disappointed to find that the best before date on both of them had already passed. Please could you send me two replacements?

5 Ask students to exchange their email with a partner and use the questions to check their partner's work. They should then write a reply.

> MODEL ANSWER
>
> I am sorry that we sent you cartridges which are out of date. I will put two new ones in the post for you immediately.

3f Augmented reality

Before you watch

1 Students work in groups. Ask them to look at the photo and say what they can see, then discuss the questions. Take feedback from the class.

2 Ask students to read the question and think of ways a headset could be used.

While you watch

3 Give students time to read through the words in the glossary. Play the whole of the video for students to check their ideas from Exercise 2 and answer the question. They should not try to understand everything at this stage.

> ANSWERS
>
> firefighters, pilots, tourists

4 Give students time to read the sentences. Play the video again for them to listen and correct the statements.

> ANSWERS
>
> 1 Professor Feiner is working with a group of **computer science** students.
> 2 The team wants to develop a virtual world that is **integrated with** the physical world.
> 3 The virtual world can provide extra information about what you **see and hear.**
> 4 A global positioning system allows the team to use the equipment **outdoors.**
> 5 The system **is very good** for people to find their way around places they don't know well.
> 6 Visitors to the campus can use the system to find out **about Bloomingdale Asylum.**
> 7 Professor Feiner developed the technology because he has a bad sense of **direction.**

5 Give students time to read the questions, then play the video again for them to listen and answer the questions.

> ANSWERS
>
> 1 integrate a virtual world with the real world, to give extra information about what you can see and hear
> 2 a to see where rooms are in a building filled with smoke
>   b to show information about their position on their windscreen
>   c to give documentaries about the history of a site
> 3 a documentary that shows where the things were that are being described
> 4 images of the old asylum building

After you watch

6 Students work in pairs to roleplay an interview with Professor Feiner, according to the instructions.

7 Students work in pairs to discuss the questions.

Videoscript

00.05–00.22 On the campus of New York's Columbia University, researchers are already looking into the future. It's part of a programme designed to change the way we see the world. Professor Steve Feiner and his group of computer science students are working to, as they say, augment reality.

00.24–00.35 *Professor Steve Feiner* The idea means essentially that we're trying to build up a virtual world that we can integrate with the physical world so the virtual world can provide extra, added information about what you see and hear.

00.36–00.59 Using a head-worn device, this prototype superimposes text and graphics over a person's normal field of vision.

Sophisticated tracking devices determine exactly where the user's head is oriented, allowing the computer to constantly update the information on display. It's a relationship all built on numbers and hard work.

01.00–01.03 *Professor Steve Feiner* And it's based on our having very laboriously measured where things are.

01.04–01.10 The system enables users to view three-dimensional graphics and imagery, mapping their location within their surroundings.

01.11–01.18 *Blaine Bell* This is actually very good for going into an environment that users are very unfamiliar with and they need to get information about.

01.19–02.02 Imagine giving firefighters a clear view of building blueprints even as their vision is obscured by smoke, or providing pilots with information on the windscreen of their cockpits.

Utilising a global positioning system, or GPS, Feiner's research team is among the first to take augmented reality technology outdoors and into the real world where it might entirely change the tourist experience, offering situated documentaries about the history of a site.

It's already begun on Columbia's campus where augmented reality users can learn about Bloomingdale Asylum, an early 19th-century asylum for psychiatric patients which previously occupied this space.

02.03–02.18 *Professor Steve Feiner* They would see the main asylum building overlaid as sort of a ghost image, on top of their view of the library. And they could actually walk around that building and look at it and see additional information about it on the hand-held display.

02.19–02.24 It's all very educational but Feiner's motivations may be a bit more pedestrian.

02.25–02.30 *Professor Steve Feiner* I have a very bad sense of direction. This is part of the reason why I want to be able to – to have this kind of technology.

02.31–02.36 If he's successful, you might never get lost ever again.

UNIT 3 Review

Grammar

1 Ask students to work in pairs to recall the global problems from the unit, without looking in their books.

> **ANSWERS**
> overpopulation, pollution, epidemics, poverty

2 Ask students to discuss wind turbines as a class.

3 Read through the questions with the class to focus their reading. Ask students to read the text and answer. Elicit answers from the class.

> **ANSWERS**
> 1 CO_2 emissions
> 2 reduce CO_2 emissions to zero
> 3 stop using electricity; use gadgets which don't need energy; generate electricity that doesn't produce CO_2
> 4 They are only intermittent energy sources.

4 Ask students to choose the correct verbs in the text individually, then check with a partner. Elicit the answers as complete sentences.

> **ANSWERS**
> 1 don't reduce   6 are not going to stop
> 2 will continue   7 will be using
> 3 will have increased   8 will consume
> 4 will come   9 will have
> 5 happens   10 will be generating

Vocabulary

5 Ask students to do this individually, then check with a partner. Elicit the answers, having one student give the first phrase, and another the synonym.

> **ANSWERS**
> 1 overload   4 neat
> 2 breakthrough   5 handy
> 3 appropriate   6 fix

6 Ask students to discuss the issues in groups of four. Circulate and monitor their discussions. Elicit answers from the groups and discuss them with the whole class.

Real life

7 Ask students to match these sentences individually, then check with a partner. Elicit the answers.

> **ANSWERS**
> 1 c   2 e   3 b   4 a   5 d

8 Ask students to prepare and act out the conversations in pairs. Circulate and monitor their roleplays.

Speaking

9 Ask students to make predictions about their life, in pairs. Remind them about the future continuous and future perfect tenses. Circulate and monitor their speaking.

10 Ask students to discuss their partner's predictions with a new partner.

Unit 4 Art and creativity

Lead-in

Personal response

Ask students: *What is your favourite kind of entertainment and why?* Ask them to get into a group of four and tell the others what they think. Elicit some responses from the whole class.

1 Read the instructions and example with the class, then read through the words in each of the three categories, and check students are familiar with them. Ask them to make who–what–where combinations individually, then compare their ideas with a partner. Elicit answers and alternatives from the whole class.

> **SAMPLE ANSWERS**
>
> a band + a gig + a live music venue / a club / a concert hall
> a comedian + a show + a theatre
> a dance company + a performance / a musical + a theatre / a concert hall
> a circus act + a show / a performance + the street / a theatre
> a drama company + a play + a theatre
> an orchestra + a classical concert + a concert hall
> an artist + an exhibition + a gallery

2 Ask the class: *What do you think is happening in the picture?* Elicit answers and have a discussion about the activity and their experience of such entertainment, of juggling in general, and of street performance.

> **SAMPLE ANSWER**
>
> A circus act is giving a performance in the street.

3 💿 [1.24] Ask students to look at the questions to focus their listening. Play the recording through once and ask for answers. If necessary, play it again.

> **ANSWERS**
>
> 1 teacher, accountant
> 2 the teacher is an acrobat / street performer, the accountant writes poetry

Audioscript 💿 [1.24]

A: People are never quite what you expect, are they? There's a teacher that I work with who's really quite a shy person … never expresses a strong view or imposes herself in a group. I worked with her for about a year before I found out that every weekend she becomes a street performer.

B: What kind of street performer?

A: Well, she turns out to be some kind of acrobat. She was brought up in a circus and she still gets together at weekends with friends and puts on shows of circus skills with them in public places, like a busy shopping street on a Saturday afternoon. She doesn't do it for money – just for fun. But it's not what you imagine her doing when you meet her …

B: That sounds a bit like my neighbour. He works for a firm of accountants, watches a lot of sport, but in his free time he writes poetry. I don't think many people have read it, because he's rather private, but he showed me a poem a while ago that he wrote when his little boy was sick in hospital and it was absolutely beautiful …

Vocabulary notes

to express a view = to give an opinion

to impose oneself = to dominate, or make people take notice of you

to turn out to be = used when you find out that somebody or something is different to what you thought

rather private = not very outgoing, keeping oneself to oneself

a while ago = some time ago

4 Ask students to work in pairs to answer the question. If they have never been *surprised*, ask them to tell their partner about something creative that somebody they know does as a hobby. Elicit some examples from the whole class.

4a All about Melbourne

Lead-in

Personal response

Say to the class: *Tell me some things you know about Australia.* Elicit some information, and ask follow-up questions as necessary to elicit more information, e.g. *What places do you know? What unusual animals come from there?*

Listening

1 Ask students to work in pairs to talk about arts in their country and in their own experiences. Elicit some answers from the whole class.

2 Ask the whole class what they know about activities and entertainment opportunities in Australia. If they don't know, encourage them to guess.

> **SAMPLE ANSWERS**
>
> surfing, trekking, watching / playing cricket, rugby, Australian rules football
> Sydney is internationally famous for its Opera House.

3 [1.25] Ask students to read through the questions to focus their listening. Then play the recording once while they listen and again for them to answer. Ask them to check their answers with a partner, before you elicit them from the class.

> **ANSWERS**
>
> 1 Sydney has natural beauty, while Melbourne has none.
> 2 easy access to lots of different cultural events
> 3 art events, sport; they enjoy the arts, but love sports

Audioscript [1.25]

'Nature has done everything for Sydney, man nothing; man has done everything for Melbourne, nature nothing,' a visitor to Australia once noted. Herein lies the essential difference between Australia's two largest cities. Melbourne is Australia's second city, but it has plenty of first-class qualities, from a buzzing arts scene to its enormous range of restaurants. It may have a few grey days, and a muddy river instead of a beautiful harbour, but don't let that worry you. The lack of natural attractions has meant that Melbourne has had to create its own man-made pleasures … and in doing so it has become Australia's cultural capital. Theatre, music, street sculpture, fashion – in fact, there are hardly any forms of artistic expression which you can't find here – all thrive, alongside a cosmopolitan mix of cafés, restaurants and pubs.

What's great about Melbourne for the visitor is how accessible all these arts are. As well as traditional museums and galleries like the National Gallery of Victoria and concert halls, like Hamer Hall, there are an enormous number of smaller art spaces and venues which cater for every kind of taste. Art is not something for a small minority. In fact, for most inhabitants of Melbourne a weekly visit to the cinema

or an art exhibition is a routine event. Several festivals take place during the winter months including the International Film Festival in July and the Fringe Festival in September which has loads of interesting (even if not always that good!) comedy, dance and theatre acts.

If the locals appreciate their art, they absolutely love their sport. Lots of people around the world will know the Australian Formula One Grand Prix and the Australian Open Tennis, which attracts over half a million spectators to Melbourne in a carnival atmosphere, but few people will be familiar with the sports Melburnians themselves follow. Australian rules football and cricket enjoy a huge amount of support and, if you have enough time, a visit to see either is well worth it just for the atmosphere. If you're looking to participate rather than just watch, why not try a bit of surfing or swimming? Cycling, jogging or a visit to one of Melbourne's many gyms are other possibilities. All this information is on our website at *thetravelshow.org* so do have a look …

4 [1.25] Read through the statements with the class to focus their listening. Play the recording again, and elicit the answers from students immediately.

> **ANSWERS**
>
> 1 F (it has grey days and not many natural attractions)
> 2 F (it is known as the cultural capital)
> 3 F (they are enjoyed by most people)
> 4 F (the festivals are in winter)
> 5 T
> 6 T
> (see also underlined phrases in the audioscript)

Background note

Australian rules football, which was founded in Melbourne in 1859, is rather like a cross between rugby, football and basketball. There are 18 players on each team. It is played on an oval pitch with an oval ball. Players are allowed to run with the ball in their hands as long as they bounce it once every 15 metres, and they can pass to another team member by kicking it, hitting it with their fist or their open hand. They cannot throw it. Players can be stopped by tackling between the shoulders and the knees. The object is to score by kicking the ball between posts similar to rugby posts. The game is divided into four 20-minute quarters.

5 Ask students for their responses to the questions about visiting Melbourne.

Grammar expressions of quantity

6 Read through the instructions with the class. Ask them to turn to page 176 and find the expressions in the audioscript individually, then check their answers with a partner. Elicit the expressions from the whole class.

> **ANSWERS**
>
> 'many or much': *plenty of, enormous range of, an enormous number of, loads of, a huge amount of, lots of*
> 'not much or many': *hardly any, few, a lack of*
> 'some': *a few, enough, a bit of*

Grammar note

Note that while *lots of* and a *lot of* have exactly the same meaning, and can be used in both formal and informal situations, *loads of* is informal and generally spoken rather than written. Other informal spoken expressions with the same meaning are: *masses of, stacks of, heaps of, piles of, tons of*.

7 Read through the grammar box with the class, then ask them to find the answers to the questions in the exercise individually. They can then check with a partner before you elicit answers from the class.

ANSWERS

1 b = some; a = only a small number of
2 yes, but *hardly any* is much more usual
3 a (*lots of*)
4 b (*a huge number of*)
5 b (*isn't much*)

8 Ask students to choose the correct option individually, then check with a partner. Elicit answers from the whole class as complete sentences.

ANSWERS

1 a lot of	5 some
2 number	6 Hardly
3 no	7 little
4 a few	8 many

Pronunciation weak form of

9a [1.26] Ask students to read through the phrases in the box to themselves, and think about how *of* is pronounced. Then play the recording while they listen. Ask them to say *of* in the strong and weak form.

9b Ask students to work on saying the phrases with the correct pronunciation.

10 Ask students to turn to page 153 and look at the charts. They should then complete the sentences about the charts with a partner. Elicit the answers from the class as complete sentences.

ANSWERS

1 few	4 Many (Lots of), hardly
2 lots, number	5 enough, amount, lack
3 no	

Speaking

11 Read through the instructions with the whole class. Ask students to get into groups and decide which area they want to research – make sure each group chooses a different area. They should then follow the instructions to make their report and present it to the class.

Homework

Ask students to write up their report findings into a paragraph.

4b Reverse graffiti

Lead-in

Personal response

Ask students: *How dirty is the town where you live? In what ways is it dirty?* You could prompt them with ideas about smoke, water pollution, litter, uncared for buildings. When they have given some responses, ask: *Does anyone do anything about it and if so, who?* (e.g. the local council or local environmental groups). Discuss the issues as a class.

Listening

1 [1.27] Ask the class to look at the four statements, and then read each one in turn. Invite comments and encourage discussion. Then ask them to listen to the recording and note the artist's ideas on the four statements. Play the recording again for them to check, complete and correct. Elicit the answers from the whole class.

ANSWERS

1 Not true – the artist's intention might be to make you feel uncomfortable.
2 Not necessarily – Monet did some of his paintings in 5 minutes.
3 Not necessarily – some can be a clever idea rather than involving technical skill.
4 Certainly not – the artist's role is simply to present an idea in a visual form.

Audioscript [1.27]

I = Interviewer; W = Will

I: OK, Will, I'm going to fire some statements at you about what various people say art should be and I want to know which of these you agree with. OK?

W: Er … OK … but I'm already a bit suspicious, because I don't actually think that 'should' has a lot to do with it. People have a very fixed idea about what art 'should be' – a certain kind of portrait or landscape very often … but, anyway, anyway, I'll play the game, so … let's hear what they say …

I: Good, here's the first one then … Art should be something pleasing for the viewer.

W: Mmm no, not necessarily – the artist's intention might be to make you feel uncomfortable, not to give you a warm feeling …

I: OK. What about this, then? … Art should involve effort on the part of the artist.

W: OK that's more interesting, but still the answer is 'not necessarily' – Monet did some of his paintings in five minutes.

I: Did he? I didn't know that. That's amazing … well, that ties in with the next one, perhaps. Art should involve technical skill.

W: Ummm … I can think of quite a lot of examples of successful art that wasn't technically difficult, but was just based on a clever idea.

I: OK … Art should have a social message or make a political point.

w: No, certainly not. Is the Mona Lisa political? I don't think so. Look, … an artist's role is simply to present an idea in a visual form. The viewer's role is to give that effort their time and attention and then they can say either 'Yes, I really like that', or … 'That moves me', or 'No, I'm afraid that doesn't do anything for me.'

2 🔘 [1.27] Read the question with the class, and then play the recording again while they listen for the answer. Elicit answers from the whole class.

> **ANSWERS**
>
> The artist's role is simply to present an idea in a visual form. The viewer's role is to give that effort their time and attention, and respond in some way.

3 Read the words for types of artwork with the class, and elicit descriptions of what each one is. Read the *Wordbuilding* box with the class and discuss the contents. See also Vocabulary note below, and refer to page 35 of the Workbook for further information and practice.

> **SAMPLE ANSWERS**
>
> *graffiti* = writing or painting on public walls or vehicles such as trains or buses
>
> *an installation* = a physical set of materials of any kind arranged in a particular way in a particular space
>
> *a landscape* = a picture of the countryside
>
> *a sculpture* uses solid materials such as wood, stone and bronze to make abstract or accurate representations of people and things.
>
> *a sketch* = a quickly drawn picture of something to give a general impression, or record a particular moment – often done in pencil

> **Vocabulary note**
>
> Ask students to give examples of words using the suffixes *-ment* (e.g. *entertainment, shipment, argument*) and *-tion* (e.g. *relation, situation, attention*), which are used for making verbs into nouns, and which are apparently without a clear meaning; and contrast this with *-scape* which means 'view of the'.
>
> Try to elicit other specific suffixes, such as *-post* (= a vertical upright support, e.g. *lamppost, gatepost, goalpost*), *-side* (= next to, e.g. *countryside, seaside, bedside (adj)*) and *-view* (= seeing, e.g. *interview, review, interview*)

Reading

4 Ask students to discuss the questions as a class, giving reasons for their opinions.

5 Invite suggestions for the meaning of *reverse graffiti*, without saying whether answers are correct or not. Ask students to read the text quickly and find the answer.

> **ANSWER**
>
> It involves inscribing images through the layer of pollution or dirt on walls to show the original colour underneath.

> **Vocabulary notes**
>
> *inspired by* = getting ideas from
>
> *share a common aim* = do something for the same reason as others
>
> *be commissioned by* = be asked to do something for someone or an organisation
>
> *to charge someone with* = to say that somebody did something (illegal)
>
> *a mural* = a wall painting
>
> *to take drastic action* = to do something serious to change a situation
>
> *to scrape away* = to remove the surface of something

6 Ask students to read the article again to find the missing words to complete the sentences. They can do this individually, then check with a partner. Elicit the answers as complete sentences.

> **ANSWERS**
>
> | | |
> |---|---|
> | 1 dirt | 4 drivers |
> | 2 pollution | 5 confused |
> | 3 advertising | 6 clean |

7 Ask students to discuss the two questions with a partner. Elicit comments from the class and create a wider discussion.

Grammar determiners

8 Ask students to decide what the nouns are in pairs. Then elicit answers from the whole class.

> **ANSWERS**
>
> *either* + singular
>
> *each* + singular
>
> *all* + plural
>
> *every* + singular
>
> *any* + singular
>
> *both* + plural
>
> *any* + plural and singular
>
> *no* + plural and singular
>
> *the whole* + singular

> **Grammar note**
>
> Explain that in grammar the word *determiner* is used to describe a word which limits the meaning of a noun or noun phrase, e.g.
>
> *some boys went* (= not all of the boys)
>
> *all the boys went* (= the whole group of boys)
>
> *Some* and *all of* limit the numbers of boys who went.

9 Ask students to read through the information in the grammar box, then answer the questions. Elicit the answers from the class as complete sentences.

> **ANSWERS**
>
> 1 b
> 2 b and c (but c is incorrect use of *both*)
> 3 a and b

10 Ask students to do this exercise individually, then check with a partner. Elicit answers from the whole class as complete sentences. Be sure to point out where two words are possible, if students do not give them both.

ANSWERS

1 each / every	5 Either
2 all	6 the whole
3 no	7 each / every
4 both	8 any

11 Ask students to get into groups of four to discuss the eight quotations, and their relationship to the statements about art. Take the quotations one by one, and elicit comments from the groups.

12 Ask students to complete the sentences using determiners from the grammar box individually, then check with a partner. Elicit answers from the whole class as complete sentences.

ANSWERS

1 All	5 No
2 Either	6 any
3 both	7 All
4 Each / Every	

Background note

The Turner Art Prize, named after the famous British painter Joseph Mallord William Turner, was started in 1984. It is the major British prize for artists under the age of 50. The £40,000 prize is awarded by a committee each year, and is related to exhibitions by artists during the previous 12 months. The winner gets £25,000 and others shortlisted get smaller sums. The prize has generally been won by art at the more extreme and experimental end of the spectrum, and entries have included Damien Hurst's shark in formaldehyde and Tracey Emin's bed. There is a lot of installation work, or events (e.g. lights going on and off in a room), and some critics refuse to take it seriously.

Speaking

13 Read through the instructions with the class and ensure that they understand what to do. Ask them to get into groups and discuss their competition and decide on the rules – they can adapt ideas from Exercise 12. When they have done this, they should write out their set of rules ready to swap with another group.

14 Ask groups to exchange rules, then discuss a proposal for the other group's competition. They should then write out their artwork idea and give it to the other group. The groups should discuss and evaluate the ideas against the criteria they set.

Homework

Write a dialogue between somebody who likes traditional paintings and somebody who likes modern installations, in which they ask for and give their opinions about the art they like.

4c Hip-hop planet

Lead-in

Personal response

Ask students: *Who is your favourite musician, and why?* Elicit some answers from the class, and invite others to ask questions about a performer someone mentions.

Reading

1 Ask students to read through the types of music and discuss the three questions in pairs. Elicit some answers from the whole class.

Ask students to say something about the characteristic of each type of music. They can do this as a whole class, helping each other to extend definitions.

Background note

blues = black music expressing unhappiness at personal situations, or else rocking along to forget the misery

classical = composed music from Mozart onwards (i.e. after Baroque), which can be solo instrumental, orchestral or choral

country = traditional country music from America, usually quite balladic, telling life stories

jazz = music branching out of the blues, based on improvisation; instrumental, or vocal, and very various in style (e.g. trad, modern, bebop)

pop = mainstream popular music

reggae = syncopated music begun by black musicians from Jamaica

rock = a driving, often blues-based, form of popular music

soul = a mixture of blues and gospel styles sung initially by black American singers

traditional / folk = the music of the people, made over centuries and passed down orally.

2 Ask for answers to the two questions from the whole class and encourage students to discuss them. Do not say whether the answers are correct or not. Then ask them to read the text to check their ideas and comment on the answers they gave before.

ANSWERS

Hip-hop and rap talk about the unfairness of society, where poor people don't have the same opportunities as the rich. (*Initially hip-hop artists produced socially-conscious songs that described life on the other side of the tracks, where people are denied the same opportunities as the rich. ... In poor urban communities around the globe, rap music is a universal expression of outrage at the injustice of the distribution of wealth.*)

Commercial rappers talk about crime and about their wealth and fame (*most commercial rappers in America brag about their lives of crime and the things that fame and money have brought them, among which women seem to be just another material possession*).

People from poor backgrounds and rich suburban kids all listen to rap and hip-hop.

3 Ask students to read through the questions to focus their reading, then read the article and answer the questions individually. They can check with a partner before you elicit answers from the whole class.

ANSWERS

1 that the rapper was the best DJ in the world
2 dance and graffiti
3 They move records backwards and forwards to make a scratching sound, or play a break over and over.
4 It's cool.
5 Because it's the music of the poor and unhappy, which is what many people in Senegal are.
6 the violence, and that women are treated as possessions

Vocabulary notes

to boom = to make a loud deep sound

to permeate = to move slowly through something

bankrupt = having no money (literally), but here having nothing of value to offer

an aspiration = a goal, or aim

outrage = great anger at injustice

macho = with characteristics considered to be typically male (e.g. strong, aggressive, not sentimental)

to embrace = to accept

4 Ask students to find the phrases in the text and write what they mean. They should do this individually, then check with a partner. Elicit the answers from the class.

ANSWERS

1 It sounded as if something was wrong with the record.
2 People sometimes avoid stepping on the cracks between stones in the pavement.
3 Life in the poorer districts (because in the US poor people – often black – lived on the far side of the railway tracks, away from the town)
4 not having a good quality of life (*second-rate* = not of good quality)
5 masculine show of bragging and superiority
*6 The society that we are passing on to our children lacks a moral basis.

Critical thinking analysing contrasts

5 Ask students to find the sentences individually.

ANSWERS

1 a I thought it was the most ridiculous thing I'd ever heard
  b I have come to embrace this music
2 a an almost bankrupt New York City
  b in poor urban communities around the globe
3 a socially-conscious songs that described life on the other side of the tracks
  b bragging about their life of crime, fame, money and women treated like material possessions
4 a the music was all about identity: I am the best
  b exposes the empty moral cupboard that we have left for our children

6 Ask students to compare their answers with a partner and discuss their feelings about hip-hop. They should then work together to write a summary paragraph about it.

Word focus *cool*

7 Ask students to match the meanings to the sentences individually, then compare answers with a partner. Elicit answers from the class, having one student read a sentence and another give the meaning.

ANSWERS

article: meaning 2

1 meaning 1	4 meaning 2
2 meaning 2	5 meaning 3
3 meaning 3	6 meaning 1

Extra activity

Ask students to tell a partner three things that they think are cool (meaning 2). Elicit some responses from the whole class.

Speaking

8 Ask students to read the two sets of lyrics and then discuss them in pairs. Elicit ideas from the whole class.

ANSWERS

Country song: family are always there for you
Rock song: be your own person, assert your rights

9 Have this discussion with the whole class. Go through the genres one by one and elicit ideas from students.

SAMPLE ANSWERS

blues: expresses pain and sorrow, origins in African-American culture

classical: conformism, conventional

country: traditional American values (white middle class), patriotic

jazz: individuality, spontaneity

pop: conformist youth culture

reggae: relaxed, often has a spiritual message, anti-establishment, origins in African-Caribbean culture

rock: anti-establishment music

soul: fight for social equality and civil rights, resistance to oppression, origins in African-American culture

traditional folk: continuity and stability, love of tradition and roots

Homework

Write 100 words about a song or piece of instrumental music that you really like. If you know, say who wrote it, who performs it. Explain why you like it.

4d Personal tastes

Lead-in

Personal response
Ask students to think about two things (not people) which they like very much and two things which they dislike, then explain to a partner why they like or dislike them. Elicit some responses from the whole class. Ask students to talk about their partner's likes and dislikes as well as their own.

Real life describing likes and dislikes

1 Ask students to ask and answer the questions with a partner. Elicit some responses from the class.

2 💿 [1.28] Read through the items in the box with the class to focus their listening. Play the recording for them to tick the boxes. Play it again if necessary. Ask students to check their answers with a partne. Then elicit the answers from the whole class.

> **ANSWERS**
>
> cost of tickets for musicals ✗
> Disney comic characters ✗
> Elton John ✓
> musicals in general ✗
> the music in musicals ✗
> the visual effects ✓
> this production of *The Lion King* ✓

Audioscript 💿 [1.28]

J = Jake; T = Tom

J: Hey, Tom, how was The Lion King?

T: <u>I loved it</u> … <u>I'm not generally a fan of</u> musicals …

J: No, me neither … <u>I never feel particularly inspired by</u> the music in them … which should really be the whole point of them … with a few exceptions perhaps … like *West Side Story* or *Grease* which have fantastic music … So what was so good about it?

T: Well, visually it's absolutely stunning, the opening scene particularly. All the animals – giraffes, wildebeest, zebra, antelope – congregate on the stage to set the scene, which is the plains of the Serengeti where the story takes place. And they're in these fabulous costumes: they're difficult to describe but the effect is that they actually seem to move like real animals. Everyone in the audience was spellbound …

J: But is the story the same as in the Disney film? I remember there were a couple of rather annoying characters in the film, like that bird, who's supposed to be there for comic effect, well at least I think it is, but actually after a while they begin to annoy you.

T: You mean Zazu. Yeah, I know what you mean about that kind of Disney character – often they can <u>get on your nerves</u> – but this production's different. It actually seems much more adult than the film … It's very well done. I found the story really moving.

J: Mmm … and what about the music?

T: It's essentially the same score as the film – I think Elton John wrote most of it, but it's all based on African rhythms and vocals …

J: <u>Doesn't really sound like my kind of thing.</u>

T: Oh .. Well, <u>I've got a lot of time for Elton John</u>. I think he catches the mood of this really well. Have you heard *Circle of Life*?

J: Er … no, don't think so …

T: Well, I'm not going to sing it … anyway I really recommend it. It's not cheap to go but if you get a chance you should. <u>I can't bear</u> the high prices they charge for musicals these days, but actually I didn't mind for this one … it was worth it.

Background note

The Lion King musical is based on the 1994 Disney film of the same name, which contains songs with music by Elton John and lyrics by Tim Rice. The musical made its stage debut in Minneapolis in spring 1997, and later that same year moved to Broadway. It has been performed in theatres around the word, collecting many prizes.

3 💿 [1.28] Ask students to read through the expressions for describing likes and dislikes in the box, and decide which of the phrases they heard.

Play the recording again and ask them to tick the phrases they hear. Point out that the form in the box may be slightly different to the form on the recording (e.g. different verb form, different pronoun etc.). Elicit the correct answers from the whole class.

> **ANSWERS**
>
> I love …
> I have a lot of time for …
> I can't bear …
> I'm not generally a fan of …
> I never feel particularly inspired by …
> It doesn't really sound like my kind of thing.
> gets on my nerves
> (See also underlined phrases in the audioscript)

Extra activity

a) Read through the phrases in the box in Exercise 3 and have students repeat them after you chorally and individually.

b) Highlight the strength of meaning of the different expressions. The ones in the *likes* column are all of similar strength. However, in the *dislikes* column there is a difference between *can't* bear and *gets on my nerves* (both quite strong), and the other expressions which suggest mild dislike. You could point out that the milder expressions are more polite and tactful.

c) Next, ask students to personalise the phrases by working in pairs, and asking and answering questions about their likes and dislikes.

Pronunciation disappearing sounds

4a [1.29] Ask students to look at the words in the box and say them to themselves. Ask them to underline the sound they think is the sound which is not voiced when we read the written word (i.e. which *disappears*). Play the recording a couple of times for them to listen, and decide whether they were correct. Elicit answers, by having students say the word correctly and indicate which sound disappeared. Play the recording again, and pause after each word for students to repeat chorally and individually.

ANSWERS

diff<u>e</u>rent, ev<u>e</u>ryone, gen<u>e</u>rally

4b [1.30] Ask students to do as they did in Exercise 4a, first reading and underlining the disappearing sounds in the words in the box, then listening to check. Elicit answers, by having students say the word correctly and indicate which sound disappeared. Play the recording again, and pause after each word for students to repeat chorally and individually.

ANSWERS

beautif<u>u</u>lly, choc<u>o</u>late, comf<u>o</u>rtable, int<u>e</u>resting, med<u>i</u>cine, ord<u>i</u>nary, secret<u>a</u>ry

Extra activity

Ask students to work in pairs. Together they should write a short sentence for each of the words in Exercise 4a and 4b (e.g. *It's generally cold in winter. She wears different shoes every day*). Then they should take it in turns to say each sentence and listen to see that their partner is making the sounds disappear.

5 Ask students to work together to complete the sentences using words from the *likes / dislikes* box in Exercise 3. Elicit answers from the class.

ANSWERS

1 very
2 really / a bit
3 very / particularly
4 really / generally
5 really / generally
6 really / a lot

6 Ask students to get into groups of four to discuss their likes and dislikes in the context of art and culture. Circulate and monitor their discussions, particularly their use of expressions for likes and dislikes, for feedback afterwards.

4e You've got to see this

Lead-in

Personal response

Ask students: *What is your favourite park? Why and when do you go there? Have you ever seen any interesting events happening there?* Elicit responses from the whole class.

Writing an online review

1 Ask students to read the review, then give their responses to it, with reasons.

2 Ask students to answer all three questions individually, then check with a partner. Elicit answers from the whole class. Check any new language from the review (see Vocabulary notes below).

ANSWERS

1 1 an introduction
2 the occasion of the visit
3 the content of the exhibition
4 the details of where and when it is on
5 the author's recommendation
2 name of the exhibition and artist, descriptions of the sculptures, date and location, cost
3 personal – she gives personal opinions and details and the language is very informal

Vocabulary notes

Check students understand these words and expressions:

at an angle = not horizontal or vertical
to check out something = to find information about
to complement = to fit in with, to match
convex = curving outward, like a section of a sphere (cf. *concave* = curving inward)
directed at = pointing at
to look out of place = to not belong to or fit in with the surroundings
reflect – a shiny surface reflects an image of things around it
reflection = the image reflected

Cultural note: Anish Kapoor

Anish Kapoor is a British sculptor who was born in Bombay, India in 1954. He studied at art colleges in the UK from 1973, and has lived in London since then. He became known in the 1980s for his geometric structures, made of granite, limestone and marble. In the 1990s he used solid quarried stone to make pieces which often had different holes and cavities in them. Since 1995 he has worked with reflection, using polished stainless steel. In 2009 he became the first living artist to have an exhibition at the Royal Academy, London. His works are exhibited in collections around the world, as well as being permanently outside in many places.

Writing skill personalising your writing

3 Read through the list with students and then ask them to work in pairs to find the personal forms in the review. Elicit examples from the whole class.

SAMPLE ANSWERS

Use pronouns: I find / my boyfriend and I / I was so glad we did

Use active verbs: I find / took a walk / they complemented / makes you see / makes you appreciate / the one I liked best

Use contracted forms: it's / we'd have missed / I'd definitely recommend

Use phrasal verbs: checking out / look out of place / trying to work out

Use conversational linking devises: as well as / and by the way

Share your feelings: I find that / absolutely exhausted / too tired to / I was so glad we did / The one I liked best / It was so funny / I'd definitely recommend

---

4 Ask students to write their review. This could be done for homework, and then in the following lesson you could continue with Exercise 5. Suggest that they can invent an exhibition or other artistic event, if they would prefer to do so.

5 Read through the checklist with the class, then ask pairs to exchange their reviews. They should then give each other feedback on their writing.

4f Urban art

Before you watch

1 Students work in groups. Ask them to look at the photo and discuss the questions. Take feedback from the class.

2 Ask students to think of other kinds of urban art, then predict what kinds of art they think they will see in the video. Take feedback from the class.

While you watch

3 Play the whole of the video for students to check their ideas from Exercise 2.

4 Give students time to read the list. Then play the video for them to put the things in the order they see them.

ANSWERS

1 e   2 c   3 g   4 b   5 f   6 a   7 d

---

5 Give students time to read the information and complete the table as far as they can remember. Then play the video again for them to check. Point out that some of the information is not specifically given on the DVD: students have to surmise which person it relates to based on other information.

ANSWERS

Nick Posada: b, e, g

Jafar Barron: a, c, d, f, h

---

6 Give students time to read the questions. Then play the video again for them to listen and answer the questions.

ANSWERS

1 it invites us to see things in a different way, e.g. playing music on buckets, showing graffiti in a traditional art gallery, mixing jazz with speaking
2 Because his art has been painted over with graffiti.
3 how to use colour and make their work distinctive
4 It's fast, uninhibited and inventive.
5 classical jazz, rap and hip-hop
6 hip-hop, poetry, friends of his

---

7 Play the last part of the video again (03.20 to 03.36) for students to complete the extract with words from the box.

ANSWERS

1 come from   5 envelope
2 emerge   6 boundaries
3 authentic   7 one more step
4 to the edge

After you watch

8 Students work in pairs to roleplay interviewing an urban artist, according to the instructions.

9 Students work in pairs to discuss the questions.

Videoscript

00.01–00.40 Urban art is all about innovation. From using buckets on a busy street, to filling an art gallery with local graffiti, to mixing jazz with spoken word – it invites us to listen with new ears, and to look with new eyes.

If you walk down this train tunnel in Washington D.C., you'll discover the bright colours of urban graffiti artists. It is Washington's Wall of Fame, and Nick Posada's work is here. But unfortunately other people have covered the art he's created with their own graffiti.

00.42–00.54 Nick Posada This is what happens when nobody respects any type of work that someone spent their paint and their time on. This is what the Wall of Fame in D.C. has come to.

00.55–01.12 Although the Wall of Fame is open to everyone, Posada says there are rules to be followed in the world of graffiti – rules that not everyone understands. He says that real graffiti artists understand how to use colour, and how to make their work distinctive.

01.13–01.20 Nick Posada So you would use colours that contrast one another. Ah, my piece is still there. I did this in, like, '99.

01.21–01.25 There is also an exhibition of Nick's work here at the Govinda Gallery in Georgetown.

01.26–01.34 Chris Murray Graffiti art has certainly brought to public art a whole new dimension.

01.35–02.05 According to Chris Murray, graffiti art is special because it's fast, uninhibited and always inventive. Murray believes that graffiti is just one more step in the development of pop art. The works have sold well – to young people, and to collectors of pop art. In the gallery, people can enjoy the art in a traditional setting – and they like it. It's good for the artists, too.

02.06–02.11 Chris Murray It was a real reversal for them because they're used to being vilified and now they're being enjoyed and that's a good thing.

02.14–02.39 People are beginning to appreciate the talents of Jafar Barron, too. The 28-year-old trumpeter grew up in this neighbourhood north of Philadelphia. Both his parents are jazz musicians. But Jafar wanted to mix more traditional, classical forms of jazz with the rap and hip-hop music of his own generation.

His first CD is an innovative mix of both worlds.

02.40–02.59 Jafar Barron I like to think the whole creation is all about music, to me, you know what I'm saying? And like, I think, I believe that the Most High is a musician.

I guess it came from my exposure to hip-hop, and the poetry that comes from that, and, you know, some friends of mine.

03.00–03.19 Jafar now plays in clubs in the city where he grew up. He also now has a deal with a major recording company.

The stories of how these two artists developed, one musical, one visual, do not surprise art history professor Don Kimes.

03.20–03.36 Don Kimes It's about sort of taking what it is that you come from, what you emerge from, what's authentic for you, and pushing it to the edge of its envelope, to the edge of its boundaries, its limits and taking one more step.

03.37–03.58 Kimes says artists need to build on their own cultural background, because anything else would be false. It is said that exploration and discovery are what art is truly about. Urban artists – both musicians and painters – can take us to places where we've never been before ... even if it's as close as a nearby city street.

UNIT 4 Review

Grammar

1 Ask students to discuss arts festivals they know about, and elicit some responses from the whole class.

2 Ask students to read the article and answer the question.

> ANSWERS
>
> It's the largest arts festival in the world, it has great variety, it is a place where young performers can try to get noticed.

3 Ask students to read and choose the correct options individually. They can then check with a partner before you elicit answers from the class.

> ANSWERS
>
> | | |
> |---|---|
> | 1 every / each | 7 A few |
> | 2 whole | 8 many |
> | 3 enough | 9 some / several |
> | 4 number | 10 no |
> | 5 a lot / much | 11 Both |
> | 6 a lot / plenty | 12 all |

Vocabulary

4 Ask students to categorise the words individually, then check with a partner. Elicit answers from the whole class.

> ANSWERS
>
> music: a gig, a band, lyrics, folk
> art: a sketch, an installation, landscape, sculpture
> theatre: a show, a musical, drama company, a play

5 Ask students to work in groups of four to discuss the questions. Circulate and monitor their discussion.

Real life

6 Ask students to do this individually, then check with a partner. Elicit the answers in order from the whole class.

> ANSWERS
>
> like: d, f
> dislike: a, b, c, e

7 Ask students to work in groups of four to discuss types of TV programmes (e.g. news, soaps, documentaries, nature programmes, cartoons, not specific named programmes).

Speaking

8 Ask students to stay in their groups of four to discuss these issues.

Unit 5 Development

Lead-in

Personal response

Say to the class: *Give me some examples of development that you know about – either in your home area, or around the world.* Elicit responses to the examples students suggest.

1 Ask the class to look at the photo and match what they can see with the types of development listed. Elicit ideas and check students' understanding of the different types of development (see Vocabulary notes below).

ANSWERS

Probably economic (building new properties for sale) and urban (building new housing in towns). Students may be able to argue for other types. The house looks as if it is built of concrete, so it is probably not sustainable.

Vocabulary notes

economic development = improving the wealth of a country, region or people

product development = researching, improving and trialling something manufactured

sustainable development = any kind of development which takes the environment into account

personal development = improving yourself through professional training, or in your private life

social development: has a range of meanings including the development of social skills in children; change and evolution in society as a whole; improving the lifestyle of people through things like better housing, health care and benefits from the state

urban development = building new houses in towns, and also improving the environment in towns so life is better

2 💿 [1.31] Ask students to match the examples with the types of development individually, then check with a partner. Elicit the answers from the class. Some examples might match more than one type of development. Then play the recording for students to decide which example from the box in Exercise 2 each speaker is talking about. You may need to play the recording twice. Elicit answers from the class.

ANSWERS

a new housing project – urban

a new university – social

a new railway line – economic / urban

a zero energy house – sustainable

a new smart phone – product

learning a language – personal

Speaker 1: a zero energy house

Speaker 2: a new railway line

Speaker 3: a new smart phone

Audioscript 💿 [1.31]

Speaker 1

It's always been our dream to have our own place in the countryside which is self-sufficient. So recently we decided to buy a small piece of land in the hills. We're going to build a home out of natural materials and try to generate our own electricity using wind and solar power so that we won't need to buy in any extra electricity from outside.

Speaker 2

At the moment a lot of students use their own cars to get to the university which is four miles outside the city and not served by regular public transport. So we hope that this new rail link with trains running every half an hour will help reduce traffic congestion around the university and also reduce pollution.

Speaker 3

I think this is the first mobile device to offer simultaneous translation. It listens to the speaker and then displays a translation of what they are saying directly onto the screen – absolutely incredible. It will transform communication between people speaking different languages.

3 💿 [1.31] Ask students to listen for the advantages that speakers say the development will bring. When they have compared their answers with a partner, elicit them from the class.

ANSWERS

1 don't need to buy electricity from outside (therefore reduce carbon footprint and reduce cost)
2 reduce traffic congestion and pollution
3 improve communication between people speaking different languages

---

4 Read the rubric and the example with the class. Ask them to think about some examples of different types of development in their own lives, and then share them with the class.

5a From reality to fantasy

Lead-in

Personal response

Ask students: *What is your ideal place to live? What sort of home, what sort of urban environment do you prefer?* Elicit and discuss answers from the class.

Reading

1 Ask students to work in pairs and discuss the questions about Dubai. Elicit answers from the whole class.

> **ANSWERS**
> 1 a plane or helicopter
> 2 buildings and roads, water, a park
> 3 Students' own answers

Background note

Dubai is a city located on the Persian Gulf and Arabian Peninsula. It has long been an important trading centre and port. After oil was discovered in 1966, it expanded exponentially, with many foreigners arriving for work. The main income is now from tourism, property and financial services. The city is famous for its spectacular buildings.

2 Read through the questions with the class to focus their reading, then ask them to read and answer them individually, then check with a partner. Elicit the answers from the class.

> **ANSWERS**
> 1 It was a sleepy village with a few people working there.
> 2 shopping, holiday villas, a luxury lifestyle, business
> 3 They are amazed but also suspicious.

Vocabulary notes

sheikh = the leader of an Arab tribe

pearl divers = people who dive in the sea for pearls from oysters

a gateway = (figurative) an entrance, a way in

to realise = to make real, to create

ambitious = difficult, complicated

intersection = a point where roads or motorways meet

landmark = a famous construction or natural feature

to abandon = to leave behind

heritage = history and culture

3 Ask the class to discuss their feelings about Dubai as a whole.

Grammar verb + infinitive or *-ing*

4 Ask students to complete the sentences with words from the text. Elicit the answers from the class.

> **ANSWERS**
> 1 creating
> 2 to realise
> 3 a neighbour to lend
> 4 Little Dubai become

5 Read through the instructions with the class, and ask students to find the examples individually, then check with a partner. Elicit answers from the whole class.

> **ANSWERS**
> 1 to carry on developing; risk losing
> 2 seemed to be; failed to sell; want to copy; decided to abandon
> 3 get people to invest
> 4 made people think again

6 Read through the grammar box with the class. If necessary, refer to page 162 of the Student's Book for further examples. Then ask students to do the exercise individually. Elicit answers from the class.

> **ANSWERS**
> 1 growing   5 shopping
> 2 to make   6 to create
> 3 reducing   7 construction slow
> 4 Dubai to become 8 building

Grammar note

It is important for students to understand that they need to learn the construction that a verb uses (i.e. *-ing* or *to* + infinitive etc.) when they learn the meaning of the verb.

There are some general patterns that will help them:

Verbs for likes and dislikes are often followed by *-ing*, e.g. *like, love, enjoy, hate, can't bear, look forward to.*

Verbs expressing hopes, intentions and decisions are often followed by *to* + infinitive, e.g. *decide, hope, intend, plan, prepare, want.*

Listening and vocabulary

7 Ask students to do this matching activity in pairs, then elicit answers from the whole class.

> **SAMPLE ANSWERS**
> green spaces / zone, high-rise building / development, leisure centre, luxury apartment / development, motorway intersection, pedestrianised zone / centre, shopping mall / centre, waterfront zone / development

8 ⊙ [1.32] Ask students to read the two questions to focus their listening. Play the recording while they listen and answer, then play it again if necessary. Elicit the answers from the class.

> **ANSWERS**
> 1 A residential area in the city centre was redeveloped to make a shopping district.
> 2 No, it wasn't.

Audioscript 💿 [1.32]

There used to be a lovely residential area right in the city centre, but in the 1960s the local authority decided to redevelop it as a shopping district. This involved demolishing all the houses and making way for huge car parks so that shoppers from out of town could park their cars. What's strange is that no one really considered opposing the idea at the time. Even the residents seemed to accept that the area had to be modernised. If you proposed converting houses into shops on such a big scale today, I don't think you would be allowed to do it.

Anyway, the result was that they spoilt the character of the centre. People shopped there in the daytime but at night everyone avoided going there because it became a centre for drug dealing and crime. Now, 50 years later, the local authority wants to transform it into a mixed area again by building new homes. The trouble is that rents are so high that ordinary people, like the ones who were moved out originally, can't afford to live there anymore.

9 💿 [1.32] Ask students to complete the sentences in pairs. Play the recording again for them to check their answers, then elicit answers from the class.

ANSWERS

1 redevelop	4 converting
2 demolishing	5 spoilt
3 modernised	6 transform

10 Ask students to replace the words individually, then check with a partner. Elicit the answers from the whole class as complete sentences.

ANSWERS

1 converted	4 modernised
2 transformed	5 demolished
3 spoilt	6 redeveloped

Speaking

11 Ask students to work in pairs to consider the questions in Exercise 10 in relation to their own town. Elicit suggestions for whole class discussion.

Homework

Ask students to write 100–150 words about a particular example of development or redevelopment that they know about. Encourage students to use the new vocabulary from this unit where appropriate.

5b The Kerala model

Lead-in

Personal response

Ask the class what they know about India. Elicit whatever information students can give you about places, people, languages, food, customs and so on.

Listening

1 Ask students to look at the two photos and the words in the box, and then decide which adjectives seem to be appropriate to each. Ask for reasons why they chose particular words.

SAMPLE ANSWERS

Photo 1: hectic, exotic

Photo 2: exotic, fertile, tranquil

2 💿 [1.33] Read the question with the class to focus their listening, then play the recording for them to find the answer. Elicit the answer from the class.

ANSWERS

The people don't earn much money, but the level of social development is surprisingly high. People are literate, well educated, and healthy.

Audioscript 💿 [1.33]

I = interviewer; J = journalist

I: I know you like exotic places – have you tried visiting India?

J: I was just there actually – in Kerala in the south-west. I was intending to go on to tour other parts of India, but Kerala was so fascinating I stayed on …

I: Were you on holiday?

J: No … well, it was meant to be a holiday, but actually it turned into more than that …

I: Oh dear …

J: Oh, no. I don't regret changing my plans … I became so interested in the place that I started to write an article about it for the newspaper I work for …

I: Really? Is it a travel article?

J: Not really. It's more sociological, I guess. I'm trying to show what a remarkable place Kerala is in the developing world. You see, it's a small state with a big population and the average income is only about $300 a year. Usually that would mean people having a fairly poor quality of life, but that's not the case. In fact, Kerala stands out as a kind of model of social development. The population is highly literate and well educated and they seem quite well-off, compared to other parts of India. They're healthy and live almost as long as Americans or Europeans; it seems that infant mortality is also very low. <u>Also, women, who've umm … always traditionally been the head of the household, continue to be very active (and equal) participants in society.</u>

I: Mmm … that's really interesting. I remember going there with my wife in the 1990s. But we were just tourists and my memories of it are as a very tranquil and beautiful place, with gorgeous beaches and lagoons …

J: Well, of course that's the part of it that tourists like to spend time visiting. But tranquil is not necessarily the adjective I would use. Trivandrum, the main city, where we stopped to visit an Indian journalist I know – a highly cultured man, by the way – is absolutely hectic. <u>The people there are very politically engaged: they never stop debating</u>; there are often strikes on the buses or parades of demonstrators – some medical students started protesting when we were there and went on protesting for four days.

I: So why do you think it's such a successful society?

J: Well, there are essentially two reasons, I think. <u>The first is that the Keralites are naturally tolerant people</u>: you find Hindus, Muslims and Christians all living peacefully alongside each other and foreigners are treated no differently to anyone else. And secondly, the government has invested a lot in health and education and goes on investing a lot. The land is incredibly fertile and well-organised – small farmers cultivate every inch of it so none is wasted, which I regret to say is not always the case in some developing countries.

I: Sounds fascinating. Please remember to send me a copy of the article when it's published …

J: Of course I will.

3 🖭 [1.33] Ask students to read through the statements to focus their listening. Play the recording for them to decide if the statements are true or false. Elicit answers and check any new language with the class (see Vocabulary notes below).

ANSWERS
1 F (she went for a holiday, but she was so interested that she wrote an article)
2 T
3 T
4 F (they are equal but not superior)
5 F (the people are very politically engaged)
6 T

Vocabulary note

sociological = having to do with society – the people and the way they work in groups

to regret = to wish the situation was different

infant mortality = death in childhood

household = the family living under one roof

lagoon = a quiet inlet of water from the sea

strike = a political protest where people don't go to work

4 Ask students to read through the definitions and think of the adjective to match each one, then turn to the audioscript on page 177 and find the words. Elicit answers from the class. Read through the information in the *Wordbuilding* box with the students. Refer to page 43 of the Workbook for further information and practice.

ANSWERS
2 well-off   5 cultured
3 well-educated   6 politically engaged
4 healthy   7 tolerant

5 Ask students to discuss the two questions in pairs and then make their suggestions for the whole class to discuss.

SAMPLE ANSWERS
1 the government providing good education and health care, the people are tolerant and politically involved
2 students' own answers

Pronunciation rhyming words

6a 🖭 [1.34] Ask students to read the words and match them individually, then check with a partner. Play the recording for them to check. Then elicit the answers. Play the recording again for students to repeat.

ANSWERS
1 e   2 h   3 d   4 i   5 f   6 b   7 c   8 g   9 a

Audioscript 🖭 [1.34]

1 state	weight
2 poor	law
3 low	though
4 head	said
5 course	force
6 main	plane
7 stopped	opt
8 none	fun
9 waste	faced

6b Ask students to think of rhyming words individually, then work in a group of four, to compare their words. Elicit answers from the class.

SAMPLE ANSWERS
break: ache, bake, cake, lake, make, shake, take,
foot: put, soot
height: bite, fight, light, night, sight, site, white
signed: bind, blind, kind, lined, mined
walk: cork, fork, pork, talk
word: bird, blurred, heard, herd, stirred

Grammar verbs with -ing and to + infinite

7 Ask students to choose the correct meaning for the verbs in bold in each pair of sentences. They can then check with a partner. Elicit the answers from the class, having students read a sentence and the correct meaning.

ANSWERS

1 b	3 b	5 a	7 b	9 a	11 b
2 a	4 a	6 b	8 a	10 b	12 a

Grammar note

With some verbs there is no difference in meaning between verb + infinitive or verb + -ing.
However, with other verbs (e.g. *stop, remember, forget*) the meaning changes, depending on which form follows it:
She stopped picking flowers in the garden.
(i.e. She was picking flowers and then she stopped.)
She stopped to pick flowers in the garden.
(i.e. She stopped walking so she could pick flowers.)
In the first sentence, the picking comes before the stopping; in the second sentence, the picking comes after the stopping.

8 Read through the grammar box with the class. If necessary, refer to page 163 of the Student's Book. Ask students to choose the correct answer in Exercise 6 individually, then check with a partner.

ANSWERS

1 maintaining	3 to tell	5 planning
2 living	4 to see	6 visiting

9 Ask students to complete the interview individually, then check with a partner. Elicit the answers from the class and check they understand all the language in the interview (see Vocabulary note below).

ANSWERS

1 reading	4 allowing	7 to say
2 to visit	5 giving	8 to work
3 to improve	6 to invest / investing	9 living

Vocabulary note

to implement = to put into practice
land reforms = improvements and modernisations in the way people are able to buy, own and use agricultural land
tenant farmers = farmers who do not own the land they farm, but rent it from a landlord
decent = well-paid, good quality

Speaking

10 Ask students to work in pairs, asking and answering the questions on page 155.

Homework

Ask students to write a 100–150 word paragraph about the happiness of their home society.

5c Sustainable development?

Lead-in

Personal response
Ask the class: *What do you understand by the term 'sustainable development'?*, and elicit some examples of it from them.

Reading

1 Ask students to look at the photo, then discuss what the effects of a dam on the river might have been. Elicit suggestions from the whole class.

2 Ask students to skim through the article to find the effects of the dam. Elicit additional problems caused by the dam that were not already mentioned by the class.

ANSWERS

People from the area had to retrain to make a living from the reservoir; they had to move to a new village, but they now have electricity, sanitation, clean water, roads and access to schools and health care. The dam may have a negative impact on water quality and fish, and there could be issues like flooding.

3 Read through the questions with the class to focus their reading. Ask them to read and answer individually, then check their answers with a partner. Elicit answers and check students understand all the key language (see Vocabulary notes below).

ANSWERS

1 the World Bank
2 Because they had stopped funding such projects 20 years before because of criticism.
3 over 1,000 megawatts
4 local people and people in Thailand
5 6,200
6 They may not be able to support themselves in the future.
7 the World Bank, but also Tiea, a villager
8 Because it could be bad for the water and the fish, and there might be flooding.

Vocabulary notes

a showpiece = a model to show people
to revitalise = to bring new life to
the pick of the bunch = the best that there is
to resettle = to move and live in another place
infrastructure = roads, transport systems, schools, hospitals
sanitation = running water for washing, toilets etc.
livelihood = your means of earning money to live on
amenities = buildings and services
grazing lands = fields where animals can eat grass (graze)
to readjust = to change to a new situation

4 Ask students to complete the sentences individually, then check with a partner. Elicit answers from the class as complete sentences.

ANSWERS

1 reservoir	4 make a living
2 showpiece	5 amenities
3 lives	6 flora and fauna

Vocabulary

5 Ask students to find the words beginning with *re-* in the article individually. Elicit the words from the whole class and write them on the board. Then look at the *Wordbuilding* box and show how the noun *redevelopment* is made from *redevelop*. Ask students to do the same with the verbs in the list. Then elicit them from the class.

ANSWERS

These are the *re-* verbs (underlined verbs mean 'to do something again'):

<u>revitalise</u>, <u>resettle</u>, reduce, <u>renew</u>, <u>rebuild</u>, <u>retrained</u>, <u>relocate</u>, <u>restore</u>, rely, <u>rehouse</u>, <u>readjust</u>.

(There are also 3 nouns: *revenue, reservoir, resources*; and one adjective: *responsive*.)

The nouns formed from the verbs above are:

revitalisation, resettlement, reduction, renewal, rebuilding, retraining, relocation, restoration, reliance, rehousing, readjustment.

Critical thinking fact or opinion

6 Read through the rubric with the whole class, and ask pairs to find the examples of fact and opinion for the three areas. Elicit answers from the whole class.

ANSWERS

economic benefits
fact: in 2010 the dam brought $5.6 million in sales
opinion: it will generate around $2 billion in revenue; money will be spent on reducing poverty and renewing and improving the country's infrastructure

effects on local people
fact: 17 villages have been rebuilt and farmers retrained; they have electricity, sanitation, clean water, new roads, schools
opinion: life is much better than before; they will not be able to support themselves economically in the future

effects on the environment
opinion: negative impact on water quality and fish
fact: established a protected area for flora and fauna

7 Ask students to discuss in pairs how they identified facts and opinions.

ANSWERS

Opinion is introduced by:
the bank **says / thinks** ... that ...
the government **has promised** ... that ...
environmental groups **warn / point** out ... that ...
according to the World Bank ...
it is estimated that ...
Facts have normal present and past verb forms:
17 villages in the flooded area **have now been rebuilt** ...
in 2010 the dam **brought** $5.6 million in sales of electricity ...

8 Ask pairs to form groups of four to discuss what they found, and whether they think the dam has brought more advantages or disadvantages to Laos. Elicit answers from the class and discuss.

SAMPLE ANSWERS

In general one could say that electricity for lots of people is a positive benefit, and better housing and facilities for the 6,200 people in 17 villages might be an improvement. However, there are all the other 110,000 people downstream of the dam yet to consider, and the long-term effects on the water and fish.

Word focus *pick*

Vocabulary note

The fundamental concept of *picking* can be either removing something (often carefully) or choosing or selecting one from among others. For example, if you *pick a colour* you choose one colour from many.

9 Ask students to find the three uses of *pick* in the text and decide what they mean in pairs. Elicit answers from the whole class. Then ask them to do the same with the six sentences; elicit answers in the same way.

ANSWERS

I picked my first bamboo (para 1) = collect or break off from the plant
the pick of the bunch (para 3) = the best one, the one you would choose
they will pick up new skills (para 9) = learn
1 criticise
2 ask for your help with ideas
3 increasing
4 chosen for unfair treatment
5 collect, come and get me in the car
6 select

Speaking

10 Ask students to discuss the topics given in pairs and make some notes about what they think the impacts will be, and how they should deal with them. Elicit answers from the whole class and open a wider discussion.

Homework

Ask students to write 100–150 words about one of the three situations, using their own ideas and others they heard presented during the discussion.

5d Evaluating a project

Lead-in

Personal response

Ask: *What rebuilding or restoration projects are going on in a town you know at the moment? What do you think of them?* Elicit some ideas and encourage discussion.

Real life reaching decisions

1 Ask students to work in pairs and consider the options, then choose three and rank them in order. Elicit suggestions and discuss the ideas as a whole class.

2 🔊 [1.35] Read the rubric with the class, then give them time to read through the notes. Play the recording twice for students to complete the notes. Elicit answers from the class as complete sentences.

> ANSWERS
> 1 £750,000
> 2 green space
> 3 recreation
> 4 trees, grass, café, play area
> 5 fountain, £80,000
> 6 tennis, mini

Audioscript 🔊 [1.35]

P = Patrick; A = Anna; I = Isabelle

P: OK, Anna, I believe you've prepared a brief summary of the Howard Park project …

A: Yup

P: Would you just like to take us through the main points?

A: Yes, sure. Well, the Howard Park project began two years ago. We agreed to lend the local authority £750,000 to redevelop a green space in the Howard's Hill area of the city. The aim was to give the local residents a nicer park, first of all, but also some new recreation facilities: a mini golf course, two tennis courts, a small café and a new children's play area. The play area was in terrible condition … full of rubbish … it was actually quite dangerous. So here we are two years on: what progress have they made? Well, they've done a good job of cleaning the area up: they've planted trees and laid new grass, so it looks much, much better. They've also built the café and the children's play area. However, they've also done some things that weren't part of the original plan. For example, they've built a fountain near the café and six months ago they also bought a sculpture, at a cost of £80,000, to place near the fountain. Now they've run out of money and are asking for a new loan of £250,000 to complete the tennis courts and mini-golf course. What do you think?

I: If you ask me, that's completely wrong. They've been spending money on things they had no right to. I don't think we should give them another penny.

P: Well hang on a minute. Let's not be too hasty. I agree that they should have told us about these other changes. But we need to consider if they are in the spirit of the original aims of the project …

A: That really depends on the opinion of the local residents. The way I see it, it's probably a good thing – if residents like it and it means they'll use the park more.

I: Well, I just find it arrogant of them, actually …

P: OK … so what ought we to do? Personally, I don't think we should lend them any more until we know what local people think of the work they've done already.

A: Yes, I'd go along with that. We need to ask them to conduct a survey of local opinion and then show us the results.

P: Exactly. Are we all agreed on that then?

I: Yes, I guess so … yes, that seems fair to me.

3 🔊 [1.35] Ask students to read the question to focus their listening. Then play the recording again. Elicit the answer from the class.

> ANSWER
> Conduct a survey of local opinion about the park before they give more money.
> They all agree.

4 🔊 [1.35] Ask students to read through the sentences in the box carefully before they listen. Play the recording (twice if necessary). Then elicit answers from the class as complete sentences.

> ANSWERS
> 1 ask me   6 way I
> 2 should   7 go along
> 3 Let's not   8 agreed on
> 4 to consider   9 seems fair
> 5 depends on

Vocabulary notes

To give someone the benefit of the doubt = to accept what someone says even though you are not sure that they are 100% right

Let's not be too hasty = let's not act too quickly

in the spirit of = with the same aim

the way I see it = in my opinion

to go along with something = to agree with

Speaking

5 Read through the instructions in the rubric with the class, then ask students to turn to page 153. Ask students to work in groups of four to discuss the project, using as many of the expressions they have practised as possible. Circulate and monitor their discussions for later feedback.

Homework

Ask students to write up a committee dialogue about the project in Exercise 5 using some of the expressions from the box in Exercise 4.

5e Big cities, big problems

Lead-in

Personal response

Ask the class to shout out some of the problems associated with living in a big city. List them on the board as they give them. Then ask them to rank the list from most to least problematic for the individual living in the city. Elicit their ideas, asking for reasons and open it up to a class discussion.

Writing an opinion essay

1 Ask students to make their lists in pairs, then elicit ideas from the whole class, and discuss them.

2 Ask students to suggest what problems are caused by increasing numbers of people living in cities – not just for the cities, but for the countryside and the country as a whole. Discuss the ideas raised with the class.

3 Ask students to read the essay and decide what the writer's opinion is; elicit the answer from the class.

> **ANSWER**
>
> The writer thinks cities are good places to live if they are well managed.

4 Ask the class to look at the essay again and say whether it follows the standard format.

> **ANSWER**
>
> 'Arguments against' come before 'arguments for'.

5 Ask students to read the opening paragraph (introduction) again, and answer the question.

> **ANSWER**
>
> Giving some statistics to illustrate the seriousness of the problem

Writing skills linking words

6a Read the table of linking phrases with the class and ask for other examples from the essay (four of them are in italics in the text, but there are others).

> **ANSWERS**
>
> Adding to an argument: *In addition, also*
> Introducing a contrasting fact: *On the other hand, however, but*
> Explaining the consequences: *As a result, because of this*

6b Ask students to complete the sentences individually, then check with a partner. Elicit the answers as complete sentences. There are various equally correct options for each answer.

> **ANSWERS**
>
> 1 As a result / Consequently / Because of this
> 2 Then again / On the other hand / However
> 3 In addition to / As well as

Vocabulary note

Draw students' attention to the fact that we have to modify these expressions depending on the structures which follow them, for example:

In addition, <u>there are</u> many poor people living there.

In addition to rich people <u>living</u> there, there are also many poor people.

As well as the rich, there are also poor people living there.

As well as this, both rich and poor live there.

Note the use of the comma to separate the introductory phrase where it is independent of the main part of the sentence.

7 Ask students to write an opinion essay on the topic given. They then exchange essays with a partner to check for structural correctness, and also for language correctness. You might give this exercise as homework, with students checking one another's work in the following lesson.

8 Ask students to swap their essay with a partner and check their partner's work, following the criteria given.

5f Aquarium on Wheels

Before you watch

1 Students work in groups. Ask them to look at the photo and the title and discuss the questions. Take feedback from the class.

2 Ask students to read the list in the box and predict which things they think they will see in the video. Take feedback from the class.

While you watch

3 Give students time to read through the words in the glossary. Play the whole of the video for students to check their ideas from Exercise 2. They should not try to understand everything at this stage.

> **ANSWERS**
>
> We see a boy dressed as a monkey, a computer, a fish tank, a frog, a necklace, seashells, a toy snake

4 Give students time to read the sentences. Then play the first part of the video (to 02.17) for them to choose the correct options.

> **ANSWERS**
>
> 1 a   2 b   3 b   4 a   5 b

5 Give students time to read the questions, then play the second part of the video (02.18 to the end) for them to answer.

> **ANSWERS**
>
> 1 communication skills, responsibility, organisation and planning
> 2 go to college
> 3 responsibility
> 4 how to organise and plan something
> 5 an environmental lawyer
> 6 It gives her satisfaction to watch the students grow and develop.

After you watch

6 Students work in pairs to roleplay an interview with Martha Schaum, according to the instructions. They should change roles and act out the conversation a second time.

7 Elicit ideas from the class about what the quote means and ask students to answer the question.

8 Students work in groups to discuss the questions.

Videoscript

Part 1

00.18–00.20   speaker on video   Let's get this stuff out and see what we've got here.

00.22–00.28   In a classroom at the National Aquarium in Baltimore, ten secondary school students are preparing for a lesson.

00.29–00.37   speakers on video   'But look at the camouflage on it …' 'The eyes …' 'Containers that are made from them …' 'We have a frog.'

00.38–00.45   They're also preparing a show-and-tell presentation to give to a group of children and creating costumes for a play that they've written.

00.48–00.50   speaker on video   And where's the poison dart frog container? OK.

00.51–01.10   Due to their age, this preparation and planning appears to be schoolwork, but it isn't. In fact, these students are employees of a very special programme called 'Aquarium on Wheels'.

01.02–01.12   DejaNé Jones   There's a lot of kids who do not have the opportunity to come to the aquarium, or see live animals or anything like that, so we bring the aquarium to them.

01.13–01.33   The overall objectives of Aquarium on Wheels are to entertain and educate. This year's goal is to explain the importance of the world's rain forests to young people.

These student teachers want to help their young audience to better understand conservation.

The play is about a species threatened by the loss of the rain forest because it relies on it for food: the monkey.

01.34–01.46   speakers on video   'They're going to cut down this tree.' 'They're going to cut down this tree?' 'Yes.' 'How am I going to find my leaves to eat? That means I'm going to have to fight other monkeys! I can't fight other monkeys; I'm going to mess up my hair!'

01.47–01.53   George Faulk   We're trying to get through to the kids that saving one tree can be important to all the animals in the rain forest.

01.54–02.06   For aquarium administrators, on the other hand, the programme is about more than just teaching biology, or even teaching about the environment; it's about offering student employees lessons for life.

Martha Schaum is the programme coordinator at the aquarium.

02.07–02.17   Martha Schaum   Most kids like to play in the water – let's be realistic – so marine biology is a really great vehicle to use to teach the other skills that they need to know.

Part 2

02.18–02.24   One set of skills that the secondary school students need are the communication skills necessary to get – and keep – a job.

02.25–02.35   Martha Schaum   I think for many of them – probably for most of them – they are probably the first in their family to go to college. And so what we're doing is coming along behind them and saying, 'You can do it.'

02.36–02.46   DejaNé Jones   I wouldn't be the person I am today if it wasn't for them.

Basically, they taught me responsibility. That's a big thing I've learned here.

02.47–03.00 Martha Schaum   They knew we were going to discuss the rain forest. That's a big topic. They had to decide how they wanted to present it, the concept that they wanted to use. They had to write the script. They had to decide the sorts of things that they wanted in the lab.

03.01–03.09 Through this work, the student teachers learned an enormous amount about organisation and planning, and they also learned a bit about themselves as well.

03.10–03.16 DejaNé Jones   It means a lot to me. Like I said, I have been here for three years and I really feel like I've helped a lot of people understand conservation.

03.17–03.24   However, for many of these teenagers, the real value of Aquarium on Wheels is more personal; it's about their dreams for their lives.

03.25–03.33 Student employee   At first it just seemed like a really cool job to work at the aquarium. Now that I've been working here, I've finally found out what I want to be. I've found out that I want to be a marine biologist.

03.34–03.37 George Faulk   I want to be an environmental lawyer, so it helps me out a lot.

03.38–03.52 Student employee   It really … the programme really means a lot to me because I want to major in marine biology. And here at the aquarium I can get the experience that most other students wouldn't be able to receive.

03.54–04.09   The programme is proving to be advantageous for these students in helping them to prepare for their future professional lives.

For Martha Schaum, the programme allows her to achieve personal and professional satisfaction from watching these teenagers grow as people.

04.10–04.16 Martha Schaum   This programme has meant more to me than anything else, because I've just, I have watched these kids grow and develop.

04.17–End   The Aquarium on Wheels programme is having a powerful impact on more than just the rain forests; it's having a positive effect on everyone involved with this very special programme.

UNIT 5 Review

Grammar

1 Ask students to discuss the main industry in their town or city and its effects on the character of the place.

2 Read the questions with the class to focus their reading, then ask them to read the interview and answer the questions. Elicit the answers from the whole class.

> ANSWERS
>
> 1 Tourism
> 2 That there should be a tourist tax so that the tourism benefits the city and not just private companies.

3 Ask students to complete the interview with the correct forms of the verbs. Elicit answers from the class.

> ANSWERS
>
> | 1 living | 4 to say | 7 create / to create |
> |---|---|---|
> | 2 building | 5 to turn | 8 earning |
> | 3 redeveloping | 6 coming | 9 to pay |

Vocabulary

4 Ask students to match the words individually, then check with a partner. Elicit answers from the whole class.

> ANSWERS
>
> 1 e   2 d   3 a   4 f   5 b   6 c

5 Ask students to complete the sentences with a suitable word in pairs. Elicit answers from the class.

> ANSWERS
>
> | 1 transform | 3 convert |
> |---|---|
> | 2 demolishing | 4 spoilt, redeveloping |

6 Ask students to work in pairs to discuss whether any of the statements in Exercise 5 are true of their city.

Real life

7 Ask students to work in pairs to complete the sentences with a suitable verb. Elicit answers from the whole class.

> ANSWERS
>
> | 1 think | 5 see |
> |---|---|
> | 2 find | 6 depends |
> | 3 ask | 7 go |
> | 4 seem | |

8 Ask students to work in groups of four to discuss the issue. Elicit ideas from the class.

Speaking

9 Ask students to work in pairs to discuss a project that they know about, covering the points listed carefully.

Unit 6 Alternative travel

Lead-in

Personal response

Ask: *Where have you been coldest? Where have you seen most ice and snow?* Invite the class to talk about their experiences in these conditions, and encourage them to ask each other questions.

1 Ask students to look at the photo of the ice hotel in Canada, read the caption and answer the questions – elicit comments from the class.

2 💿 [1.36] Read the questions with the class to focus their listening. Play the recording and elicit answers. If there are problems play the recording again.

> **ANSWERS**
> 1 The hotel is a work of art; the coloured light is beautiful.
> 2 It is cold and sleeping is difficult.

Audioscript 💿 [1.36]

I only get three weeks' holiday a year so I always choose the places I go to carefully. I try to go to places with dramatic scenery … and unusual places. It can take time to get to these, but it's generally worth it. I've visited a few ice hotels in my time in Scandinavia, but Hotel de Glace is something special. It's a real work of art. The furniture and fittings are all made of ice – there's even an ice chandelier in the lobby – and the walls are decorated with pictures carved out of the snow. Once the sun goes down and all the coloured lighting is switched on, the effect is stunning. But … there is a but, I'm afraid – as a place to get a comfortable night, I'm not sure I'd recommend it. I know it sounds obvious, but the place is really cold. Unless you have a sauna before going to bed, you'll probably wake up in the night feeling chilly, even in the special minus 40 degree sleeping bags you are given. I guess it's a bit like high class camping, if you like that kind of thing.

Background notes

The Hotel de Glace (Ice Hotel) is located 5km north of Quebec City, on the slopes of the Laurentian mountains. It is rebuilt each December, and lasts for four months until it is demolished in April. The beds are all made of ice and lined with deer furs, covered with mattresses and with Arctic sleeping bags to sleep in. Only the bathrooms are heated, and they are located in a separate insulated structure. The hotel also has a nightclub, a cinema and a chapel, which is a popular place to get married.

3 Ask students to work with a partner to complete the questions. Check that they understand *to travel light* (to travel with little luggage). Elicit answers from the whole class. Then ask students to ask and answer the questions.

> **ANSWERS**
>
> | | | |
> |---|---|---|
> | 1 holiday | 4 luggage | 7 airline |
> | 2 self-catering | 5 countryside / scenery | 8 take |
> | 3 view | 6 journey | |

6a Staycations

Lead-in

Personal response

Ask students to tell a partner about a recent holiday they had, giving details about travel and the place(s) they stayed. Elicit some examples from the whole class.

Speaking

1 Ask students to work in pairs to ask and answer all the questions about their capital city. Elicit answers and discuss them with the rest of the class.

2 Ask students to talk about this as a class. You can extend 'local area' to cover region or country when it comes to discussing taking holidays.

Reading

3 Ask students to read through the statements to focus their reading, then read the blog and answer. They can check with a partner before you elicit the answers.

> **ANSWERS**
> 1 F (you can camp at a local campsite.)
> 2 T
> 3 F (*you don't have any of the problems associated with travel*)
> 4 T

4 Ask students to read the blog again and complete the sentences. They should check with a partner. Elicit the answers from the whole class as complete sentences.

> **ANSWERS**
> 1 … the financial crisis in 2008.
> 2 … people spend money locally, at restaurants for example.
> 3 … holidaying in other, new places.
> 4 … complete Japanese experience.

Vocabulary notes

You might need to explain the origins of the title *Staycation* as a shortening of 'stay-at-home-vacation'.

to be put off = to get a negative idea of something

to catch on = to become popular

to base oneself somewhere = to live in one place and move around from there

to take something a step further = to do more than you are doing

ramen = a thin Japanese soup with noodles and sometimes a little meat or vegetables

bonsai = trees which are cultivated to remain very small

taiko drumming = a type of Japanese drumming, usually with several people playing drums together.

Vocabulary phrasal verbs with *in* and *out*

5 Ask students to work in pairs to find and explain the meaning of the four phrasal verbs with *in* and *out*. Elicit answers from the whole class.

ANSWERS

1 *to stay in* (to stay at home rather than go out somewhere for entertainment)
2 *to get out* (to leave one's home to do something interesting)
3 *to eat out* (to eat at a restaurant rather than at home)
4 *to join in* (to take part in something organised by others)

---

6 Ask students to complete the sentences with *in* or *out*; they may need a monolingual dictionary to help them. Elicit the answers from the class as complete sentences. Point out that while the verb to *fill in* a form is used in British English, in American English *fill out* a form is preferred. Read through the *Wordbuilding* box with the class. See also the Vocabulary notes below, and page 51 of the Workbook for further information and practice.

ANSWERS

1 out   2 in   3 in   4 out   5 out   6 in

Extra activity

Ask students to give synonyms for the phrasal verbs in Exercise 5:

1 *to try out* = to try something for the first time
2 *to eat in* = to eat at home
3 *to drop in* = to go into a building quickly (possibly to visit someone)
4 *to get out* = to leave the house to go to some entertainment or to socialise
5 *to stay out* = to not come home
6 *to fill in* = to complete

Vocabulary notes

Sometimes the same verb has a completely different meaning when used with *in* or *out*:

to drop in = to make a short visit to somebody, often unexpectedly

to drop out = to stop taking part in something, e.g. a competition, a course, or a club (often because it is too difficult)

Sometimes the same verbs are the opposite of each other with *in* or *out*:

to eat in = to eat at home

to eat out = to eat in a restaurant

Sometimes you can only use the verb with one of the prepositions:

to join in = to take part (but we cannot say *to join out*).

Sometimes a different verb is used to mean the opposite:

*to **stay** in* = to spend time at home

*to **go** out* = to leave home for entertainment or activity

---

7 Ask students to work in their pairs to ask and answer all the questions. Circulate and monitor their conversations for later feedback.

Grammar *not*

8 Ask students to find the examples of *not* in the text, reminding them that in some cases it may be contracted. Then ask them to match the examples to the descriptions 1–7. Elicit answers from the whole class.

ANSWERS

1 decided <u>not</u> to go (after first verb, before infinitive)
2 If you do<u>n't</u> want to stay at home (with auxiliary before *want*)
3 you must<u>n't</u> be put off (after *must*)
4 you do<u>n't</u> have to (with auxiliary before *have to*)
5 The only people who hope this kind of holiday wo<u>n't</u> catch on (with second verb)
6 I do<u>n't</u> think many people would want to take this much trouble (with auxiliary before *think*)
7 Let's <u>not</u> ignore the other benefits (after *Let's*)

---

9 Read through the examples in the grammar box with the class. Ask them to change each sentence in Exercise 9 to a negative sentence individually, then check with a partner. Elicit answers from the whole class. If you think students need further examples and practice, turn to page 163 of the Student's Book.

ANSWERS

1 Let's not spend a lot of money on a foreign holiday.
2 I don't want to stay in a big modern hotel.
3 I don't think staycations can replace foreign holidays.
4 I hope the accommodation isn't all booked up.
5 I told them not to wait until the last minute before booking their holiday.
6 We don't have to go swimming – if you don't want to, that is.

Grammar note

The position of *not* with verbs is as follows:
After the verb *to be*:

 It isn't a nice place.   They weren't with us.

After an auxiliary:

 She hasn't booked yet.   They didn't go to Spain.
 We don't like camping.

After modal verbs:

 You mustn't eat that!   He can't explain it.

With an infinitive verb + *to*, *not* is before *to*

 *It's cheaper **not to go** abroad.* (not *It's cheaper to not go abroad.*)

In sentences with more than one verb, *not* is generally with the verb which is negative, e.g. *They advised us not to stay at that hotel.* (They <u>did</u> advise us, but the advice was <u>not</u> to stay at that hotel.)

The main exceptions to this are *think* and *want*. With a negative opinion, *not* is always with *think* or *want*, even though we might logically expect it to be with the other verb.

 *I **don't want** to go to the party tomorrow.* (Not *I want not to go to the party tomorrow.*)

 *I **don't think** that's right.* (Not *I think that's not right*).

10 Ask students to read the article and choose the correct forms individually, then check with a partner. Elicit the answers from the class as complete sentences.

> **ANSWERS**
> 1 not forget
> 2 don't have to spend
> 3 don't want to spend
> 4 doesn't have to be
> 5 not to choose
> 6 don't think you'll enjoy
> 7 hope it isn't

Speaking

11 Ask students to work in groups of four to plan their staycation, following the instructions. Ask them to prepare a presentation of their itinerary, making sure that all four members of the group explain part of the plan.

12 Ask two groups to get together, and make their presentations and exchange their ideas about their staycation. If you wish the class to vote on the best staycation ideas, groups will need to make their presentation to the whole class. Circulate and monitor the language used for later feedback.

Homework

Ask students to do a 100–150 word description of their staycation plan.

6b Voluntourism

Lead-in

Personal response

Ask: *When was the last time you volunteered to do something, and what was it?* Ask for comments and questions from other students as they listen.

Listening

1 Ask students to discuss the proverb *A change is as good as a rest* in pairs, and then elicit comments on it. If you have a monolingual class find out what the translation is and whether it has a different literal meaning. With multilingual classes, ask them to back-translate their version from their own languages and compare them.

> **ANSWER**
>
> It means that if you do something completely different; although it might be hard work, it feels like you've had a holiday from what you usually do.

Vocabulary notes

You may wish to preteach this vocabulary from the listening text:

a gap year = a year between ending school and going to university, when students travel around the world

to be conscious of something = to be aware of, to know about

the point of = the objective, the aim

to lend a hand = to help

to poach = to kill animals illegally

a bush walk = a walk in the African countryside

a monastery = a religious building where monks live

orphaned = with no mother or father

2 [1.37] Ask students to look at the photo and speculate about what people might volunteer to do there. Elicit suggestions from the class without saying whether they are correct. Play the recording for students to check their predictions.

> **ANSWER**
>
> They help local people to find ways of making a living that don't involve poaching or killing local wildlife

Audioscript [1.37]

P = Presenter; K = Katie Samuel

P: … Now, have you ever thought of doing a bit of building work during your holidays? Or helping to look after animals on a wildlife reserve? You probably thought that sort of vacation was for eighteen-year-olds on their gap year, didn't you? But it seems more and more working adults are opting for volunteer vacations. With us today is Katie Samuél, author of *Good Travel*, a guide to alternative holidays. Katie, I can see that this might attract a few people, but for most of us, who only get a few weeks off a year ... wouldn't they prefer a more relaxing option?

K: Well, that depends very much on how your volunteer vacation is organised. The good companies in this field are certainly conscious of the fact that this should be a rewarding travel experience ... and not just a work trip.

P: But isn't the whole point of it to go and lend a hand to people in need of help? It's not really a holiday as we know it, is it?

K: Well, no, perhaps it isn't, but it is more like what real travel should be about: a cultural experience where each side gives something and takes something. A good example is a programme next to Kenya's Tsavo National Park, where volunteers help local people to find ways of making a living that don't involve poaching or killing local wildlife. So they help them to plant crops, build fences, develop ideas for tourist businesses and so on. In return the locals take them for bush walks, which are like mini-safaris, teach them about local wildlife, talk about the history of their community ...

P: But the volunteers pay for the trip, don't they?

K: Yes, of course, they have to pay for their air fares, their living expenses and something to cover the organisation costs.

P: And do you need to be qualified to volunteer? I imagine organisations don't want people turning up to teach or build or whatever who have no idea of what they're doing, do they?

K: Again it depends ... There are a few projects which are only open to people with professional experience ... um ... like people with a medical background ... but for the most part, volunteers can be trained to do the work. The Cultural Restoration Tourism Project (CRTP), which helps to restore cultural heritage sites around the world, gives volunteers the chance to work with local architects and artists. They have a project restoring a 300-year-old monastery in Nepal where you can get training in doing wall paintings from a world-famous painter.

P: So, you could actually come back with a skill you didn't have when you left?

K: Absolutely. It might not be a skill you'll ever use again: helping to bottle-feed milk to orphaned lion cubs – that's a project in Zambia – is unlikely to be of direct use to you back at the office in the UK, but we all benefit from new and different experiences, wouldn't you agree?

P: Yeah, I'm sure that's true. So could you tell us a bit more about ...

3 Ask students to decide which statement best sums up Katie's opinion.

> ANSWER
> b

4 [1.37] Ask students to read the gapped sentences to focus their listening. Play the recording while they complete the sentences. If necessary, play it again for them to check, correct and complete. Elicit the answers from the class as complete sentences.

> ANSWERS
> 1 gap   4 bush
> 2 off   5 living
> 3 rewarding / trip   6 heritage

5 Ask students to get into groups of four to discuss the three questions about this type of holiday. Elicit ideas from the whole class and open a wider discussion.

Grammar negative and tag questions

6 Read through the rubric and sentences with the class, and ask students to match them with the expectations (a–c) of the speaker individually. When they have checked with a partner, elicit the answers from the whole class.

> ANSWERS
> 1 a   2 b   3 b   4 c

Grammar note

Discuss the way that we indicate the answer we expect with questions tags:

Affirmative main verb + negative question tag expects a *yes* answer:

> *You like football, don't you?*
> *She enjoys reggae, doesn't she?*

Negative main verb + affirmative question tag expects a *no* answer:

> *They don't play well, do they?*
> *We don't want to go, do we?*

Note that the tag often relates to the answer we expect rather than the answer we hope for, e.g. *I can't do that online, can I?* (= I **hope** that I might be able to do it online, but I don't really **expect** a positive answer).

7 Ask students to find four more examples of questions expecting a particular answer from the audioscript on page 177. Elicit them from the class.

> ANSWERS
>
> It's not really a holiday as we know it, is it? (expects *no* answer)
>
> But the volunteers pay for the trip, don't they? (expects *yes* answer)
>
> I imagine organisations don't want people turning up to teach or build or whatever who have no idea of what they're doing, do they? (expects *no* answer)
>
> We all benefit from new and different experiences. Wouldn't you agree? (expects *yes* answer)

8 Read through the grammar box with the class and check that they understand how these questions work. If they need more examples and practice, see page 164 of the Student's Book.

Ask students to do the exercise individually, then check with a partner. Elicit answers from the whole class.

> **ANSWERS**
> 1 You like the idea of volunteer vacations, don't you?
> 2 Don't you think it's an interesting idea?
> 3 You've been on a volunteer vacation, haven't you?
> 4 Didn't it seem strange to pay money in order to work?
> 5 You won't be going again this year, will you?

Pronunciation intonation in questions

9a [1.38] Ask students to read the sentences in the grammar box and say them to themselves, thinking about how they might sound. Play the recordings and let students listen and follow a couple of times. Then ask the class for answers to the three questions.

> **ANSWERS**
> 1 rises   2 rises   3 falls

Audioscript [1.38]

Do you like visiting new places? [rising]   Yes, now and again.

Don't you like visiting new places? [rising]   No, not at all.

You like visiting new places, don't you? [falling]   Yes, I love it.

You don't like visiting new places, do you? [falling]   No, you're right. I don't.

9b [1.39] Ask students to ask the questions in Exercise 8 in pairs – they should both ask all the questions.

> **ANSWERS**
> 1 falling   2 rising   3 falling   4 rising   5 falling

Audioscript [1.39]

1 You like the idea of volunteer vacations, don't you?

2 Don't you think it's an interesting idea?

3 You've been on a volunteer vacation, haven't you?

4 Didn't it seem strange to pay money in order to work?

5 You won't be going again this year, will you?

10 [1.40] Read the rubric with the class and check that they understand what to do. Then ask them to make negative or tag questions from the prompts in bold individually. They can check with a partner. Elicit answers from the class and encourage discussion where there are different ideas. Finally play the recording for students to check.

> **ANSWERS**
> 1 I can work for just a few days, can't I? (falling intonation)
> 2 Don't I have to pay for my accommodation? (rising intonation)
> 3 I can't do that online, can I? (falling intonation)
> 4 You've visited our website, haven't you? (falling intonation)
> 5 Don't you have something in Colorado? (rising intonation)
> 6 And you give training first, don't you? (falling intonation)
> 7 You don't want to be a chef, do you? (falling intonation)

Audioscript [1.40]

M = Mike; **J** = Jeff

M: Hi, I'm interested in helping out on the Great Continental Divide this summer. My friend did four days last summer. I can work for just a few days, can't I?

J: Absolutely. Anything from two days to two months.

M: That's great. I have about a week in June. How much does it cost to take part?

J: It's free.

M: Sorry? Don't I have to pay for my accommodation?

J: No, it's completely free. You just have to register by filling out a form and sending it to us.

M: I can't do that online, can I?

J: Sure, you can. It's on our website. You've visited our website, haven't you?

M: Yes, I've had a quick look. And where on the trail can I work?

J: New Mexico, Montana, Wyoming …

M: Don't you have something in Colorado? That's where I live.

J: Yes, we do. We have spaces in Winfield and a few in Mount Elbert.

M: And you give training first, don't you?

J: It's on the job training, unless it's very specific. We're looking for a chef at the moment. You don't want to be a chef, do you?

M: No. I just want to help build some trails …

Extra activity

Ask students to work in pairs to practise the dialogue. When they have finished it, they should change roles and partners and do it again.

Speaking

11 Ask students to do this activity in pairs at first, then change pairs and do it again. They can change partner as often as they want. Circulate and monitor their questions and intonation for later feedback.

6c Unusual places to stay

Lead-in

Personal response

Ask students to tell their partner about the most unusual place they have ever stayed – it doesn't have to have been on a holiday. After students have discussed their experiences in pairs, elicit some descriptions of the places from students, and encourage questions and comments from the others.

Reading

1 Ask pairs to make a list of their holiday preferences, then compare the list with another pair.

2 Ask students to read about the four hotels and answer the questions with their own opinions. Elicit answers from the whole class, with reasons.

> **ANSWERS**
>
> 1 period hotels and cave hotels
> 2 prison hotels (except for the price) and art hotels

3 Ask students to read through the sentences first to focus their reading of the article, then read the article again and complete the sentences. When they have finished they can check with a partner. Elicit answers from the class as complete sentences. Check any new vocabulary with the students (see Vocabulary notes below).

> **ANSWERS**
>
> 1 a   2 b   3 a   4 b   5 a   6 b   7 b   8 a

Vocabulary notes

mutinous = soldiers or sailors who attack their officers and try to take over control

period (adj) = in keeping with a particular time in history

a gold-rush = the time when thousands of miners arrived because gold had been found

a ghost town = a town where no one lives, and there are just the buildings

Stetson hat = a tall cowboy hat (as worn in the photo)

rustic = as in the country, simple, old-fashioned

a sheriff = a kind of early policeman looking after the law in a town

a gold prospector = someone looking for gold

a balustrade = = an elaborate railing on a balcony or in front of a window

vaulted ceilings = ceilings with pointed arches and made of stone, like in a church

terracotta = a kind of ceramic made from red clay

a peasant = a poor land worker

claustrophobic = feeling small, enclosed and shut in

4 Ask students to tell a partner the meaning of these words, or use a dictionary to find their meaning first. Elicit answers from the whole class.

> **ANSWERS**
>
> *balcony:* a flat area projecting out from a building, on which you can stand or sit
> *a balustrade:* an elaborate railing around a balcony
> *corridor:* a long narrow space with doors into rooms along it
> *earth roofs:* roofs on the top of the house that are made of earth
> *saloon:* a bar
> *vaulted ceilings:* ceilings with pointed arches and made of stone, like in a church

5 Ask pairs to discuss which of the four hotels they prefer and why. Elicit some responses from the whole class. Make sure they give reasons for their preferences.

Critical thinking claims and justifications

6 Read through the rubric with the class and ensure students understand what to do. It might be a good idea to have them do this in pairs so they can confer. Elicit answers from the whole class.

> **SAMPLE ANSWERS**
>
> **Prison hotel**
> Claims to be: a naval jail
> Supporting facts: unfriendly, unheated, uncomfortable, former prison guard, bread and tea, strict rules, make own beds on a wooden bench and thin mattress
> Contradictory facts: none
>
> **Period hotel**
> Claims to be: authentic gold-rush town from 150 years ago
> Supporting facts: Victorian furniture, Wild West saloon, earth roofs
> Contradictory facts: large double beds, private bathrooms
>
> **Cave hotel**
> Claims to be: primitive cave dwellings, inhabited since the bronze age, homes of peasants
> Supporting facts: no TVs and fridges, antique furniture, terracotta tiles
> Contradictory facts: comfortably furnished
>
> **Art hotel**
> Claims to be: art gallery and hotel combined
> Supporting facts: rooms extreme in design
> Contradictory facts: not very comfortable

7 Ask students to discuss the three questions about hotels in pairs, then tell the rest of the class what they feel; others should comment and discuss their conclusions.

Word focus *mind*

Extra activity

Ask students what meanings of the word *mind* they know. You might expect that they would know *mind* as a noun, meaning 'brain'. You might also try to elicit the verb phrase: *Would / Do you mind if I open the window?* meaning 'object'.

Elicit some examples of each, e.g. *She has a very creative mind – she's full of ideas. Do you mind if I leave my car here for 10 minutes?*

8 Ask students first to look at the article and find the expression with *mind* in each paragraph. In pairs, they should decide what the word class is (noun or verb) and what the expression means. They should then look at the sentences in Exercise 8 and work out the meaning of these expressions with *mind*. Elicit answers from the whole class.

> ANSWERS
>
> Text:
> 1 *mind you* (verb): used to make a concession, to soften a criticism
> 2 *bear in mind* (noun): remember, be aware that
> 3 *if you had ... in mind* (noun): wanted, intended
> Sentences:
> 1 noun: I am undecided
> 2 verb: be careful
> 3 noun: decide to do something different
> 4 noun: think hard about something
> 5 noun: a lot to think about, often worries or difficulties
> 6 noun: I couldn't think

9 Ask students to prepare a quiz with three examples of expressions with *mind* in it, and exchange it with a partner. They can then discuss the answers together. They can change partners and do it again.

Speaking and writing

10 Ask students to get into groups of four to invent their unusual place to stay. Ask them to make notes on the different aspects of the hotel, and give it a name.

11 Ask students to write up their notes into a short description, like the ones on page 75. One of each group should read their description to the rest of the class; note the hotel names on the board. When they have all been read out, the class can vote on which is the most interesting.

Homework

Ask students to write 100–150 words on the most unusual place they have ever spent a night (they may have introduced this place in the lead-in to the lesson).

6d Couch surfing

Lead-in

Using words

Start by asking: *Do you know what surfing is?* And elicit the original meaning of the word (riding on the surf on top of a wave on a board). Then ask students what they understand by *surfing the net* (looking at different websites on the Internet). Elicit ideas from students about why the surfing image is used to talk about Internet use (because people often skim the surface of websites rather than exploring them in depth).

Real life getting around

1 Before they look at the text, ask students: *What is a couch?* Elicit that it's another word for sofa.

Ask students to work in pairs and quickly read the article and answer the questions. Elicit the answers from the whole class.

> ANSWER
>
> Couch surfing is planning a journey where you sleep on different people's couches; you have to be part of the network and allow others to sleep on your couch when they need to.

2 Ask students to look at the box and decide who says which phrase – the host or the couch surfer. Elicit answers, but do not say if they are correct or not.

> ANSWERS
>
> Couch surfer: sentences 1, 3, 4, 11
> Host: sentences 2, 5, 6, 7, 8, 9, 10

3 🎧 [1.41] Ask students to listen to the conversation and check their answers to Exercise 2.

Audioscript 🎧 [1.41]

M = Malcolm; P = Paul

M: Hi Paul, this is Malcolm, your host. You emailed me about staying next Thursday for a couple of nights.

P: Oh hi, hi Malcolm. Thanks for getting back to me. Is that still OK?

M: No, that's all fine. I just thought I'd give you a call to explain how to get here, because it's a bit complicated. How are you getting to Hamilton, first of all?

P: I'm coming in by train sometime in the afternoon.

M: OK. I wanted to pick you up, but my car's at the garage that day.

P: Hey, that's kind of you, but I can make my own way.

M: OK. Well I'm at work 'til about five thirty, so feel free to come over any time after six.

P: That sounds perfect. And how do I get to you from the town centre?

M: Well you could just get a taxi, but it's about eleven kilometres from the centre, so it won't be cheap. Alternatively, you can hop on a bus to Stoney Creek. Look out for the Stoney Creek Arena on your right and get off there. It's only a twenty minute ride. From there, Cherry Heights is another fifteen minutes on foot, straight up King Street. Once you reach the crossroads at Gray Road, the easiest thing is to give me a call and I'll come out and meet you.

P: So bus to Stoney Creek, walk up King Street to Cherry Heights and call from there?

M: Yup. Call when you get to the crossroads at Gray Road.

P: OK. Got it. That sounds great. If I get held up in any way I'll let you know, but otherwise expect a call around six thirty.

M: Great. See you next Thursday then. Bye.

P: Bye.

4 🔘 [1.41] Ask students to listen to the recording again, and complete the sentences in the box. You will probably need to play it twice. Ask them to check with a partner before you elicit answers from the class as complete sentences.

> ANSWERS
> 1 train
> 2 my car's at the garage that day
> 3 kind of you
> 4 you from the town centre
> 5 a taxi
> 6 a bus to Stoney Creek
> 7 Stoney Creek arena
> 8 ride
> 9 give me a call
> 10 meet you
> 11 let you know

Pronunciation intonation in sentences with two clauses

5a 🔘 [1.42] Read the rubric with the class. Ask students to read the two sentences to themselves and think about what they should sound like. Then play the extracts from the recording for students to hear. Play them several times, then pause for students to repeat chorally and individually.

5b Say the sentences, and have students repeat them chorally and individually. Ask students to practise the five sentences individually, then with a partner. Encourage them to help each other get the correct intonation. Circulate and monitor their intonation for later feedback.

6 Ask students to work out a roleplay using the information given and examples from the conversation they have heard. Weaker students can write down their script and read it. Circulate and monitor their conversations for later feedback.

6e A disappointed customer

Lead-in

Personal response

Ask: *Have you ever been disappointed by the service you got somewhere – for example, in a shop, a restaurant or a public office?* Elicit some examples from the class, asking for details of what the situation was and why the student was disappointed. (If they want to talk about hotels, ask them to keep it for the next activity.)

Writing a letter of complaint

1 Ask: *Have you ever had any bad experiences on holiday?* If some students answer in the affirmative, ask them to tell the class about it. Then ask if they complained, and if so, what happened.

2 Read through the rubric and questions to focus students' reading. Then ask them to read the letter and answer the questions. Check students understand the key language in the letter (see Vocabulary notes below).

> ANSWERS
> 1 Because she was not treated well at a hotel.
> 2 She suggests the hotel investigates the situation so it doesn't happen to others.
> 3 In general, yes; however, the restaurant could have really been fully booked.

Vocabulary notes

an impression = an idea, a feeling

discounted = at a special, lower price

hospitality = the good treatment of guests

to opt to do something = to choose

compensation = money paid to make up for a problem

thoroughly = completely, fully

3 Ask students to answer the questions about writing formal letters in pairs. Elicit answers from the whole class.

> ANSWERS
> 1 writer's address: top right corner
> recipient's address: below that on the left-hand side
> 2 *Yours faithfully* is for somebody we do not know (when we start *Dear Sir / Madam*)
> *Yours sincerely* is for someone we do know (when we start *Dear Mr Smith*)
> 3 in the opening paragraph
> 4 in the final paragraph

Writing skill formal language

4a Ask students to find the formal phrases in the letter that mean the same as the words and phrases 1–10. Elicit the answers from the whole class.

ANSWERS

1 to express my dissatisfaction
2 we were informed
3 a discounted offer
4 to receive
5 after some discussion with
6 we opted to dine
7 wished
8 my principal concern
9 investigate
10 ensure

4b Read the example with the class so that they can see what to do. Ask students to do the exercise individually, then check with a partner. Elicit the answers as complete sentences. There will be different correct possibilities.

SAMPLE ANSWERS

2 I informed the receptionist that the room had been reserved for two nights, not one.
3 After I had discussed the issue with the manager, she apologised and promised to investigate the problem with the shower. However, no action was taken.
4 I would have expected the safety of the guests to be the principal concern of the staff.
5 Given the inconvenience this caused us, we expected some compensation.
6 The manager told us that no rooms were available, but that if the opportunity arose, she would move us.

5 Ask students to read through the situation and then write a letter of complaint to the manager. Ask them to lay out the letter correctly, including addresses. They should use some of the expressions from the model letter and the exercises where appropriate, and organise it in a similar way to the model.

You could give this exercise as homework, and do Exercise 6 in the following lesson.

6 Ask students to exchange letters with a partner, and use the criteria given to check their partner's work.

6f East Timor

Before you watch

1 Students work in groups. Ask them to look at the photo and discuss the questions. Take feedback from the class.

2 Ask students to read about the four scenes and predict which two of them they think they will see in the video. Take feedback from the class.

While you watch

3 Give students time to read through the words in the glossary. Play the whole of the video for students to check their ideas from Exercise 2. They should not try to understand everything at this stage.

ANSWERS

b and c

4 Give students time to read the conversation. Then play the first part of the video (to 00.45) for them to write Ann's part of the conversation.

ANSWERS

1 In East Timor.
2 We first came for a week's holiday.
3 After about 36 hours.
4 The quality of the marine life, the healthy coral, the lack of environmental damage, the huge diversity of marine life.
5 Hundreds.
6 Because there is deep water close to the shore.

5 Give students time to read the questions. Then play the second part of the video (00.46 to the end) for them to answer.

ANSWERS

1 lack of infrastructure and poor economy because of the damage caused by war
2 since 1999
3 The militia rampaged through the island (causing damage).
4 preserving the natural environment
5 environmental protection
6 They should talk to the government and make sure they have their agreement before they do anything.

6 Give students time to read the extracts. Then play the whole video again for them to number the extracts in the order they hear them.

ANSWERS

1 b   2 d   3 a   4 e   5 c

After you watch

7 Students work in pairs to roleplay an interview with a government official according to the instructions.

8 Students work in pairs to discuss the questions.

Videoscript

00.00–00.12   Welcome to East Timor, one of the world's newest countries. And, for the intrepid few, an emerging tourist destination with unspoiled natural beauty.

00.13–00.37   Ann Turner   We just booked a week's holiday here and went for three or four dives, and I think it took us 36 hours to make up our minds that this would be where we'd hope to spend the rest of our lives.

We were absolutely stunned by the quality of the marine life here, the healthy coral, the lack of environmental damage and a huge diversity of marine life.

00.38–00.45   Hundreds of fish species have been recorded in East Timor's waters, a diversity that's enhanced by having very deep water so close to shore.

00.46–01.15   East Timor is a former war zone and lacks a lot of basic infrastructure.

After East Timor's vote for independence in 1999, Indonesia's militias rampaged through the island. The subsequent recovery effort has been painfully slow.

There are many changes to be made if tourism run by expatriates is to boost East Timor's meagre economy.

The government is anxious that new tourism developments don't ruin East Timor's greatest asset: it's natural beauty. A spokesperson for the Ministry of Tourism has this message for developers.

01.16–01.35   Jose Teixeira   We are still developing policies and regulations in relation to, say, the environment, for example, and environment protection. So what they should do is they should be very careful to talk to government and not to move ahead without government and local administration knowing exactly what they are doing and then getting the full go-ahead.

01.36–01.48   So as this new nation struggles to build its economy, it faces an age-old predicament: how to make the most of its natural assets without destroying them in the process.

UNIT 6 Review

Grammar

1 and 2   Ask students in pairs to look at the photo and suggest what it is, then read the conversation and find the answer.

> ANSWER
>
> Giverny, France – the garden of the artist Monet

3   Ask students to find the answer to this question.

> ANSWER
>
> She's going to stay in France and visit some places there. She wants to spend more time finding out about her own country instead of travelling to exotic places.

4   Ask students to complete the conversation with phrases with *not* in them. Elicit answers from the class.

> ANSWERS
>
> | | |
> |---|---|
> | 1 aren't you | 6 hope it doesn't rain |
> | 2 decided not to go | 7 haven't you decided |
> | 3 not find | 8 don't think I will use |
> | 4 isn't it | 9 not be |
> | 5 don't want to | 10 don't have to |

Vocabulary

5   Ask students to complete the sentences with the correct preposition individually, then check with a partner. Elicit the answers as complete sentences.

> ANSWERS
>
> 1 out   2 out   3 in   4 off   5 in   6 out

6   Ask students to work in pairs to ask and answer the questions in Exercise 5.

Real life

7   Ask students to match the phrases in the two columns in pairs. Elicit answers from the whole class.

> ANSWERS
>
> 1 I'm coming in by train.
> 2 The easiest thing is to hop on a bus.
> 3 I'll pick you up from the station.
> 4 I'll call if I get held up in traffic.
> 5 Look out for the Hoover building on your right.
> 6 I can easily make my own way.
> 7 It's only a ten-minute ride.
> 8 How do I get to your house?

8   Ask students to work in pairs to give directions from public transport points to meeting places.

Speaking

9   Ask students to discuss in pairs what they think is most important for a holiday.

Unit 7 Natural resources

Lead-in

Personal response

Ask: *What do you like most about the natural world? Where do you enjoy going? What do you like seeing?* Elicit some responses from the whole class, and encourage comments and questions from the others.

1 Ask students to look at the picture and the vocabulary box, and identify as many natural resources as they can. Elicit answers from the whole class.

> **ANSWERS**
> Air, animals (fish), trees, sunlight, water

2 Ask students to match the words and definitions individually, then check with a partner.

> **ANSWERS**
> 1 b   2 c   3 e   4 a   5 d

3 💿 [2.1] Ask students to discuss in pairs what the three 'R's' might mean. Elicit suggestions then play the recording for them to check their ideas.

> **ANSWERS**
> reduce, reuse, recycle

Audioscript 💿 [2.1]

... so if you always keep these three things in mind, it's actually quite simple to make a difference to your own personal consumption of natural resources. Number one and most important is reduce. In other words, try to buy and use fewer goods. In the UK we throw away a third of the food we buy. If we only bought the food we really needed, this wouldn't happen. Umm ... try to reduce the energy you use too, for example switching the lights off when you leave the room or umm ... walking somewhere instead of taking the car. The second thing is to reuse. Mend things that are broken. Think how you can reuse old things, such as those old jeans you threw out. If you hadn't thrown them away, you could have worn them the next time there was some gardening or decorating to do. And lastly recycle. Only buy products that are made of recyclable materials: like glass bottles or certain plastics; and when you have finished with them, take them to a recycling point. OK, so that's three things to remember: reduce, reuse, recycle.

4 💿 [2.1] Ask students to listen again and list the examples the speaker gives for each of the three R's

> **ANSWERS**
> Reduce: don't buy as much; switch off lights
> Reuse: mend things that are broken; wear old jeans for decorating or gardening
> Recycle: take glass bottles etc. to a recycling point

7a Water conservation

Lead-in

Personal response

Ask: *In what ways do you use water, in your home and outside?* Elicit all the different ways from the class and list them on the board (e.g. *washing yourself – shower or bath, flushing toilets, washing clothes, washing dishes, drinking, watering plants, watering the garden, washing the car, cleaning around the house*).

Speaking

1 Ask students to work in pairs to discuss why we need to save water. Elicit ideas from the whole class for wider discussion, without commenting on what they say. Then ask students to read the text and check their ideas. Take feedback from the class. Ask: *Why can't we use all the sea water on the planet?* Take the opportunity to introduce some of the key language from the listening exercise on this topic (*brine, salty / saline, desalination;* see Vocabulary notes below).

> **ANSWERS**
> The majority of the Earth's water is sea water, which we can't use for many things.
> We use more fresh water than can be replaced by nature, so we have to use a lot of energy to purify used water.

2 Ask the class to look at the table of facts and answer the questions.

Listening

3 💿 [2.2] Read the two questions with the class to focus their listening. Play the recording for students to answer as much as they can. Check students' understanding of the key language (see Vocabulary notes below) and play the recording again if necessary. Elicit answers from the class.

> **SAMPLE ANSWERS**
> | | | |
> |---|---|---|
> | Liam | 1 | wastes a lot of water |
> | | 2 | water companies have to use more energy to treat water |
> | Gemal | 1 | is interested in finding farming techniques to use salt water |
> | | 2 | dangerous waste from desalination could destroy life in the sea |
> | Daniel | 1 | thinks we waste too much water (including himself) |
> | | 2 | rivers will get smaller, deltas will dry up |
> | Carmen | 1 | is careful and saves water |
> | | 2 | water will have to be transported from one part of the world to another |

Audioscript 🔘 [2.2]

Speaker 1 (Liam)

I live in Manchester, which is probably one of the wettest places in the UK. If I had been brought up somewhere like Saharan Africa, where I had to walk miles each day just to fetch water, I'd obviously be a lot more conscious of water conservation. But I'm afraid I don't set a very good example – er ... I probably waste a lot – leaving the tap running when I brush my teeth and so on. Clearly we're not going to run out of water in the UK, but I know water conservation is important. If we all used less water, the water companies wouldn't have to use so much energy treating water to make it clean. And of course that would be more environmentally friendly.

Speaker 2 (Gemal)

I'm not saying the idea of desalination plants is wrong. If desalination methods didn't exist, this country would not have been able to develop in the way it has. Nowadays we use water in our homes more or less as we want to. But I don't think we can continue like this. You see, the waste from the desalination process is a kind of brine with a dangerously high salt content ... which will eventually destroy life in the sea. I am interested in discovering farming techniques that use salt water. There are grasses and other types of plant that can grow with sea water. If we were to use more of these, it would give our natural fresh water springs a chance to recharge.

Speaker 3 (Daniel)

Americans (and I'm as guilty as the rest) use water like there is no tomorrow. I think it's well-known that the Colorado River doesn't reach the sea anymore. If you had visited the area around the old delta in Mexico 100 years ago – rich wetlands, full of wildlife – you'd be shocked to see it now. It's all dried up, ... a kind of salt flat. The reason is agriculture. The river has been dammed and diverted in various places along its route to irrigate fields and provide enough water for people living in the desert areas of Nevada and California. Unless we change the way we think about water and stop wasting so much, the river will carry on getting smaller.

Speaker 4 (Carmen)

My water needs are the same as most people's, I think: I have a small vegetable garden; I have to wash myself and my clothes. I don't have to save water, but I want to, you know. I collect rainwater for the garden, I fill a basin to wash in rather than running the tap, I wash my dishes every other day. But now governments are discussing big projects for transporting water from one part of the world to another using huge pipes and tankers. I think if more people thought and acted like me, things would not have come to this point, you know.

Vocabulary notes

to be conscious of something = to be aware of, think about something

desalination = removing salt

a plant = a factory

brine = salty water

to be guilty = to do something wrong

delta = the area where a river branches to go into the sea

wetlands = areas of marsh, reeds and pools

a salt flat = flat salty area of land (e.g. in Utah)

to dam = to block a river

to divert = to have the direction of movement changed

to irrigate = to water cultivated land

a basin = a bowl

4 🔘 [2.2] Ask students to read through the questions to focus their listening. Play the recording once or twice for students to answer. Elicit answers from the class.

ANSWERS

1 probably one of the wettest places in the UK
2 He leaves the tap running.
3 It leaves behind concentrated brine.
4 farming techniques for plants that can be grown with sea water
5 It has dried up and become a salt flat.
6 irrigating crops and drinking water
7 She collects rainwater for the garden, washes in a basin and does the washing up every two days.
8 If more people did what she does, then the situation would not have got so serious.

5 Ask the class to comment on this question and discuss any answers that come up.

Grammar mixed conditional sentences

6 Read the rubric with the class and do the example together. If they find it difficult, use page 165 of the Student's Book to review conditional sentences before students do the rest of the exercise. It will help them to understand whether the clauses refer to past or present if they change each condition into a statement, as in the example. Ask students to work in pairs, and then elicit answers from the class.

ANSWERS

1 b: past situation and past consequences.
2 c: past situation with present consequences (I wasn't brought up in Saharan Africa, I am not conscious of water conservation)
3 a: present situation, present consequences (we don't use less water, the water companies do have to use a lot of energy)
4 c: present situation, past consequences (desalination methods do exist, the country did develop the way it has)
5 c: past situation, present consequences (you didn't visit the area 100 years ago, you aren't shocked to see it now)
6 c: present (unreal) situation, past consequences (people don't act like me, things have come to this point)

7 Read through the grammar box with the class. If they seem unsure about any of the points, ask them to turn to page 165 of the Student's Book and read the additional information and do the practice. Ask students to read the information in Exercise 7 and write the conditional sentences individually, then check with a partner. Elicit the answers from the whole class.

ANSWERS
1 If we hadn't bought such a cheap dishwasher, we would use much less water.
2 If someone had told me that washing dishes by hand uses more water, I would have used the dishwasher more.
3 If you had used a car wash in the past, you wouldn't have wasted so much water.
4 If automatic carwashes were not so expensive, I would have used them more.
5 If we hadn't built a big swimming pool in the garden, we wouldn't use so much water.
6 If we didn't water the garden when it was cool, the water would just evaporate away.
7 If the United States hadn't tried to cultivate areas with a desert climate, they wouldn't have a water shortage.
8 If we hadn't seen a shocking TV programme about how much water is wasted, we wouldn't have changed our habits.

Pronunciation contractions in conditionals

8a [2.3] Play the recording and ask students to listen and read, paying attention to the pronunciation of the contracted forms. Then play the track again for students to listen and repeat.

9 Ask students to read the facts and make appropriate conditional sentences about them. They should do this individually, then check with a partner. Elicit the answers from the whole class.

ANSWERS
1 If farmers hadn't used the water to irrigate their fields, the Aral Sea wouldn't be one tenth of its original size.
2 If they didn't have so many golf courses, Las Vegas wouldn't have to import so much water.
3 If fewer tourists visited Greece each year, there wouldn't be water shortages on many of its islands.
4 If Britain hadn't used its North Sea gas immediately, it wouldn't have to import 50% of its gas now.

Extra activity

Extend Exercise 9 by asking students to create a chain of conditions, e.g. for sentence 2:

If they didn't have so many golf courses, Las Vegas wouldn't have to import so much water.

If people didn't play golf, there wouldn't be so many golf courses.

If people didn't have so much money and time, they wouldn't play golf.

See how long a chain of sentences they can make.

Background notes

The Aral Sea is situated between Kazakhstan and Uzbekistan, and the name means 'the sea of islands' because there were once 1,534 of them. It was one of the four largest lakes in the world. However, the two major rivers that feed the lake were diverted to irrigate fields, mostly to grow cotton. Unfortunately, the channels were not well-made, and lost up to 75% of the water before it reached the crops. By 2007, the Aral Sea was 10% of its original size, and had divided into four separate lakes, and by 2009 there were really only two lakes left. Because of this, the former fishing industry was destroyed, bringing economic hardship and unemployment. Climate change also contributed to the problem, with hotter, drier summers and colder, longer winters. The Kazakhs have been trying to remedy the situation, and by 2008 had managed to raise water levels, reduce salinity and encourage the return of fish.

Vocabulary and speaking

10 Ask students to work with a partner to match the verbs and nouns to form common collocations relating to conservation. Elicit the answers from the class. Then ask students to tell their partner whether they have ever been involved in any such actions, and if so how. Elicit answers from the whole class.

ANSWERS
consume: energy / water / food / petrol
conserve: energy / water / food / petrol / forests
preserve: food / forests
protect: animals / land / forests
run out of: money / time / energy / water / food / petrol
save: money / time / energy / water / petrol
spend: money / time
waste: money / time / energy / water / land / food / petrol

11 Ask students to write some sentences, and then share them with others. They can use the answers to Exercise 9 as models for their sentences. Discuss some of the sentences and ideas as a whole class.

7b The minister for no oil

Lead-in

Personal response

Ask: *What petroleum-based products do you use regularly?* Ask students to list the products and talk about how they use them. (Petroleum, or crude oil, is used to produce petrol for different fuels, oil for lubrication, oil for heating, pesticides and fertilizers.)

Vocabulary oil

1 Ask the class to look at the expressions in the box, and say which ones they know. If the class are not familiar with many of these, ask groups to pick an expression and check the meaning in a dictionary, then feed back to the class. Read the *Wordbuilding* box with the class, and ask students to look at page 59 of the Workbook for further information and practice if you feel it is necessary at this point.

> ANSWERS
>
> *oil field* = the underground 'lakes' of petroleum (crude oil)
> *oil refinery* = the factory where petroleum is turned into petrol – impurities are taken out of it
> *oil reserves* = the amount of oil left underground
> *oil rig* = the platform on which equipment is put to extract undersea or underground oil (*drilling rig*)
> *oil slick* = the layer of oil on water when there has been an oil spill
> *oil tanker* = the enormous ships which are used to transport oil
> *oil well* = the hole in the ground which goes down to the oil fields and through which oil is extracted
> The photo shows an oil refinery.

Extra activity

Ask students if they can think of any other nouns which have many words which collocate with them. As an example you could give them the words *farm* or *book* and ask them to think of as many collocations as possible (*farmhouse, farm buildings, farm animals, farm worker, farm labourer, farmyard, farm produce; bookshop, bookshelf, bookcase, bookends, book token, bookstall, bookworm*).

Background note

Petroleum (otherwise known as *crude oil*) is a naturally occurring substance which lies under the surface of the earth. The world extracts it from many places, but the three main producers are Saudi Arabia, Russia and the USA, with Iran, China and Canada next, but producing less than half as much as the big three producers. The world uses more than 30 billion barrels (= 4.8 cubic km) every year, for a variety of purposes. The USA uses around 20% of all oil produced.

2 Ask students to discuss these questions in pairs and then tell the class what they think. Open it up as a whole class discussion.

Reading

3 Read the three statements with the class to focus their reading, then ask them to read the text and answer. Elicit answers from the whole class. Check any difficult language from the text (see Vocabulary notes below).

> ANSWER
> b

Vocabulary notes

madness = foolishness, a strange thing to do
biodiversity = the interlinking ecosystem of plants and animals in the environment
unspoiled = (also *unspoilt*) natural and original
innovative = new and exciting
to suspect = to believe someone is doing something bad
to exploit = to abuse, to use badly
to make a deal = to do business
a spokesperson = a representative who talks to the media
an initiative = a plan, a project
to absorb = to take in

4 Ask students to read the four questions to focus their reading, then read the text again to find the answers. Elicit the answers from the whole class, having one student read a question and another answer it.

> ANSWERS
> 1 Because Ecuador is quite poor, and the oil money would have helped the economy.
> 2 Because it was half of the total value of the oil.
> 3 Only a few countries have shown an interest and only Germany has promised any money.
> 4 They are very pleased by it.

Background note

Ecuador is a democratic republic of 15 million people in South America. *Ecuador* is the Spanish word for the equator. It is bordered on the north by Columbia, to the east and south by Peru, and to the west by the Pacific Ocean. The Galapagos Islands, 1,000 km to the west, are also part of Ecuador. Ecuador has the greatest biodiversity per square kilometre of any country in the world, and in 2008 was the first country in the world to build a clause about the rights of nature into its constitution.

5 Ask students to complete the sentences individually, then check their answers with a partner. Elicit the answers from the class as complete sentences.

> ANSWERS
> 1 biodiversity   3 Petroecuador   5 appreciate
> 2 reserves   4 exploit   6 long-term

6 Ask students to discuss these questions in pairs, then share their ideas with the class for further discussion.

Grammar *wish, would rather* and *if only*

7 Read through the grammar box with the class and write some examples on the board (see Grammar note below). For further information and practice, refer to page 166 of the Student's Book. Ask students to choose the correct option in the sentences individually, then discuss their answers with a partner. Elicit the answers from the class.

> ANSWERS
>
> | | |
> |---|---|
> | 1 don't destroy | 3 don't appreciate |
> | 2 supported | 4 won't |

Grammar note

Wish is used to talk about something that you would like to be different to the real situation, in the present or the past. It usually expresses a sense of regret that things are not different.

I wish we had more forests in this country.
I wish we had not cut down all our forests.
I wish people would use their water more carefully.

Wish can also express a sense of anger or irritation:
I wish you wouldn't waste so much water!

For strong wishes we can use *if only*:
If only we had more forests in this country!
If only we had not cut down all our forests!
If only people would use their water more carefully!

Would rather is used to say what you would prefer to do, or what you would prefer someone else to do. This usually expresses a real possibility and is more neutral than *wish*.

I would rather cycle to work than take the car.
I would rather they planted more trees on the land.

8 Ask students to choose the correct forms individually, and then check with a partner. Elicit answers from the whole class as complete sentences.

> ANSWERS
>
> | | | |
> |---|---|---|
> | 1 would stop | 4 had | 7 had taken, work |
> | 2 hadn't cut down | 5 didn't have | 8 would wake up |
> | 3 walk, went | 6 could speak | |

Speaking

9 Ask students to write their sentences, then read them to a partner. Elicit answers from the whole class.

> SAMPLE ANSWERS
>
> 1 I wish I had enough money to buy a new car.
>   If only my car didn't use so much petrol.
> 2 If only my company gave me more holidays.
>   I wish my company gave me more holidays.
>   I would rather work for a company that gave me more holidays.
> 3 I wish I had more time to do some exercise.
>   If only I got home earlier in the evening.
>   I would rather get home earlier in the evening.

7c A world of its own

Lead-in

Personal response
Ask students with closed books: *Can you name the four largest islands in the world?* Elicit suggestions from the class and see what they come up with. (Answer: 1 Greenland, 2 New Guinea, 3 Borneo, 4 Madagascar. Great Britain is eighth.)

Reading

1 Read through the instructions with the class. Give them two minutes to read the facts. Then ask them to cover their books and ask and answer questions with a partner.

2 Read through the questions with the class to focus their reading, then ask them to read the article and answer the questions. Elicit answers from the class. Check any words they are unsure of (see Vocabulary notes below).

> ANSWERS
>
> 1 the rosewood and ebony trees
> 2 It is cut down with great difficulty, shipped down the rivers, and then on to China (for furniture) and western Europe (for musical instruments).
> 3 the collection of medicinal plants; guiding tourists to see lemurs; visiting a wild orchid conservatory

Vocabulary notes

unique = there is only one thing like it

a lemur = a special type of primate found only in Madagascar

a logger = a person who cuts down trees

to harvest = to collect a crop

tension = stress or aggression

to deplore = to express disapproval

slash-and-burn = the cutting and burning of trees and other vegetation in order to plant a crop in the space cleared

to reverse = to change back

hardwood = wood of deciduous trees as opposed to conifers (pine trees)

a cyclone = a strong tropical storm

a rosewood tree = a tropical tree giving hard, dark wood, with a rose-like scent

an ebony tree = a tropical tree with very dark, hard wood

sacred = holy, having religious significance

back-breaking work = extremely hard physical work

a hand axe = a small tool used for cutting wood

to erode = to move the earth or rock by constant water or wind on it

to silt up = when earth is washed down a river and blocks it

bleak = bare and unattractive

to be obsessed = to think about only one thing

a conservatory = a glass and iron construction for keeping plants in

mafia = organised criminals

3 Ask students to complete the sentences individually, then check with a partner. Elicit the answers from the class as complete sentences.

ANSWERS

1 c	2 a	3 b	4 a	5 c	6 c	7 c	8 b

Critical thinking emotive language

4 Read through the rubric and the phrases with the class. Ask them to find the words in the text individually, then check with a partner. Elicit the answers from the whole class.

ANSWERS

1 unique ecosystems / exceptional riches
2 desperate situation / caught in a trap
3 alarmed / deploring
4 to rob the forests
5 precious / majestic
6 bleak landscape / the rosewood mafia

5 Ask the class to discuss their ideas about the language used, and answer the questions.

Vocabulary strong feelings

6 Ask students to work in pairs to replace the words in bold with more emotive ones.

Elicit the answers from the class as complete sentences.

ANSWERS

1 unique	5 majestic
2 desperate	6 back-breaking
3 deplores	7 bleak
4 rob	8 obsessed

7 Read the rubric with the class, then ask students to work in pairs to write a description of a place or community needing protection. They could do this for homework, in order to be able to do some research. When the texts are complete, they can read them to the rest of the class (or if you have a big class, divide them into smaller groups of four or five pairs).

7d The climate change debate

Lead-in

Personal response
Ask: *How do you think people can be made to understand environmental problems like those in Madagascar?* Elicit some suggestions from the whole class.

Real life making your point

1 Read through the words in the box with the class and check that students understand their meaning before they discuss the issues in pairs (see Vocabulary notes below).

Vocabulary notes

CO_2 emissions = giving off / producing carbon dioxide

fossil fuels = coal and oil

global warming = the idea that the Earth's temperature is increasing

the greenhouse effect: a lot of the radiation from the Sun which warms the Earth is bounced back away from the Earth, but so-called greenhouse gases (water vapour, carbon dioxide, methane and others) trap the warmth and send it back to Earth, so raising the temperature. It is rather similar to what happens in a greenhouse.

natural weather cycle = the natural variations in weather, including warming and cooling, from one period of time to another.

2 🔊 [2.4] Ask students to read the instructions, then play the recording for them to put a tick or cross next to the names. If necessary play the recording again. Elicit the answers from the class.

ANSWERS

1 Erika: doesn't know	3 Jane: ✗
2 Andy: ✗	4 Ralph: doesn't say

Audioscript 🔊 [2.4]

E = Erika; A = Andy; J = Jane; R = Ralph

A: Erika, what do you think about all these people who say that there's no proof that climate change is man-made?

E: OK, I'll tell you my position. I don't know if climate change is man-made and I'm not sure anyone can say for sure. Let me give you an example ... umm ... an analogy. Imagine you were losing your hair and I told you that some people had found that if they ate a banana every day it prevented hair loss. Even though you had no proof it worked, you would probably try eating a banana each day, wouldn't you? Well, it's the same with global warming. We don't know that we're causing it, but some people say we might be with all the fossil fuels we burn. And I, for one, am happy to be a little more careful in how I pollute in case they're right.

A: Mmm ... well, I don't accept that. I used to believe in climate change, but the last few winters here in the UK have been much colder than normal. To be honest with you, I'd believe it more if I wasn't getting up in the morning and scraping ice off the inside of my windows rather the outside.

E: Yeah, but that's not the point, Andy, is it? You know, regional temperatures may be lower, but average global temperatures carry on rising.

J: Mmm ... Look – there's no doubt that the weather's changing, but I don't believe it's a man-made problem. It's just part of a natural weather cycle. Yeah, I know you'll say, 'Oh, that's just your excuse to drive a big car and fly to exotic places for your holidays,' but actually that's not the reason. I don't believe it simply because no scientist has successfully proved it yet.

R: We're approaching this debate all wrong by saying, 'It's a big environmental problem that we need to address.' Because it's not just an environmental problem. It's an economic problem, a social problem, even an ethical problem.

3 [2.4] Ask students to read through the box to see the phrases they need to complete. Then play the recording again. Play it again if necessary. Elicit answers from the class as complete phrases.

ANSWERS

1 you were losing your
2 am happy to be a little more careful
3 in climate change
4 the weather's changing
5 no scientist has successfully proved it yet
6 it's a big environmental

Extra activity

Refer students to the audioscript in the back of their Student's Book (page 178), and play the recording while students follow. Then play it again and pause after the key phrases in the box for students to repeat them chorally and individually. After that, ask students to practise saying the different sections in pairs, and help each other with their expression.

4 [2.4] Read the list of techniques the speakers use with the class. Ask them to listen and say who uses what.

ANSWERS

a Andy (ice on the inside of windows)
b Ralph
c Erika
d Erika (banana example) and Andy (illustration of ice on the windows)
e Jane (*I know you'll say ...*)

5 Ask the class to comment on these questions about what was most effective.

Pronunciation sentence stress

6a [2.5] Ask students to read the sentence and think about how it sounds. Then play the recording a couple of times for them to listen. Then ask them to repeat it chorally and individually.

6b [2.6] Ask students to underline the stressed words in the four sentences individually, then check with a partner. Elicit suggestions from the class without saying whether they are right or wrong (you could write the four sentences on the board and mark where they say the stress falls). Then play the recording and check, and correct what is on the board, if necessary.

ANSWERS

1 We don't <u>know</u> that we're causing it, but some people say we <u>might</u> be.
2 ... scraping ice off the <u>inside</u> of my windows rather than the <u>outside</u>.
3 <u>Regional</u> temperatures may be lower, but average <u>global</u> temperatures carry on rising.
4 Because it's <u>not</u> just an environmental problem. It's an <u>economic</u> problem, a <u>social</u> problem, even an <u>ethical</u> problem.

7 Read through the whole rubric with the class and then ask them to get into pairs to choose a topic and work out their arguments in favour of that solution. Suggest that they make notes to help them later. Also, suggest they think about what others might say against their argument and decide how to defend it. When they are ready, ask pairs with different solutions to get together and discuss their ideas. Circulate and monitor their arguments for later comment.

Homework

Ask students to write up their arguments into a 100–150 word paragraph.

7e Waste of energy

Lead-in

Personal response

Ask: *When was the last time you wrote a letter with a pen on paper, and posted it?* Elicit answers and details from the class, and encourage them to ask questions (e.g. *Who was it to? Why did you write it? When did you send it?*).

Writing a letter to the press

1 Ask the class to answer these questions as a continuation of the lead-in activity. Discuss why they do / don't read the letters pages of newspapers.

2 Read the three questions with the class to focus their reading, then ask them to read the letter and answer the questions. Elicit answers from the class.

> ANSWERS
>
> 1 Mr V. Dupeyrat
> 2 to comment on the way that energy is wasted in different situations
> 3 The letter uses various rhetorical devices quite effectively to persuade the reader:
>   – rhetorical questions (*why stop with hotels? Would it not be better to mention ...*)
>   – strong language and exaggeration (*mindless waste, overheated rooms, wide open, fully-lit, enormous, completely open*)
>   – repetition (*In the morning I walk ... at night I walk ... ; past ... past ...*)
>   – the presentation of a series of personal examples followed by impersonal 'facts'
>   – the example of speed limits to illustrate the need for legal measures

3 Ask students to decide on the organisation of the letter individually, then check with a partner. Elicit answers from the whole class.

> ANSWERS
>
> 1 c   2 a   3 d   4 b

Word focus *better*

4 Ask students to find all the examples of phrases with *better* in them in the letter individually, then check with a partner. Elicit the examples from the class – you may want to write them on the board. Then ask students to match the phrases with the five definitions.

> ANSWERS
>
> 1 would it not be better to mention (c)
> 2 advertisers try to go one better than their competitors (d)
> 3 they should know better (a)
> 4 we had better increase its price (e)
> 5 we would all be better off if (b)

Writing skills giving vivid examples

5a Ask students to find the examples about lights and towels and elicit them from the class.

> ANSWERS
>
> lights that are left on all night, towels that are used once and then sent to be washed

5b Ask students to find the examples of energy waste and then elicit them from the class.

> ANSWERS
>
> 1 shop doors wide open blowing hot air into the street
> 2 fully-lit office buildings when the workers have left
> 3 enormous flashing advertising screens
> 4 a cooling cabinet in the supermarket that is completely open

6 Read the rubric and the example with the class, then ask students to expand on three more phrases in the same way individually. Elicit examples from the class.

> SAMPLE ANSWERS
>
> 1 trains which are never on time
> 2 mobile phones that ring loudly in public places
> 3 TV shows about cookery / house makeovers / reality shows
> 4 supermarket food that has too much packaging
> 5 computer programs which crash the first time you use them

7 Ask students to choose a topic from Exercise 6 and write a letter based on the model in Exercise 2. They could do this for homework. When the letters are ready, ask them to exchange them with a partner for comment (see below).

8 Ask students to comment on the organisation of their partner's letter, their use of examples, and how persuasive it is.

7f Galapagos energy

Before you watch

1 Students work in groups. Ask them to look at the photo and discuss the questions. Take feedback from the class.

2 Ask students to read the summary and complete it using words from the glossary.

ANSWERS

1 haven	3 mainland	5 conservationist
2 sky-rocketed	4 emissions	

While you watch

3 Play the whole of the video for students to check their ideas from Exercises 1 and 2.

4 Give students time to read the questions. Then play the first part of the video (to 02.41) for them to answer.

ANSWERS

1 Because the islands were isolated, a thousand kilometres from the mainland.
2 It's a living laboratory of evolution.
3 On different sides of a volcanic eruption, plants and animals have evolved differently.
4 a hundred years
5 from 3,000 to 25,000 (700%)
6 It brings in money.
7 It killed 60% of nearby iguanas, but it made people aware of the dangers of pollution.

5 Give students time to read the list, then play the second part of the video (02.42 to the end) for them to tick the things they see.

ANSWERS

We see everything except a bird with a red beak and a turtle (we do see a tortoise).

6 Give students time to read the questions. Then play the second part of the video again for them to write the answers.

ANSWERS

1 to stop using fossil fuels and use renewable, clean energy, which will reduce our impact on the environment
2 a a modern oil depot which removes contaminants in the fuel
  b an ultra-modern petrol station with barriers to contain leaks
  c a plan to use cleaner boat engines and low emissions vehicles instead of cars
  d a World Wildlife Fund recycling campaign

After you watch

7 Students work in pairs to roleplay an interview with Leopoldo Bocheri More according to the instructions.

8 Students work in groups to discuss the questions.

Videoscript

Part 1

00.09–00.16 In splendid isolation, animals on the Galapagos evolved into unique species found nowhere else in the world.

00.21–00.30 This archipelago of 13 main islands is a thousand kilometres or six hundred miles from the coast of Ecuador.

00.32–00.37 Remote, contained, a world unto itself.

00.42–01.04 Alan Tye The cliché about Galapagos of course is that it's a living laboratory of evolution. And the volcanoes, their eruptions, actually show us that. You can see how the plants and animals have developed in these areas either side of a lava flow created by an eruption.

01.06–01.12 But an alien species has invaded this tropical haven: humans.

01.13–01.19 … They've been living here for more than a century. But in the past few decades, tourism has skyrocketed.

01.24–01.38 And workers from the mainland have followed in their wake to open businesses and provide services.

Some estimate the permanent population on the islands has increased by as much as 300%.

01.40–01.49 Lauren Spurrier In the 1980s there was a local population of about 3,000 people living here in the islands and today we have a local population of more than 25,000 people.

01.52–02.06 Tourism brings much needed revenue but all these people generate pollution through vehicle emissions and energy consumption. And like almost all humans, they create rubbish.

02.08–02.13 Conservationists worry the newcomers are having an adverse impact on the old-timers.

02.17–02.28 Recently, an oil tanker ran aground trying to deliver fuel to the Galapagos, creating a spill that eventually killed an estimated 60 per cent of nearby iguanas.

02.32–02.39 Researchers now say even a small amount of pollution can harm the island's legendary species.

Part 2

02.42–03.25 Fortunately, the oil spill turned out to be a wake-up call.

Now, with a series of ambitious projects, conservationists and corporations are working together with the Ecuadorian government to minimise human impact.

The goal is to end the use of fossil fuels on the Galapagos in the next decade and to use only renewable, non-polluting energy.

In terms of conservation, as well as appearance, the islands would be 'green'.

An example, this modern oil depot replaces a rusty relic that was about to fall into the sea.

Contaminants in the fuel are removed to reduce pollution.

03.26–03.38 William Reinert The more we can work together to provide advanced fuel so we can get closer and closer to zero emissions vehicles, the more we can do that, the more we can approach the idea of a zero footprint.

03.40–03.56 An ultra-modern petrol station has barriers to contain leaks.

There's an ambitious plan to convert boat engines to cleaner and more efficient models and to replace cars on the islands with low emissions vehicles.

03.58–04.13 A World Wildlife Fund recycling campaign is teaching islanders about the importance of keeping their domain pristine.

Lourdes Peñaherrera and her family have won a World Wildlife Fund award for reducing the amount of waste they produce.

04.15–04.29 'Not only us, but the whole community has to recycle,' she says. 'It's to protect the environment. Almost everybody in our neighbourhood does it now.'

04.33–04.42 Conservationists say humans will continue to have an impact on the Galapagos but that combined efforts may help keep destruction in check.

04.43–04.57 'It's a big challenge because we need many resources,' says one of the islands' mayors.

'We need our people to cooperate and we also need international organisations to help with conservation.'

04.59–05.15 Naturalist Charles Darwin once called the islands a 'little world within itself'.

Now the rest of the world has arrived.

They can be the ruin of the Galapagos, or, perhaps with a united effort, they could be its salvation.

UNIT 7 Review

Grammar

1 Ask students to discuss the question in pairs.

2 Ask students to read the two questions to focus their reading, then read the blog. Elicit answers from the class. Check their understanding of the language.

> ANSWERS
>
> They are aware of global environmental problems (e.g. deforestation), but they are not aware of how their own actions affect the world situation.

3 Ask students to choose the correct forms of the verbs individually, then check with a partner. Elicit answers from the class as complete sentences.

> ANSWERS
>
> | | | |
> |---|---|---|
> | 1 will say | 4 switch | 7 would know |
> | 2 would stop | 5 would be | 8 had had |
> | 3 leave | 6 had been | 9 taught |

Vocabulary

4 Ask students to find the odd one out.

> ANSWERS
>
> 1 waste: the other three are about protecting things
> 2 natural: the other three are about quantity
> 3 oil slick: the other three are all equipment
> 4 minerals: the others are all in the atmosphere
> 5 tall: the other three are all extreme adjectives

5 Ask students to work in groups of four to discuss two natural resources.

Real life

6 Ask students to work with a partner to decide which speakers agree and which disagree with the statement. Elicit answers from the whole class.

> ANSWERS
>
> 1, 2, 3 and 4 disagree, 5 partly agrees

7 Ask students to decide which of the techniques the speakers use in Exercise 6 to make their point.

> ANSWERS
>
> 1 a   2 c   3 d   4 e   5 b

8 Ask students to prepare a two- or three-sentence statement like the ones in Exercise 6.

Speaking

9 Ask students to work in groups of four to discuss the three issues raised.

Unit 8 The news

Lead-in

Personal response

Ask a series of questions about students' newspaper habits: *Do you read a newspaper? Which one? Where and when do you read it? Do you read it in print or online? What do you read?* Elicit answers and encourage discussion about it.

1 Ask students to match the two halves of each sentence about news. Elicit answers from the class. Ask students to discuss the meanings of the three English sayings. Then ask them to translate back any sayings about news from their mother tongue(s).

> ANSWERS
> 1 *Good news doesn't sell.* (= newspapers make money out of disasters, deaths and accidents, not out of the nice things that happen in life)
> 2 *Bad news travels fast.* (= we tend to hear about bad things sooner than good things)
> 3 *No news is good news.* (= when you hear nothing, it usually means that the situation is OK – this can be related to the first saying)

2 [2.7] Ask students to work in pairs to look at the photo and caption and answer the two questions. Elicit possible answers from the class, without saying what is the correct answer. You might write their suggestions on the board for later reference. Play the recording for students to check their answers. Discuss the real answers with the class.

> ANSWERS
> 1 to be near their children during their first days at college
> 2 because they can't afford to sleep in a hotel

Audioscript [2.7]

N = Newsreader; MC = Martha Cash

N: And in China, hundreds of parents of first-year students at the University of Wuhan have been sleeping on the floor of the university's gym so that they can be near their children in their first anxious days at college. As Martha Cash, our Far East correspondent, reports.

MC: China's policy of urging families to have only one child has meant that parents, already ambitious for the success of their children, become even more intensely focused on helping a single son or daughter to make it in the world. Going to university is of course seen as a necessary first step in this journey, but most Chinese families are not particularly well-off and they often make great sacrifices to support their children. So staying in a local hotel during their children's first days at college is not really an option. That was how, on a recent visit to Wuhan in the centre of China, we witnessed this extraordinary scene: a mass adult sleep-in on the university gym floor. It seems odd to us in the west to find parents so involved in their children's education and lives when they are already adults, but as an expression of parental concern, you can't help but be impressed by it.

3 Ask the class to answer the first question as a whole class. Ask them then to look at the six examples individually before discussing them with a partner. Elicit the answers from the class.

> ANSWERS
> The Chinese parents story is soft news.
> celebrity gossip: soft news
> new housing: soft news
> political scandal: hard news
> interest rates: hard news
> travel feature: soft news
> science story: hard news

Extra activity

Ask students to tell a recent news story they have read or heard about. Elicit stories from students and ask them whether they are soft or hard.

8a A life revealed

Lead-in

Personal response

Ask: *Are you interested in other people's lives? Do you ever read biographies, or newspaper and magazine articles about people? Why / why not?* Elicit some answers from the whole class, and encourage questions and comments.

Vocabulary photography

1 Ask students to read the quotations and find the words. They can then check with a partner before you elicit them from the class.

> **ANSWERS**
>
> photograph: shot, snapshot, picture
>
> parts of a camera: shutter, lens
>
> what a camera does: record, caught on film, takes a shot

2 Ask students to comment on the quotations as a class.

Reading

3 Ask students to look carefully at the two photos, and then answer the questions with a partner. Elicit answers from the class without saying whether they are right or wrong. Then ask students to read the article and check their answers. Elicit answers 2–4 again in the light of the reading. Check that students are familiar with all the words and expressions (see Vocabulary notes below).

Vocabulary notes

a refugee = a person who leaves their home to seek refuge (safety) somewhere else

to stare = to look with a fixed expression for a long time

iconic = well known and a symbol

intense = very strong

carefree = without worries or problems

to erase = to rub out, to remove

weathered = made brown and hard by the weather

to blame = to say who or what was responsible

to force someone out = to make somebody move away from where they were

to flee = to run away to escape something bad

to beg = to ask people for help

to bring up children = to raise, to help them grow up

4 Ask students to complete the sentences individually, then check with a partner. Elicit the answers from the class as complete sentences.

> **SAMPLE ANSWERS**
>
> 1 she had never been photographed before.
> 2 nobody knew who the girl was.
> 3 he had not seen her for seventeen years.
> 4 it is very hard.

Background notes

Steve McCurry is an American photojournalist, born in 1950. He is best-known for his photo *The Afghan Girl* which appeared on the cover of National Geographic magazine in 1985. In order to report on the Afghan war situation, McCurry had disguised himself in local clothes in order to cross the Pakistan border into rebel-held Afghanistan just before the Russian invasion. He sewed his rolls of film into his clothing in order to get them back safely. McCurry has won many prizes for his colour photography, including the coveted Robert Capa Prize for Best Photographic Reporting from Abroad.

Sharbat Gula (born c. 1972) was orphaned by Soviet bombing in Afghanistan. She was sent to the Nasir Bagh refugee camp in Pakistan in 1984, where McCurry met and photographed her in 1985. in the late 1980s she married Rahmat Gal, and they returned to Afghanistan in 1992. She has three daughters: Robina, Zahida and Alia – a fourth girl died in infancy. McCurry tried to trace her unsuccessfully several times in the 1990s. He didn't find her until 2002. Her identity was confirmed by biometric technology, matching the patterns of her iris to those in the photo. McCurry took more photos of her for the April 2002 National Geographic magazine, and a documentary called *Search for the Afghan Girl* was released in March 2002. Because of Sharbat Gula, National Geographic set up a charitable organisation called the Afghan Girl's Fund, aimed at educating girls and young women from the country; in 2008, this was renamed the Afghan Children's Fund, and was widened to include boys.

Grammar reporting verbs

5 Ask students to find the sentences in the article individually, then complete the sentences and check with a partner. Elicit the answers from the class as complete sentences. Ask students what the two basic forms are that follow the reporting verbs (the infinitive with *to*, preposition + *-ing*).

> **ANSWERS**
>
> | | | |
> |---|---|---|
> | 1 to let | 4 to return | 7 to give |
> | 2 thinking | 5 to fetch | 8 about having |
> | 3 not to ignore | 6 for forcing | |

6 Read the rubric and the example with the class. Ask students to work in pairs and decide what actual words were spoken for the speech reported in Exercise 5. Elicit the answers from the pairs, having one student read the reported version and the other the actual speech.

> **ANSWERS**
>
> 2 I don't think this picture will be anything special.
> 3 Don't ignore the victims of war.
> 4 Please return to Pakistan.
> 5 I will fetch her from her home in the Tora Bora mountains.
> 6 The war forced us out of our homeland.
> 7 Please give us food and blankets.
> 8 I haven't had a hard life.

Grammar note

Remind students about the other necessary changes in changing direct to reported speech, as well as verb tense.

Pronouns and possessive adjectives:

'My car doesn't work.'   **She** said (that) **her** car didn't work.

Places:

'I live here.'   He said (that) he lived **there**.

Times:

'We're going tomorrow.'   They said (that) they were going **the next day.**

'Mike arrived yesterday.'   He said (that) Mike had arrived **the day before.**

7 Read through the forms and examples in the grammar box with the class. If you feel they need more information and practice, refer to page 167 of the Student's Book. Then ask students to report the sentences individually, and check with a partner. Elicit the answers from the class. Note that different object pronouns are possible.

SAMPLE ANSWERS

1 She complimented him on his amazing photos.
2 She encouraged me to do this professionally.
3 She accused her of being far too modest about her own talents.
4 She suggested I went on a proper photography course.
5 She promised to introduce me to her friend who is a wildlife photographer.
6 She apologised for not having introduced me to him sooner.
7 She urged me to enter the photographic competition in National Geographic.
8 She offered to lend me her camera if I didn't think mine was good enough.

8 Ask students to do this activity individually. They should check with a partner before you elicit the answers from the class as complete sentences. Check students know the meanings of the words (see Vocabulary notes below).

ANSWERS

1 of being   5 to pose   8 to asking
2 doing   6 to let   9 to talk
3 for doing   7 on being   10 getting
4 to take

Vocabulary notes

ethics = moral correctness (opposite = unethical)

sneaky = in a cheating or crafty way

a telephoto lens = a lens that makes distant things bigger

to pose = to get into a particular position for a photo

Speaking

9 Ask students to discuss the questions in groups of four.

Homework

Ask students to write 100–150 words entitled 'My Experience of Photography' stressing that this can be about them as a photographer or as photographer's subject.

8b And finally ...

Lead-in

Personal response

Ask students about their experience of radio and TV news, e.g. Are there any programmes you particularly like? Why? Elicit responses from the whole class about programmes they regularly watch, newsreaders they like and so on. Encourage questions and comments.

Vocabulary the feel-good factor

1 Ensure students are familiar with the adjectives in the box; quirky (meaning unusual, eccentric and different) may be a new word for them. Ask them to decide which adjectives fit into the spaces individually, then compare their ideas with a partner. Elicit answers from the whole class as complete sentences. Read the Wordbuilding box with the class and elicit some examples of -ing adjectives made from verbs (e.g. interesting, terrifying, worrying). Look at the information and exercises on page 67 of the Workbook if you feel they need more practice.

ANSWERS

1 optimistic / encouraging   4 quirky
2 amusing   5 appealing, charming
3 inspiring

2 Read the rubric and the example with the class, then ask them to think of a news story to tell their partner. Ask some students to tell theirs to the rest of the class.

Listening

3 [2.8] Ask students to have pen and paper ready to make notes on the four news stories they hear. When they have finished, ask them to get into threes to compare their notes. Elicit ideas from the class about the key points of each story. Check students understand the key words on the recording (see Vocabulary notes below).

Audioscript [2.8]

And finally ... It was thought that the large blue butterfly was extinct in Britain, but it seems to have made a remarkable return. The large blue, which disappeared 30 years ago, is only found in certain fields. What these fields have in common is that their grass is very short, because rabbits, sheep and cows graze there. Originally it was believed that greedy butterfly hunters had killed off the large blue butterfly, but it is now agreed that changes in farming techniques were responsible for its decline. As a result of recent efforts to protect its natural habitat, it is estimated that around 20,000 of these beautiful creatures will be seen in the British countryside this summer.

And finally, researchers believe they may have found a cure – or at least some relief – for the common cold. In tests it was reported that people who started taking zinc at the first signs of a common cold got well sooner. There have been many previous studies into the effectiveness of zinc but they were inconclusive.

The new study, involving over 1,000 people of various ages, found that on average people who took zinc supplements recovered from their colds one day earlier than those who took nothing. The effectiveness of zinc in preventing a cold in the first place was less certain, although it was said that those who took it regularly suffered less serious symptoms than those who didn't.

And finally, believe it or not, eating chocolate might be good for you after all. In the past it was thought that eating sweets would result in tooth decay and putting on weight. But now it is claimed that a new chocolate bar, invented by the world's largest chocolate maker, can actually slow the ageing process of your skin. The special chocolate contains antioxidants, which help hydrate the skin and fight wrinkles. The market for healthy foods has grown by over five per cent a year in recent years and it seems now that even the sellers of traditionally unhealthy snacks are trying to get in on the act. However, doctors have warned against rushing out to buy extra chocolate – good skin and chocolate are not generally natural partners, they say.

And finally, Costa Rica today has the honour of being named the world's happiest nation. According to the latest Happy Planet Index, it is said that Costa Rica has the best balance of human well-being – that is to say, good health, a long life, low levels of poverty – and a low ecological footprint, in other words the amount of natural resources it uses. In fact, Latin American countries took nine of the top ten places, while richer, so-called developed countries, like the US at number 74, were much further down in the list.

Vocabulary notes

extinct = a species which no longer exists

to graze = to eat the grass in a field

greedy = wanting too much

a cure = a way to make an illness better

a supplement = something extra

inconclusive = not showing a clear result

to prevent = to stop something happening

symptoms = the outward signs of being ill (e.g. headache, high temperature)

tooth decay = when teeth go bad

antioxidants = substances which stop the effects of oxidation inside the body

to hydrate = to stop from drying out

a wrinkle = a line in the skin, usually a sign of getting older

an ecological footprint = how much pollution you create and resources you use

4 🔘 [2.8] Ask students to read through the four gapped texts to focus their listening. Play the recording for them to listen and complete the summaries.

ANSWERS
1 large blue butterfly was extinct, it has made a return, many more of them.
2 a cure for the common cold, zinc supplements, they recovered one day sooner.
3 chocolate manufacturers, a chocolate bar which can slow the ageing process of human skin, that good skin and chocolate are not natural partners.
4 the world's happiest nation, the best balance of human well-being, the USA, are a long way down the list.

5 Ask students to work with a new partner (not one they worked with for Exercise 3) and retell the stories. Then discuss what they thought of them, according to the questions. Elicit responses from the whole class.

Grammar passive reporting verbs

6 Ask the class to answer the two questions about the sentences from the text. Read through the grammar box with the class. If you feel students need further explanation and practice, turn to page 167 of the Student's Book.

ANSWERS
1 We think that the large blue butterfly is extinct. We estimate that we will see 20,000 large blue butterflies this summer.
2 first sentence: said in the past
  second sentence: said in the present

Grammar note

Note how the same stem (*It was thought*) can introduce ideas related to past, present and future, depending on the tenses used in the main part of the sentence. Note also that in passive reporting structures, the speaker (agent) is almost always unimportant and not mentioned; for this reason these structures are frequently used when we want to avoid saying who the speaker is.

7 Ask students to work with a partner to find and underline passive reporting verbs in the audioscript on page 179. Elicit the list of verbs from the class. Then ask students to decide when the reporting happened and when the event happened for each example.

ANSWERS
1 *it was reported that people who started taking zinc at the first signs of a common cold got well sooner*
  reporting – past   event – past (same time as report)
2 *it was said that those who took it regularly suffered less serious symptoms than those who didn't*
  reporting – past   event – past (same time as report)
3 *it is claimed that a new chocolate bar ... can actually slow the ageing process of your skin*
  reporting – present   event – present
4 *it is said that Costa Rica has the best balance of human well-being*
  reporting – present   event – present
5 *it was believed that greedy butterfly hunters had killed off the large blue butterfly*
  reporting – past   event – past (before reporting)
6 *it is now agreed that changes in farming techniques were responsible for its decline*
  reporting – present   event – past
7 *it was thought that eating sweets would result in tooth decay and putting on weight*
  reporting – past   event – future (relative to report)

Pronunciation weak forms in verbs

8a 🔘 [2.9] Ask students to read the sentences and mark where they expect the stress to be. Elicit answers from the class, but do not say what is correct. You could write up the sentences on the board and have students come and mark where they think the stress is. Then play the recording and discuss what they heard. Finally, ask what rules they can make.

> **ANSWERS**
>
> It was <u>said</u> that none of the previous studies had <u>given</u> a clear answer.
>
> It is <u>believed</u> that 100,000 chocolate bars have been <u>sold</u> in the first week.
>
> Rule: auxiliary verbs like *is, was, have, had* are not stressed.

8b Ask students to practise saying the five sentences in pairs, and check each other's pronunciation. Circulate and monitor their pronunciation and stress.

9 Read the rubric and example with the class, and then ask students to change the sentences into passive reporting sentences with *it* individually. They can check with a partner before you elicit answers from the class.

> **ANSWERS**
>
> 2 Thirty years ago it was said that the large blue was a common species.
> 3 It was said that hunters had caused the butterfly to die out.
> 4 It was thought in the past that Costa Rica was a poor country.
> 5 It is claimed that taking zinc helps if you have a cold.
> 6 It was said that none of the previous experiments had been conclusive.
> 7 It was claimed that eating the new chocolate would improve your health.
> 8 It is known that eating too much chocolate is actually bad for you.

10 Ask students to use the cues to make passive reporting sentences. Elicit the answers from the whole class. Then ask students to discuss in pairs how true they think the statements are. Elicit answers from the class, with reasons why they think they are true or not. Finally, their suggestions can be checked on page 155.

> **ANSWERS**
>
> 1 It is believed that chewing gum when you peel onions prevents you from crying.
> 2 It is said that Google's name originally came from 'Googol', meaning a number with 100 zeros.
> 3 It is known that laughing regularly increases life expectancy by up to ten years.
> 4 In 2008 it was reported that air pollution in the US had fallen by 40 per cent since 1980.
> 5 It was claimed recently that scientists studying the Zebra fish had discovered a way for the human heart to heal itself.
> 6 In 2011 it was reported that a man whose house had been crushed by a huge rock in the New Zealand earthquake had sold the rock for $10,000.

Writing and speaking

11 Ask students to work in groups of three to write their news story as directed. They need to make three copies of their text, and after practising reading it aloud, join a new group to read it, and listen to the other stories.

8c From hero to zero

Lead-in

Personal response

Ask: *What has your experience of flying been like? Tell us some good and bad things that have happened to you on planes.* Elicit some stories from the class, and encourage others to ask questions and comment.

Reading

1 Ask students to read the headlines and discuss their content in pairs. Elicit suggestions about what happened from the class, without saying whether the ideas are correct.

2 Ask students to read the story and compare it to their version(s) in pairs. Did any pairs come up with the right story? Check that students understand the key vocabulary (see Vocabulary notes below).

Vocabulary notes

to freeze = (of a person) to be unable to move or act, usually through fear
a villain = a wrong-doer, a criminal
ultimately = in the end, finally
risky = quite dangerous
a runway = the place where an aeroplane lands and takes off
to skid = to slide along the ground out of control
to gossip = to talk about somebody behind their back
incompetent = unable to do a job
a mayday call = the emergency call for help
to evacuate = to get people out of a place of danger
to ban someone from doing something = to legally prevent someone from acting in a particular way
to be betrayed = to have no support from others
wrongdoing = the act of doing something wrong
a rumour = an unofficial story
to reduce the flap setting = to move the flat parts on the edge of the plane's wing down (the flaps are moved up and down to help the plane take off and land)
to take voluntary redundancy = to leave employment of your own choice

3 Ask students to read through the six statements and decide if they are true or false – they should reread the relevant sections of the text if they are unsure. Ask them to check with a partner before you elicit answers from the class: have them read out the statement before they say if it is true or false, and if possible correct the false sentences.

> **ANSWERS**
>
> 1 F (he let his co-pilot take the controls while he adjusted the wing flaps)
> 2 F (*The passengers escaped without serious injury.*)
> 3 F (this was what the press reported)
> 4 F (*it was only read by the senior management*)
> 5 T
> 6 F (*He began applying for jobs with other airlines*)

4 Ask students to find the missing words in the text individually, then check with a partner. Elicit answers from the class as complete sentences.

ANSWERS

1 villain	3 incompetent	5 betrayed
2 miraculously	4 let down	6 awarded

Critical thinking different perspectives

5 Ask students to complete the table individually, then check with a partner. Elicit answers from the whole class.

ANSWERS

BA staff	he was incompetent	gossip
BA management	banned him from speaking and refused to clear his name	to avoid bad publicity
AAIB	he had saved lives by his action	to give a true account of the incident
The newspapers	incompetent	increase newspaper sales

6 Ask the whole class to comment on these two questions.

Word focus word

7 Ask students to find the four expressions with *word*, and match them to the definitions individually, then check with a partner. Elicit the answers from the whole class.

ANSWERS

1 had the last word	3 his word against theirs
2 word went round	4 no word of it

8 Ask students to work in pairs to decide what the expressions with *word* mean. Elicit answers from the whole class.

ANSWERS

1 don't believe what I say
2 I didn't know what to say
3 people telling others about it
4 they promised

Speaking

9 Ask students to work in groups of four to discuss the questions about the media. If you have a multinational group, try to make sure you have students from a range of countries in each group, so that they can explore similarities and differences in media coverage.

Homework

Ask students to write 100–150 words on the media in their country, using the ideas raised in Exercise 9.

8d Spreading the news

Lead-in

Personal response

Ask: *Can you tell us about a traffic accident you saw or have heard about? Where and why did it happen? Who was involved?* Elicit some examples from the class.

Real life reporting what you heard

1 🎵 [2.10] Ask students to look carefully at the three pictures, and discuss with a partner what they think is happening in each. Then play the recording for them to decide which picture the people are talking about. Play it twice if necessary. Check that students understand the key language (see Vocabulary notes below).

ANSWER

The middle picture is the right one

Audioscript 🎵 [2.10]

J = Jess; **P** = Phil

J: Hi Phil. Did all that noise in the street wake you up last night?

P: No, it didn't but then I'm a deep sleeper. What happened?

J: Well, I didn't see it myself but I heard that it was an argument between two car drivers and supposedly it got quite heated.

P: Really?? Who told you about it?

J: Tara at number 42. It seems that both drivers got out of their cars and started shouting at each other. She says they almost started fighting.

P: Hmm … well I'd take what Tara says with a pinch of salt if I were you. She tends to blow things out of proportion.

J: No, I believe her actually – people do get very frustrated by not being able to pass each other on this street. Anyway, the police were called …

P: The police? It wasn't that serious, was it?

J: Well, no. The cars didn't crash or anything. But Tara says that they got out of their cars and started arguing. She reckons that if the police hadn't arrived there would have been a fight.

P: Did the cars make contact?

J: No … they were just coming in opposite directions and they met where the street gets narrow and neither one would reverse to let the other pass. So they just stayed there, in the middle of the road, with neither one giving way.

P: How childish.

J: Yeah, it is rather. Someone said they'd seen one of the drivers before. Apparently he's a local politician.

P: It wasn't Tara getting her facts mixed up again, was it?

J: No it was Chris … I think I'd take his word for it; he's not the type to spread gossip.

P: So what did the police do about it?

J: Well, according to Chris, they took them both away for questioning … surprisingly …

Vocabulary notes

a deep sleeper = someone who is not easily disturbed when asleep

heated = (of an argument) aggressive

to take something someone says with a pinch of salt = to not automatically believe it

to blow things out of proportion = to exaggerate the extent or importance of things

to get frustrated = to get annoyed, upset

to make contact = (of cars) to hit each other

to spread gossip = to talk about others to many people

2 🔊 [2.10] Ask students to discuss the six questions with a partner and answer them. Elicit answers from the whole class, but don't say what is right or wrong. Play the recording for students to check their answers.

> ANSWERS
> 1 He was asleep.
> 2 Tara
> 3 by one of them reversing into a space to let the other pass
> 4 a local politician
> 5 The police took them both away for questioning.
> 6 He thinks Tara cannot be trusted because she exaggerates. He doesn't give an opinion of Chris, but Jess says he's not the type to gossip.

3 🔊 [2.10] Read through the expressions in the box with the class and make sure that they are familiar with them and the way they are used. Ask them to use some of them to complete sentences 1–7 individually, then check with a partner. Elicit answers from the whole class, without saying what is correct. Note that various answers are correct, though they may not be the same phrases as those on the recording. Play the recording for them to check their answers.

> ANSWERS
> 1 I heard, supposedly / apparently
> 2 it seems that / Apparently, / Supposedly,
> 3 a pinch of salt if I were you, blow ... out of proportion
> 4 reckons
> 5 said, Apparently
> 6 his word for it, spread gossip
> 7 According to

Pronunciation the schwa

4a 🔊 [2.11] Ask students to look at the two words (*apparently, supposedly*) and think about how they are said. Then play the recording two or three times for them to listen. Play it again and pause for them to repeat chorally and individually.

4b 🔊 [2.12] Ask students to mark the words with the schwa and the stress individually, then check with a partner. Elicit their suggestions – you might write the words on the board and have students come out and mark the schwa and stresses on them. Do not say what is correct. Play the recording for them to check.

> ANSWERS
> (a)ccording
> gener(a)lly
> happ(e)ned
> inf(o)rmati(o)n
> pr(o)porti(o)n
> reck(o)n
> s(u)rprisingly

4c Play the recording again, and pause after each word for students to repeat chorally and individually. Ask students to practise saying the words with a partner.

5 Read through the rules of this activity with the class and ensure they understand what to do. Give them a minute or two to think up their true and false facts about themselves. Then ask them to mingle and start exchanging information. Stop the activity after a few minutes, and ask students to say what information they have heard about others, and whether they think it was true or false. The students involved should reveal what is true or false.

Homework

Ask students to write a monologue of about 75–100 words in which they are spreading some gossip (real or imagined) about someone; they should use phrases from the box to give the information.

8e A residents' meeting

Lead-in

Personal response

Ask: *Do you have a residents' association in the block or street where you live? If so, what does it do? If not, why not and would it be a good idea?* Elicit ideas from the class, with questions and comments from others.

Writing minutes from a meeting

1 Ask students to read the report and answer the two questions individually, then check with a partner. Elicit answers from the whole class. Check that students understand the key language (see Vocabulary notes below).

> ANSWERS
>
> 1 Make Essex Street one-way; reduce the number of parking spaces in the street; put up signs asking for care and consideration from drivers.
> 2 Putting up signs – because making the street one-way and reducing parking spaces would be inconvenient for residents.

Vocabulary notes

a confrontation = a serious argument, even a physical fight

road rage = when one driver gets very angry with another and is aggressive to them

the minutes = official notes on what people said and decided to do at a meeting

an incident = an event, an interaction, usually with negative associations

consideration = care for others

2 Ask students to think about the structure of the report, and discuss it with a partner. Elicit answers from the whole class.

> ANSWERS
>
> 1 the aim of the meeting
> 2 what action was decided
> 3 follow-up action

Writing skill impersonal language

3a Ask students to find the phrases, and discuss the question with a partner. Elicit answers from the class.

> ANSWERS
>
> *one proposal was to ask ...*
> *most people thought that ...*
> *another suggestion was to ...*
> *the objection to this was ...*
> *it was agreed that ...*
> She uses these phrases to keep the minutes impersonal, so it comes across as being a joint discussion and decision by all the residents.

3b Ask students to rewrite the six sentences individually to make them less personal, then check with a partner.

> ANSWERS
>
> 1 One suggestion was to put speed bumps along the road.
> 2 It was decided that this was not a good idea.
> 3 Another idea was that the speed limit should be reduced to 15mph.
> 4 It was agreed that probably no one would keep to that speed limit.
> 5 Another proposal was to have signs with arrows giving priority to drivers from one direction.
> 6 The objection to that was that it would be impossible to enforce.

4 Ask students to read the report, and look at the suggestions on page 153. They should then work with a partner to write a report of a meeting at which the problems and solutions were discussed, saying which was chosen and what will happen next. You might ask students to do this writing for homework.

5 When they have written their reports, ask pairs to exchange them. They should answer the questions about the report they are reading.

8f Mount Fuji

Before you watch

1 Students work in groups. Ask them to look at the photo and discuss the questions. Take feedback from the class.

2 Ask students to read the words in the box and predict which things they think they will see in the video. Take feedback from the class.

While you watch

3 Give students time to read through the words in the glossary. Play the whole of the video for students to check their ideas from Exercise 2.

> **ANSWERS**
>
> We see all the things in the list except a bear.

4 Give students time to read the question. Then play the video for them to write the descriptions.

> **SAMPLE ANSWERS**
>
> 1 Mount Fuji is a significant symbol of Japanese culture. It is big and very steep.
> 2 They include lots of dancing and fire, and they are to keep the mountain happy.
> 3 It's misty and wet.

5 Give students time to read the sentences. Then play the first part of the video (to 02.07) for them to decide if the sentences are true or false. They should then correct the false sentences.

> **ANSWERS**
>
> 1 F (it's a typhoon)
> 2 F (because it's big and it dominates everything)
> 3 T
> 4 F (among the tourist attractions at the base of the mountain)
> 5 T
> 6 F (it is spiritually significant and very important for Japanese tourists)

6 Give students time to read the topics. Then play the second part of the video (02.08 to the end) for them to write notes.

> **ANSWERS**
>
> 1 She feels emotional
> 2 Women weren't allowed to climb it until 1930. Climbing the mountain used to be a purification process, but now it is like an amusement park.
> 3 It's a big operation and a lot of work is needed to get food and drink up the mountain.
> 4 People come to clean up the rubbish.

After you watch

7 Students work in pairs to roleplay an interview with a *National Geographic* photographer, according to the instructions.

8 Elicit ideas from the class about what the quote means and ask students to answer the question.

9 Students work in pairs to discuss the questions.

Videoscript

Part 1

00.16–00.24 Mount Fuji is one of the most significant symbols of Japanese culture.

Karen Kasmauski, a *National Geographic* photographer, has travelled to Japan to photograph the mountain.

00.25–00.35 Karen Kasmauski I can't believe I'm looking for Fuji in the middle of a typhoon. I have three more days to go before I have to leave back for the States, and hopefully between now and then I'll be able to see the mountain.

00.36–00.41 Mount Fuji is very important for Japanese people. Karen feels that this may be because of its size.

00.42–00.47 Karen Kasmauski The mountain dominates everything, and you can easily see how people would come to worship the mountain.

00.48–00.58 Another reason for Fuji's importance is that some people feel that Mount Fuji is a goddess. Many festivals are held to celebrate this goddess, and they usually include lots of dancing and fire.

00.59–01.10 Karen Kasmauski These festivals, called 'fire and water festivals', are to sort of appease the mountain, give celebration and gifts to the goddess Mount Fuji, so that she will not destroy them.

01.11–01.22 Karen starts her photography shoot at the base of the mountain, where many tourist attractions can be found.

Mount Fuji attracts a huge number of tourists, and after a visit, most want to go home with a gift.

01.23–01.32 Karen Kasmauski You can have cookies, cakes, candies, bento boxes, coffee cups, teacups ... whatever. Whatever you can think of, that you can put Fuji on, you'll find it.

01.33–01.37 For most Japanese people, climbing Mount Fuji still represents more than tourism.

01.38–02.06 Karen Kasmauski Climbing Mount Fuji is a mind exercise. It's really mind over matter more than anything.

There's a word they use, it's called 'gambatte', which is 'persevere'. 'Persevere' is a big word in Japanese culture and language.

I think it's good that it's a misty day, because it's actually been able to cut down on the heat. And stopping to take pictures is a good excuse to take a break.

Part 2

02.08–02.10 Climbing Mount Fuji has been spiritually significant for a long time.

02.11–02.16 Karen Kasmauski So the original purpose of climbing Mount Fuji was a religious pilgrimage.

02.24–02.33 Karen Kasmauski I think it's always kind of an amazing event when you climb for 12 hours, or whatever, and you come up and you see this gorgeous sunrise. It just really is quite an emotional event.

02.35–02.40 These days, Mount Fuji is a busy place that's full of climbers. In the past, it was different.

02.41–03.00 Karen Kasmauski The women were not allowed on the mountain until 1930, so these would be men climbing the mountain ... usually with 'tabis', which are these little white socks, and a white outfit with the straw conical hat.

So people would climb on the mountain sort of as a purification process of their soul.

03.02–03.12 Karen feels that climbing Mount Fuji is an amazing adventure that's almost like an amusement park. She also feels that it's a national 'bonding experience' that brings the people of Japan closer together.

*03.13–03.39 **Karen Kasmauski** There's a whole group of people who operate … or who live on the mountain for about six to eight weeks at a time that make this adventure possible for the 400,000 plus people that climb it during that six-week period.

How do they get the food up there? I mean, there's vending machines at the top of the mountain. How are the cans of sodas brought to the top? Obviously there's some vehicle that has to bring it to the top and it's the bulldozers.

03.40–03.45 Managing Mount Fuji is a huge operation. At the end of the climbing season, there's still more to do.

*03.46–03.53 **Karen Kasmauski** Toward the end of the season, they have a bunch of groups that come and clean up the mountain, because … you know a lot of trash and litter is left.

03.54–04.12 Karen explains that cleaning up the mountain is a kind of community duty for most of these people.

When one looks at Fuji, it's easy to see the hard work that keeps it in good condition. It's also easy to see that the effort is well worth it. Mount Fuji is as beautiful as ever!

UNIT 8 Review

Grammar

1 Ask students to discuss the picture and the idea in pairs. Elicit ideas about it from the whole class.

2 Ask students to read the text and find out if they were correct. Check students understand the key language in the article (see Vocabulary notes below).

Vocabulary notes

a railway corridor = the route of a railway line

striking = interesting and unusual

to submit = (a document) to present

a photovoltaic cell = a cell making electricity by electromagnetic radiation

sceptical = to feel that something is not as good as people say

3 Ask students to complete the text individually, then check with a partner. Elicit answers from the class.

ANSWERS	
1 for being	5 will be covered
2 is	6 to submit
3 to think	7 on coming
4 turning	8 (to) feeling

Vocabulary

4 Ask students to find the odd one out in pairs. Elicit answers from the whole class.

ANSWERS

1 film (the others are all words for photo)
2 column (the others are all types of article)
3 amusing (the others all look to a better future)
4 camera (the others are all parts of a camera)
5 promise (the others are to make someone else do something)
6 objection (the others are all giving ideas)

5 Ask students to discuss this in pairs, and then elicit some examples from the class.

Real life

6 Ask students to do this individually, then check with a partner. Elicit answers from the whole class.

ANSWERS							
1 R	2 D	3 R	4 D	5 R	6 R	7 B	8 D

7 Ask students to work in groups of four, choose an event and discuss the media coverage of it.

Speaking

8 Ask students to create their news items in pairs, including reporting verbs.

Unit 9 Talented people

Lead-in

Personal response

Ask: *Can you name some people you think are talented, and say what their particular talent is?* Elicit some suggestions from the whole class.

1 Ask students to work in pairs to match the words in the box to the definitions. Elicit answers from the class.

> ANSWERS
>
> a talents   e experience
> b skills   f knowledge
> c qualities   g background
> d qualifications

Pronunciation note

Note the position of the stress in the multi-syllable words: *experience, qualifications*

2 Ask the class to look at the photo and suggest what a mahout needs to be like. Elicit suggestions from the whole class, and encourage discussion.

3 ⊙ [2.13] Ask students to listen to the description of the mahout's job and compare it with their ideas.

> SAMPLE ANSWERS
>
> knowledge and experience from the family, patience, understanding of the elephant, ability to do hard physical work, no formal qualifications

Audioscript ⊙ [2.13]

Both the mahout and the elephant start their training at a young age. A mahout generally begins to learn his trade when he's about ten years old and is assigned a baby elephant to look after. He'll probably be paired with this elephant for the rest of his life. It's traditionally a family trade, with knowledge being passed down from one generation to another. There are no formal qualifications for the job, but extreme patience is required. An elephant will learn up to 65 commands in its life – depending on what work it's expected to do – and the mahout has to teach these. The mahout must also develop an intimate understanding of his elephant – something that only comes with time and experience – so that he knows when it's sick or unhappy. In this way he can get the best out of his elephant. It's a very physical job and extremely hard work. The elephant must be fed and bathed daily and watched so that it doesn't run away.

4 Ask students to make notes about themselves under the various headings from the box in Exercise 1, then work with a partner to ask and answer questions.

9a An ordinary man

Lead-in

Personal response

Ask: *Who is the most talented person you know personally? Describe their talents.* Ask students to tell the class, and encourage questions and comments.

Listening and reading

1 ⊙ [2.14] Ask students to look at the photo and discuss what they know about the event and the person involved. Elicit some answers from the whole class, but do not say if they are correct. Then play the first part of the conversation for them to check.

> ANSWERS
>
> Buzz Aldrin and the first Moon landing in 1969

Audioscript ⊙ [2.14]

A: Do you know this photo?

B: Of course. It's the first man on the Moon, Neil Armstrong. The guy who said 'That's one small step for man, one giant leap for mankind.'

A: That's what everyone thinks, but actually it's his fellow astronaut, Buzz Aldrin. Neil Armstrong took the photo – you can see his reflection in Aldrin's visor. But you're right. It was that mission: Apollo 11 in 1969.

B: Amazing to think that was over 40 years ago ... but what happened to Neil Armstrong after that?

A: He probably toured the world getting paid huge amounts of money for public speaking at corporate dinners and official openings and that sort of thing.

Background notes

Apollo 11 was launched from the Kennedy Space Centre, Florida on 16 July, 1969. It was manned by three astronauts: Neil Armstrong (commander), Edwin 'Buzz' Aldrin (Lunar Module Pilot) and Michael Collins (Command Module Pilot). All three had been in space once before. It was the fifth manned mission and third lunar mission of the Apollo programme. The lunar module *Eagle* landed on the moon in the Sea of Tranquility on 20 July, and Neil Armstrong and Buzz Aldrin walked on the Moon on 21 July. The module was on the moon for 21 hours 31 minutes. While they were there, the astronauts tested equipment, took films, tried different ways of moving, collected 21.5 kg of lunar rocks. They also left behind a number of Earth objects. The lunar module then returned to the command module which had been orbiting the Moon, and they returned to Earth, landing in the Pacific Ocean on 24 July. They then spent 21 days in quarantine as it was feared they might bring pathogens from the Moon (it was later found there was no life on the Moon). 600 million people watched the first space walk on TV. The astronauts later toured 25 countries, meeting heads of state such as Queen Elizabeth II of the UK.

2 Ask students to read the article and give the information about Armstrong.

> **ANSWERS**
>
> He was ordinary because he went back to a normal job and only gave two interviews after the historic Moon landing.
>
> He was extraordinary because of flying so young, his Korean War record, the experimental flying he did, leading the Apollo 11 mission, being the first man on the Moon.

3 Ask students to answer the questions individually, then check with a partner. Elicit answers from the class, having one student read a question and another answer. Check students understand the key language in the text (see Vocabulary notes, below).

> **ANSWERS**
>
> 1 Because he did the job he was hired to do, then kept quiet about it.
> 2 the US Navy; in return, Armstrong did service as a naval pilot for three years
> 3 his passion for flying; 'to push the boundaries of flight'
> 4 We all know what happened after that.
> 5 he went flying
> 6 the thousands of people who worked in the space programme

Vocabulary notes

the ultimate = the most perfect example of

to hire someone = to employ them

to be obliged to do something = to have to do it

a mission = (military) taking part in a wartime attack

to push the boundaries of something = to go further, do more

the attention = media wanting photos and interviews

avionics = the science and technology of electronics applied to flight and space flight

a firm = a company, a business

Vocabulary careers

4 Ask students to work together to find the missing career words in the article. Elicit answers from the whole class. Read the *Wordbuilding* box with the class, and note the constructions with and without a preposition. If students seem to need more practice and explanation, refer to page 75 of the Workbook.

> **ANSWERS**
>
> 1 follow   4 serve   6 work for
> 2 graduate from   5 become   7 do, get, apply for
> 3 do

Vocabulary note

Note that other verbs which can go with *career* are: *plan, start, end / finish, cut short.* You might also ask students for any other work-related expressions they know (e.g. *to get a promotion, to lose your job, to be unemployed, to get a pay rise, to change jobs*).

Grammar article: *the* or zero article?

5 Ask students to do the matching individually, then check with a partner. Elicit the answers from the whole class, having them read the use, then the example. Read through the information in the grammar box. See page 168 of the Student's Book for further information and practice.

> **ANSWERS**
>
> 1 superlative adjective
> 2 specific things or people
> 3 already mentioned thing
> 4 before *home*
> 5 specific person
> 6 something unique
> 7 people in general

Grammar note

Point out the difference between these two sentences:

*She went **to school** on Saturdays when she was young.*

*She went **to the school** on Saturday to take her son to play football.*

With *school, university, hospital, church, prison* and other similar words we do not usually use the definite article after *go* to talk about normal attendance. However, we do use the definite article in other contexts, e.g. to talk about the building or place rather than the whole institution.

*The robbers were caught and went **to prison**.*

*I go **to the prison** every Thursday to see my brother.*

*My mother was very ill and had to go **to hospital**.*

*I am going **to the hospital** to pick up my test results.*

6 Ask students to work with a partner to find other examples of each use in the article. Elicit the answers from the whole class.

> **ANSWERS**
>
> a the job
> b the navy, the war in Korea, the Lewis Flight Propulsion Laboratory, the Apollo 11 Moon landing, the University of Cincinnati, the Apollo Space programme; the USA
> c (no true superlatives, but *the ultimate professional; the man who first set foot on the moon*)
> d The rest, the weekend, the chance, the pilot
> e the 1930s, the astronauts, the thousands of people, the boundaries of flight
> f speeds, altitudes, TV shows, experimental aircraft
> g graduated from high school, at Purdue University

7 Ask students to find the examples individually, then check with a partner. Elicit answers from the whole class.

> **ANSWERS**
>
> 1 a) Korea   b) aerospace engineering   c) July
> 2 a) the USA   b) the astronauts   c) the 1930s

8 Ask students to complete the sentences individually, then check with a partner. Elicit answers from the class as complete sentences.

ANSWERS

1 the, zero, the, the
2 the, the
3 zero, zero, zero, zero
4 The, zero, zero
5 The, the, zero, the, zero
6 the, zero, zero

Pronunciation linking vowels

9a [2.15] Read the rubric with the class. Ask them to read the phrases to themselves and decide which sound links the marked words. Then play the recording for them to listen and check. Play the recording again, pausing after each phrase for the class to repeat chorally and individually. Ask students to get into pairs and check and help each other with pronunciation of the phrases.

ANSWERS

1 /j/   2 /w/   3 /r/   4 /r/   5 /j/, /w/   6 /w/

9b Ask students to work in pairs and think of some phrases which require the linking sound. They should then compare their phrases with those of another pair and practise saying the other pair's sentences.

Speaking

10 Ask students to illustrate their career or that of a parent in a diagram, perhaps as homework, and prepare to explain it. When it is ready, ask them to show it to a partner and talk about it.

9b Pushing the boundaries

Lead-in
Personal response
Neil Armstrong's aim was 'to push the boundaries of flight'. Ask: *What other people have pushed boundaries, and which ones?* Elicit some examples from the class. If they are stuck, you might suggest Bill Gates (computing) as an example.

Listening

1 [2.16] Read through the questions with the class to focus their listening. Play the recording once, or twice if necessary. Elicit answers from the whole class.

ANSWERS

1 to encourage young adventurers, scientists, photographers and storytellers to realise their potential
2 *National Geographic* awards each one of them US$10,000, for research and exploration; their articles and news appear in *National Geographic*.
3 many different fields, including anthropology, space exploration, mountaineering, music, storytelling

---

Audioscript [2.16]

Q: Can you tell us something about the Emerging Explorers programme?

A: It's an award scheme set up by the *National Geographic Society* to encourage young adventurers, scientists, photographers and storytellers to continue their work and to realise their potential. Each year between eight and fifteen explorers, whose work is really outstanding, are selected and given money to help them continue their research and exploration.

Q: So Emerging Explorers are generally young people, are they?

A: Not necessarily. Emerging Explorers are generally people who are at an early stage of their careers. What they have in common is that they are all people who are pushing at the boundaries of their field, whether that's exploring undiscovered deep water caves or watching the stars through a telescope.

Q: And how does *National Geographic* encourage them?

A: Well, first of all *National Geographic* awards each one of them US$10,000, which is intended to go towards further research and exploration. Of course their profiles are also raised by the articles and news that appear in *National Geographic*. In other words, the magazine is a place where other interested people can read about their work.

Q: And what kind of fields do the winners come from?

A: We have so many different types of explorer, chosen from fields as diverse as anthropology, space exploration, mountaineering and music.

Q: You mentioned storytellers earlier. What did you mean by that, exactly?

A: Well, there are all these people doing important work out there in the various fields that I have described. And that's great, but it's also very important that everyone hears about this work. That's the skill of the storytellers, communicating with pictures and words important facts about the planet and life on the planet in a way that grabs everyone's attention. A really good example is Alexandra Cousteau, whose grandfather Jacques Cousteau was well-known for his films about marine life. She works as a conservationist, trying to persuade people to protect scarce resources like water. Alexandra, inspired by her grandfather's success as a storyteller, is researching ways in which the environmental community can use new media – social networks, video games – to communicate its message.

2 🔘 [2.16] Ask students to read through the statements to focus their listening. Then play the recording again for them to answer. Ask students to check with a partner before you elicit answers from the class. Ask students to correct the false sentences if possible.

ANSWERS
1 T
2 T
3 F (they come from fields as diverse as anthropology, space exploration, mountaineering and music)
4 F (their skill is communicating with pictures and words important facts about the planet)
5 F (her grandfather made films about marine life)
6 T

Background notes

Alexandra Cousteau was born on March 21, 1976, grand-daughter of world famous undersea explorer Jacques Cousteau, who taught her to scuba dive aged 7. She grew up travelling with her explorer father Philippe Cousteau. She studied in the USA, and in 2000 founded *EarthEcho International* with her brother Philippe Junior. Then, in 2008, she established the *Blue Legacy* organisation to continue her family's work in protecting the world's oceans. She was named as a *National Geographic Emerging Explorer* in 2008.

Grammar relative clauses

3 Ask students to read the sentences a–e, and then discuss questions 1–4 in pairs. Elicit answers from the whole class. Read through the information in the grammar box with students and check that they understand it. Refer to page 169 of the Student's Book for further information and practice.

ANSWERS
1 b / c
2 b / d
3 a / c – the commas
4 e

Grammar note

Make sure students know that:
– the relative clause **always** follows the noun it is defining
– a defining relative clause contains *essential* information
– a non-defining relative clause contains *extra* information, and requires commas.

4 Ask students to use the information in the grammar box to complete the sentences individually, then check with a partner. Elicit answers from the whole class.

ANSWERS
1 Alexandra Cousteau, who is a conservationist, believes …
2 Alexandra Cousteau, whose father was an oceanographer, is a …
3 which
4 whose
5 which
6 The problem, which she says was created by people, is a problem which people can …

Grammar reduced relative clauses

5 Ask students to read the five sentences and decide which participles are active and passive. They should do this individually, then check with a partner. Elicit answers from the whole class.

ANSWERS
1 passive   4 active
2 active   5 passive
3 active

6 Read through the explanation in the grammar box. Refer to page 169 of the Student's Book for more information and practice. Ask students to change the reduced relative clauses from Exercise 5 into full relative clauses individually, then check with a partner. Elicit answers from the whole class.

ANSWERS
1 We have so many different types of explorer, who are chosen from diverse fields.
2 There are all these people who are doing important work out there in the various fields.
3 That's the skill of the storytellers, who are communicating important facts about the planet.
4 She works as a conservationist who is trying to persuade people to protect resources like water.
5 Alexandra Cousteau, who was inspired by her father's success as a storyteller, is researching ways in which the environmental community can use new media.

7 Ask students to complete the three profiles at the foot of the page individually, then check with a partner. Elicit answers from the class as complete sentences.

> **ANSWERS**
> 1 called the real-life Lara Croft by the New York Times
> 2 cycling a distance of 700 miles
> 3 threatening to harm her
> 4 fascinated by the truly big questions
> 5 playing music to take his mind off problems
> 6 who spends his time diving into water caves deep under the ground (a reduced relative clause could be used after a comma, *spending his time …*)
> 7 undisturbed for 3.5 million years
> 8 provided by these dark and wonderful places

8 Ask students to find the eight adjectives individually, then check with a partner. Elicit answers from the whole class.

> **ANSWERS**
> independent, adaptable, analytical, patient, daring, easy-going, articulate, passionate

9 Ask students to consider the question for a few minutes, then tell a partner, giving reasons for their choice. Elicit some responses from the whole class.

Background notes

Kira Salak was born in Chicago, USA in 1971. She studied writing and literature to PhD level, and has published prize-winning short stories and a novel. In 1995 she became the first woman to backpack across Papua New Guinea, which is chronicled in her *Four Corners* book. Her 2004 book *The Cruellest Journey* recounts her trip to Niger.

Stephon Alexander was born in Trinidad, but his family moved to New York City when he was eight. He did a PhD in Theoretical Physics at Brown University, then post-doctoral research at Imperial College, London. He is currently an Assistant Professor at Penn State University.

Kenny Broad is a professor at the Rosenstiel School of Marine and Atmospheric Science in Miami, and Director of the University of Miami's Center for Ecosystem Science and Policy. In 2011 he was made *National Geographic* Explorer of the Year.

Speaking and writing

10 Ask students to write a description of someone they admire, then share their work in groups of four.

9c The king herself

Lead-in

Personal response

Ask: *What can you tell me about Ancient Egypt?* Elicit any facts and information about the civilisation which students can give you.

Reading

1 Ask students to read the title in pairs and discuss it. Then elicit their suggestions.

> **ANSWERS**
> *King* is masculine, so one would expect *the king himself* (or *the queen herself*).

2 Ask students to read through the list of events, and then read the article and order the events correctly individually. They can check with a partner before you elicit the answers in the correct order. Check any language students don't understand (see Vocabulary notes below).

> **ANSWERS**
> 1 g   2 f   3 d   4 c   5 b   6 a   7 e

Vocabulary notes

irony = an amusing or strange situation when things turn out differently from what you would expect

a dynasty = the family which rules a country

a shrine = a holy place in memory of a religious person

an account = a story

to inscribe = to write in a hard surface

an obelisk = a square stone column which tapers to the top

to erase someone's memory = to make people forget about someone

a cult = a group who look up to a particular person

a pit = a deep hole in the ground

to proclaim = to make a public announcement

to assume control = to take over and be in charge

a regent = a person who takes the position of king or queen while a prince or princess is too young to do the job

intriguing = causing great interest

to act on someone's behalf = to do something instead of another person, with their consent

a convention = a traditional way of behaving

to learn the ropes = to learn how to do something new

to have a claim to something = to believe that something is yours by right, legally

to be depicted = to be shown in a drawing or painting

imposingly = in a way which dominates and looks powerful

to take one's revenge = to punish someone for something they did to you

to wipe something out = to destroy something completely

3 Ask the class to suggest what different roles Hatshepsut had in life.

> **SAMPLE ANSWERS**
> wife, mother, regent, ruler, Pharaoh, politician, cult leader

4 Ask students to read through the multiple-choice options to focus their reading before they read the article again. They should do the exercise individually, then check with a partner. Elicit the answers from the class as complete sentences.

> **ANSWERS**
> 1 b   2 c   3 a   4 a   5 b   6 b

Background note

The Karnak Temple Complex is situated near Luxor, 500 km south of Cairo. It is the largest religious site in the world. The site was developed over very many years, not least by Hatshepsut. She restored the Precinct of Mut (the ancient mother goddess of Egypt). Hatshepsut had two obelisks erected at the entrance – at the time they were the tallest in the world. One of them still stands, while the other lies broken into two. She also constructed the Red Chapel and had two more obelisks made to celebrate her 16th year as pharaoh. However, one broke in construction, and it still lies in the quarries at Aswan, enabling us to see how they quarried obelisks.

Critical thinking weighing the evidence

5 Read through the rubric with the class and explain that they have to allocate a percentage according to how clearly the evidence given in the text supports the statement. Ask them to weigh the evidence individually and decide a percentage for each statement. You could ask them to underline the supporting sentences in the text.

> **SAMPLE ANSWERS**
> 1 100%   2 100%   3 50%   4 30%   5 50%   6 80%

6 Ask students to check their answers with a partner before you elicit them from the class. Ask them to explain the evidence they found. In feedback, discuss with the class what percentages they think should be allocated. If there is definite factual evidence, they might write 100%. If there is quite strong evidence to support the statement, but it is not a definite fact, they might write 80%.

Word focus long

7 Ask students to match the expressions with the meanings individually, then check with a partner. Elicit the answers from the whole class, with one student reading a phrase, and another giving the definition.

> **ANSWERS**
> 1 c   2 d   3 f   4 e   5 a   6 b

8 Ask students to complete the sentences with one of the phrases from Exercise 7 individually, then check with a partner. Elicit answers from the whole class as complete sentences.

> **ANSWERS**
> 1 longed for
> 2 long after / in the long term
> 3 As long as
> 4 and before long
> 5 at long last
> 6 long after

Speaking

9 Ask students to read through the jobs in the box, and check that they are familiar with them all. Ask them to work in groups of four to discuss whether they think more women or more men do each job. Elicit answers from the whole class, and open it up as a wider discussion.

10 Ask students to look at the statistics on page 154, and discuss the jobs with their group. Elicit answers from the class.

> **SAMPLE ANSWERS**
> **Managers:** company director, prime minister
> **Skilled trades:** plumber
> **Professional:** doctor, lawyer, nurse, teacher
> **Associate professional and technical:** IT technician
> **Low skilled:** cleaner
> **Process, plant and machine operatives:** machine operator
> **Sales:** florist
> **Administrative:** secretary, senior civil servant
> **Personal service:** nurse

Homework

Ask students to write around 150 words on *Women at work* in which they discuss whether there are some jobs women cannot or shouldn't do, what the situation for women in work is and what things they think need changing.

9d Right for the job

Lead-in

Personal response

Ask: *Which skills and talents do you think kept Hatshepsut in power for 21 years?* Elicit suggestion from the class and discuss them.

Real life describing skills, talents and experience

1 Ask students to read about Shelterbox and answer the question. Check that they understand all the key language (see Vocabulary notes below).

> **ANSWER**
>
> It is a charity. It provides essential basic equipment for victims of a disaster.

Vocabulary notes

a charity = an organisation which helps people in difficult situations

essential = absolutely necessary

cooking utensils = equipment used to prepare food (e.g. knives, pots, pans)

a kit = a set of equipment for a specific purpose

2 ⊙ [2.17] Read the rubric and the questions with the class to focus their listening. Play the recording and elicit the answers from the class. Check students understand the key language (see Vocabulary notes below).

> **ANSWERS**
>
> 1 working abroad
> 2 that the candidate will soon leave for a better-paid job

Audioscript ⊙ [2.17]

S = Sarah; **P** = Phil

S: So, you're 24 years old, you graduated a year ago and you're looking for work with a charity. What attracted you to Shelterbox?

P: Well, I'm familiar with your work because I have a friend who volunteered for you last year – packing boxes – and I think it's a fantastic concept. But umm … mainly I'm very keen on the idea of working abroad, … in different countries …

S: Mm, I see … and what makes you think you'd be suited to that? I see you studied economics at Cambridge … Don't you think that's a rather different world?

P: Yes, it's true that I specialised in economics but, actually, I'm good at coping with difficult environments. I spent three months helping to build a school in Chennai in India last summer. And the year before that I trekked across the Mojave Desert. So I think I'd be suited to the work.

S: OK – well … they're certainly not easy places to adapt to … although in fact you'd also be spending a good part of the time here in the office doing paperwork.

P: Yeah, that's also fine. I was expecting that. I have quite a lot of experience of sitting at a desk … for my studies. What sort of paperwork is it?

S: Well, each trip involves a lot of preparation and a certain amount of follow-up too. Keeping spreadsheets, writing reports. Are you OK doing that sort of thing?

P: Yeah, I'm quite good with computers. I'm comfortable with all the usual programs – Excel, Word, some financial software …

S: OK. There's just one thing that's worrying me though. You're clearly a bright person and you have a good degree. How do I know that you won't just do this job for a few months and then go and get a better paid job with a bank or consultancy business?

P: That's a good question. It's actually what a lot of my friends from university have done but I'll tell you why that's not for me. Firstly, I'm really serious about wanting to help people in need. Secondly, I think I need to become more knowledgeable about the world, before I use my economics degree to do something else … If you put your faith in me, I will be absolutely committed to doing the best job that I can … for two or three years at least.

Vocabulary notes

to be suited to = to have the right skills and personality

to cope with = to be able to do something difficult

to do paperwork = to do office work (work on paper)

follow-up = collecting information and checking after something has ended

a spreadsheet = software for numerical information

bright = intelligent (in this context)

to put one's faith in something / somebody = to trust or believe in something / somebody

to be committed to something = to take on a task or responsibility and do it as well as you can

3 ⊙ [2.17] Ask students to read through the list of phrases in the box. Play the recording while they complete the phrases. Then play the recording again for students to check and complete their answers. Elicit the final answers from the class.

> **ANSWERS**
>
> 1 volunteered for you last year
> 2 working abroad
> 3 economics
> 4 the work
> 5 difficult environments
> 6 sitting at a desk
> 7 computers
> 8 the usual programs
> 9 help people in need
> 10 the world

4 Ask students to discuss how well they think the candidate presented himself in pairs. Elicit ideas from the whole class and discuss it further.

SAMPLE ANSWER

He sounds as if he has experience in all the relevant areas (coping with difficult environments, paperwork, computer programs), but also seemed committed to the work of the charity. He sounded convincing when he responded to the interviewer's concerns.

Pronunciation difficult words

5a 🎧 [2.18] Ask students to think about the pronunciation of the words in the box individually, and decide how confident they are about the pronunciation of each one. Play the recording for them to check whether they were right, nearly right, or wrong.

Extra activity

Play the recording again, pausing after each word for students to repeat chorally and individually. Then check for syllable stress – have them underline the stressed syllable in each word. Next elicit the words from them, with pronunciation and stress correct.

5b 🎧 [2.19] Ask students to listen to the words on the recording and write them down with the correct spelling. They can then check with a partner before you ask students to spell them out to you, while you write them on the board. Ask students to work in pairs to practise saying the words in Exercises 5a and 5b.

Audioscript 🎧 [2.19]

clothes, February, folk, island, lengths, receipt, surface, thorough

6 Read through the rubric and the jobs with the whole class. Ask students to choose a job, and make sure it is different from their partner. They can make a few notes about it if they wish, especially the weaker students. Then ask them to do the roleplay, using the Shelterbox interview as a model. When they have done it once, they should swap roles and do it again. Circulate and monitor their interviews for later feedback.

9e Professional networking

Lead-in

Personal response

Ask: *What sort of relationship do you have with colleagues at work? Do you meet outside the workplace? Do you meet others in your profession socially? Why or why not?* Ask students to answer and comment and ask questions.

Writing an online profile

1 Ask the whole class to discuss these questions about professional networking sites.

2 Ask students to read the profile individually and summarise the man's skills and qualities, then discuss their ideas with a partner. Elicit responses from the class for further discussion.

SAMPLE ANSWERS

Main skills: identifying and responding to learning needs, designing online programmes

His profile gives general information about what he does, but does not say much about the skills and qualities he needs in his job.

---

3 Ask students to read through the tips individually, and decide if Barton McCready has followed each tip or not. They can then compare their ideas with a partner. Elicit answers and discuss them with the whole class.

ANSWERS

1 ? (includes photo but no recommendations)
2 ✔
3 ✔
4 ? (doesn't include school)
5 ? (does not describe what he did in each job in much detail)

Writing skill writing in note form

4a Ask students to read the four extracts from the profile and decide which is a proper sentence individually, then check with a partner and discuss why this is. Elicit answers from the whole class.

ANSWERS

2 is a proper sentence (it has a subject and verb, it has a capital letter and full stop). 1, 3 and 4 are written in note form. This is done to save space and avoid repetition, and to make it easier for the reader to find the important information.

4b Ask the class to complete extracts 1, 3 and 4 so that they are written as full sentences.

> **ANSWERS**
>
> 1 I am responsible for new products.
> 3 I published (the book) *Learning in the 21st Century*.
> 4 I am involved in developing an innovative e-learning programme for the car industry.

4c Ask students to shorten the six statements into note form individually, then check with a partner. Elicit the answers from the whole class.

> **ANSWERS**
>
> 1 worked as PA to Marketing Director
> 2 currently writing article for *National Geographic*
> 3 in charge of organising corporate social events
> 4 took official photos for National Basketball Championships
> 5 working for various charities
> 6 employed by local college to raise money

5 Ask students to write their own profile, using the one on the page as a model. They can do this for homework. When they have finished, they should exchange it with a partner, and read it quickly to gain a first impression.

6 Ask students to read each other's profile again in more detail and check the three points. They should tell each other about anything they think could be improved.

9f Queen of Egypt

Before you watch

1 Students work in groups. Ask them to make notes about what they know about Cleopatra. Take feedback from the class.

2 Ask students to predict three kinds of image they think they will see in the video. Take feedback from the class.

While you watch

3 Give students time to read through the words in the glossary. Play the whole of the video for students to check their ideas from Exercises 1 and 2. They should not try to understand everything at this stage.

> **ANSWERS**
>
> 1 Cleopatra was Queen of Egypt, she ruled Egypt around 50 BC. She was married to Marc Antony and committed suicide when she thought she was going to lose Alexandria to the Romans.

4 Give students time to read the questions. Then play the video for them to write the answers.

> **SAMPLE ANSWERS**
>
> 1 They didn't have a good relationship.
> 2 When he was in Alexandria in pursuit of a Roman general, she smuggled herself into his court.
> 3 Her influence prevented the Romans from taking control of Egypt.
> 4 He was angry that Cleopatra's son was declared the successor to Caesar.
> 5 at the Battle of Actium in 31 BC
> 6 He killed himself because he thought Cleopatra was dead.
> 7 She let herself be bitten by a poisonous snake.

5 Give students time to match the sentence beginnings with the endings, then play the video again for them to check.

> **ANSWERS**
>
> 1 d   2 a   3 e   4 g   5 f   6 b   7 c

After you watch

6 Students work in pairs to roleplay a first meeting with Caesar, according to the instructions. They should change roles and act out the conversation a second time.

7 Read the quote with the class and ask students to answer the questions.

8 Students work in groups to discuss the questions.

Videoscript

00.01–01.15 She has a reputation for beauty, power, controversy and, ultimately, tragedy.

In 69 BC, Cleopatra was born into Egypt's Ptolemaic dynasty; a dynasty in decline and under the protection of Rome.

At the age of 18, she became queen, and ruled Egypt with her younger brother, Ptolemy the 13th. But the royal couple did not have a good relationship and Cleopatra was soon forced from power. But losing did not suit Cleopatra and she waited for a chance to prove her capabilities.

That opportunity came when Julius Caesar, the winner in Rome's recent civil war, arrived in Alexandria, Egypt, in pursuit of a rival Roman general.

According to legend, Cleopatra managed to get herself into Caesar's court rolled up inside a rug.

Caesar was completely charmed. He defeated Cleopatra's rivals and helped her seize the throne.

Shortly after, she gave birth to a boy, Caesarion, whom she claimed was Caesar's son.

01.16–01.34 Egypt was a very rich country and Cleopatra was fiercely determined to keep it independent of Rome. Her relationship with Caesar kept the Romans from taking direct control of Egypt. But after Caesar's murder, her position, and the future of her country, became uncertain.

01.36–02.02 Searching for people who could help her among Rome's new leaders, she was overjoyed when Mark Antony, one of Caesar's potential successors, sent for her.

Like Caesar before him, Mark Antony was charmed by the elegant Egyptian queen ... and her riches.

Together they ruled Alexandria, an arrangement that made Cleopatra a fully independent ruler.

02.05–02.30 Cleopatra and Antony shared a hunger for power.

They eventually married and became the power couple of the eastern Mediterranean.

Antony tried to help her acquire some Roman lands. And he declared Cleopatra's son Caesarion to be the son and true successor to Julius Caesar.

02.32–03.03 That insulted and infuriated Mark Antony's Roman rival, Octavian, who went to war against them.

Antony and Cleopatra were quickly beaten at the Battle of Actium in 31 BC.

Legend tells us that Cleopatra spread numerous false rumours of her death.

His mind distorted by grief, Antony killed himself. But word came she was still alive, and Antony's followers carried him to Cleopatra where he died in her arms.

03.05–03.25 After 22 years as queen, Cleopatra was fighting a losing battle. She tried unsuccessfully to make peace with Octavian. Utterly unable to bear the pain of losing to the Romans, she took hold of a poisonous snake and let it kill her with its bite.

03.26–03.48 With her death, the Ptolemaic dynasty was finished, and Egypt fell firmly into Roman hands.

Although her ambitions were never realised, Cleopatra lives on in history through her personal story of love and tragedy.

UNIT 9 Review

Grammar

1 Ask students to write *the* where necessary in the text individually, then check with a partner. Elicit answers from the class as complete sentences.

ANSWERS		
1 –	5 the	9 the / –
2 –	6 the	10 –
3 –	7 the	11 –
4 –	8 the	12 –

2 Ask students to complete the two paragraphs with relative pronouns and participles individually. They can then check with a partner before you elicit the answers.

ANSWERS	
1 whose	6 composed
2 which	7 hitting
3 who	8 causing
4 which	9 used
5 where	10 worn

3 Ask students to close their books, then describe the module to a partner.

Vocabulary

4 Ask students to complete the sentences individually, then check with a partner. Elicit answers from the class.

ANSWERS	
1 qualification, graduated	4 skills, did
2 experience, served	5 background, follow
3 quality, do	6 knowledge, become

5 Ask students to make notes on their skills and experience, then use their notes to tell a partner about themselves.

Real life

6 Ask students to complete the sentences with the correct preposition individually, then check with a partner. Elicit the answers from the class as complete sentences.

ANSWERS	
1 with	5 at
2 in	6 about
3 to	7 on
4 with	8 about

7 Ask students to discuss jobs that would and wouldn't be good for them. Encourage them to give reasons for their statements.

Speaking

Ask students to describe someone they admire, including the points given.

Unit 10 Customs and behaviour

Lead-in

Personal response

Ask: *Does your family follow any customs which are traditional? If so, which ones and why? If not, why not?* Elicit answers, questions and comments from the whole class.

1 Ask the class to look at the picture and discuss the question as a whole class.

> SAMPLE ANSWER
>
> One of them is talking on her mobile phone, and the other is reading or sending texts or emails. Perhaps the behaviour is deemed incorrect and disrespectful in the Forbidden City by the older ladies.

2 Ask the class to make suggestions about the quotation. Make sure they understand the meaning of *manners* (polite ways of treating other people and behaving in public). Don't comment on their ideas at present, just encourage them to express their ideas. Possible interpretations will follow in the next exercise.

3 [2.20] Ask students to read the questions. Play the recording for them to answer. Elicit answers from the whole class and check students understand the key language (see Vocabulary notes below).

> ANSWERS
>
> 1 Good manners help you get on in society.
> 2 The customs of our society form who we are.

Audioscript [2.20]

Well, a narrow view of this quotation is that you need to have good manners or you won't get far in life … Good manners meaning the kind that we teach our children: you know the kind of thing – don't talk with your mouth full; don't interrupt when grown-ups are speaking; don't point or stare at people; don't slouch or chew gum; don't wear clothes that are inappropriate or offensive; in a nutshell, be polite, well-behaved and show courtesy to others.

But I think what William of Wykeham really meant is that each society creates its own code of behaviour and customs, and that is what makes people what they are. So each culture defines itself by the way it behaves socially – how we eat, how we dress, how we celebrate, how we interact with one another. In fact, the different ways we all find of doing essentially the same things.

Vocabulary notes

a narrow view = a limited set of ideas about something

to interrupt = to speak when someone else is speaking

to point at someone = to hold out one's index finger towards them

to stare at someone = to look at someone continuously for a long time

to slouch = to walk in a lazy way with rounded shoulders

in a nutshell = simply

courtesy = politeness, respect

a code = a set of rules

4 [2.20] Ask students to read the gapped sentences. Then play the recording so that they can listen and complete them. If necessary, play the recording twice. They can check with a partner before you elicit the answers as complete sentences.

> ANSWERS
>
> 1 talk
> 2 interrupt
> 3 point, stare
> 4 slouch, chew
> 5 inappropriate, offensive
> 6 well-behaved, respect

Homework

Ask students to write 100 words on the rules that their parents made for their behaviour at home when they were children.

10a Cruel to be kind

Lead-in

Personal response
Ask the class to discuss the meaning of the section title. (It means to do something which seems to be hard or damaging, but which will make things better in the end.)

Reading

1 Ask students to look at the picture and then answer the three questions in pairs. Elicit answers from the class.

> **SAMPLE ANSWERS**
> 1 The mother is saying something to her daughter about doing her cello practice.
> 2 The mother looks quite relaxed, but firm, perhaps strict; the daughter is smiling. Perhaps the mother is telling her to do her cello practice.
> 3 Students' own answers

2 Ask students to work in groups of four to discuss the parental control issues. Elicit answers and encourage a wider class discussion.

3 Ask students to read the text and answer the questions individually, then check with a partner. Elicit answers from the whole class. Check students understand the key language in the text (see Vocabulary notes below).

> **ANSWERS**
> 1 strict and ambitious Chinese mothers
> 2 TV and computer games only come after homework, music practice etc., and are banned if those things are not done; music practice has to be done well; going out with friends is banned if duties are not completed; homework comes first, and top grades are expected.
> 3 Western parents are laid-back, give too much praise for poor performance.

Vocabulary notes

instinct = your own basic feelings about how to behave

to rear a child (child-rearing) = same as *to bring up*

to highlight = to make something noticeable

to ban = to stop or prevent

harsh = unreasonably strong

to resent = to dislike someone for something

laid-back = relaxed

self-discipline = the ability to organise oneself

4 Ask students to discuss the questions with a partner. Elicit answers from the whole class.

> **ANSWERS**
> 1 Tiger mothers get good results from their children.
> 2 She says it *seems harsh* and *perhaps it works* which suggests she is not completely sure.
> 3 Students' own answers

Vocabulary raising children: verbs

5 Ask students to compare the verbs in pairs; you may want them to use dictionaries.

Elicit the differences from the whole class.

> **ANSWERS**
> 1 *bring up* means helping with all aspects of the child's development; *educate* refers only to mental (and perhaps social) knowledge
> 2 *praise* mean saying things are good; *reward* means that something is given for good performance
> 3 *rebel* means to fight against a system as a whole; *disobey* means to deliberately do something you have been told not to do
> 4 *push oneself* means to try your hardest even when it is difficult; *discipline oneself* means setting one's own rules and keeping to them
> 5 *give in* means to not stand up to people when they want their own way; *spoil children* means to let them do and have whatever they want all the time
> 6 *nag* means to keep on telling people what to do and complaining about their behaviour; *pester* means to continually interrupt with questions and demands
> 7 *shame* means to make someone feel bad for what they have done or not done; *punish* means to make someone suffer for what they have done

Grammar habitual actions: present tenses, *will*

6 Read through the examples in the grammar box with the class, then ask the class to answer the three questions. Refer to page 169 of the Student's Book for further information and practice.

> **ANSWERS**
> 1 will
> 2 present continuous with *always*
> 3 present simple

Grammar note

The present continuous with *always* is used to express annoyance at something somebody regularly does. It emphasises and exaggerates the frequency with which the behaviour takes place, by suggesting it is happening continuously.

> John **is always leaving** the lights on!

In more formal English, the same idea can also be expressed by *will + keep + -ing*:

> John **will keep leaving** the lights on!

7 Ask students to find the relevant phrases in the text individually, then check with a partner. Elicit the answers from the whole class.

8 Explain the word *a chore* (a unenjoyable task one has to do) before students start. Ask students to underline the correct verb forms individually, then check with a partner. Elicit answers and comments from the class.

ANSWERS

1 are always telling	4 hopes, won't always admit
2 will do	5 respond, need
3 want, perform	6 are always trying, buy

9 [2.21] Ask students to put the verbs in the correct form individually, then check with a partner. Play the recording for students to check the answers.

ANSWERS

(alternative correct answers are given in brackets)

1 beg	5 are always misbehaving
2 will say (say)	6 depend
3 will pester (pesters)	7 play
4 will do (do)	8 assume

Audioscript [2.21]

1 I've seen this situation so many times in Mexico. What happens is children beg their parents for some sweets. At first the parent will say no. So then the child will pester and pester until the parent finally gives in – which they always do. It's against all the rules of parenting.

2 I teach in a school in San Francisco where we have quite a lot of ethnic Chinese and Japanese kids. By and large they will do what you tell them. But the other kids – wow – they are always misbehaving. You can tell them ten times to sit down before they do.

3 Where I live in India, it's common for young children to work. Kids still depend on their parents, but they have a different attitude to responsibility. Just as children in every culture play naturally, so children in India naturally assume responsibility for working and earning money.

Speaking

10 Ask students to discuss the questions about the three texts in Exercise 9 in pairs, then report their ideas to the rest of the class. Encourage questions and comments.

11 Ask the pairs to think of three examples.

12 Ask pairs to get together to discuss their examples. Circulate and monitor their discussion for future feedback.

10b A matter of taste

Lead-in

Personal response

Ask: *What is your favourite food, and why?* and elicit answers from the class; encourage questions and discussion.

Listening

1 Ask the class to answer the questions about strange foods, and encourage questions and comments.

2 [2.22] Ask students to read the three questions to focus their listening. Play the recording and elicit the answers from the class. Play the recording again if necessary. Explain any of the key language.

ANSWERS

1 the Nicobar Islands in the Indian Ocean
2 insects
3 They cultivate certain fungi and moss for the insects to eat.

Audioscript [2.22]

Different people's diets rarely surprise me these days. We didn't use to think so much about what we ate. But today, well ... we live in an age where people are just very conscious of their diets. A day hardly ever passes without a story in the news about a particular food that's good for your health or bad for you if you eat too much of it.

So I was very interested to read a story the other day about the diet of the Nochmani tribe of the Nicobar Islands in the Indian Ocean. People used to think that these tiny islands – which are about 600 miles from the coast of India – that they were uninhabited by humans. But in 2004 aid workers in helicopters spotted some tribespeople on a mountainside.

Scientists were particularly surprised that there were inhabitants there, because people usually need mammals – you know, cows, goats and so on – and their produce – meat, milk, etcetera – in order to live. But the Nicobar islands have almost no mammals. So what were the Nochmani surviving on? Fish, perhaps? No. Amazingly, their diet consisted largely of insects, in particular beetles, of which there were over 1,700 varieties on the islands, but also other insects and spiders.

This presented a problem for the aid workers, who'd brought with them standard survival meals, including chicken, beef and pork. The Nochmani, who weren't used to eating meat at all, were disgusted by these offerings. All they'd take from the aid workers were sweets and cakes. It wasn't just a matter of taste either. If you're used to a certain type of food – even insects – other types may be completely indigestible.

Insects are in fact very nutritious: high in protein and fat and low in carbohydrates, making them an ideal food source for humans. But what was even more amazing was that just as we usually help our animals to live by providing food for them, so the Nochmani cultivate certain fungi and mosses to attract and feed the insects they eat. Perhaps we can learn from this tribe. If more of us could get used to eating unconventional foods such as insects, it might help the world's food problems.

Background note

The Nicobar Islands are an archipelago in the eastern Indian Ocean, 150 km north of Sumatra. They have a warm tropical climate, with heavy rainfall due to the monsoons. They are largely covered by rain forests and mangrove forests, with some areas of grassland. The inhabitants speak 6 dialects of Nicobarese, but they are part of India. The people chiefly live by horticulture. In the aftermath of the 2004 earthquake, on December 26th, a 10–15 m tsunami hit the islands, destroying property, breaking up some islands altogehter, and causing huge loss of life.

Vocabulary notes

to spot someone = to notice them unexpectedly or with difficulty

standard = normal, basic

to be disgusted by something = to find something extremely unpleasant

indigestible = not able to be eaten and used by the body

nutritious = (of food) full of goodness

protein = compounds that are essential for life

carbohydrates = organic compounds supplying energy from food

fungus (plural – fungi) = flowerless plant (e.g. mushrooms)

moss = low-growing green plant, in bogs, on walls

unconventional = not normal or usual

3 🔘 [2.22] Ask students to read the gapped sentences carefully and think what might be a suitable word or phrase to complete them. Play the recording for them to write the answers, then play it again for them to check, and complete their answers. They can then compare with a partner. Elicit the answers from the class as complete sentences.

ANSWERS

1 b	2 c	3 a	4 b	5 c	6 c

4 Ask students to think about the questions raised for a few minutes, then work in a group of four to discuss them. Ask one student in each group to act as secretary and record what is said. Have a class feedback session where the secretaries report their group's ideas.

Grammar *used to, usually, be used to and get used to*

5 Ask students to read the five sentences (1–5) and match the verb forms to the meanings (a–e) individually, then check with a partner. Elicit the answers from the class, having them read the complete sentence before giving the meaning. Read through the grammar box with the class and make sure they understand the structures and their use. See page 170 of the Student's Book for further information and practice.

ANSWERS

1 d	2 b	3 a	4 e	5 c

6 Ask students to work individually and use the information from the grammar box to help them choose the correct forms to complete in the three texts. They can check with a partner before you elicit the answers from the class as complete sentences.

ANSWERS

1 do not usually finish
2 get used to
3 are used to eating
4 usually assumes
5 used to sit
6 usually eat
7 get used to dining
8 used to be
9 didn't use to eat

Background note

The basic form of the traditional English breakfast consists of fried egg and fried or grilled sausages and bacon, with toast, or fried bread. Other foods that are often included are fried black pudding (a blood sausage), mushrooms, tomatoes and baked beans (haricot beans in sweetish tomato sauce). The traditional breakfast has fallen out of favour in homes because it is very high in cholesterol, very fattening, and generally unhealthy. However, it is still served and enjoyed in hotels and guest houses throughout the country, and many people enjoy it at home as a weekend treat, or on special occasions.

7 Ask students to complete the sentences individually, then check with a partner. Elicit the sentences from the class as complete sentences.

ANSWERS

1 used to eat	3 used to take, get used to
2 usually have	4 am used to eating

8 Ask students to reflect on their experiences relating to the sentences in Exercise 7, and then tell a partner about it. Elicit some comments from the whole class.

Pronunciation /u:/ and /ju:/

9a 💿 [2.23] Ask students to read the three sentences to themselves and think about the pronunciation of the words in bold. Then play the recording for them to listen to several times. Play the recording again, pausing after each sentence for students to repeat it chorally and individually.

9b Ask students to practise saying the /ju:/ words in the box to a partner, and help each other to get the pronunciation right.

9c 💿 [2.24] Ask students to practise the /u:/ words in the box individually, then listen and check.

> **ANSWER**
>
> /u:/ follows /r/ and /dʒ/

Vocabulary and speaking

10 Ask students to work in pairs to categorise the food, then check and share their answers with another pair. Elicit answers from the whole class.

> **ANSWERS**
>
> (possible other examples in brackets)
> a yoghurt (cheese, cream, milk)
> b breakfast cereals (tinned foods, prepared meals, packet foods)
> c rice (pasta, bread)
> d chocolate bars (sweets, biscuits)

11 Ask students to complete the statements individually. Then ask them to circulate and compare what they have written – the results will be very different depending on whether you are teaching a monolingual or a multilingual class.

Homework

Ask students to write 120–150 words on one of these topics to do with food.

My favourite meal

The best meal I ever ate

A traditional meal in my country

Changing eating trends in my country

10c A universal language

Lead-in

Personal response

Invite students to show the others an everyday gesture (e.g. waving hello, thumbs up etc.), and ask them to explain what it means. Discuss the gestures. If you have students from different countries, or ethnicities, do the gestures mean the same thing for all of them?

Reading

1 Ask students to get into pairs to decide what the actions are like and what they mean by demonstrating them to each other, then classify them. Elicit the answers from the whole class.

> **ANSWERS**
>
> Posture: sitting back in your chair; standing with arms crossed
> Gesture: waving; a handshake
> Facial expression: smiling; biting your bottom lip
> Possible meanings:
> Sitting back in your chair = feeling relaxed or feeling in charge
> Standing with arms crossed = feeling impatient, intolerant or defensive
> Waving = saying hello or goodbye
> A handshake = saying hello or goodbye
> Biting your bottom lip = nervousness or fear
> Smiling = friendliness or feeling happy

2 Ask students to read the three summary sentences to focus their reading, then read the text and decide which summary is correct. Elicit answers from the class. Check students understand the key language in the article (see Vocabulary notes below).

> **ANSWER**
>
> c

Vocabulary notes

to exploit = to fully make use of

to adopt = to use, to take on

a case in point = a typical example

outstretched = reaching out

to bow = to lean the top part of the body forward

a profitable route = a more productive way

to be distracted = to be thinking about other things

to tense up = to become tight and ready for action (opposite of relaxed)

to apply = to use

to invade = to move into

3 Ask students to choose the correct answer individually, then check with a partner. Elicit answers from the class as complete sentences.

> **ANSWERS**
>
> 1 a   2 b   3 b   4 c   5 c   6 a

4 Ask students to find the gestures described, and then demonstrate them to each other in pairs. Have some students demonstrate them to the whole class for comment.

> **ANSWERS**
>
> Paragraph 3: sitting cross-legged with foot outstretched; raising the eyebrows quickly as a greeting
>
> Paragraph 4: bowing; shaking hands
>
> Paragraph 5: boredom: people look at other things, e.g. watches, move feet restlessly, tap fingers, scratch head
>
> anger: the face muscles tense up causing a frown, the eyes stare, the face goes red, the body tenses

5 Ask the class to comment on the two questions as a class, and encourage discussion about them.

Critical thinking sources

6 Ask students to underline the references to other cultures individually. Elicit answers from the whole class.

> **ANSWERS**
>
> Para 1: buying bus tickets in England, France and Australia
>
> Para 2: distance from speaker in Latin cultures, China, Nordic cultures
>
> Para 3: sitting in Europe, in Arab countries; greeting in the Philippines and the USA

7 Ask students to look at the text to find sources for the examples listed in Exercise 6. They should note them and give a number as indicated. Elicit answers from the whole class and discuss them with students.

> **ANSWERS**
>
> Para 1: bus tickets: 0
>
> Para 2: distance: 3 (Proxemics, Statistics)
>
> Para 3: sitting: 2/3 (personal experience); greeting: 1 (it is said …)

Word focus common

8 Ask students to match the sentences and the meanings individually, then check with a partner. Elicit answers from the whole class.

> **ANSWERS**
>
> a 1   b 2   c 2   d 1

9 Ask students to match expressions e–h with meanings 1–2 in Exercise 8, then check with a partner. Elicit answers from the whole class.

> **ANSWERS**
>
> e 2   f 1   g 1   h 2

Speaking

10 Ask students to work in pairs to describe customs from their country. If you have a monolingual, mono-ethnic class, then put pairs together to discuss their ideas. If you have a multi-ethnic group, try to pair people from the same country, and then pair them with another pair from somewhere different. If you have some single students, let them make notes by themselves to describe the customs, and then talk to someone from a different country. Elicit answers from the whole class.

Homework

Ask students to write 120–150 words about some interesting gestures from their culture.

10d A pre-wedding ritual

Lead-in

Personal response

Ask: *When was the last time you went to a wedding?
What was it like?* Elicit some descriptions from students,
and encourage questions and discussion.

Introducing the theme: weddings

Ask students to work in pairs to list as many words
connected to weddings as they can. Elicit answers from the
whole class and make a list on the board (e.g. wedding /
wedding dress / wedding guest / wedding breakfast /
bridesmaid / best man / wedding cake / wedding ceremony /
wedding presents / marriage / to get married / bouquet /
church / registry office / temple / wedding ring / to give
away the bride / confetti / rice)

Vocabulary weddings

1 Ask the class to discuss the question as a class. Invite
comments and questions on what is said. Provide any
wedding vocabulary students need to help them along.

2 Ask students to answer the questions in pairs, then
check with another pair. Elicit answers from the whole
class.

> ANSWERS
>
> 1 stag night (for the man) hen night (for the woman)
> 2 bride (woman) groom (man)
> 3 veil

Vocabulary note

The stag party and hen night traditionally used to take
place the night before the wedding, although nowadays
they are usually held about a week before. Sometimes
people now go away – even abroad – for a weekend the
week before the wedding. In general, these parties often
involve noisy public behaviour, and sometimes friends play
pranks or tricks on the groom (less often on the bride).
Some groups nowadays wear unusual costumes, with
special T-shirts for everyone to wear naming the bride or
groom to be. The parties are supposed to be symbolic of
the last night of freedom with your friends before settling
down into married life.

Real life describing traditions

3 [2.25] Read the rubric and question with the
class to focus their listening. Make sure they know what
henna is (a reddish dye obtained from a plant, which is
used to colour hair and to decorate the body). Play the
recording through once and elicit the answer. Play it again
if necessary.

> ANSWERS
>
> The women of both families attend; they play music, sing
> and dance.

Audioscript [2.25]

M = Marie; E = Esther

M: I know of henna painting as a custom from Indian
weddings … but you came across it in Turkey, didn't
you?

E: Yes, in eastern Turkey when I was travelling there. It
takes place a few nights before the wedding.

M: Was it a bit like a hen night?

E: Well, in the sense that it marks the last evening that a
bride spends with female family and friends, I suppose
it is a bit like that. What happens is, typically, the
women from both families get together, with the bride,
to celebrate with music, song, and dance. But it's not
just a party. It's an occasion for sadness too, because
it symbolises the end of life as a single person and the
start of another stage.

4 Read through the first four sentence stems in the
box with the class. Play the recording again for them to
complete the sentences. Play it again for them to check
and complete their answers. Elicit answers from the class
as complete sentences.

> ANSWERS
>
> 1 a few nights before the wedding
> 2 last evening that a bride spends with female family and
> friends
> 3 sadness too
> 4 end of life as a single person and the start of another
> stage

5 [2.26] Ask students to read the six sentences to
focus their listening. Play the recording and ask students
to order the sentences by writing the numbers 1–6.

> ANSWERS
>
> a 6   b 2   c 5   d 3   e 4   f 1

Audioscript [2.26]

M: So what happens exactly?

E: Well, the ceremony begins with preparation of the
henna. It's traditional for this to be done by the
daughter of a couple who have had a successful
marriage themselves. Then, after the bride's head
has been covered in a red veil, her hands and feet are
decorated with henna. After that, a gold coin is put
into the remaining henna. While this is happening, the
guests sing … umm … separation songs – these are
rather sad, as you can imagine. The party continues well
into the night. Then, on the morning of the wedding,
a child presents the hennaed coin to the groom as a
symbol of future prosperity and good fortune.

6 💿 [2.27] Read through the linking words in the box in Exercise 4 with the class.

Ask students to work in pairs and tell each other what happens in the pre-wedding festivities in the correct order, adding the appropriate linking words. Circulate and monitor their speaking for later feedback. Play the whole recording and let them listen and check.

Audioscript 💿 [2.27]

See audioscripts 2.25 and 2.26 above.

Pronunciation the letter s

7a 💿 [2.28] Ask students to read the words in the box and decide for themselves how the letter 's' is pronounced in each case. Then play the recording for them to listen and check. Elicit the answers from the whole class.

> ANSWERS
>
> /s/: custom / dress / suppose (first 's') / symbolise (first 's')
>
> /z/: friends / music / suppose (second 's') / symbolise (second 's') / weddings

7b 💿 [2.29] Ask students to decide on the pronunciation of the words in the box, then listen and check. Ask them to think of three other words for each pronunciation and compare them with another pair.

> ANSWERS
>
> /s/: across / eastern / single / spends (first 's') / surprise (first 's')
>
> /z/: lose / rings / spends (second 's') / surprise (second 's')

Extra activity

Play the recordings of all the words, pausing after each one for students to repeat chorally and individually. Then ask them to practise with a partner, and help each other with their pronunciation.

Speaking

8 Ask students to do this activity individually. If people don't know what happens in a wedding ceremony in their country, ask them to think about another ceremony with many traditions associated.

9 Ask students to get together in groups of four and describe the customs; if the others in the group share the same culture, they should listen and add anything which they think is missing. If they are from different cultures, they should listen and ask questions.

Homework

Ask students to write 120–150 words describing a wedding ceremony (or other traditional ceremony).

10e Business customs

Lead-in

Personal response

Ask: *What customs do you know connected to business in this country?* Elicit ideas from the students (if students are at a loss for ideas suggest: being punctual, not taking mobile calls in meetings, exchanging business cards) and discuss what they say.

Writing an informal email

1 Ask students to read the question about business customs in other countries and discuss ideas as a class. Elicit any examples they can give of business customs in different countries.

2 Ask students to read the first email and answer the questions, then check with a partner. Elicit answers from the class.

> ANSWERS
>
> 1 advice about how to behave in China
> 2 He doesn't want to upset his business partners.

Vocabulary notes

Ensure students are familiar with these words and phrases:

briefly = for a short time

to put one's foot in it = to make a mistake, to do the wrong thing

to be aware of = to understand and know

3 Ask students to read the reply and answer the question, then check with a partner. Elicit answers from the whole class.

> ANSWERS
>
> Take business cards; eat whatever you are offered.

Writing skill elision in informal writing

4a Ask students to find four examples of elision and share them with a partner. Elicit answers from the whole class.

> ANSWERS
>
> **First email**
> 1 Forgot to tell you
> 2 Just wondered what to expect
> 3 Don't want to put my foot in it.
> 4 Thanks
>
> **Second email**
> 1 Glad to hear you're going out to China
> 2 Not Shanghai, is it?
> 3 Anyway, my advice:
> 4 Good luck and speak soon

4b Ask students to write the eight shortened sentences as full formal sentences individually, then check with a partner. Elicit the full versions from the class.

ANSWERS

First email

1 I forgot to tell you
2 I just wondered what to expect
3 I don't want to put my foot in it.
4 Thank you in advance for your help.

Second email

1 I'm glad to hear you're going out to China.
2 It isn't Shanghai you're going to, is it?
3 Anyway, this is my advice:
4 Good luck and I will speak to you soon.

4c Ask students to write the sentences as shorter informal versions individually. They can then check with a partner before you elicit answers from the whole class.

SAMPLE ANSWERS

1 Hope we can meet soon.
2 Bad luck that you didn't get the job.
3 Back Tuesday night.
4 My New York address:
5 Look forward to hearing all about it.
6 Not a bad result, was it?

---

5 Ask students to read the email, then reply to it in an informal style, making appropriate suggestions for how things are done in their country.

6 Ask students to work in pairs, exchange emails and check them against the four criteria listed.

Homework

Students reply to the email they checked in Exercise 6. They then give it to their partner, who checks it for the same criteria.

10f Eating insects

Before you watch

1 Students work in groups. Ask them to look at the photo and discuss the questions. Take feedback from the class.

2 Ask students to work in pairs to discuss their childhood experience of sweets.

3 Elicit ideas from the class about the questions asked.

While you watch

4 Play the whole video for students to check their ideas from Exercise 3.

ANSWERS

1 countries in Asia, Africa, Australia, and Latin America
2 No, it's a very old habit, dating back to the earliest humans.
3 Yes, insects brim with vitamins and minerals.
4 Yes, it is: producing a pound of caterpillar takes a tenth of the resources needed for a pound of beef.

---

5 Give students time to read the list. Then play the video for them to number the foods in the order they see them.

ANSWERS

1 g	2 b	3 e	4 c	5 h	6 d	7 f	8 a

---

6 Give students time to read the questions. Then play the video again for them to complete their answers.

ANSWERS

1 Pismo beach, California
2 for more than 10 years
3 Because they are taught to avoid insects from an early age.
4 more than 1,400 / fourteen hundred
5 It has snob appeal, people can enjoy tasting gourmet insects.

After you watch

7 Students work in pairs to roleplay a meal at Larry's restaurant, according to the instructions. They should change roles and act out the conversation a second time.

8 Read the quote with the class and discuss what it means.

ANSWER

Something that has 'snob appeal' makes people feel superior in some way. Gourmet insects might have snob appeal because they are unusual, and because they are very good for the environment.

---

9 Discuss the question briefly and ask students to give their opinion by a show of hands.

10 Students work in groups to discuss the questions.

Videoscript

00.01–00.20 Every resort town in the US has a candy store. But one store in Pismo Beach, California goes beyond the usual toffee and caramel apples. If Hotlix has its way, Americans will be snacking on everything from caterpillars and cockroaches … to mealworm-covered apples.

00.22–00.29 Larry Peterman is a candy man on a mission. For more than a decade, he's been promoting a valuable food source that most Americans find revolting.

00.31–00.39 In a land of plenty, people resist. Larry knows why. From an early age, parents teach children to avoid insects.

00.40–00.49 Larry Peterman In our culture, from the time we're really small, we're taught to avoid insects. They might bite you like a mosquito, you swat them.

This was kind of good … this has kind of a good cricket in it.

00.50–00.57 But kids aren't the only ones munching on bugs. Around the world, more than fourteen hundred insect species show up on menus.

00.58–01.12 Insect-eating or entomophagy is part of healthy diets in Asia, Africa, Australia, and Latin America. This trend is anything but new. Archaeologists have found evidence of it dating to the earliest humans.

01.15–01.35 Advocates of insect eating like to note that it's environmentally sound. Producing a pound of caterpillar takes a tenth of the resources needed to produce a pound of beef. And insects brim with vitamins and minerals. But despite all the benefits, most Americans can't stomach bugs.

01.36–01.38 Larry Peterman Welcome, welcome, welcome! Have a seat!

01.39–01.48 Unlike Larry Peterman, who celebrates them at his dinner parties. The evening begins with Larry's version of the classic shrimp cocktail.

01.49–02.16 Larry Peterman We just finished preparing a cricket cocktail. It's a lot like a shrimp cocktail, only instead of shrimp we use crickets. OK, folks. Here's the first course.

'Oh yum!' 'Now enjoy.' 'My God, I just ate a cricket!' 'While you're enjoying this, I'm going down and get your next course.'

02.18–02.20 The main course is a stir-fry, a special garnish.

02.22–02.37 Larry Peterman Here we go. Dinner is served. 'Here we go, ready?' 'OK' 'Uno, dos, tres, go.' 'Yeah, they're terrific. Yeah. All right.' 'Oh, thank you so much. Yeah, you want the cricket.'

02.38–02.41 Several courses later, Larry presents his pièce de resistance.

'This is the best dinner I've had.'

02.44–03.10 Larry Peterman OK. Here it is, folks, what you've been waiting for. Now don't let anybody dive in until everyone's been served, please. We call them a Pismo Surfer and what it is is a banana with whipped cream and a really good cockroach on it. You don't have to eat the wings. You don't have to eat the head. Unless you want to.

'Do you know, do you know where this cockroach has been?'

'Probably not. How is the taste?'

Larry Peterman We can do another one next week if you like!

03.11–03.13 Larry predicts he'll eventually win people over.

03.14–03.32 Larry Peterman As we become more and more insect-food oriented, our taste is going to change and so I see a niche for somebody that does gourmet insects. It could have some snob appeal, like, people taste wine, hmm, this is a good one. Why, this bug is good.

UNIT 10 Review

Grammar

1 Ask students to discuss in pairs what they know about Spanish eating habits. Elicit some ideas.

2 Ask students to read the text and find the information about Spanish meal times. Elicit answers from the class.

ANSWERS

Breakfast: 8–9.30 a.m. Lunch: 1.00–3.30 p.m.
Dinner: 09.00–11.00 p.m.

3 Ask students to choose the correct forms of the verbs individually, then check with a partner. Elicit answers from the whole class as complete sentences.

ANSWERS

1 get used to	5 close
2 aren't used to	6 will rest
3 used to live	7 used to be
4 usually eat	8 won't eat

Vocabulary

4 Ask students to work in pairs to find the odd word out in each group, and the reason for it.

ANSWERS

1 spoil – the others are things parents do to get their children to behave correctly
2 educate – the others are about looking after children
3 shame – the others are positive
4 cheese – it is dairy, the others are carbohydrates
5 sit back – it is a posture, the others are gestures
6 smile –the others are all bad manners
7 offensive – the other three are all good behaviour

5 Ask students to tell a partner about their postures, gestures and facial expressions.

Real life

6 Ask students to match the phrases in the two columns with a partner.

ANSWERS

1 It marks the moment when a child becomes an adult.
2 It takes place on the child's 16th birthday.
3 It is an occasion for celebration.
4 It symbolises leaving childish things behind.
5 It's customary for the child to stand up and give a short speech.
6 Typically the ceremony begins with the parent walking into the hall with the child.
7 Once the child has given their speech people in the audience can also say a few words.

7 Ask students to talk about a traditional celebration in their own country. Elicit some examples from the class.

Speaking

8 Ask students to discuss the questions in groups of four.

Unit 11 Knowledge and learning

Lead-in

Personal response

Ask: *What have you enjoyed learning most in your life, and why?* Elicit answers from the class and encourage others to comment and ask questions.

1 Ask students to work in pairs to match the phrases; they may need a dictionary. Elicit answers from the class.

> ANSWERS
>
> 1 d   2 c   3 b   4 a

2 🔊 [2.30] Read the rubric and the two questions with the class to focus their listening. Then play the recording for them to answer. Play it again if necessary.

> ANSWERS
>
> 1 buying a second-hand car
> 2 consult an authority, do some research, study the facts, make some reasoned judgements, process the information, trust your instinct

Audioscript 🔊 [2.30]

We rely on our intuition all the time. Let me give you a couple of examples. Imagine you're going to buy a second-hand car. You have a basic grasp of car mechanics. So, first you consult an authority on the subject … like a motoring magazine. You do a bit of research to find out what the best kind of car is, and try to pick up some tips from experts and journalists. Then you study the facts about the car – how big the engine is, how economical it is and so on – and make some reasoned judgements from the information you read about whether it's a suitable car for you or not. In other words, you process the information.

But when it actually comes down to buying a particular car from a particular person, then … in the end you have to trust your instinct or gut feeling. Do I trust this person? Is a car of this age going to give me any trouble? No one else can answer these questions. And that's how it is with many situations in life. Our knowledge is rarely perfect enough to mean we can make a purely objective decision.

3 🔊 [2.30] Ask students to read through the phrases. Play the recording for students to complete the sentences.

> ANSWERS
>
> 1 grasp   3 process
> 2 find, pick   4 gut
>
> *grasp* = understanding
> *find out* = get information
> *pick up* = to get ideas, sometimes in unexpected ways
> *process* = take all the information and make sense of it
> *gut feeling*: an instinct, or a feeling you have that you cannot explain by logic

11a Knowledge conservation

Lead-in

Personal response

Ask: *Have you learnt more from working in jobs, or from your formal school and university studies? Why?* Elicit answers from students, and encourage comments and questions from others.

Reading

1 Ask students to answer the question in pairs, then elicit the answer from the class.

> ANSWER
>
> A botanist studies plants.

2 Ask students in pairs to make a list of plants and plant products they use regularly. They should then compare their list with another pair. Elicit ideas from the class.

> SAMPLE ANSWERS
>
> fruit and vegetables in food; plant oil (olive, maize, sunflower); plant extracts in shampoos and other cosmetics (e.g. nettle); herbal medicines; pot plants for decoration; coconut matting on the floor; wood for fuel, building, furniture, etc.; paper

3 Read through the questions with the class to focus their reading, then ask them to read the article and answer the questions individually. Elicit the answers from the class. Check students understand the key language in the article (see Vocabulary notes below).

> ANSWERS
>
> 1 She looks at the way people interact with plants.
> 2 in the rain forests of Ecuador and at Florida Atlantic University
> 3 medicine and food

Vocabulary notes

to distinguish = to separate one thing from another
a cash-crop = a cultivated plant grown for money
to engage with = to make connections with, interact

4 Ask students to answer the questions individually, then check with a partner. Elicit answers from the class, having one student ask and another answer the questions.

> ANSWERS
>
> 1 She writes down information that they give her.
> 2 They pass it on by word of mouth from one generation to another.
> 3 She tells stories about her life in the rain forest.

5 Ask students to discuss the questions in pairs. Then elicit ideas from the class. Read the *Wordbuilding* box with the class, and point out that idiomatic expressions can make texts more interesting and convey more subtle meaning. For more explanation and practice, see page 91 of the Workbook.

Grammar *could, was able to, manage to and succeed in*

6 Ask students to work in pairs to find the forms in the text, then match each one to a use. Elicit answers from the class.

> ANSWERS
> 1 could distinguish – b
> 2 were able to pick out, were able to engage – b
> 3 couldn't easily absorb – c
> 4 weren't able to remember – c
> 5 Fadiman managed to persuade – a
> 6 Fadiman succeeded in getting – a

Grammar note

Explain that, to talk about ability in the past, *could* and *was able to* are virtually interchangeable, as are *couldn't* and *wasn't able to*.

> He **could / was able to** run very fast as a boy.
> They **couldn't / weren't able to** leave because of the snow.

However, we use *was able to*, not *could*, to talk about a particular action that someone succeeded in doing.

> After he fell, he **was able to** reach the telephone to call for help.

Manage to do and *succeed in doing*, when used in the past, both imply that something was difficult to do, but that in the end, the desired result was achieved:

> He didn't want to come with us at first, but eventually we **managed to persuade / succeeded in persuading** him to join us.

7 Read through the grammar box with students. For further practice and explanation, see page 171 of the Student's Book. Ask students to complete the sentences individually, then check with a partner. Elicit answers from the class.

> ANSWERS
> 1 distinguish   4 to work
> 2 to say   5 in passing
> 3 to use   6 save

8 Ask students to underline the correct forms individually, then check with a partner. Elicit answers from the whole class as complete sentences.

> ANSWERS
> 1 was able to combine / succeeded in combining
> 2 could look at
> 3 managed to record
> 4 wasn't able to do
> 5 was able to visit
> 6 were able to make

Vocabulary learning

9 Ask students to work in pairs to decide which words are synonyms. Elicit answers from the whole class.

> ANSWERS
> absorb – take in   connect with – engage with
> acquire – pick up   grasp – understand
> be ignorant (of) – not know inspire – motivate

10 Ask students to complete the sentences about their own experiences of learning at school. Then ask them to get into pairs to ask and answer the questions.

> SAMPLE ANSWERS
> 1 succeeded in inspiring
> 2 could you absorb / were you able to absorb
> 3 could you engage with
> 4 Did you manage to pass / Did you succeed in passing
> 5 did you manage to acquire / did you succeed in acquiring
> 6 you couldn't grasp / you weren't able to grasp

Speaking

11 🔊 [2.31] Read the questions with the class to focus their listening. Play the recording and let them note their answers. Elicit answers from the whole class.

> ANSWERS
> 1 growing vegetables
> 2 She read a book by Joy Larkcom.

Audioscript 🔊 [2.31]

I became interested in growing my own vegetables a few years ago because I was aware of how expensive vegetables were in the shops. It also struck me that a lot of the vegetables we buy are imported. It occurred to me that if more people grew their own, we wouldn't have to import so many. I was really ignorant of the subject – I couldn't grow a thing – but luckily I managed to discover a fantastic book written by a woman called Joy Larkcom. That was six years ago and it's become more than a hobby. It never crossed my mind that I would become an expert, but now I get a lot of neighbours coming to ask me for my advice.

12 Ask students to choose a subject they know a lot about (e.g. a hobby or interest) and answer the questions, then discuss it with a partner.

Homework

Ask students to write 120–150 words on *How I learnt to …* They can choose a work area or a hobby that they have already talked about in this section.

11b Memory

Lead-in

Personal response

Ask: *What is the earliest memory you have from childhood?* Elicit answers from the whole class and encourage questions and comments.

Speaking

1 Ask students to look at the picture for ten seconds – count the seconds out yourself – then close their books and write down all the objects they can remember. They should then combine their list with a partner.

2 Ask the pairs to share their lists with another pair. Elicit the list from the class with books still closed – try to get as much information as you can about colour, shape, material and so on. You might want to write it on the board. Discuss any techniques students used for memorising the items, and any other applications these techniques might have.

> ANSWERS
> a red toy sports car
> a book: Homer's *The Iliad*
> a box of matches with *Peace* written on it
> a metal badge
> a silver cigarette lighter
> a locket on a chain
> a baseball with writing on it
> 2 photos (one colour, one black-and-white)
> an airmail letter and envelope
> 2 metal tags (one red, one silver)
> a plastic toy figure
> a white fan with signatures on it
> 6 medals: 1 round one with a long tricolour neckband
>   1 Maltese cross with stars & stripes flag
>   2 small heart-shaped ones with a head on a blue background
>   2 small circular ones with striped cloth attachment
> something unrecognisable, black / khaki and red, mostly out of picture on the left

Listening

3 Ask the class to discuss what sort of things they often forget. Encourage questions and comments.

4 💿 [2.32] Ask students to listen and compare their own memory problems with those discussed on the recording. Elicit comments from the class.

Audioscript 💿 [2.32]

Do these situations sound familiar to you? Have any of these things happened to you? You were about to give a speech or make a comment at a meeting, and then your mind went blank. You were supposed to send a friend a card for their birthday, but then you forgot. You recognised someone in the street and would have spoken to them, but you didn't because you couldn't remember their name. You promised you would post a letter for someone and two days later you found it still in your pocket. You were going to write down a great idea you had, but when you found a pen and paper, the idea had gone. I could go on, … but I won't because I'm sure everyone recognises these common failures of memory.

5 💿 [2.33] Read through the questions with the class to focus their listening. Play the recording and ask them to find the answers. If necessary, play it again. Elicit answers from the whole class. Check students understand the key language (see Vocabulary notes below).

> ANSWERS
> 1 dates and the events related to them
> 2 She finds it is a burden.
> 3 Because we store things externally on computers and mobile phones, and don't use our memories as much.

Audioscript 💿 [2.33]

Everyone would like to remember more but would it actually make us any happier?

I want to tell you the story of a 41-year-old woman from California known in medical literature as 'AJ', who remembers almost every day of her life since the age of 11. She remembers that at 12.34 p.m. on Sunday, the 3rd of August 1986, a young man she was attracted to called her on the telephone. She remembers that on the 28th of March 1992, she had lunch with her father at the Beverly Hills Hotel. It's a bit like certain smells that evoke strong memories … AJ's memory is stimulated in the most intense way by dates.

You'd think that being able to retrieve facts and knowledge in this way would make us more confident and wiser. But in fact for AJ an incredible memory is as much a burden as it is a benefit. That's because most memories are selective: they remember mostly important things and mostly good things too. AJ remembers every detail, good or bad, important or not.

So when we curse our poor memories for forgetting to send a birthday card, actually we should be grateful also for all the things that our memories hide away because they don't need to be remembered or thought about. Umm … technology of course helps us with this. We don't need to remember the precise content of a report or the exact time of a meeting, because it's stored on our computer or in our mobile phone.

But interestingly, the growth of this technology – what psychologists call our external memory – is having an effect on what and how much we remember. Even our memories of happy events – like parties or holidays – get stored in photograph albums on our computers. So our internal memories are probably worse than those of people 100 years ago. Medical science is trying to address the problem of poor memory and this is what I want to talk about next …

Vocabulary notes

medical literature = medical articles and reports in professional journals and books

to evoke = to make you remember and think about

to stimulate = to cause something to react in some way

to retrieve = to get back, to find again

wise = having a great deal of useful knowledge about life

a burden = something which is physically or figuratively 'heavy', and becomes a problem

a benefit = something which helps us

selective = partial, incomplete

to curse something = to regret or be annoyed by something, to wish a situation was different from what it is

6 [2.34] Ask students to read through the sentences and complete what they can individually. Play the recording for them to check and complete their answers. They can then check with a partner. Elicit the answers from the class as complete sentences.

> ANSWERS
> 1 dates, smells
> 2 confident and wiser
> 3 important, good
> 4 grateful
> 5 external
> 6 poor

Audioscript [2.34]

(See audioscripts 2.32 and 2.33)

7 Ask students to work in groups of four to discuss the three questions. Ask the groups to appoint a secretary to keep notes on their ideas. Elicit suggestions from the secretaries and encourage comments and questions from the rest of the class.

Grammar future in the past

8 [2.35] Ask students to read through the five sentences and think about what should be in the gaps. Play the recording and ask them to complete the sentences. Play it again if necessary. Elicit answers from the whole class as complete sentences.

> ANSWERS
> 1 were about
> 2 were supposed
> 3 would have
> 4 would
> 5 were going

Audioscript [2.35]

(See audioscript 2.32)

9 Ask students to discuss the questions about the sentences in Exercise 8 in pairs. Elicit ideas from the whole class.

> ANSWERS
> 1 your mind went blank (you couldn't remember what to say).
> 2 you forgot.
> 3 you couldn't remember their name.
> 4 you found it still in your pocket.
> 5 you'd forgotten what it was.
> None of the actions were completed because the person forgot to do what they had planned, or they couldn't remember what they were going to do.

10 Ask students to choose the verb forms individually, then check with a partner. Elicit the answers from the class as complete sentences.

> ANSWERS
> 1 was going to ask
> 2 was supposed to be
> 3 would have told
> 4 it would have meant
> 5 was about to ask
> 6 would be frustrated

Grammar note

The future in the past is used for various reasons:

To talk about an intention which may or may not have been completed:

> I **was going to** visit them, but then they went away for the weekend.
> I **was going to** visit them whether they wanted me to or not.

To talk about a plan or appointment that changed:

> We **were going to** meet at six, but he rang to say he couldn't come.

To talk about other actions in the past (not intentions) that didn't happen as expected:

> I **would have said** hello, but I didn't see him.

To report our thoughts in the past:

> I knew what **she was going** to say, but I kept quiet.
> It was **going to be** a wonderful party.

In reported speech:

> I told them (that) **it was going** to rain.

11 [2.36] Read through the information and examples in the grammar box with students. If they need more explanations and practice, refer to page 172 of the Student's Book. Then ask students to complete the sentences in Exercise 11 using the future in the past. Elicit answers from the class, and play the recording for them to listen and check.

> ANSWERS
> 1 I was going to ask Sarah to come, but I asked Kate instead.
> 2 She was supposed to be in Cairo this week, but she's ill.
> 3 He promised he would send me the original, but he sent me a copy.
> 4 We would have been there by ten o'clock, but the train didn't get in until eleven fifteen.
> 5 He was about to announce that he would retire this year, but now he thinks he'll stay.
> 6 The council were going to build a new shopping mall in the centre, but residents opposed the idea.

Pronunciation contrastive sentence stress

12a 🎵 [2.36] Ask students to underline the words in pairs. Elicit answers from the whole class without saying if they are correct or not. Play the recording for them to listen and check. Then ask them to practise saying the sentences to each other and getting the stress correct.

> **ANSWERS**
> 1 I was going to ask <u>Sarah</u> to come, but I asked <u>Kate</u> <u>instead</u>.
> 2 She was supposed to be in <u>Cairo</u> this week, but she's <u>ill</u>.
> 3 He promised he would send me the <u>original</u>, but he sent me a <u>copy</u>.
> 4 We would have been there by <u>ten o'clock</u>, but the train didn't get in until <u>eleven fifteen</u>.
> 5 He was about to announce that he would <u>retire this year</u>, but now he thinks he'll <u>stay</u> until <u>next year.</u>
> 6 The <u>council</u> were <u>going to build</u> a new <u>shopping mall</u> in the centre, but <u>residents opposed</u> the idea.

12b Ask students to complete the sentences individually, then say them to a partner and ask them which words were stressed.

> **SAMPLE ANSWERS**
> 1 I was going to order a <u>steak</u>, but I decided to have <u>chicken</u> instead.
> 2 They were supposed to be going on holiday to <u>Italy</u>, but they went to <u>Greece</u> instead.
> 3 <u>I</u> would have driven, but <u>Jane</u> wanted to drive.
> 4 He said he would <u>wait</u> for me, but he went <u>without</u> me.
> 5 We were about to <u>buy</u> a <u>new</u> TV, but Jimmy <u>gave</u> us an <u>old</u> one.

Speaking

13 Ask students to choose a situation in pairs and make up an excuse to explain what happened, using the future in the past. They can write down what they plan to say, or make short notes. They then tell another pair and listen to their excuses. Elicit examples from the whole class and ask students to vote for the best ones.

Homework

Ask students to write 100–120 words about their memory – what they remember and forget, and how they help themselves remember things.

11c Who's a clever bird, then?

Lead-in

Personal response
Ask: *What is your experience of parrots? What do you know about them?* Elicit some responses, questions and comments from the whole class.

Using words
Ask students to look at the heading and the picture in the article and explain what they think the title means. Explain that this a stock phrase used to animals and small children. For example, a grandparent might say to a small grandchild, *'Who's a lovely boy, then?'* or *'Who's a lucky girl, then?'* It is one of the phrases that speaking parrots are often taught or are expected to say. It is also used ironically to adults, e.g. an adult might say to a male friend who has won some money, *'Who's a lucky boy, then?'*

Reading

1 Ask students to work in pairs to discuss the intelligence of any domestic animals they know about, and what things they do that show they are intelligent. Elicit some examples and observations from the whole class and encourage comment and questions.

2 Ask students to read the article and say how Alex showed his intelligence. Elicit the answer from the whole class. Check students understand the key language in the article (see Vocabulary notes below).

> **ANSWER**
> by separation of objects by shape and colour, by doing arithmetic, by telling other parrots to 'talk clearly'

Vocabulary notes

deliberately = on purpose, intentionally

futile = of no use

to imitate = to copy, to do the same thing as someone else

to learn by heart = to memorise

a perch = a wooden bar for a bird to sit on

rare = uncommon, not normal

the dynamics = the changes

a predator = a hunting, meat-eating animal

moody = changing from a good to bad state of mind regularly

3 Ask students to work individually to decide if the statements are true, false, or not in the article, then check with a partner. Elicit answers from the whole class.

> **ANSWERS**
> 1 NA   2 T   3 T   4 F   5 T   6 NA

4 Ask students to discuss the questions in pairs. Then elicit some answers from the whole class.

Background notes

Dr Irene Pepperberg was born in Brooklyn, New York on 1st April 1949. She studied chemistry at university, eventually completing a PhD in chemical physics at Harvard in 1976. However, she made her name through her studies of language, cognition and communication with an African Grey Parrot whom she called Alex. Her studies broke new ground in the field of animal communication, but also drew a great deal of criticism from fellow researchers. Pepperberg, who is currently an adjunct associate professor at Brandeis University, and a lecturer and research associate at Harvard, set up The Alex Foundation to support her research studies. When Alex died prematurely on September 6th, 2008 aged 31, she wrote a book called *Alex & Me*, about her life with the parrot. She has also published *The Alex Studies* about her research.

The African Grey Parrot lives in rain forest in west and central Africa. Adults grow to 33 cm, and have light grey feathers, a cherry-red tail and an all-black beak. The oldest reliable age known for a captive bird is 49.7 years, though records of 73 and 93 have been suggested. They are very popular as pets, not least because of their ability to imitate human sound, and their general intelligence. However, they have been over-exploited by the legal and illegal pet trade, with 350,000 wild birds taken between 1994 and 2003. There are bans and limits worldwide, but this does not always help. Also, their preferred nesting trees are those which are most important for the wood trade, so their habitat is being reduced all the time.

Critical thinking reinforcing ideas

5 Read the rubric with the class and ensure that they understand the concept of the reinforcement of ideas in text. Ask students to find the eight ideas in the text and underline them, then think about how they are reinforced. Elicit the answers from the class.

ANSWERS

1 Para 1: *How does a scientist find out to what extent an animal is capable of thinking?* (reinforced by paraphrase in the next question)
2 Para 2: *decided to investigate the thought processes of another creature by talking to it.* (reinforced by explanation of how, then a quote from Pepperberg)
3 Para 3: *most researchers thought Pepperberg's communication study would be futile.* (reinforced by quote from Pepperberg)
4 Para 4: *Pepperberg wanted to get inside his mind …* (reinforced by examples)
5 Para 5 (top of column 2): *Many of Alex's cognitive skills, such as his ability to understand concepts of 'same' and 'different' are rare …* (reinforced by paraphrase, *Very few animals …*)
6 Para 5: *But parrots, like humans, live a long time in complex societies.* (reinforced by another example of similarity and repetition of 'like humans')
7 Para 7: *Alex ran through various tests* (reinforced by examples of the tests)
8 Para 8: *Alex knew all the answers himself and was getting bored* (reinforced by examples of how he behaves to show this)

6 Elicit suggestions from the class about which method they found most effective. If necessary, explain that the most effective methods are those that get an idea across most clearly. Discuss the ideas put forward.

Word focus *learn*

7 Ask students to find the expressions with *learn* in the text and decide on the meaning in pairs. Elicit answers from the whole class.

ANSWERS

learn as you go along = to learn as you do something (compared to more formal learning, or learning the theory first, then putting it into practice)
learn by heart = to memorise something so you can repeat it exactly (e.g. a poem, a set of facts or dates; *to learn by rote* has a similar meaning)
learn the hard way = to learn something through bad experiences (this is often used about people who stubbornly refuse to take good advice, but then find out by making mistakes)

8 Ask students to read the sentences and decide on the meaning of the expressions with *learn*. They should check with a partner before you elicit answers from the class.

ANSWERS

1 learn the techniques that professionals know
2 learn to do the simpler things before the more difficult ones
3 You can always learn something new, whatever your age.
4 What I did – the mistakes I made – have taught me to be more careful in future (= to learn the hard way).
5 to accept the situation even if we don't like it
6 look at the mistakes that happened in the past and change their behaviour / policy to avoid making the same mistakes

9 Ask students to write two sentences individually, then read them out to a partner, missing out the expressions with *learn*. Their partner has to work out what the missing expression is.

Speaking

10 Ask students to do the quiz on page 154 in pairs. They can then check the answers on page 155. Elicit students' opinions of the results – was the quiz accurate about what kind of learner they think they are?

11 Ask students to work in groups of four to discuss the issues raised. Ask each group to appoint a secretary to note their answers. Elicit ideas from the secretaries, and discuss learning ideas as a class.

Homework

Write 120–150 words about something you would like to learn about, and how you would go about learning it.

11d Keep learning

Materials

Dictionaries for Exercise 1.

Lead-in

Personal response

Ask: *Have you ever done an evening course in something?* Encourage students to talk about what courses they have done, and where and when they did them, and discuss what the teaching and learning was like.

Real life getting clarification

1 Ask students to look at the list of courses at Rousham Adult Education Centre, find out what the courses are and decide which ones they would like to do. Elicit some feedback from the class.

Vocabulary notes

A-level = the exam which UK students take before they leave school at 18, and which qualifies them for university. The exams can also be taken at any time in special colleges.

appreciation = study and understanding of something

composition = how things are positioned in a painting

references = what other paintings, events, people the painting is connected to

to catch = to hear

no worries = (colloquial) that is not a problem

2 [2.37] Read the rubric and questions with the class to focus their listening. Play the recording for them to answer. Play it again, if necessary, and ask students to check their answers with a partner. Elicit answers from the class.

> **ANSWERS**
> 1 history of art
> 2 art appreciation
> 3 He wants to think about it.

Audioscript [2.37]

A = Ahmad (student); **L** = Liz (college receptionist)

A: Hi there, I'm interested in taking a class at your college – umm ... the history of art course.

L: Is that the two-year A-level course?

A: Sorry, what do you mean by A-level?

L: The A-level art history course is a two-year pre-university course with examinations at the end of each year.

A: Oh no, no, no … I don't want to take any exams. It's just for interest.

L: OK. In that case, we have a one-year art appreciation course.

A: Sorry. Could you speak up a little? I can't hear you very well.

L: Yes, we have a one-year art appreciation course.

A: Umm … can you explain what the course involves?

L: Yeah, it's a two-hour class once a week and, basically, it teaches you how to look at art so that you get the most from the experience.

A: No, sorry, I'm not really with you. Are you saying that it doesn't really deal with the history of art?

L: No … there's some history of art in it, of course, but it's mainly learning about composition, techniques, references and so on.

A: Hmm … Could you give me an example of the kind of thing students do in the class?

L: Sure. Typically, students look at works of art and then comment on them. Then they're told more about the artist, what he or she was trying to achieve and then they look at their work again, … with fresh eyes as it were.

A: Mmm, OK. It sounds quite interesting. What was the course called again?

L: Art appreciation.

A: And when is it?

L: Every Tuesday – in term time, that is – from 7 p.m. til 9 p.m., starting on … one minute … yeah, starting on the 29th of September. The cost is £298 for the year, unless you're a registered student.

A: Hang on a second. That's too much to take in all at once. I'm trying to write it down. I didn't catch the start date. Did you say the 29th of November?

L: No, the 29th of September.

A: OK. Well, thanks. I'll have a think about it, but it sounds good.

L: No worries, bye.

3 Read through the phrases in the box with the class to focus their listening. Make sure students understand that Ahmad uses them to ask for repetition or explanation from the receptionist. Play the recording, and have students decide on the use of the phrases and mark them accordingly. If necessary, play the recording again for them to check and complete their answers. Elicit answers from the whole class, having students read a phrase, then say what its use is.

> **ANSWERS**
> 1 What do you mean by…? E
> 2 Can you speak up a little? R
> 3 Can you explain what …? E
> 4 I'm not really with you. E
> 5 Are you saying that …? E
> 6 Could you give me an example of …? E
> 7 What was … again? R
> 8 Hang on a second. That's too much to take in all at once. R
> 9 I didn't catch … R
> 10 Did you say …? R

4 💿 [2.37] Ask students to listen to the recording again and complete the phrases with missing parts. You may need to play it twice. Elicit answers as complete sentences.

ANSWERS

1 What do you mean by A-level?
3 Can you explain what the course involves?
5 Are you saying that it doesn't really deal with the history of art?
6 Could you give me an example of the kind of things the students do in the class?
7 What was the course called again?
9 I didn't catch the start date.
10 Did you say the 29th of November?

Pronunciation linking in question forms

5a 💿 [2.38] Ask students to listen to the recording of the linked questions a couple of times.

Play the recording again, pausing after each phrase for students to repeat chorally and individually.

5b Ask students to say the phrases in the box to a partner, and help each other to use the appropriate linking. If necessary, replay the dialogue (track 2.37), pausing after each of the phrases in Exercise 3 for students to repeat them chorally and individually.

6 Read through the rubric and notes for each role with the class, and ensure that they know what to do. Ask them to get into pairs and act out the dialogue. When they have done it once, ask them to change partners and do it again in the other role. Circulate and monitor their conversations for later feedback.

Homework

Ask students to write 100 words on *An evening course I would like to do* explaining why they would be interested in doing this course.

11e The wrong course

Lead-in

Personal response
Ask: *Have you ever written a letter of complaint? If so, to whom and what about?* Elicit some examples from the class, including what response the students got.

Writing an email about a misunderstanding

1 Ask students to read through the questions to focus their reading of the email. Ensure they are familiar with the words in the multiple choice options. Ask them to read the email and answer the questions individually, then check with a partner. Elicit the answers from the whole class.

ANSWERS

1 b   2 c   3 b

2 Ask the class to give their responses to the question and explain their reasons; discuss any different answers.

SAMPLE ANSWER

The request for a refund is justifiable: the course is more advanced than was originally intended, so it is no longer appropriate for Karen. She is finding it hard to keep up and feels uncomfortable that she is holding other people back.

The tone of the email is very reasonable; Karen is sympathetic to the teacher and the other students. Her reasons for requesting a refund are well explained.

The administrator would be likely to react positively and give a refund.

Extra activity

In the light of the discussion in Exercise 2, ask students to write a letter as the college administrator to Karen Redman, discussing her problem and responding to her request.

Writing skill linking contrasting ideas

3a Ask students to read and find the linking words or phrases individually, then check with a partner. Elicit the answers from the class.

ANSWERS

1 but in fact
2 so despite the fact that
3 on the contrary
4 whereas
5 While

3b Ask students to match the words and phrases individually, then check with a partner. Elicit answers from the whole class.

ANSWERS

1 whereas / while
2 while / So despite the fact that
3 On the contrary / But in fact
4 whereas
5 But in fact

3c Ask students to fill the gaps individually, then check with a partner. Elicit answers from the whole class as complete sentences.

ANSWERS

1 Despite the fact that / although / whilst
2 but in fact / but in reality
3 Although / while
4 but on the other hand
5 whereas / whilst
6 On the contrary

4 Ask students to choose a course from the Rousham College list on page 136, and then write a letter about a misunderstanding that occurred when they enrolled for the course. They might do this for homework.

5 Ask students to exchange letters with a partner and check them using the listed criteria. They should tell their partner what they think.

Extra activity

Students write a reply to the letter they have just read, on behalf of the administrator at Rousham College. They then give it to their partner to read.

11f Paraguay shaman

Before you watch

1 Students work in groups. Ask them to look at the photo and discuss the questions. Take feedback from the class.

2 Ask students to work in pairs to discuss the questions and write their predictions. Elicit ideas from the class.

While you watch

3 Give students time to read through the words in the glossary. Play the whole of the video for students to check their ideas from Exercise 2. They should not try to understand everything at this stage.

ANSWERS

1 The plants are becoming extinct because of deforestation.
2 recording the properties of the plants before they disappear
3 a shaman, his wife, scientific researchers

4 Give students time to read the sentences and underline the information they think is false. Then play the video for them to check and to note the correct information. Give them time to rewrite the sentences correctly, then check the answers as a class.

ANSWERS

1 Before going into the forest, a scientist travels to a local village by **motorbike**.
2 When they arrive, Gervasio, the local shaman, is **chanting and praying.**
3 Gervasio and the team set off to look for **a root / a plant** the scientists are interested in.
4 **Gervasio and his wife** lead the way.
5 The root **is used to treat and cure various illnesses.**
6 Later, back in the village, **Gervasio** looks at a book **the scientist have published.**

5 Give students time to read the questions and answer as many as they can. Then play the video again for them to check and complete their answers.

ANSWERS

1 diabetes, malaria, common fevers and colds, cancer
2 by showing them where the plants are and sharing their knowledge of the plants and their healing properties
3 Because the plants are disappearing quickly.
4 to establish a spiritual connection with the forest
5 Because they think it might be useful for cancer research.
6 help people to identify and study local plants

6 Give students time to read the extracts. Then play the video again for them to number them in the order they hear them.

ANSWERS

1 c   2 e   3 b   4 d   5 a

After you watch

7 Students work in pairs to roleplay interviewing a scientist, according to the instructions. They should change roles and act out the conversation a second time.

8 Students work in groups to discuss the questions.

Videoscript

00.04–00.20 Somewhere in this forest, maybe in this plant or that herb, there could be a cure for an illness like diabetes, malaria, or even common fevers and colds.

But as the plants disappear, the potential cures disappear with them.

00.22–00.54 The rain forests of Paraguay have been a source of medicinal cures for a long time. Traditional folk healers often show us where to find the plants that provide the medicines. Paraguay's famous healers, called 'shamans', have a deep knowledge of local medicinal plants – the equivalent of the knowledge contained in an entire medical library.

But Paraguay has one of the highest deforestation rates in the world.

That's why researchers believe it's a priority to record the shaman's extensive knowledge before the forest disappears.

00.55–01.27 The journey begins in Paraguay's isolated Mbaracayu Forest Nature Reserve and the nearby native community of Tekoha Ryapu, where shaman Gervasio lives.

To reach Gervasio, a group of researchers set out on a long journey through the reserve.

Meanwhile, at the village, Gervasio is using chants and prayers, perhaps to make a spiritual connection with the forest.

When he feels ready, Gervasio and his wife take the group on the search.

01.31–02.03 They are looking for a plant called Suruvi, also known as Jatropha isabelli, which is used to treat and cure various illnesses. Scientists are very interested in this family of plants for cancer research. Gervasio brings the root back to the village where his wife puts it in a pot of water to prepare tea.

Scientists have published a book to help record and transmit Gervasio's forest knowledge. The book helps people to easily identify and study local plants.

02.04–02.24 Recording and studying Paraguayan plants for possible medical cures is urgent business, some may even call it an emergency.

Medicinal plants that were once healthy and multiplying are now disappearing – and the possibility of finding new medical cures is disappearing with them.

UNIT 11 Review

Grammar

1 Ask the class to discuss these questions as a whole. Encourage ideas, comments and questions.

2 Ask students to read the three questions to focus their reading, then read quickly to find the answers. Elicit the answers from the whole class.

> ANSWERS
> 1 someone who speaks several languages well
> 2 teaching languages to people
> 3 54

3 Ask students to underline the correct forms individually, then check with a partner.

> ANSWERS
> 1 was able to explain
> 2 could speak
> 3 succeeded in getting
> 4 couldn't pay
> 5 were going to use
> 6 would have remained
> 7 Was he really able
> 8 was supposed to show

Vocabulary

4 Ask students to complete the passage in pairs, then check with another pair. Elicit answers from the class.

> ANSWERS
> 1 acquire
> 2 trial
> 3 observation
> 4 feeling
> 5 pick
> 6 grasp
> 7 ignorant
> 8 engage

5 Ask students to tell each other about something they can do in pairs, and explain how they learnt to do it.

Real life

6 Ask students to work in pairs to match each pair of phrases which have a similar meaning. Elicit the answers from the class.

> ANSWERS
> 1 d   2 c   3 e   4 a   5 b

7 Ask students to work in pairs to give instructions and ask for clarification and repetition.

Speaking

8 Ask students to work in groups of four to discuss learning experiences.

Unit 12 The economy

Lead-in

Personal response

Ask: *What do you know about the current state of the world economy?* Elicit ideas and information from the whole class, and discuss the present and future global financial situation and the reasons for it.

1 Ask students to work in pairs, looking at the picture and discussing the questions. Elicit answers from the whole class.

2 [2.39] Read through the rubric and questions with the class to focus their listening. Play the recording for them to answer. If necessary, play it again.

> **ANSWERS**
> 1 you spend more than 10 per cent of your earnings on energy; if you earn less than 60 per cent of the average
> 2 if you have all that you need, a good work-life balance and a happy family life.

Audioscript [2.39]

Poverty is a relative concept. For some people being poor may mean not having enough to eat; others consider themselves hard up if they can't afford to go on holiday. Much depends of course on the cost of living, in other words how pricey basic goods and services are. In the UK one definition of poverty is that you spend more than ten per cent of your earnings on energy – that is, the gas and electricity you use in your home. The trouble with this kind of definition is that something like energy might be much more reasonable in one country than another. So sometimes poverty is expressed as a percentage of average national income – for example, if you earn less than 60 per cent of the average, you are classified as poor. Wealth is also a relative concept. Being well off doesn't necessarily mean being loaded and surrounded by luxuries – two cars and a second home in the country. Wealth can also be measured by people's quality of life. You can be considered rich if you have all that you need – the basic necessities – a good work-life balance and a happy family life.

3 Ask students to match the synonyms individually, then check with a partner. Elicit answers from the whole class.

> **ANSWERS**
> 1 b   2 a   3 g   4 e   5 c   6 d   7 f

4 Ask students to work in groups of four and discuss the questions about *rich* and *poor*. Elicit answers from the class for wider discussion.

12a Saving for a rainy day

Lead-in

Using words

Ask students to look at the page heading and article title, *Saving for a rainy day,* and ask them to discuss in pairs what they think the expression means. (*A rainy day* is a metaphor for difficult times: the expression means to save money when you have it, in case there is a time in the future when things aren't so good and you need the extra money.)

Reading

1 Ask students to look at the picture and discuss what they know about Norway in pairs. Elicit answers from the whole class, and discuss the country further.

2 Ask students to read the article and answer the question.

> **ANSWER**
> People have a very good quality of life and the country has a lot of money invested for the future.

Vocabulary note

work ethic = a strong belief in the value of hard work

productivity rates = the amount of goods produced in a particular time

to redefine = changing the way something is seen

maternity / paternity leave = time off work for new mothers and fathers

subsidised = the individual does not pay the full price – the rest is paid by the government

3 Ask students to complete the summaries in pairs, then check with another pair. Elicit answers from the whole class as complete sentences.

> **SAMPLE ANSWERS**
> 1 quality of life
> 2 their natural thrift, strong work ethic
> 3 a good family life, social benefits and long holidays
> 4 its pension fund

4 Ask the class to comment on this question, and discuss the issue together.

Grammar focus adverbs *only, just, even*

5 Read through the examples in the grammar box with the class and ask students to work in pairs to answer the question. Elicit answers from the class. See also the Grammar notes below, and page 172 of the Student's Book for further information and practice.

> **ANSWER**
> c

Grammar note

Point out that *focus adverbs* are so called because they emphasise (or focus on) a particular piece of information. All three adverbs come before the word (noun, verb or adjective) they are focusing on.

Only is used to focus on one thing to the exclusion of all others:

> **Only** *Mike could play the guitar.* (Nobody else could play it.)

> *Mike could* **only** *play the guitar.* (He couldn't play any other instruments.)

> *She's* **only** *joking.* (She isn't serious.)

Note that the change in position of *only* in the same sentence above radically changes the meaning.

Just has a similar meaning and use, but it is slightly less emphatic.

> *She's* **just** *joking.*

> **Just** *Mike's playing the guitar tonight.* (Nobody else is playing.)

Even is used to show we are surprised or shocked.

> *Mike* **even** *writes the songs himself.* (as well as playing the guitar and singing)

> **Even** *Liz couldn't answer it!*

> *Sue's birthday party was* **even** *better than last year's.*

Note that *even* + comparative adjective is quite a common way of showing surprise at a situation.

6 Ask students to find other examples individually, then answer the question. Elicit answers from the class.

> ANSWERS
>
> Para 2: Norway's success is not **only** the result of its huge reserves of oil.
> Para 3: Laws **just** recently passed by the government …
> Para 4: It is not **even** invested in new schools and hospitals
> Yes, they all come before the word they are emphasising.

7 Ask students to work in a group of four to match the sentences to the clauses that would follow. Elicit answers from the whole class, having one student read the sentence and another read the meaning.

> ANSWERS
>
> 1 g   2 e   3 d   4 b   5 f   6 a   7 h   8 c

8 Ask students to complete the sentences with the focus adverbs individually, then check with a partner. Elicit answers from the whole class as complete sentences. Discuss whether the facts are true for the students' countries.

> ANSWERS
>
> 1 … so they **only** see their children …
> 2 **Even** people with university degrees …
> 3 … a job is **just** a way to make money …
> 4 The rich **only** represent … / The rich represent **only** about 5%
> 5 **Even** poor people usually have …
> 6 The state pension **only** gives you … / The state pension gives you **just** enough to live on …

Grammar focus adverbs *too, as well, also*

9 Ask students to read the sentences, and then find similar ones in the article with *also* in them. Elicit from the class what they notice about the position of the words.

> ANSWERS
>
> 1 Norwegians can **also** expect to get a good education.
> 2 It is **also** due to the Norwegians' natural thrift.
> 3 Norwegians **also** work hard.
> 4 **Also**, the country is saving for the future.
>
> *Also* comes before the main verb or after *be* or an auxiliary verb. It can be used at the start of the sentence, followed by a comma.

Grammar note

Point out that these focus adverbs have a similar emphasising function to *just, only* and *even*, but each adverb has fewer possible positions in the sentence, as explained in the grammar box in the Student's Book.

We use *also, as well* and *too* to emphasise something which is additional information to what has already been said.

Note that can also use *as well* and *too* in short sentences:

> Paul: I'm going to the match on Saturday.
> Bill: Me, *too*!
> Paul: I hope our team wins this time!
> Mike and John: We do *as well*!

10 Read through the grammar box with students. Ask students to find the patterns in the article individually, then check with a partner. Elicit the answers from the whole class. If you feel students need more information and practice, refer to page 172 of the Student's Book.

> ANSWERS
>
> 1 sentence + *too*: *the prisons are quite comfortable too!*
> 2 sentence + *as well*: *and long holidays as well.*
> 3 *Also*, + sentence: *Also, the country is saving …*
> 4 *also* + main verb: *Norwegians also work hard …*
> 5 *be* + *also*: *It is also due to …*
> 6 auxiliary verb + *also* + main verb: *Norwegians can also expect …*

11 Explain to students that they need to rewrite each sentence twice, using one of the focus adverbs in each sentence. Ask students to rewrite the sentences in pairs, then check with another pair. Elicit the answers from the whole class as complete sentences.

> SAMPLE ANSWERS
>
> 1 Norwegians are happy that the country is saving for the future, but they would *also* like to see the government increase spending on healthcare. / they would like to see the government increase spending on healthcare *as well*.
> 2 Most countries have high public borrowing and a lot of debt *too*. / and *also* a lot of debt. Norway has neither.
> 3 Teachers in Norway receive a good salary and if they teach 'heavy' subjects, they get extra payments, *too*. / they *also* get extra payments.
> 4 Artists can get a grant – not a loan – from the government of around $20,000 a year and *also* support with childcare. / support with childcare *as well*.
> 5 The prices for food and drink seem very high to outsiders and fuel is expensive, *too*. / fuel is also expensive. However, house prices are relatively low and so property is a good investment.
> 6 Nurses in Norway get 42 weeks' maternity leave on full pay. They *also* have access to the hospital kindergarten when they return to work. / They have access to the hospital kindergarten when they return to work *as well*.

Vocabulary money

12 Ask students to complete the eight phrases with nouns from Exercise 11. They should do this individually, then check with a partner. Elicit answers from the class, having one student read the original phrase and another student the new one.

> ANSWERS
>
> 1 payment   5 loan
> 2 investment   6 debt
> 3 borrowing   7 salary
> 4 spending   8 grant (loan)

Speaking

13 Ask students to work in pairs to prepare questions to ask other pairs about the economy of their countries. They might also make notes about their own countries so they are ready to answer the questions from other students.

14 Ask them to work with a new partner to ask and answer questions.

12b Don't do it yourself

Lead-in

Personal response

Ask: *What would your ideal job be?* Ask for ideas from the whole class, and reasons for their choice. Encourage questions and comments from other students.

Vocabulary domestic help

1 Read through the list of jobs in the box, and ensure that students are familiar with them all. Ask students to look at the picture and tell you what job the woman does.

> ANSWER
>
> a maid

2 Ask students to talk to a partner about the issues raised. Elicit some feedback from the whole class.

Listening

3 [2.40] Read the rubric and the questions with the class to focus their listening. Then play the recording for them to answer. Play it again if necessary. Elicit answers from the whole class. Check any key vocabulary that students need to understand (see Vocabulary notes below).

> ANSWERS
>
> 1 2 million; mostly Eastern Europeans
> 2 He thinks it is a good thing.

Audioscript [2.40]

I = Interviewer, A = male author

I: Thirty years ago, the idea of getting a worker to hand wash your car would have been unthinkable – except to the very rich. Either you washed it yourself at home on a Sunday morning or you took it down to the automatic carwash at your local garage. Nowadays, you can have it washed inside and out by a team of willing and capable workers for as little as £6. So, what's changed? I have here with me David Stiles, author of *The Servant Economy*. David, are we just getting too lazy to do our own domestic chores or is this part of some new economic phenomenon?

A: Well, first of all hello and thanks for inviting onto your programme … um so, yes in answer to your question, it's said that in Britain today there are more workers doing domestic jobs than there were in the 19th century – um … perhaps as many as two million: gardeners, nannies etcetera. And this is a direct consequence of globalisation and the freeing up of the labour market. You see, many of these workers are migrants – in the case of Britain mostly Eastern Europeans. Umm and I think that in capitalist economies, at any rate, the richer classes will always provide employment for the poorer classes. As the Victorian satirist Hilaire Belloc famously said, 'it is the duty of the wealthy man to give employment to the artisan'.

I: Yes, … but that's the point, isn't it? A 19th-century style servant economy actually emphasises the inequalities between rich and poor in a society.

A: Well, hmm … yes, it can do, but it also creates employment. You don't have to be especially rich to have a cleaner come once a week and tidy your house. Quite a lot of working people do that. A lot of so-called ordinary people get their windows cleaned every few months. But there are some – er … rich – people who get it into their heads that they're too busy or important to do any domestic chores. So they'll hire a personal shopper, and have someone walk their dog every day. If they're having a party at home, they'll get an outside catering company to prepare the food. I know some people who even have their Christmas tree installed in their living room and then decorated for them. That really is a statement of wealth.

I: Hmm … it seems more a statement of confused priorities to me. Walking the dog and decorating the Christmas tree are supposed to be a pleasure, aren't they?

A: Mmm … of course, they are. But look at it another way … these are all things that create employment. As long as staff are treated well – you know, as employees, not as servants – and are fairly paid and their skills are valued, just as you would show respect to your hairdresser when you get your hair cut, then I don't see a problem.

Vocabulary notes

unthinkable = nobody would even think of doing it

willing = happy to do something

capable = good at doing something

a servant = somebody who is employed to work in the house

a phenomenon = a situation, an event

globalisation = the increased interaction between different parts of the world

a catering company = a company that cooks meals

a priority = the most important thing

4 [2.40] Ask students to read the three questions, then listen to the recording and answer. If necessary, play the recording again. Elicit answers from the whole class. Read the information in the *Wordbuilding* box with students and discuss this use of *the* + adjective. Other adjectives which are commonly used in this way are *the old, the young, the sick, the infirm, the unemployed*. See also Workbook page 99.

ANSWER

1 gardener, nanny, cleaner, personal shopper, dog walker
2 car washer, servant, hairdresser, Christmas tree decorator, outside caterer
3 Many people employ people like cleaners and car washers, but few people employ outside caterers, Christmas tree decorators, personal shoppers.

5 Ask students to discuss this in pairs, then as a class. Encourage wider discussion of the issue.

ANSWER

The interviewer said: *it seems more a statement of confused priorities to me. Walking the dog and decorating the Christmas tree are supposed to be a pleasure, aren't they?*

6 Ask students to complete the quotation (play that part of the recording again if necessary), then discuss it as a class. Note that the true meaning of *artisan* is a craft person, or someone who makes things with their hands. In the recording the quote is interpreted in the wider context of giving employment to working people.

ANSWER

It is the duty of the **wealthy** man to give employment to the **artisan**.

Grammar causative *have* and *get*

7 Ask students to match the four examples to the two questions individually, then check with a partner.

ANSWERS

1 b, d   2 a, c

8 Read through the grammar box with the class. Point out that *get* constructions are considered more informal than those with *have*.

Ask students to complete the passage individually, then check with a partner. Elicit answers from the class as complete sentences. Refer to page 173 of the Student's Book for further information and practice.

ANSWERS

1 to do	5 to do
2 to help	6 fix
3 done	7 organise
4 cleaned	8 looked

9 Ask students to complete the sentences individually, then check with a partner. Elicit answers from the class as complete sentences. Note that all the sentences can be completed in two ways except the first.

ANSWERS

1 got someone to organise
2 have a personal trainer take their children / have their children taken
3 have a driver pick up their children / have their children picked up
4 have a travel consultant choose their holidays / have their holidays chosen for them
5 they get a nanny to look after their children / get their children looked after
6 get someone to pack their bags / get their bags packed

10 Ask students to choose their two things individually, then compare them with a partner's. Elicit some from the class.

Pronunciation the sounds /ʃ/, /tʃ/, /ʒ/ and /dʒ/

11a ⊙ [2.41] Ask students to read the words and think about how they are said. Play the recording two or three times, while students listen and follow. Ask them to practise saying them with a partner.

11b ⊙ [2.42] Ask students to look at the words in the box and think about how they are pronounced. Play the recording and ask them to discuss with a partner which of the four sounds in Exercise 11a are in each word. Elicit answers from the class. Then ask students to practise them with their partner.

ANSWERS

/ʃ/	/tʃ/	/ʒ/	/dʒ/
fashion	cheese	television	agent
sugar	choice	usual	arrange
champagne			general
			January

Vocabulary and speaking

12 Ask students to match the verbs and the nouns to create DIY jobs in pairs. They can then check with another pair. Elicit answers from the whole class. Make sure students are familiar with some of the less common words (see Vocabulary notes below).

ANSWERS

assemble – some shelves, a bed
clean – a carpet, the bathroom
decorate – the bathroom
do – the garden, the roof
fit – a carpet, some shelves, a tap
fix – a tap, the roof
hang – a picture, some curtains
plaster – a wall
put up – some shelves, a picture, some curtains
tile – a wall, the bathroom

Vocabulary notes

to plaster = to use a mixture of lime, sand and water for making a smooth covering on walls

to fit = to put something into place by making it exactly the right size and shape (e.g. kitchen cupboards, carpet)

to put up = to attach to a wall

13 Ask students to look at the picture in pairs, and list the jobs that need to be done. Then they should decide what they will do themselves and what they will get help for. They should then exchange ideas with another pair.

12c The gift economy

Lead-in

Personal response
Ask: *What do you know about contemporary life in Japan?* Elicit anything students can tell you about customs, traditions, politics, problems, the economy.

Reading

1 Ask the class what they think the title of the section and the article means. Don't say whether they are correct or not, just encourage them to discuss ideas.

2 Ask students to read the article and find out what a gift economy is, and three examples of it. Elicit answers from the whole class.

ANSWERS

A gift economy is where people work for each other and share everything.
examples: stone-age hunter-gatherers; Japanese companies; neighbourhood groups on the Internet

---

3 Ask students to choose the correct options individually, then check with a partner. Elicit the answers from the class. Check that students are familiar with the key words in the text (see Vocabulary notes).

ANSWERS

1 a   2 b   3 c   4 b   5 c   6 b

Vocabulary notes

greed = wanting more than you really need

the essence of = the basic nature of

social bonds = interpersonal connections

to strive for = to try very hard

sound (adj) = solid, good quality

abundance = plenty, when there is lots

to thrive = to flourish, to do well

excess = too much

gain = benefit

4 Ask students to match the words and meanings individually, then check with a partner.

ANSWERS

1 a gain	b reward
2 a thrive	b strive
3 a mutual	b common
4 a excess	b abundance
5 a prospects	b aspects
6 a accuracy	b promptness

---

5 Ask students to work in groups of four to discuss the nature of employer–employee relationships in their own country. Elicit ideas from the whole class.

Critical thinking signposts to key information

6 Ask students to find the phrases in the article, and decide what the key information is that they refer to.

7 Students should check with a partner. Elicit answers from the whole class.

ANSWERS

The real essence of human nature lies in the social bonds … (paragraph 1) – social bonds are what is most important for humans

shared social interests that is at the heart of the gift economy (paragraph 1) – the gift economy is based fundamentally on shared social interests

But this is not only an idea that applies to a more primitive way of life. There are also many recent examples … (paragraph 2) – the idea is still valid today as well as being something that dates from early human society

Rather, they felt they were entering into a long-term – 'gift exchange' – relationship (paragraph 3) – contrasts with US system and emphasises the importance of the long-term relationship to the Japanese

the main gift given by the employees (paragraph 4) – the most important thing that the workers gave the company

---

Word focus hard

8 Ask students to work in pairs to find the three expressions with *hard* and then discuss their meanings. Elicit meanings from the whole class.

ANSWERS

Paragraph 4: *their hard work*: conscientious work, effort
Paragraph 6: *these are hard times*: difficult times
Paragraph 6: *drive the hardest bargain:* get the outcome that is the most profitable for them

---

9 Ask students in pairs to discuss the meanings of the six expression with *hard*, then discuss their ideas with another pair. Elicit ideas on meaning from the whole class.

ANSWERS

1 bad feelings (resentment, jealousy)
2 poor / short of money
3 bad luck (an expression for showing sympathy)
4 badly or unfairly treated
5 be critical, without understanding the other person
6 focused on the financial or commercial benefits, not affected by sentiment or personal considerations

---

Speaking

10 Ask students to work in groups of three to discuss gift giving customs.

12d The bottom line

Lead-in

Personal response
Ask: *What do you understand by the word 'negotiating'? What types of negotiations have you been involved in?* Elicit examples from students' work and personal life for questions and comment.

Using words
Make sure students understand the section title *the bottom line*, meaning the point beyond which someone will not go. For example, if you are trying to sell a painting, you might think, '*I am asking £12,000 for it, and I am prepared to negotiate down a bit, but £10,000 is the bottom line.*'

Real life negotiating

1 Ask students to read the Herb Cohen quote, and then discuss their views on it as a class.

Background notes

Herb Cohen was an internationally important American negotiator. He worked with major companies such as General Motors, government organisations such as the CIA and FBI, and at the US – Soviet Union START Arms Control Negotiations. He began formally teaching negotiation in 1963, and went on to work for many US universities. His two main publications are the bestseller *You Can Negotiate Anything,* which has been translated into 30 languages, and his 2003 book *Negotiate This! By Caring Not T-H-A-T Much.*

2 🔘 **[2.43]** Read through the rubric and the questions with the class to focus their listening. Make sure students understand all the language in the rubric, and what the woman is doing (trying to make an agreement about the use of a building for her business – she is speaking to the letting agent, or the person who manages the lease on the building and liaises with the owner). Play the recording for them to answer the questions; play it again if necessary. Elicit answers from the whole class.

ANSWERS

1 The woman seems to really want the building, she cares a lot. The agent doesn't seem to care at all, he says there are other people who are interested and that they can find someone else (though this might not be true).
2 how long the lease should be for, and whether it can be changed
3 a get-out clause with a forfeit after six years
4 The woman phones her partner to see what he thinks about the situation.

Audioscript 💿 [2.43]

LA = letting agent; W = woman

LA: So, you've had a look at the offices. What do you think?

W: Well, yeah, I really like the building. To be honest, it's absolutely perfect for our needs.

LA: That's wonderful. So you'd like to take it then?

W: Well, yes, ideally I would but … mmm a key thing for us is how long we'd be tied into the lease.

LA: Er … It's a fifteen-year lease. I think that was on the details I sent you.

W: Yes, it was but I was hoping we could negotiate that down. Because if you look at it from our point of view … we're a young business … umm … we don't really know how things are going to go over the next few years … who does? … and let's face it, fifteen years is a big commitment. So if your client could move a bit on that …

LA: Hmm … I think what you have to appreciate is that our client's main concern is to secure a rental for a reasonable length of time. You know, at the end of the day, it gives them some security. To tell you the truth, that's why the rent is so low. The fifteen-year period is a kind of compensation for that. So I'm not at all sure we're going to get anywhere there …

W: Oh … that's a bit of a sticking point then, isn't it? Is there not some way around that?

LA: Er … Not that I can think of offhand. What did you have in mind?

W: Well, perhaps if we signed a fifteen-year lease but with a get-out clause after, say, six years, then we could pay some kind of forfeit to get out of the contract.

LA: Um … well the normal forfeit would be that you paid the remaining nine years' rent, so I don't really think that would work …

W: Oh, I see. Well, that's a shame because I really like it and we need somewhere pretty urgently.

LA: Look, we have other people interested in the premises, so someone will take it … If I were in your shoes … you know … and found the terms of the lease difficult, I think I'd just leave it. When all's said and done, it has to feel right for you.

W: But that's just the problem it does feel right for us. Give me a moment. I'm just going to call my business partner and see what he thinks …

LA: OK no problem …

Vocabulary notes

a lease = a contract for the rent of a property for a set number of years

to be tied to = committed to something (e.g. by contract)

a sticking point = a point on which you cannot reach agreement

to be offhand = to take something lightly, not seriously

a get-out clause = a part of the contract which fixes terms if one person breaks the contract

a forfeit = an amount of money to pay as compensation

3 💿 [2.43] Read through the phrases in the box with the whole class, and make sure they understand them. Play the recording and ask students to fill the gaps. If necessary play it again for them to complete and check their answers. Elicit answers from the class as complete sentences.

> **ANSWERS**
>
> 1 perfect for our needs   6 move a bit
> 2 tied into   7 is so low
> 3 negotiate that down   8 leave it
> 4 young business   9 feel right
> 5 big commitment

4 Ask students to discuss the uses of the phrases in the box with a partner. Elicit suggestions from the whole class.

> **ANSWERS**
>
> Say what the important thing is: *A key thing for us is / Our client's main concern is*
>
> Be direct: *To be honest / Let's face it / At the end of the day / To tell you the truth / If I were in your shoes / When all's said and done*
>
> Talk about an obstacle to the agreement: *That's a bit of a sticking point / Is there not some way around that? / Perhaps if we … , then we could …*
>
> Ask the other person to see your side: *If you look at it from our point of view / I think what you have to appreciate is that …*

5 Ask students to discuss in pairs how the negotiators could have done better. Elicit suggestions from the whole class, and encourage discussion and comments.

> **ANSWER**
>
> The woman showed that she wanted the property too much: she wasn't prepared to walk away. The agent didn't make any compromise, but he might have ended up getting a better deal in the end because of this.

Pronunciation sentence stress in idiomatic phrases

6a 💿 [2.44] Ask students to look at the five phrases and try to decide which words are most stressed in each of them. Play the recording, and ask them to underline the stressed words. Play it again for them to check and complete their answers. Elicit answers from the whole class. Play the recording again, pausing after each phrase for students to repeat chorally and individually.

> **ANSWERS**
>
> 1 To be honest …
> 2 A key thing for us is …
> 3 Let's face it …
> 4 At the end of the day, …
> 5 To tell you the truth …

6b 💿 [2.44] Ask students to look at the six phrases and try to decide which words are most stressed. Play the recording, and ask them to underline the stressed words. Play it again for them to check and complete their answers. Elicit answers from the whole class. You may need to explain that phrases 2 and 3 mean the same as *When all's said and done* and *At the end of the day*. Play the recording again, pausing after each phrase for students to repeat chorally and individually. Then ask students to work in pairs to practise saying the phrases from Exercises 6a and b.

ANSWERS

1 The <u>bottom</u> line for <u>us</u> is …
2 The <u>long</u> and <u>short</u> of it is …
3 The <u>fact</u> of the <u>matter</u> is …
4 <u>One</u> thing that's <u>bothering</u> me is …
5 To be <u>frank</u>, …
6 Am <u>I</u> <u>right</u> in <u>thinking</u> that … ?

7 Read through the rubric with the class to set the scene, then ask them to get into pairs and look at the relevant pages (153 and 155) to find their instructions. Ask them to do the roleplay together. Then they can change partners and play the other role. Circulate and monitor their negotiations for later feedback.

12e This is what I propose

Lead-in

Personal response

Ask: *Have you ever written a report?* Elicit some responses and encourage students to ask each other for details.

Writing a report

1 Ask the class to read and comment on the quotation by Pascal as a class.

ANSWER

What he meant was that it takes longer to write something short, because one has to be more careful and precise with one's words, and the drafting and cutting process takes time.

2 Ask the class to look at the four qualities and say which one Pascal was referring to. Also check students understand the significance of the other three elements mentioned.

ANSWER

conciseness

Background note

Pascal (1623–1662) was a French child prodigy, who became an important mathematician, physicist, inventor and philosopher. As a teenager he invented the world's first mechanical calculator, after three years' work and 50 prototypes. He went on to build 20 of them over the next ten years. He wrote influential papers on projective geometry and probability theory. His writings on religious philosophy – the *Provincial Letters* and the more famous *Pensées (Thoughts)* published after his death – were very influential, and the latter is among the classics of French prose writing. He worked on the barometer and pressure, invented the hydraulic press and the syringe, and also inaugurated the first bus route in the world in Paris. In his honour we still have the Pascal (a unit of pressure), Pascal (a computer programming language), Pascal's Law (relating to hydrostatic pressure) and Pascal's Triangle (mathematics).

3 Ask students to read the report individually and decide what the aim and the recommendation are, then tell a partner. Elicit the answers from the whole class.

ANSWERS

Aim: to report on potential new office space
Recommendation: to rent the premises

Writing skill sub-headings and bullet points

4a Ask the class to read the report in Exercise 3 again and answer the question about organisation.

> **ANSWER**
>
> It is in note form, not in full sentences (noun phrases, few verbs)

4b Ask students to read the unformatted report below the rubric and rewrite it as indicated. Point out to students that they should write a summary and an advantages section. The disadvantages will be dealt with in the next exercise.

> **SAMPLE ANSWER**
>
> **Summary**
>
> Last month the company sent me on a two-week 'professional English' course at Falcon Business Language Training in London, staying with a host family in west London. I was very impressed by the course:
>
> **Advantages**
> * well organised
> * spoke English in school and at home
> * teachers very professional – good knowledge of business world
> * small groups – individual attention

4c Ask students to compare their report with a partner, and comment on the similarities and differences.

5 Ask students to complete the report with disadvantages and a recommendation. They should then exchange it with a partner.

> **SAMPLE ANSWER**
>
> **Disadvantages**
> * little focus on my particular job (engineer)
>
> **Recommendation**
>
> I would recommend Falcon Business Language Training as a suitable school for other colleagues to attend an English language course. Not only are the staff very professional, and the teaching personalised, but living with a host family is also very beneficial for maximising English speaking time. The lack of focus on language for a particular job is not really a major issue, as the rest more than makes up for this.

6 Ask students to read their partner's report and make comments based on the three criteria given.

12f Japan

Before you watch

1 Students work in groups. Ask them to look at the photos and discuss the questions.

> **SAMPLE ANSWERS**
>
> The main photo shows a man pouring tea in what looks like a Japanese tea ceremony. He is in a Japanese garden. The smaller photo shows a busy Japanese city at night. The caption refers to the traditional Japanese identity, and the modern identity of an international city.

2 Ask students to write down the things they associate with Japan. Take feedback from the class.

While you watch

3 Play the whole of the video for students to check their ideas from Exercise 2.

4 Give students time to read the numbers. Then play the first part of the video (to 02.04) for them to write what they refer to.

> **ANSWERS**
>
> 1 the population of Japan
> 2 the number of main islands that make up Japan
> 3 the population of Tokyo
> 4 the Meiji restoration
> 5 the bombing of Pearl Harbour
> 6 the bombing of Hiroshima and Nagasaki, the surrender of Japan

5 Give students time to read the questions. Then play the second part of the video (02.05 to the end) for them to write the answers.

> **ANSWERS**
>
> 1 a democratic constitution
> 2 its cultural emphasis on education
> 3 a ritual   b simplicity   c the beauty of daily routine
> 4 European Impressionist painters

6 Give students time to match the sentence beginnings with the endings. Then play the video for them to check.

> **ANSWERS**
>
> 1 a   2 d   3 b   4 e   5 c

7 Ask students to work in pairs to describe the painting.

> **SAMPLE ANSWER**
>
> The painting shows two women standing in the foreground. One is holding an umbrella. There are also some trees and part of a building or shrine. In the background there is a lake with a bridge, and a small boat. There are three birds in the sky. Everything is covered with fresh snow.

After you watch

8 Students work in pairs to roleplay a conversation between two generations, according to the instructions.

9 Students work in pairs to discuss the questions.

Videoscript

Part 1

00.15–01.10 It is a land of dual identities, one of neon glitz and industrial innovation, the other given to the quiet shrines of Kyoto and honoured tea ceremonies.

With a population of over 127 million people, Japan is a country that harmonises the forces of what is western and modern with those that are traditional Japanese.

It is a place where American baseball isn't out of place next to Sumo wrestling.

The country of Japan is comprised of a chain of islands stretching from north to south in the Pacific Ocean just off the Asian mainland.

Honshu is the largest of the four main islands. The country's capital, Tokyo, is here.

The bustling urban area of greater Tokyo is the largest metropolitan area on Earth with a population of 35 million people.

01.11–01.48 The path to modernisation was forged under the Meiji restoration of 1868. It was at this time, warlords known as shogun returned power to the Emperor Meiji and Japan began moving away from its feudal past.

It looked to the West for a new, more modern political and industrial model. Before long, Japan was one of the dominant powers in Asia and began expanding its influence in the region, occupying parts of Korea, and gaining influence over parts of China in the early 20th century.

01.49–02.05 When World War II broke out, Japan sided with the Axis powers of Italy and Germany. Its bombing raid on the US naval station at Pearl Harbour, Hawaii, on December 7th 1941, brought the United States into World War II.

02.06–02.19 The Japanese war effort came to an end when US Allied Forces dropped atomic bombs on Hiroshima and Nagasaki in August 1945. A week later, Japan surrendered.

Part 2

02.20–03.01 The post-war period has been one of incredible prosperity for Japan. The government is firmly rooted in democracy under a constitution based on drafts prepared by the Allied Forces.

Although it is a land of few natural resources, Japan has become one of the most industrialised countries in the world.

Its cultural emphasis on education has helped it become a world leader in technology, manufacturing and finance. Its products are exported around the world with brands like Sony and Toyota virtually ubiquitous.

03.02–03.43 But beyond the bullet trains and neon of Tokyo, there lies a rich cultural tradition.

In private life, guests may be honoured in a tea ceremony. The emphasis in this ceremony is on ritual, simplicity and the beauty of daily routine.

Those themes are echoed in the arts, where painters like Hiroshige captured moments of life and were a great influence on European Impressionist painters.

03.44–03.57 Today, Japan continues to be a source of industrial innovation and an important leader in the international community, while keeping its traditions and culture always in focus.

UNIT 12 Review

Grammar

1 Ask students to read the article quickly and say what caused Japan's poverty problem.

> ANSWERS
>
> Workers had no social security benefits, and older people had to live on their savings when they retired.

2 Ask students to decide where the focus adverbs should go in the sentences individually, then check with a partner.

> ANSWERS
>
> 1 But *even* the so-called advanced economies …
> 2 Japan, for example, *just* a few decades ago …
> 3 … with *only* the USA having a higher rate.
> 4 One reason was that Japan *also* had one of the …
> 5 … contributed to the problem *as well*.
> 6 It is *even* beginning to be a problem already.

3 Ask students to put the correct verb form to complete the advice.

> ANSWERS
>
> 1 checked   2 play, to ask   3 cut, to help   4 to see

Vocabulary

4 Ask students to match words in the two columns individually, then check with a partner.

> ANSWERS
>
> hard up – poor; hang – put up; decorate – paint; borrow from the bank – take out a loan; cheap – reasonable; income – earnings; nanny – child-minder; owe money – have a debt

5 Ask students to work in pairs to make these two lists.

Real life

6 Ask students to order the conversation with a partner, then check with another pair.

> ANSWERS
>
> 1 TA: So we're suggesting …
> 2 C: Yes it is, but to be honest …
> 3 TA: What you have to appreciate …
> 4 C: I know they aren't …
> 5 TA: I understand that …
> 6 C: I was hoping …
> 7 TA: To tell you the truth …
> 8 C: Perhaps if we stayed …
> 9 TA: OK, I'll give them a call …

7 Ask students to continue the negotiation in pairs.

Speaking

8 Ask students to work in groups of four and discuss the idea, then think of another domestic service idea.

Grammar summary: answer key

Unit 1

1

2 c   3 c   4 c   5 b   6 c   7 a   8 b

2

2 New plans are made all the time.
3 Some new laws are being brought in (by the government).
4 The whole system has been changed since I was a student.
5 The old way of life is being forgotten (by young people).
6 Good manners haven't been seen for a very long time.
7 A lot of the old customs are still being respected.
8 Is the way that people used to live being respected?

Unit 2

1

2 have you ever read
3 didn't like
4 enjoyed
5 hasn't studied
6 wrote
7 have told
8 did you find out

2

1 was walking
2 was
3 had been shining
4 was setting
5 heard
6 had come
7 ran
8 reached
9 saw
10 had slipped
11 had fallen
12 was struggling
13 took
14 jumped
15 caught
16 dragged

Unit 3

1

1 starts
2 Are … going to go
3 'll give
4 will be
5 'm meeting
6 are giving
7 start
8 's
9 'll try
10 is about to / is going to

2

2 will have designed
3 will have made
4 will have discovered
5 will be working
6 will be studying

Unit 4

1

2 lots of
3 much
4 few
5 many
6 a little
7 almost no
8 enough

2

2 Every / Each
3 both
4 either
5 No
6 Each

Unit 5

1

2 growing
3 to lend
4 to invest
5 starting
6 to give

2

2 borrowing
3 to inform
4 to ask
5 to bring
6 changing

Unit 6

1

2 doesn't (didn't) want
3 not tell
4 not to book
5 don't think
6 not to stop

2

3 did she
4 Haven't
5 will they
6 would they
7 Didn't he
8 Wouldn't she

Unit 7

1

2 hadn't protested, would be
3 would have applied, knew
4 had, would join / would have joined
5 hadn't worked, wouldn't have been
6 hadn't written, wouldn't feel

2

2 would stop
3 hadn't flooded
4 understood
5 had considered
6 weren't / wasn't
7 didn't let
8 had left

Unit 8

1

2 admitted that she had informed the press.
3 thanked me for reading her article.
4 complained about having to write business reports.
5 apologised for making the mistake.
6 invited me to come to the newspaper office the next day.
7 offered to give me a lift to the press conference.
8 told me that I shouldn't send that email.

2

2 It is understood that those people lived there for twenty years.
3 It is suggested that people will travel to Mars next year.
4 It was thought that women were less intelligent.
5 It was said that men had not seen the Arctic ice then.
6 It was not believed that newspapers would become so powerful.

Unit 9

1

2 –
3 the
4 the
5 –
6 –
7 the
8 –
9 –
10 The

2

2 This is the desert where the fossils were discovered.
3 Equipment left on Mount Everest is regularly removed.
4 That is the biologist whose papers were lost in the storm.
5 Lake Titicaca, on the border of Bolivia and Peru, is very large.
6 The prototype created by GreenSpace was copied by a rival company.

Unit 10

1

2 They will do anything to avoid getting wet.
3 James always rides his bike everywhere.
4 Nicola is always talking with her mouth full.
5 He always stays at work until 7.00 or 8.00 in the evening.
6 Cats will sleep all day rather than go out.
7 My mum is always complaining about the mess in my bedroom.
8 Jack gets to work early most days.

2

2 c   3 b   4 c   5 a   6 b   7 b   8 a

Unit 11

1

2 b   3 a   4 a   5 a

2

2 would work
3 would have told
4 was supposed to bring
5 were going to start
6 was about to say
7 would have told
8 would pass

Unit 12

1

2 too
3 even
4 as well
5 only
6 just
7 also
8 too

2

2 I had the accountant go over my accounts on Saturday.
3 We got the mortgage rate fixed last week.
4 She got her neighbour to pay for the new fence this afternoon.
5 He got a friend to open an account last summer.
6 She had a new credit card sent out this morning.

Photocopiable tests

Unit 1 Test

Grammar

1 Complete the sentences with the correct form of the verb. Use the present simple, continuous, perfect simple or perfect continuous.

1 Paul _____ in a bank. (work)
2 Jane _____ in Australia for two years now. (live)
3 Mike can't come to the phone – he _____ a shower. (have)
4 Jim _____ never _____ to the USA. (be)
5 Where _____ Peter _____ tennis at the weekend? (play)
6 _____ you _____ the new James Bond film? (see)
7 How _____ he _____ on at school at the moment? (get)

(14 points)

2 Rewrite the sentences in the passive. Do not include *by + agent.*

1 The aid workers always give food to the children first.
_____

2 The guide is showing the guests around the hospital.
_____

3 My friends have helped me a lot with my English.
_____

4 The man often tells me news about our neighbours.
_____

(8 points)

3 Rewrite the passive sentences as active sentences.

1 Foxes are regularly seen around here by the residents.
_____

2 All the flats are being used by holidaymakers.
_____

3 The car has been used by several people recently.
_____

4 My mother is being helped by my sister this week.
_____

(8 points)

Vocabulary

4 Circle the word which matches the description.

1 A person you meet every day at the office.
   a a flatmate   **b** a workmate   **c** a fellow student
2 Someone you've known for a very long time.
   a an old friend   **b** a true friend   **c** a mutual friend
3 A person who lives in the same place as you.
   a a fair-weather friend   **b** a workmate   **c** a flatmate
4 Someone who is a friend in good and bad times.
   a an old friend   **b** a true friend   **c** a mutual friend
5 Someone who studies at the same place as you.
   a a flatmate   **b** a workmate   **c** a fellow student

(10 points)

5 Read the sentences. Match the uses of *get* to a word with similar meaning in the box.

be (in passive sentences)   catch   do / manage   persuade
reach   receive

1 We got the train from London to Glasgow.
2 We got to the office in time for the meeting.
3 Jon is getting on very well at school.
4 I couldn't get him to agree to the plan.
5 I got a phone call from the bank today.
6 We got introduced to some interesting people.

(12 points)

6 Match the words 1–9 with the words a–i.

1 mutual	**a** acquaintance
2 passing	**b** friend
3 strong	**c** companion
4 true	**d** bond
5 faithful	**e** relative
6 blood	**f** mate
7 fellow	**g** student
8 flat	**h** respect

(8 points)

Functions

7 Put the expressions in the box into the correct spaces in the conversation.

Do you see much of	What have you been up to?
a nice surprise!	I don't mean to be rude
You're looking well	

CAROL: Jane! What [1] _____
JANE: Carol! How nice to see you! [2] _____
CAROL: I've been working up in Yorkshire.
JANE: Oh, how interesting! [3] _____
CAROL: Thank you. And what about you?
         [4] _____ Peter these days?
JANE: No, I haven't seen him for ages! Look, Carol,
         [5] _____, but I need to get back to work.
         Why don't we meet up one evening – I'll give you a ring!
CAROL: OK, that'll be great!

(10 points)

Unit 1 Test

Writing

8a Read this informal email. Circle the most suitable expressions.

> Dear [1] *Mike / Sir*,
>
> I hope all's well with you. I'm fine. As we've not been in touch for a while, I just wanted to let you know what I [2] *'m up to / 'm occupied with* at present.
>
> I've been staying with Larry Jones for the last month up here in Scotland. It's been pretty cold lately, although without much rain, so I have been able to get out and do some sketches and watercolours for my exhibition.
>
> [3] *It is my intention / My plan is* to come back to London in early June, so that I have a month to prepare everything for the exhibition. I hope you and Suzie will be around at that time, so we can do some things together. Write 12th July in your diary and keep the evening free for the opening! [4] *I hope we can arrange a meeting / I'm looking forward to seeing you* when I get back.
>
> [5] *All the best / Yours faithfully*,
>
> Jonny

(5 points)

8b Now write a similar letter to a friend, with three paragraphs, as follows:

1 introduction
2 your present situation
3 your future plans

_____
_____
_____
_____
_____
_____
_____
_____
_____

(15 points)

Speaking

9 Talk about three people you know in different ways. Explain your relationship with each one, and how the relationships are different.

(10 points)

Unit 2 Test

Writing

7a Complete the extract from the story with the words from the box.

screamed	stumbled	muttered	wearily	apprehensively

The weather was getting worse as the boys [1] _____ along the mountain path.

'I'm so tired,' said Steve [2] _____ . 'Is there much further to go?'

'About a kilometre,' answered Kate, 'but it's not easy going, I'm afraid.'

Steve [3] _____ something about stopping for a rest, but nobody bothered to comment because we knew we had to get back to the camp before night.

Kate lead the way, but as she turned the corner, she [4] _____ and jumped back.

'What is it?' asked Robert, running up to where she was standing and pointing.

He looked down [5] _____ to where our camp had been.

'Oh no,' he said quietly. The rain had washed everything away.

(5 points)

7b Continue the story, describing what the people did next, and how the story ended. Use as many descriptive verbs and adjectives as you can.

_____
_____
_____
_____
_____
_____
_____
_____
_____
_____

(15 points)

Speaking

8 Tell a story about something interesting that happened to a member of your family, or someone you know. Include as many details as possible and use interesting language.

(10 points)

Unit 2

Grammar

1 Complete the sentences with the past simple or present perfect form of the verbs.

1 _____ he ever _____ the Ayrton Senna film? (watch)

2 Paul _____ me the story yesterday. (not tell)

3 I _____ her about three times. (meet)

4 When _____ they _____ the story for the first time? (hear)

5 We _____ carefully to what the old man told us. (listen)

6 The girls _____ what they were doing there yet. (not explain)

7 They _____ several good new novels last week. (buy)

8 Mike still _____ us his African diary. (not send)

(16 points)

2 Circle the correct form of the verb in these sentences.

1 Mike *was / had been* living there for two months when I met him.

2 The boys *were / had been* walking along the road when they saw the bear.

3 I *was / had been* having a shower when the phone rang.

4 My sister *was / had been* applying for jobs for months when she finally got one.

5 Martina *went / had been* there twice last year.

6 I was bored because Steve *told / had told* us this story many times before.

7 Sally *visited / had visited* them several times before she took me.

(14 points)

Vocabulary

3 Complete the sentences with the adjectives from the box.

objective	scary	gripping	touching
thought-provoking		original	

1 The film gave my friends and me a lot to discuss over the next few days. It was really _____ .

2 I think the director was very _____ – he gave the facts, and didn't give his own feelings.

3 It was such a _____ love story – the audience were in tears for half the film!

4 I think he's a very _____ director – he is always experimenting with different genres and styles.

5 I couldn't sleep after watching that horror film – it was so _____ !

6 I enjoyed that thriller – the story was so _____ I just couldn't look away.

(12 points)

4 Circle the correct word to complete each sentence.

1 They chose a really good _____ in which to make the film.
   a scene   b storyline   c setting

2 This film is going to be very popular – it might even be a _____ .
   a best-seller   b blockbuster   c box office

3 I love working with John – he's such a good _____ .
   a director   b cast   c audience

4 Her _____ of the heroine was absolutely brilliant.
   a portrayal   b character   c actor

5 I enjoy his books. All his _____ are really believable.
   a audience   b cast   c characters

6 It's an exciting story with a fast-moving _____ .
   a location   b plot   c theme

(6 points)

5 Complete the sentences with the words in the box.

an eye on	his chin up	a secret	track of	you	a diary

1 It's very hard to keep _____ our customers if we don't have a good database.

2 In traditional stories, the hero always has to keep _____ in the face of problems.

3 I can easily find out what I was doing then, because I keep _____ every day.

4 The new girl should be OK, but can you keep _____ her for me, please?

5 I'm sorry to keep _____ after five o'clock, but I need to ask you about the accounts.

6 I want to tell you about Dick, but I need to know that you can keep _____ first.

(12 points)

Functions

6 Circle the phrase which best completes the conversation.

JIM: How are you this morning, Liz?

LIZ: Well, my car broke down on the way to work.

JIM: Oh, no! ¹*That's odd! / That's awful! / That's lucky!*

LIZ: I know. I was on a very busy road, too.

JIM: Really? ²*How strange! / That was a relief. / Poor you!*

LIZ: Luckily John came past and he stopped to help me.

JIM: Well, ³*that was lucky. / well done! / that was clever.*

LIZ: Yeah, it was. He got a mechanic to look at the car, but he found there was no petrol in it!

JIM: Oh, dear. ⁴*Phew! / How embarrassing! / That was lucky.*

LIZ: Yeah, I felt really stupid.

JIM: Well, I once had the ⁵*similar thing / same experience / a nightmare …*

(10 points)

Unit 3 Test

Grammar

1 Circle the correct future verb forms.

1 You need a microphone? I _____ one for you.
   a am getting   b get   c will get

2 Ladies and Gentlemen, quiet please.
   The lecture _____ .
   a starts   b is about to start   c will start

3 We _____ the speakers at ten o'clock.
   a meet   b are about to meet   c are meeting

4 The train _____ early in the morning.
   a leaves   b is about to leave   c is going to leave

5 I am afraid you _____ late for the opening lecture.
   a are about to be   b are being   c are going to be

6 Many cities _____ twice as big in the next twenty years.
   a are growing   b will grow   c grow

7 Most people already know what _____ next.
   a is going to happen   b is happening   c happens

(14 points)

2 Complete the sentences with the future continuous or the future perfect simple.

1 In twenty years' time everyone _____ (drive) electric cars.

2 The town centre _____ (changed) completely by 2040.

3 _____ they _____ (complete) the new hospital by next spring?

4 By 2050 people _____ (not use) PC computers.

5 _____ we still _____ (wear) clothes like these in ten years' time?

6 I don't think I _____ (work) for this company in five years' time.

7 I'm afraid we _____ (not finish) paying for our house until I'm 60.

8 I don't think I _____ retire before I'm 70.

(16 points)

Vocabulary

3 Complete the words using one of the prefixes in the box.

bio	nano	mega	micro	semi	ultra

1 Milk which is half-skimmed is _____skimmed milk.

2 The manufacture of artificial parts for living creatures is called _____ engineering.

3 Extremely high sounds that cannot be heard are known as _____sonic sounds.

4 One thousand millionth of a second is a _____ second.

5 Pop stars who are very well-known and popular everywhere are called _____stars.

6 The climate which operates in a very small region is called a _____ climate.

(12 points)

4 Circle the correct word to complete the sentences.

1 Doing it like that is very _____. This way is much faster.
   a cutting-edge   b appropriate   c time-consuming

2 Quick solutions are not always the best in the _____ .
   a time   b long-term   c past

3 Look at this little tool, it's a really _____ gadget.
   a handy   b appropriate   c renewable

4 This is a new machine, using _____ technology.
   a time-consuming   b cutting-edge   c easy

5 This saves a lot of work. It's a _____ device.
   a labour-saving   b time-consuming   c long-term

6 It's made of _____ materials like wood.
   a long-term   b cutting-edge   c renewable

7 The machine should be _____ to the job.
   a long-term   b appropriate   c time-consuming

8 This device uses only a little energy and is very _____ .
   a efficient   b renewable   c easy

(8 points)

5 Complete the sentences with a word from the box.

business	the blue	your way	interest	my depth
time	his hands	order	luck	date

1 We stop now because we're out of _____ .

2 That shop's gone. It went out of _____ last month.

3 You don't need to drive me home – I don't want you to go out of _____ .

4 Don't buy that milk – it's out of _____ !

5 I really don't know – I'm completely out of _____ .

6 He won't be able to help you because the project is out of _____ now.

7 I didn't expect a pay rise – it came out of _____ .

8 We just sold the last one, so you're out of _____ .

9 The coffee machine is out of _____ again.

10 Just out of _____ , why did you think that?

(10 points)

Functions

6 Complete the conversation with the phrases in the box.

do the trick	give that a try	having trouble
feel free to	have a look	

SUE: Hi, Jill. I wonder if you can help me? I'm [1] _____ with this program.

JILL: Sure, Let me [2] _____ .

SUE: It's this file. It doesn't seem to be working.

JILL: Let's see … have you tried pressing F4?

SUE: No. Hold on and I'll [3] _____ .

JILL: That's it. Now press this key here, that should [4] _____ .

SUE: Oh, yes. That's great. Thanks!

JILL: No problem. [5] _____ ask if you have any more problems.

(10 points)

Unit 3 Test

Writing

7a Read this short email requesting information. Match the phrases in bold (1–4) with the descriptions in the box (a–d).

a phrase introducing a request	**c** stating the problem
b details of the product	**d** additional details

Two months ago I bought one of your ¹ **DT900 printers** from XL Computers in Manchester, a shop which has since gone out of business. The printer works very well, but ² **there are some buttons on it which I don't understand, and there was no user manual in the box.** ³ **I thought there would be one on the Internet, but I cannot find anything.** ⁴ **Please could you tell me where I can get one?** Thank you.

(5 points)

7b Now write a similar short email using this information:

- you bought a PV 2003 digital camera 2 weeks ago
- the photos come out well
- the films come out badly
- you want to return it and get a new one
- ask how to do this

_____

_____

_____

_____

_____

_____

_____

_____

_____

_____

(15 points)

Speaking

8 Use the future continuous and future perfect simple to talk about what changes you think will have happened in the world by 2050.

(10 points)

Unit 4 Test

Writing

7a Read the online review and complete it with the phrases in the box.

One reason I liked it	The entrance price varies	
Last week I visited	I recommend it	There's a large exhibit

¹ _____ a new museum in south London. It's called *The Tennis Club* and it's not far from the Wimbledon Park underground station. The museum is in a lovely old house in a pretty garden. You can recognise it from outside by the tennis net they use as a fence, and the giant tennis racquets on either side of the gates.

You get a friendly welcome from the staff. ² _____, depending on whether you are an adult, a child or a student. Also, members of any tennis club get a special discount if they bring their card.

³ _____ about Wimbledon, of course, which you would expect as the museum is close to the club, which hosts the biggest tournament in Britain.

⁴ _____ was because everything is very clearly labelled, and many of the exhibits are interactive, so you can touch things and press buttons to make things happen. In one room, you can actually hit a tennis ball to see how fast the ball travels.

⁵ _____ for people who like tennis, or sport in general. It is also good for families with children, as there is plenty to do there.

(5 points)

7b Now write an online review of a new art gallery you visited. Say when you went, where it is, what it looks like, what exhibition was on, how much it cost, what the atmosphere was like, and why you would recommend it or not recommend it.

_____

_____

_____

_____

_____

_____

_____

_____

_____

_____

(15 points)

Speaking

8 Talk about your favourite and least favourite area of the arts, explaining in detail what it is you like and dislike about them and why.

(10 points)

Unit 4 Test

Grammar

1 Circle the correct expression of quantity to complete each sentence.

1 _____ painters use colour in the way that she does.
   a a little   b few   c not much

2 _____ of people came to see the exhibition.
   a several   b some   c lots

3 _____ sculptures were accepted for the competition.
   a several   b a bit of   c not much

4 There _____ information about the artists in the catalogue.
   a aren't many   b isn't much   c isn't many

5 _____ young dancers won prizes this year.
   a hardly any   b only a little   c a small amount of

6 _____ the exhibits were installations, not paintings or sculptures.
   a much of   b some   c a large number of

7 There is _____ interest in your work, John.
   a many   b no lack of   c several

8 A surprising _____ of artists are working with batik this year.
   a number   b many   c lots

(16 points)

2 Complete each sentence with one of the determiners from the box. Use each word once.

all	any	each	both	no	either	any

1 _____ of the two artists could win the Turner Prize this year.

2 _____ paintings are very beautiful, but I prefer the dancer.

3 Do you think _____ of these sculptures are good?

4 There was _____ information about his technique.

5 _____ artists try to say something new and different.

6 They didn't buy _____ of my paintings last week.

7 They _____ won 1,000 euros for their work.

(14 points)

Vocabulary

3 Complete each sentence with the correct word from the box.

with	to	lost	really	keep	down

1 We went to a _____ cool party last Saturday at Pete's.

2 We argued last week and she's very cool _____ me now.

3 If the computer crashes, just _____ your cool and try to fix it.

4 Don't try and eat it yet – wait for it to cool _____ a bit first.

5 It's not very cool _____ talk about school at the weekend!

6 When he said that to me, I'm afraid I _____ my cool and was very rude to him.

(12 points)

4 Circle the correct answer.

1 Who plays rock music?
   a a band   b an orchestra

2 Who puts on a play?
   a a dance company   b a drama company

3 Where do you see an art exhibition?
   a a gallery   b a club

4 Who tells jokes?
   a an artist   b a comedian

5 Who plays a gig?
   a an orchestra   b a band

(10 points)

5 Add a suitable suffix from the box to the nouns below to change them into another noun. Write the complete word.

-dom	-ian	-hood	-ness	-ism	-ist	-scape	-ship

1 art   _____
2 kind   _____
3 vandal   _____
4 bore   _____
5 friend   _____
6 neighbour _____
7 Brazil   _____
8 land   _____

(8 points)

Functions

6 Circle the correct phrases to complete the conversation.

JIM: Have you heard the new songs by Trisha?

ANNE: I'm [1] _____ the kind of music she sings, I'm afraid.
   a not very inspiring   c a big fan of
   b not very keen on

JIM: Oh, I didn't know.

ANNE: Yes, her voice really [2] _____. It's so harsh.
   a gets on my nerves   c gets a bit tired of
   b does something for me

JIM: Oh, well, I just bought her new CD and I [3] _____!
   a sounds right up my street   c can't bear it
   b could listen to it all day

ANNE: I'm [4] _____ soul and jazz, but rap just irritates me.
   a very inspiring   b love   c really into

JIM: I see. I never [5] _____ by jazz, but I love 1960s soul.
   a feel particularly inspired   c sound up my street
   b like my kind of thing

(10 points)

Unit 5 Test

Grammar

1 Put the verb in brackets into the infinitive or the *-ing* form, as appropriate.

1 What do you want _____ on Saturday? (do)

2 His plans involved _____ a large office. (build)

3 He imagined _____ the region to develop. (help)

4 His friends all wanted _____ shopping centres. (construct)

5 She has managed _____ a small business. (start)

6 Paul has kept on _____ money into agricultural development. (put)

7 They have decided _____ their revenue to the project. (donate)

8 We will enjoy _____ time in the new parks. (spend)

(8 points)

2 Make sentences using the cues, and the infinitive, only using *to* when necessary.

1 Michael / paid / me / design / his first house.

_____

2 She / asked / her sister / lend / her £20,000.

_____

3 He helped / Walton / become / an important city.

_____

4 They invited / Jill / submit / plans for a golf course.

_____

5 She / wanted / us / work / on the project with them.

_____

6 We / watched / the city / grow larger / in a few months.

_____

(12 points)

3 Write S if the two sentences have the same meaning, and D if they have a different meaning.

1 We should stop eating. We should stop to eat. _____

2 I hate swimming in the lake. I hate to swim in the lake. _____

3 He's just started running. He's just started to run. _____

4 I tried getting a job at the supermarket. I tried to get a job at the supermarket. _____

5 I regret saying he was ill. I regret to say he was ill. _____

(10 points)

Vocabulary

4 Match the words 1–8 with a–h to make urban features.

1 motorway	**a** spaces
2 shopping	**b** centre
3 green	**c** intersection
4 pedestrianised	**d** development
5 leisure	**e** apartment
6 high-rise	**f** mall
7 luxury	**g** building
8 waterfront	**h** zone

(8 points)

5 Complete the sentences using the words in the box.

holes in	your brains	up	of the bunch	on
you up	and choose			

1 Business picks _____ when it gets warmer.

2 My boss always picks _____ my ideas – it's really annoying!

3 I can pick _____ from the station.

4 I'm having problems with this and I'd like to pick _____ .

5 They were all good, but Miss Jones was the pick _____ .

6 Don't worry, you'll soon pick _____ the skills.

(12 points)

6 Circle the correct word to complete each sentence.

1 Jane's leaving her job to _____ as a nurse.
   a renew   **b** retrain   **c** rebuild

2 We are going to _____ to a quieter part of town.
   a relocate   **b** rehouse   **c** rebuild

3 Shall we _____ the house next summer?
   a rehouse   **b** rebuild   **c** redecorate

4 We had to _____ the garden wall.
   a rebuild   **b** redevelop   **c** redecorate

5 If it isn't right, you will have to _____ it!
   a readjust   **b** redo   **c** redevelop

(10 points)

Functions

7 Ask students to complete the dialogue with the phrases from the box.

we ought to	be too hasty	the opinion of
do you think we should do	that's completely wrong	

JACK: What [1] _____?

JILL: I think [2] _____ ask them for more money.

JACK: You know they won't give us any.

JILL: But [3] _____ ! How can we continue with the development if they don't finance it?

JACK: I know that, but we need to consider [4] _____ the directors. We shouldn't [5] _____ about this. Let's think about all the possibilities first …

(10 points)

Unit 5 Test

Writing

8a Complete the opinion essay with the linking phrases from the box.

> however   on the other hand   as a result   furthermore
> because of this

> Smoking has long been a major social problem. Originally people saw it as a problem for the smokers themselves; they were concerned with the individual smoker's health problems. [1]_____, in the last twenty years there has been a change of view, as research has shown that smoking also harms non-smokers. [2]_____, recent public legislation has been in favour of the non-smokers, with actions such as the banning of smoking in the workplace and public buildings, and the extension of the ban to social places such as restaurants and clubs.
>
> These moves have been welcomed, especially by the majority of the public who are non-smokers. [3]_____, restaurant owners have not been pleased by these moves, because they now have fewer customers. There has been a significant drop in the number of smokers going to restaurants, and the industry claims that there are many closures every week. [4]_____, unemployment has increased.
>
> [5]_____, some people suggest that the smoking ban actually hasn't helped reduce the number of smokers. What it certainly has done is reduce the damage from passive smoking to non-smokers and staff working in public places.

(5 points)

8b Write an opinion essay about the use of public transport in big cities, compared to people using their own cars. Discuss issues such as parking, rising fuel costs, congestion, pollution, and government funding of bus, train and metro services.

_____
_____
_____
_____
_____
_____
_____
_____
_____
_____

(15 points)

Speaking

9 Talk about what types of development you would like to see in the place where you live, to help improve the lives of the residents. Consider other people's views in your arguments.

(10 points)

Unit 6 Test

Writing

8a Read the letter of complaint and match the parts of the letter (1–5) to the descriptions a–e in the box.

> **a** a formal greeting
> **b** a formal ending
> **c** a brief explanation of the reason for writing
> **d** a formal request for action
> **e** details of the complaint

> Dear [1] Sir / Madam,
>
> [2] I am writing to complain about the service I got from your taxi company on Friday 17th May.
>
> [3] I had booked a taxi to leave for Heathrow Airport at 14.30. The car actually arrived at 15.10 after I had phoned twice to ask where it was. Not only was the car late, but it was very dirty and the driver had obviously been smoking in it on his way to collect me. Despite having said I needed to go to Terminal 2, the driver first took me to Terminal 3. All of this meant that I had to rush my check-in and that I was nearly late for my plane. [4] Because of this very inadequate service, I request a refund of the £30 fare.
>
> I look forward to a prompt response from you on this matter.
>
> [5] Yours faithfully,
>
> Gerald Hamstone

(5 points)

8b Write a similar letter to a travel agent with whom you booked a holiday in Italy, using the following information. Decide what compensation to ask for.

- there were no rooms at the hotel you had booked, so you had to stay in another
- you had paid extra for a view, but you had no view
- transport to and from the airport was supposed to be included, but you had to pay
- food was poor

_____
_____
_____
_____
_____
_____
_____
_____
_____

(15 points)

Speaking

10 Describe a holiday you had, giving details about when and where it was, and what was good and bad about it.

(10 points)

Unit 6 Test

Grammar

1 Write ^ to show where *not* goes in these sentences.

1 The warden   asked   us   to   walk   on the grass.

2 I told them that I   did   want   to   stay   there any longer.

3 There's only a little money left so   let's   buy   expensive presents.

4 I'm sorry but   I   do   think   that's   correct.

5 Tell her that she   must   cook   anything for us tonight.

6 Remember that   you   do   have   to   go   there.

(6 points)

2 Write the correct question tag.

1 You like living in France, _____ ?

2 She enjoys reading novels, _____ ?

3 They don't go camping, _____ ?

4 He doesn't do voluntary work, _____ ?

5 She's got a lot of money, _____ ?

6 You'll come with us, _____ ?

7 They went to Africa last year, _____ ?

8 You didn't invite me, _____ ?

(16 points)

3 Write open or negative questions in the tense indicated and using the cues.

1 you / like / eat / Chinese food ? (open: present simple)

_____

2 they / want / go / with him ? (negative: past simple)

_____

3 he / visit / us / next week ? (open: *will* future)

_____

4 she / tell / you / her news ? (negative: present perfect)

_____

(8 points)

Vocabulary

4 Complete the sentences and expressions with *mind* with the words from the box.

in	how you go	change	put	on
went blank				

1 She's busy all day long, and has so much _____ her mind, she often forgets things.

2 It's very cold and icy out there tonight, so mind _____ .

3 I knew exactly what I was going to say, but when I saw her my mind _____ .

4 The weather was so strange that I was _____ two minds about what to wear.

5 I'm sure he could pass his exams if he really _____ his mind to it.

6 We don't have to go; there's still time for you to _____ your mind.

(6 points)

5 Complete the sentences with *in* or *out*.

1 Let's not go _____ anywhere tonight. I'd really like to stay _____ for a change.

2 I dropped _____ at John and Sue's on the way home to tell them about the new drama society we're starting and ask if they'd like to join _____ .

3 Our daughter is trying _____ a new club tonight, so I suppose she'll be staying _____ very late.

4 The only time grandpa seems to get _____ these days is when we take him to eat _____ at a restaurant for Sunday lunch.

(8 points)

6 Complete the sentences with the correct word. The first letter has been given for you.

1 I really don't like staying in hotels, so I usually book self-c_____ accommodation.

2 I hate hotels where I don't have a v_____ from my window.

3 Last time I flew to Italy, they lost my l_____ .

4 I can't afford to go abroad, so I'm having a s_____ this summer.

5 Do you get a d_____ off as holiday if you work an extra Saturday?

6 I really don't like holidaying in towns, so I find a place in the c_____ .

7 It was a really long j_____ to get there by bus.

8 The a_____ gave us a great discount on all our flights last year.

(16 points)

Functions

7 Complete this conversation with the expressions in the box.

the easiest thing is to	can make my own way
how do I get to	look out for	wanted to pick you up

CAROL: Hi, Sarah. It's Carol. I'm at the airport.
¹ _____ your place?

SARAH: Oh, hi! I'm sorry, I ² _____ , but Jim's using the car.

CAROL: That's fine. Don't worry. I ³ _____ . Just tell me what to do.

SARAH: ⁴ _____ get the airport bus to the central bus station.

CAROL: OK. and what do I do at the bus station?

SARAH: You need to get the 45 bus to Fairmont.

CAROL: Right … and where do I get off?

SARAH: ⁵ _____ the Mercedes car showroom and it's the next stop after that. I'll wait for you there.

(10 points)

Unit 7 Test

Grammar

1 Complete the conditional sentences with the correct form of the verbs in brackets.

1 If Jane uses all the water, we _____ (be) angry.

2 If the boys had thought about it, they _____ (see) the problems.

3 Mike will go with us if we _____ (travel) by train.

4 People won't have enough water if they _____ (not stop) wasting it.

5 The crops would have grown if you _____ (water) them.

6 They would be more careful if they _____ (know) what could happen to the oil.

(12 points)

2 Complete the mixed conditional sentences with the correct form of the verbs in brackets.

1 I went to India last year. I now have malaria.
If I _____ (not go) to India, I _____ (not have) malaria.

2 Paul drives everywhere. He used a lot of petrol last week.
If Paul _____ (not drive) everywhere, he _____ (use) so much petrol last week.

3 Sue used to eat lots of junk food, and now she's on a diet.
If Sue _____ (not eat) so much junk food, she _____ (not be) on a diet now.

4 People always leave the lights on, so we wasted a lot of electricity last month.
If people _____ (not leave) the lights on, we _____ (not waste) so much electricity last month.

(8 points)

3 Circle the correct form of the verb.

1 I wish people *tried / would try* to use less water.

2 Would you rather *eat / ate* organic food?

3 Many councils wish they *didn't have / wouldn't have* to deal with green issues.

4 If only she *could use / had used* a computer, she might get a better job.

5 Mike wishes he *had saved / would save* his money.

(10 points)

Vocabulary

4 Complete each sentence with one word from the box.

exhaustible	abundant	scarce	renewable

1 Those butterflies used to be everywhere, but they have become very _____ now.

2 Have another apple, they are really _____ this autumn.

3 I buy paper made from _____ sources.

4 Oil is an _____ resource, just as coal was.

(4 points)

5 Complete the sentences with a suitable verb.

1 I want to _____ a year travelling.

2 We need to _____ tigers or they will soon be extinct.

3 We should not _____ water by leaving taps on.

4 We ought to _____ the forests as they are.

5 If you don't _____ your money, you won't be able to buy a house later.

6 If we keep using oil, we will soon _____ of it.

(12 points)

6 Circle the correct word to complete these sentences.

1 A machine for extracting oil from the ground is called an oil _____ .
   a rag   b rig   c rug

2 An oil _____ crashed into another ship last night.
   a boat   b tanker   c liner

3 The oil comes out of an oil _____ .
   a well   b hole   c mine

4 The ship sank, leaving an oil _____ on the water.
   a lick   b trick   c slick

5 They make the oil useable at an oil _____ .
   a factory   b refinery   c workshop

6 The oil lies underground in an oil _____ .
   a field   b lake   c pool

(6 points)

7 Match the words and phrases 1–8 with synonyms a–h.

1 individual		a desperate
2 to disapprove of		b obsessed with
3 very anxious		c majestic
4 hopeless		d back-breaking
5 very interested in		e unique
6 hard and tiring		f to rob
7 to take from		g bleak
8 tall and elegant		h to deplore

(8 points)

Functions

8 Complete the conversation with these expressions.

Look, there's no doubt that   take   the point is that
To be honest with you   I don't accept that

ANDY: I think the council has done a great job by putting recycling bins everywhere. Don't you agree?

JUDY: ¹ _____ , no, I don't.

ANDY: Oh, really … why is that?

JUDY: Well, ² _____ the city centre, for example. There are almost no recycling bins there.

ANDY: ³ _____ . There are bins around the market.

JUDY: That's true, but ⁴ _____ there are not enough bins in the areas where people live.

ANDY: ⁵ _____ we still need more bins, but at least they are doing something at last.

(10 points)

Unit 7 Test

Writing

9a Read this letter to a newspaper. Underline:

1 the reason for writing

2 two examples that illustrate the problems

3 two suggestions for action

> From Ms Judy Roberts
>
> Sir, whilst applauding the idea behind the recent changes, your report (Council recycling initiative, 12th April) about the Town Council's installation of recycling bins ignores a number of important issues about what the Council have actually done.
>
> From what I have seen, the Council has put large numbers of bins on the housing estates to the north of the town centre, although the positioning of some of them could have been better – for example, it is not pleasant to have two rows of bins right next to a children's playground. They have also provided many bins around the market and the town centre shops, which is very good for stall and shop workers.
>
> However, there is no doubt that the provision of recycling bins for those of us who live in the town centre is inadequate. The point is that no residents want to walk a long distance with piles of old newspapers or bags full of glass bottles and jars, so they will just put them into their own household bins. Equally, driving to deposit waste in recycling bins negates the green objectives of the Council's project.
>
> Would it not be better for the Council firstly, to think about where they place the bins? Secondly, I would ask them to provide further bins in suitable places around the town centre housing areas.
>
> Ms J Roberts
>
> Town Centre Resident

(5 points)

9b Using this letter as a model, write a letter to a local newspaper about the following situation.

- The Council has banned smoking from all its offices.

- There are special smoking areas, but these are in the halls where everyone has to walk, outside the main doors through which all staff pass, and next to the staff kitchens which everyone uses.

- You are pleased about the ban in general, but want the smoking areas moved to places which are more suitable.

_____

_____

_____

_____

_____

_____

(15 points)

Speaking

10 Talk about the positive and negative things about recycling where you live, and make some suggestions for what could be done better.

(10 points)

Unit 8 Test

Writing

7a Read the minutes and complete them with the words from the box.

agreed	suggestion	apologies	objection	proposal

> Residents of Apartment Block 10, Victoria Road
>
> From: John Roberts
>
> Re: the car-parking facilities
>
> Thanks to everyone who wrote with [1] _____ for not attending Wednesday evening's meeting. These are the minutes from that meeting.
>
> We met to discuss what to do about the car-parking facilities outside our block, following an increasing number of residents being unable to park their cars in the spaces provided. One [2] _____ was to ask the Council to install a barrier so that only residents could enter, but many residents felt it would cause problems with deliveries to the block. Another [3] _____ was to put up a sign with the registration number of each resident's car on it. The [4] _____ to this was that when people went away, the space would be unused, and other visiting cars would have nowhere to park.
>
> In the end, it was [5] _____ that the best thing would be to put up some signs asking delivery vehicles and visitors to park in the large space opposite the entrance, and other signs pointing out that the main set of spaces were exclusively for the use of the residents. Jackie Brown offered to write a letter to the Council to ask if this would be possible.

7b Write minutes for a meeting at which the following discussion takes place.

> Residents meet to discuss the Council providing a children's playground near their apartments.
>
> Idea 1: it would be too noisy and would disturb people
>
> Idea 2: it would be very helpful for mothers with young children; the nearest playground is 1 km away in the park
>
> Agree: to place it at the far end of the gardens, not close to the apartments.
>
> Steve Jones will write to the Council

_____

_____

_____

_____

_____

_____

_____

_____

_____

_____

_____

(15 points)

Speaking

8 Talk about a recent local, national or international news item you have heard about. Explain what journalists and reporters have said, and say what your opinion of the situation is.

(10 points)

Unit 8 Test

Grammar

1 Complete the sentences with the correct form of the words in brackets. Use the past simple where appropriate.

1 We _____ (agree / tell) the journalist what had happened.

2 I _____ (persuade / the photographer / take) the photos we needed.

3 The editor _____ (admit / believe) the director's story at first.

4 Young reporters always _____ (complain / about / work) long hours.

5 The article _____ (blame / the politician / for / cause) the situation.

6 The photographer _____ (beg / the refugees / let) him take photos of them.

7 The demonstrators _____ (accuse / the journalist / of / lie) about events.

8 The reporter _____ (offer / lend) me her phone when mine got broken.

(16 points)

2 Rewrite the direct speech using passive reporting verbs and *it*.

1 People report: 'There aren't many sparrows in our towns now.'

_____

2 In the past people said: 'Radio will never be replaced by TV.'

_____

3 People thought: 'Computers are only for specialists.'

_____

4 Everyone knows: 'Drinking lots of water is good for you.'

_____

5 People believed: 'Tigers have been saved for ever.'

_____

6 Some people think: 'Life was better fifty years ago.'

_____

7 My friends said: 'That job isn't good for Jake.'

_____

(14 points)

Vocabulary

3 Match the words to the definitions.

1 to record		**a**	a person who takes pictures professionally
2 a lens		**b**	an ordinary or simple photograph, taken by an amateur
3 a photographer		**c**	the special glass which you look through
4 a shot		**d**	a part inside the camera that moves to take the photo
5 snapshot		**e**	to take photos of things in order to remember them
6 the shutter		**f**	a general term for a photograph

(6 points)

4 Complete the sentences with a word from the box.

amusing	charming	encouraging	inspiring
optimistic	quirky	amazing	appealing

1 He's really a very strange person. Everything he does is _____ and different.

2 She is so friendly and pleasant, and really is a _____ woman.

3 I love being at a party with Bill. He makes us all laugh with his _____ comments.

4 I often feel depressed, but half an hour with Liz makes me feel _____ about the future.

5 I couldn't resist buying one of these toy cats – they make such _____ presents.

6 I thought my essay was bad, but the tutor made some _____ remarks about it.

7 I have heard her talk several times, and she is always very _____ in what she says.

8 It's an _____ story, and I'm not sure that I believe it.

(8 points)

5 Complete the sentences with one word.

1 He didn't know what to say – he was _____ for words.

2 Why did they change their minds? They promised – they _____ their word.

3 Read about it in the paper, don't _____ my word for it.

4 We didn't read about how good it was, we heard by word of _____.

5 Whenever we argue, Peter always has to have the _____ word.

6 I don't know – I have heard _____ word of it.

7 You can't prove it – it's just his word _____ yours.

8 Everyone in the office knew because word went _____.

(16 points)

Functions

6 Complete the sentences with one of these phrases.

take that with a pinch of salt	I heard that
apparently	according to	take no notice

JAMES: [1] _____ there was a problem in the office yesterday.

ANNIE: Really? What happened?

JAMES: Well, [2] _____ Mike, there was an argument between Janet and the boss.

ANNIE: I would [3] _____ of what Mike says – he always invents stories.

JAMES: Yes, but [4] _____, the boss asked Janet to leave and she refused.

ANNIE: I'd [5] _____ . Janet is very good friends with the boss, and Mike doesn't like either of them!

(10 points)

Unit 9 Test

Grammar

1 Complete the text with *the* where necessary.

Bear Grylls is one of [1] _____ most famous British adventurers. He grew up in [2] _____ UK and studied [3] _____ Hispanic studies at [4] _____ University of London, then joined [5] _____ British Army. He has practised many extreme sports and in [6] _____ 1996 he had a serious parachuting accident in Zambia. [7] _____ accident resulted in serious injury to his back and he spent a long time in [8] _____ hospital, but amazingly, just 18 months later he climbed to the summit of [9] _____ Mount Everest. He has led expeditions to [10] _____ Antarctic, [11] _____ Himalayas and [12] _____ South America. He has also worked for [13] _____ charities and made [14] _____ TV programmes about survival.

(14 points)

2 Complete the sentences with a relative pronoun. Do not use *that*.

1 He is the man _____ wife won a million euros.

2 Is that the woman _____ made that sculpture?

3 These are the books _____ my uncle wrote.

4 This is the place _____ he studied.

5 These are the physicists _____ work won the Nobel Prize.

6 Are these the fields _____ he painted his first masterpieces?

7 My brother, _____ lives in America, has invented a new kind of pen.

8 Their inventions, _____ changed the course of history, are on display in the museum.

(8 points)

3 Write reduced relative clauses using the present or past participles.

1 He lives in France, where he sells his paintings to earn money.

_____

2 It is an interesting topic, which is written about rarely.

_____

3 They work for an energy company, where they are trying to promote green energy.

_____

4 Alice, who was inspired by her teachers, went on to study physics.

_____

(8 points)

Vocabulary

5 Match the words 1–6 with the definitions a–f.

1 background	**a**	what you know from doing things
2 experience	**b**	certificates and degrees
3 qualifications	**c**	what you are like as a person
4 qualities	**d**	everything about you: family, education, experience
5 talents	**e**	your natural abilities

(10 points)

6 Complete the sentences with the correct form of a verb from the box.

follow	graduate	do	serve
become	work for	apply for	get

1 Do you think John _____ the job that he wants in accounts?

2 She worked very hard in the company and eventually _____ a director.

3 Petra _____ a career in education after university.

4 My father _____ the same company all his life.

5 Jane _____ from college next summer.

6 I _____ 25 jobs before I finally got this one.

7 My uncle _____ in the army during the 1990s.

8 Are you planning _____ a specialist course?

(8 points)

7 Circle the phrase which can be used in each sentence.

1 _____, I have received the payment.
  a As long as   **b** At long last   **c** Before long

2 I finally saw the film _____ it first came out.
  a long after   **b** long for   **c** before long

3 I will go with you _____ it doesn't rain.
  a at long last   **b** in the long term   c as long as

4 When I am away from home I always _____ my mother's cooking.
  a long after   **b** long for   **c** before long

5 You will have to get a job _____ .
  a long after   **b** long for   **c** before long

6 It looks as though the situation will be all right _____ .
  a in the long term   **b** as long as   **c** long after

(12 points)

Functions

8 Match the prepositions a–e with the expressions 1–5, then use the phrases to complete sentences A–E.

1 I am very familiar	**a**	to
2 He's not so keen	**b**	in
3 She specialised	**c**	on
4 We're more suited	**d**	of
5 I've lots of experience	**e**	with

A _____ doing a boring office job.

B _____ accounts – I've been here for years.

C _____ practical work than theoretical things.

D _____ this kind of engine, as I helped design it.

E _____ this very particular area of plant sciences.

(10 points)

Unit 9 Test

Writing

9a Complete the online profile with the correct headings from the box.

Location	Industry	Current
Past	Education	Summary

Profile

James Robinson

Assistant Director, Sadler Plant Technology

1 _____: Bristol, UK

2 _____: Plant technology

3 _____: developing innovative ways of improving plant growth, flowering and fruiting indoors

4 _____

- Research Assistant at Southampton University Department of Botany
- Assistant Development Officer, Dorset Tree Nurseries
- Technical Director, Wilson's Plant Sciences

5 _____

B.Sc. Experimental Botany, University of Leeds

M.Sc. Photosynthesis Research, University of Southampton

6 _____

I have been fascinated by plants since I was a child, and have always studied British wild plants. After a university degree in experimental botany, I went on to do research into photosynthesis at Southampton University for three years, which led to my M.Sc. I then had three years of practical experience working with trees for a nationally important nursery specialising in trees. After that I spent five years directing the development work in the fruit production of apple and pear trees for Wilson's Plant Sciences. Now, as Assistant Director at Sadler's Plant Technology, I am able to put my research and practical experience to good use across the range of areas which we are working on.

(5 points)

9b Now write a similar profile for Anna Lake, who went to Brighton College of Art, practised as a painter for 10 years, having several important exhibitions, but then moved into the restoration of old paintings at Birmingham Art Gallery, and is currently Director of the Leeds Art Gallery.

_____

_____

_____

_____

_____

(15 points)

Speaking

10 Talk about the education and career of somebody you know, giving full details of their qualities, qualifications and experience.

(10 points)

Unit 10 Test

Writing

8a Read this informal email, and underline five things which show that it is written in informal English.

Hi Josie

Hope you're well. Haven't written for some time as I was away.

Just wondered if we could meet up some time next week?

Let me know.

Speak soon

Jenny

(5 points)

8b Now write an informal email to a friend. Include these things:

- you haven't met for some time
- you have tickets for a concert on 22nd June
- if not free then, party at Steve's on 24th June

_____

_____

_____

_____

_____

_____

_____

_____

_____

_____

(15 points)

Speaking

9 Talk about a festival or a tradition you know about, and say what people do and what the sequence and timing of the events is. Include details about when, where and why it takes place, and what people are involved.

(10 points)

Unit 10 Test

Grammar

1 Choose the correct present tense form of the verbs.

1 Mike's parents *take / are taking* him to a football match every week.

2 Sue's dad *is always saying / will always say* how clever she is.

3 Some kids *are never doing / will never do* what their parents tell them.

4 His mum *always tries / is always trying* to make him play the piano.

5 Her father *always attends / will always attend* courses on bringing up children.

6 My parents *are always telling / will always tell* my friends all my secrets.

7 My aunt *lives / will live* in a very strange way.

8 Those children *break / are breaking* their father's rules again.

(8 points)

2 Complete the sentences with the correct form of *used to*, *be used to* or *get used to*.

1 When I was little, I _____ eat a lot of sweets, but now I don't.

2 I didn't like to eat the local food at first, but I am starting to _____ it now.

3 _____ you _____ drink a lot of milk when you were a child?

4 He _____ not _____ the way of life here.

5 _____ Peter _____ the food in China when he was there last August?

6 We _____ not _____ swim in the river when we were young, but we do now.

(6 points)

3 Write ^ to show where *usually* goes in these sentences.

1 Do you go to the seaside for your holidays?

2 They eat rice with all their meals.

3 The children don't go to school on Saturdays.

4 Does she practise the piano after dinner?

5 Michael doesn't like eating different kinds of meat.

6 We drink tea with milk in it.

(6 points)

Vocabulary

4 Complete the sentences with the correct form of the verbs in the box.

bring up	reward	rebel against	spoil
nag	punish	disobey	

1 If children behave badly, parents need to _____ them.

2 All parents _____ their children in different ways.

3 It is important to _____ children when they do something really good.

4 If you always give children what they want, you _____ them.

5 My mother used to _____ us all day about tidying our room and doing our homework.

6 It is natural for teenagers to _____ what their parents want them to do.

7 You get into trouble when you _____ the school rules.

(14 points)

5 Write the food words from the box in the correct list.

pasta	cheese	sweets	potatoes	rice
crisps	frozen hamburgers	yoghurt	chocolate bars	
breakfast cereal				

Dairy products:

_____

_____

Processed food:

_____

_____

Staple foods:

_____

_____

Snacks:

_____

_____

(10 points)

6 Decide if the expressions with *common* mean *shared* or *normal*. Write *shared* or *normal*.

1 _____ I don't have anything in common with Jason.

2 _____ It is common for you to take off your shoes in people's houses here.

3 _____ Eating with your fingers is common practice there.

4 _____ It is common knowledge that John hates the boss.

5 _____ Everyone can put their animals there – it is common land.

6 _____ It is quite common to see people eating insects in the street.

(6 points)

Functions

7 Complete the text with sequencing words from the box.

then	next	after that	finally	first

A Traditional British Wedding

[1] _____ the groom and the best man arrive at the registry office. [2] _____ the guests start to arrive, and the ushers show them where to sit. [3] _____ the bride and her father arrive, usually in a special car. [4] _____ the ceremony takes place. [5] _____ everyone goes to a hotel or restaurant for a meal.

(10 points)

Unit 11 Test

Grammar

1 Complete the sentences with the past forms of the verbs.

1 He _____ (could / understand) difficult maths problems easily.

2 The students _____ (succeed / complete) their project in time.

3 Carol _____ (not manage / pass) her history exam first time.

4 The boys _____ (able / find) the solution after a lot of work.

5 Bill _____ (could / not / do) his homework last night.

6 The girls all _____ (manage / finish) their course with high marks.

7 Jake _____ (not / able / solve) the difficult task the tutor had set.

8 My sister _____ (not / succeed / get) her university degree.

(16 points)

2 Underline the correct form of the verb in these future in the past sentences.

1 I *would / was going to* call you, but my mobile didn't work.

2 Paul said he *would play / would have played* in the match, but then he didn't come.

3 Jane *would play / was supposed to* tell them about it, but then she forgot.

4 The girls *were going / would have come*, but the snow prevented them.

5 He *would / was about to* leave when the phone rang.

6 What *would you do / would you have done* in that situation yesterday?

7 *Were they supposed to / Would they* come to tea yesterday afternoon?

(14 points)

Vocabulary

3 Circle the correct verb to complete the sentences.

1 It is the teacher who has to _____ the students.
   a absorb   b acquire   c motivate

2 Students need to _____ the ideas that are presented to them.
   a inspire   b grasp   c motivate

3 If students are to _____ a foreign language, they need to hear it spoken lots.
   a inspire   b motivate   c acquire

4 Students won't understand the game if they _____ the rules.
   a are ignorant of   c don't engage with
   b don't connect with

5 Good teachers _____ their students to study hard.
   a acquire   b inspire   c understand

6 I find it easy to _____ the interesting facts the teacher tells us.
   a absorb   b inspire   c connect with

(6 points)

4 Match the expressions 1–8 with the definitions a–h.

1 to learn the tricks of the trade
2 to learn to walk before you can run
3 to learn one's lesson
4 to learn to live with a situation
5 to learn from one's mistakes
6 to learn something by heart
7 to learn something as you go along
8 to learn something the hard way

a to find out you were wrong
b to memorise something
c to have many problems while you learn
d to get better through making errors
e to learn how professionals do things
f to learn how to do something as you do it
g to accept things without making complaints
h to learn to do the simple things first

(16 points)

5 Match one of the phrases in the box to each description of types of learning.

to learn by trial and error	to learn by authority
to learn by observation	to learn by reasoning

1 I learnt from the lectures of our professors at university. They had all done a lot of research and written many important books. _____

2 I thought about all the different information I had, and examined it carefully from all possible sides before I came to my conclusion. _____

3 At teacher training college we spent hours watching teachers teach in their own classrooms, and studying films of teachers in different situations. _____

4 In the laboratory we tested our theories in practical ways. We tried things out and if they didn't work, we tried again in a different way. _____

(8 points)

Functions

6 Complete the extract from the conversation with the phrases in the box.

you explain	do you mean	you speak up
catch that	Hang on	

B: I'd like some information about your Spanish course.

A: Are you a beginner or do you have some experience?

B: What [1] _____ by beginner? I did some Spanish at school.

A: It's probably best if you join the intermediate group then.

B: Sorry. can [2] _____ a bit, please?

A: I said you should probably join the intermediate group. It starts on 12th September at 7.30 in Room 501, and if you ….

B: [3] _____ a second. Could [4] _____ what we will do in the course first, please?

A: The website has all the details. It's www.weston/Spanish/intermediate.com.

B: I'm afraid I didn't [5] _____. Can you spell it, please?

(10 points)

Unit 11 Test

Writing

7a Underline the five linking phrases in this letter about an evening course.

Dear Sir/Madam

I started a course in Spanish at the college on 12th September. The person I spoke to at registration suggested I went into the intermediate group, but in fact I find that everyone is much better than me. Despite the fact that the teacher is very helpful, I find that I don't understand much. I think it would be better if I moved down into the beginner's group.

While I like the teacher and what he says is interesting, I cannot grasp some of the things that the class talks about, whereas I know from someone in the beginner's group that they are talking at my level. The teacher says he is sure I will pick things up if I stay a bit longer, but on the contrary, I think the situation will just get worse.

I would be very pleased if you could arrange for me to attend the beginner's class from next week.

I look forward to hearing from you.

Yours faithfully

John Giles

(5 points)

8 Now write a similar letter to Weston College using this information:

- You enrolled in the Tuesday Italian Cookery course
- After three weeks, you find your basic cooking skills aren't good enough for this class, and your cooking hasn't been very successful
- You like the teacher and the classes are fun
- You want to change to General Cooking Skills on Thursdays with the same teacher

(15 points)

Speaking

9 Talk about a course or workshop that you attended. What was good and bad about it. What was the tutor like? What did you learn from it?

(10 points)

Unit 12 Test

Writing

9a Read this report and write the section headings (summary, advantages, disadvantages, recommendation) in the correct place.

1 _____

I visited the land where we are proposing to build 24 houses yesterday, 3rd June, and was generally impressed by the site. It seems to be very suitable for the kind of development we are planning. However, location and access seem to be something of a problem. These are the details:

2 _____

- The price is lower than we expected and budgeted for
- The land is ideal for building – well-drained and flat
- It has a number of natural features which we can keep to make the development more attractive – trees, a pond and hedges

3 _____

- The actual location of the land is close to a large industrial area, which makes it less attractive
- Because of the layout of existing roads, access would have to be through the industrial area

4 _____

I propose buying the land, and designing our houses around the existing natural features. Because it costs less than expected, we might be able to pay for the building of a new access road which avoids the industrial area. We would need to consult with the Town Council over this first.

(4 points)

9b Now write a similar report, using the following details:

- your company is going to buy and restore a house
- the price of the one you visited is more than you wanted to pay
- it needs less work doing on it than expected, though it will need a new roof
- it is in a nice part of town, with big gardens back and front – they need work

(16 points)

Speaking

10 Work with a partner. You run a business which provides different services for homes (gardening, cleaning, decorating). Try to persuade your partner to use your services, explaining why he or she should use your company.

(10 points)

Unit 12 Test

Grammar

1 Write ^ to show where the phrase in brackets goes in each sentence.

1 I wanted to go to the party . (too)
2 Did Steve go there ? (as well)
3 They visited Nancy when in France . (also)
4 Did she get some money ? (too)
5 Have you bought an expensive car ? (also)
6 Pete opened a new bank account . (as well)

(6 points)

2 Complete the sentences with *only, just* or *even*.

1 It was _____ 40 years ago that man first walked on the moon.
2 Quite a lot of people have been in space, but _____ a few have walked on the moon.
3 When times are hard, _____ rich people notice the difficulties.
4 I _____ eat ice cream in July and August.
5 Paul _____ isn't good enough for the team.
6 I got up so late, I didn't _____ have time for a cup of coffee before I left home.
7 He was late getting to the airport but he _____ managed to catch the plane.
8 I don't trust the banks, so I _____ invest in private companies.

(16 points)

3 Write sentences using causative *have* or *get*.

1 yesterday / I / get / cleaner / wash / windows

_____

2 They / always / have / a gardener / cut / grass

_____

3 We need / get / a plumber / fix / the bathroom

_____

4 Paul / want / have / an architect / design / an extension / to his house

_____

(8 points)

Vocabulary

4 Complete the sentences with one of the words in the box.

pricey	hard up	loaded	reasonable
well off	afford	income	

1 I am surprised he can _____ to run a Ferrari!
2 I wanted to buy a coat, but they were too _____ .
3 His annual _____ comes not just from his job, but also from the flats he rents out.
4 It's been a bad year, so everyone is _____ now.
5 After he won the lottery, John was really _____ .
6 I shop here because the prices are very _____ .

(6 points)

5 Complete each sentence with the correct form of a verb in the box.

give	spend	earn	borrow
lend	invest	owe	pay

1 He _____ a lot of money in that new travel company.
2 They had to _____ a lot of money from the bank.
3 I haven't got any money – can you _____ me £50?
4 When times are hard, people _____ less in the shops.
5 We _____ quite a lot to charities like Oxfam.
6 How much money do you _____ in your new job?
7 Peter is in trouble – he _____ money to a lot of people.
8 I have to _____ all those bills by Friday.

(8 points)

6 Match the verbs 1–7 with the words a–g.

1 fit   a the living room
2 decorate   b the bathroom
3 tile   c some shelves
4 put up   d a picture
5 hang   e a carpet
6 plaster   f a wall

(6 points)

7 Complete these expressions. Use one suitable word in each space.

1 Mick didn't feel bad about not getting the contract. He had no hard _____ .
2 My cousin lost her job – she's really hard _____ now.
3 It was hard _____ that the other team got a penalty – we didn't deserve to lose.
4 He's really tough – a very hard-_____ director.
5 She's feeling really hard _____ _____ because she knows she was the best but didn't win.

(10 points)

Functions

8 Complete the conversation with the phrases in the box.

to be honest	is there not some way around that?
if I were in your shoes	at the end of the day a key thing

A: Look, John, [1] _____ for our company is to invest well.
B: I realise that, but [2] _____ , the amount you have to invest is small. No banks are interested.
A: [3] _____ I mean, if the banks are not interested, isn't there somewhere else we could invest our money?
B: [4] _____ , I would try buying some shares in one of the top 100 companies.
But [5] _____ , it's your company and your money, so you will have to decide.

(10 points)

Photocopiable tests: answer key

Unit 1 Test

Grammar

1

1 works
2 has been living
3 is having
4 has … been

5 does … play
6 Have … seen
7 is … getting

2

1 The children are always given food first.
2 The guests are being shown around the hospital.
3 I have been helped a lot with my English.
4 I am often told news about our neighbours.

3

1 The residents regularly see foxes around here.
2 Holidaymakers are using all the flats.
3 Several people have used the car recently.
4 My sister is helping my mother this week.

Vocabulary

4

1 b   2 a   3 c   4 b   5 c

5

1 catch
2 reach
3 do/manage

4 persuade
5 receive
6 be

6

1 h
2 a
3 d

4 b
5 c
6 e

7 g
8 f

Functions

7

1 a nice surprise!
2 What have you been up to?
3 You're looking well
4 Do you see much of
5 I don't mean to be rude

Writing

8a

1 Mike
2 a'm up to
3 My plan is
4 I'm looking forward to seeing you
5 All the best

Unit 2 Test

Grammar

1

1 Has … watched
2 didn't tell
3 have met
4 did … hear

5 listened
6 haven't explained
7 bought
8 hasn't sent

2

1 had been
2 were
3 was
4 had been

5 went
6 had told
7 had visited

Vocabulary

3

1 thought-provoking
2 objective
3 touching

4 original
5 scary
6 gripping

4

1 c   2 b   3 a   4 a   5 c   6 b

5

1 track of
2 his chin up
3 a diary

4 an eye on
5 you
6 a secret

Functions

6

1 That's awful!
2 Poor you!
3 that was lucky.

4 How embarrassing!
5 same experience

Writing

7a

1 stumbled
2 wearily
3 muttered

4 screamed
5 apprehensively

Unit 3 Test

Grammar

1

1 c   2 b   3 c   4 a   5 c   6 b   7 a

2

1 will be driving
2 will have changed
3 will … have completed
4 won't (will not) be using

5 Will … be wearing
6 will be working
7 won't have finished
8 will have retired

Vocabulary

3

1 semi-skimmed
2 bio-engineering
3 ultrasonic

4 nanosecond
5 megastars
6 microclimate

4

1 c   2 b   3 a   4 b   5 a   6 c   7 b   8 a

5

1 time	6 his hands
2 business	7 the blue
3 your way	8 luck
4 date	9 order
5 my depth	10 interest

Functions

6

1 having trouble	4 do the trick
2 have a look	5 Feel free to
3 give that a try	

Writing

7a

1 b   2 c   3 d   4 a

Unit 4 Test

Grammar

1

1 b   2 c   3 a   4 b   5 a   6 c   7 b   8 a

2

1 either	5 all
2 both	6 any
3 any	7 each
4 no	

Vocabulary

3

1 really	4 down
2 with	5 to
3 keep	6 lost

4

1 a   2 b   3 a   4 b   5 b

5

1 artist	5 friendship
2 kindness	6 neighbourhood
3 vandalism	7 Brazilian
4 boredom	8 landscape

Functions

6

1 b   2 a   3 b   4 c   5 a

Writing

7a

1 Last week I visited
2 The entrance price varies
3 There's a large exhibit
4 One reason I liked it
5 I recommend it

Unit 5 Test

Grammar

1

1 to do	5 to start
2 building	6 putting
3 helping	7 to donate
4 to construct	8 spending

2

1 Michael paid me **to design** his first house.
2 She asked her sister **to lend** her £ 20,000.
3 He helped Walton **become** an important city.
4 They invited Jill **to submit** plans for a golf course.
5 She wanted us **to work** on the project with them.
6 We watched the city **grow** larger in a few months.

3

1 D   2 S   3 S   4 D   5 D

Vocabulary

4

1 c	3 a	5 b	7 d/e
2 f	4 h	6 g	8 e/d

5

1 up	4 your brains
2 holes in	5 of the bunch
3 you up	6 up

6

1 b   2 a   3 c   4 a   5 b

Functions

7

1 do you think we should do
2 we ought to
3 that's completely wrong
4 the opinion of
5 be too hasty

Writing

8a

1 However
2 Because of this (As a result)
3 On the other hand
4 As a result (Because of this)
5 Furthermore

Unit 6 Test

Grammar

1

1 us not to	4 do not think
2 did not want	5 must not cook
3 let's not buy	6 do not have

2

1 don't you	5 hasn't she
2 doesn't she	6 won't you
3 do they	7 didn't they
4 does he	8 did you

3

1 Do you like eating / to eat Chinese food?
2 Didn't they want to go with him?
3 Will he visit us next week?
4 Hasn't she told you her news?

Vocabulary

4

1	on	4	in
2	how you go	5	put
3	went blank	6	change

5

1	out, in	3	out, out
2	in, in	4	out, out

6

1	self-catering	5	day off
2	view	6	countryside
3	luggage	7	journey
4	staycation	8	airline

Functions

7

1 How do I get to
2 wanted to pick you up
3 can make my own way
4 the easiest thing is to
5 Look out for

Writing

8a

1 a   2 c   3 e   4 d   5 b

Unit 7 Test

Grammar

1

1	will be	4	don't stop
2	would have seen	5	had watered
3	travel	6	knew

2

1 hadn't gone, wouldn't have
2 didn't drive, wouldn't have used
3 hadn't eaten, wouldn't be
4 didn't leave, wouldn't have wasted

3

1	would try	4	could use
2	eat	5	had saved
3	didn't have		

Vocabulary

4

1	scarce	3	renewable
2	abundant	4	exhaustible

5

1	spend	4	preserve
2	protect	5	save
3	waste	6	run out of

6

1 b   2 b   3 a   4 c   5 b   6 a

7

1 e   2 h   3 a   4 g   5 b   6 d   7 f   8 c

Functions

8

1 To be honest with you
2 Take
3 I don't accept that.
4 the point is that
5 Look, there's no doubt that

Writing

9a

1 Your report … ignores a number of important issues …
2 … for example, it is not pleasant to have two rows of bins right next to a children's playground; no residents want to walk a long distance with piles of old newspapers; driving to deposit waste in recycling bins negates the green objectives …
3 … to think about where they place the bins; … to provide further bins …

Unit 8 Test

Grammar

1

1 agreed to tell
2 persuaded the photographer to take
3 admitted believing
4 complain about working
5 blamed the politician for causing the situation.
6 begged the refugees to let
7 accused the journalist of lying
8 offered to lend

2

1 It is reported that there aren't many sparrows in our towns now.
2 In the past it was said that radio would never be replaced by TV.
3 It was thought that computers were only for specialists.
4 It is known that drinking lots of water is good for you.
5 It was believed that tigers had been saved for ever.
6 It is thought that life was better fifty years ago.
7 It was said that that job wasn't good for Jake.

Vocabulary

3

1 e   2 c   3 a   4 f   5 b   6 d

4

1	quirky	5	appealing
2	charming	6	encouraging
3	amusing	7	inspiring
4	optimistic	8	amazing

5

1 lost	5 last
2 gave	6 no
3 take	7 against
4 mouth	8 around

Functions

6

1 I heard that	4 apparently
2 according to	5 take that with a pinch of salt
3 take no notice	

Writing

7a

1 apologies	4 objection
2 proposal/suggestion	5 agreed
3 suggestion/proposal	

Unit 9 Test

Grammar

1

1 the	4 the	7 The	10 the	13 –
2 the	5 the	8 –	11 the	14 –
3 –	6 –	9 –	12 –	

2

1 whose	5 whose
2 who	6 where
3 which	7 who
4 where	8 which

3

1 He lives in France, selling paintings to earn money.
2 It is an interesting topic, written about rarely/rarely written about.
3 They work for an energy company, trying to promote green energy.
4 Alice, inspired by her teachers, went on to study physics.

Vocabulary

5

1 d   2 a   3 b   4 c   5 e

6

1 will get	4 worked for	7 served
2 became	5 will graduate	8 to do
3 followed	6 applied for	

7

1 b   2 a   3 c   4 b   5 c   6 a

Functions

8

1 e   2 c   3 b   4 a   5 d

A He's not so keen on
B I've lots of experience of
C We're more suited to
D I am very familiar with
E She specialised in

Writing

9a

1 Location	3 Current	5 Education
2 Industry	4 Past	6 Summary

Unit 10 Test

Grammar

1

1 take	5 always attends
2 is always saying	6 are always telling
3 will never do	7 lives
4 is always trying	8 are breaking

2

1 used to	4 is … used to
2 to get used to	5 Did … get used to
3 Did … use to	6 did … use to

3

1 you usually go	4 she usually practise
2 They usually eat	5 doesn't usually like
3 don't usually go	6 We usually drink

Vocabulary

4

1 punish	5 nag
2 bring up	6 rebel against
3 reward	7 disobey
4 spoil	

5

Dairy products: cheese, yoghurt
Processed food: frozen hamburgers, breakfast cereal
Staple foods: potatoes, pasta, rice
Snacks: crisps, sweets, chocolate bars

6

1 shared	4 shared
2 normal	5 shared
3 normal	6 normal

Functions

7

1 First	4 After that
2 Then	5 Finally
3 Next	

Writing

8a

Hi Josie

Hope you're well. Haven't written for some time as I was away.

Just wondered if we could meet up some time next week?

Let me know.

Speak soon

Jenny

Unit 11 Test

Grammar

1
1. could understand
2. succeeded in completing
3. didn't manage to pass
4. were able to find
5. could not do
6. managed to finish
7. was not able to solve
8. didn't succeed in getting

2
1. was going to
2. would
3. was supposed to
4. would have
5. was about to
6. would you have done
7. Were they supposed to

Vocabulary

3
1 c   2 b   3 c   4 a   5 b   6 a

4
1 e   2 h   3 a   4 g   5 d   6 b   7 f   8 c

5
1. to learn by authority
2. to learn by reasoning
3. to learn by observation
4. to learn by trial and error

Functions

6
1. do you mean
2. you speak up
3. Hang on
4. you explain
5. catch that

Writing

7a
but in fact
Despite the fact that
While
whereas
on the contrary

Unit 12 Test

Grammar

1
1. the party too
2. go there as well
3. They also visited
4. some money too
5. you also bought
6. bank account as well

2
1 just   3 even   5 just   7 just
2 only   4 only   6 even   8 only

3
1. Yesterday I got the cleaner to wash the windows.
2. They always have a gardener cut the grass.
3. We need to get a plumber to fix the bathroom.
4. Paul wants to have an architect design an extension to his house.

Vocabulary

4
1. afford
2. pricey
3. income
4. hard up
5. loaded
6. reasonable

5
1. invested
2. borrow
3. lend
4. spend
5. give
6. earn
7. owes
8. pay

6
1 e   2 a   3 b   4 c   5 d   6 f

7
1. feelings
2. up
3. luck
4. headed
5. done by

Functions

8
1. a key thing
2. to be honest
3. Is there not some way round that?
4. If I were in your shoes
5. at the end of the day

Writing

9a
1. Summary
2. Advantages
3. Disadvantages
4. Recommendations

Photocopiable communicative activities

Unit 1 Communicative activity
Meeting an old friend

Read the information on your role card about yourself and your partner. Then roleplay the situation in which you meet by chance after five years.

Role-card

You:

- married for three years, with a one-year-old baby girl
- live in a house in Salton which you bought two years ago
- still in the same job (Smith's Paper Factory), but you are now head of Exports – you were promoted last year
- still interested in watching tennis, but you had to give up playing last year because of knee problems; started to play golf
- still like photography, films, reading; stopped going to rock concerts because of baby
- you still keep in touch with Janet, another old school friend, who moved to Manchester after University. She got divorced last year, and is thinking of taking up a new job in Leeds

Your friend:

- you were at school together from 11–18 in Salton; you stayed friends though you went to different universities
- you both started working for Smith's Paper Factory when you were both 22; your friend left after two years, getting promotion to a paper company in Canada
- you have kept in touch on and off, but recently haven't exchanged emails

✂ -

Read the information on your role card about yourself and your partner. Then roleplay the situation in which you meet by chance after five years.

Role-card

You:

- single, no current relationship
- just moved back to stay with your parents at Salton
- you worked for Old Pines Paper Works in Canada for four years, but they have just been bought buy an American company, so you left – you didn't like the new conditions. You are looking for a new job now.
- you still play tennis regularly and play the guitar; in Canada you were in a blues band, and you hope to join a band back in Salton
- you have lost touch with your mutual friend Janet

Your friend:

- you were at school together from 11–18 in Salton; you stayed friends though you went to different universities
- you both started working for Smith's paper Factory when you were both 22; your friend stayed there when you got promotion to a paper company in Canada
- you have kept in touch on and off, but recently haven't exchanged emails

Unit 2 Communicative activity

Telling a story

Think about a story which you have read or seen recently, e.g. a novel or short story, a film or a TV programme. Make some notes about the details in the table below, and then tell your partner your story while they make brief notes about it. Answer any questions they may have about the details carefully. Then listen to your partner's story, and make brief notes about their story. Make comments, and ask questions for clarification, if necessary. Afterwards, compare notes about your stories.

	My story	My partner's story
Story title		
Where is it from? (book / film / TV, author / director)		
Setting / location		
Main characters		
Story: start		
Story: middle		
Story: end		

Unit 3 Communicative activity

Making predictions about the future

Work in a group of four.

Each of you should choose one of the following topics:

- transport and travel
- food and drink
- computers and technology
- homes and home life

Make some notes below about what will and won't have happened and what people will and won't be doing in the area you have chosen by 2050, using the verbs given and any others you can think of. Then give a brief talk to the other three about the changes you expect in your area.

Listen to the talks by the other three members of your group. Then discuss the ideas presented and say whether you think they are possible, probable or unlikely.

Notes about my talk	
Use	
Replace	
Become	
Invent	
Discover	
Introduce	
Increase	
Decrease	
Disappear	

Unit 4 Communicative activity

Talking about likes and dislikes

Think about the many different areas of the arts (e.g. theatre, opera, musicals, classical music, ballet, modern dance, painting, sculpture, installation art, jazz, blues and other different types of music).

Choose one genre which you like and one which you dislike. Think carefully about what it is about them that you like and dislike, and make some notes under the relevant areas in the table below.

When you have completed the table, work with two other students and ask and answer questions about your likes and dislikes.

	The art form I like is: _____	The art form I dislike is: _____
music / sound		
words		
venue		
action / movement		
colour / visual effects		
other		

Unit 5 Communicative activity

Deciding on a development project

A rich benefactor has donated one million euros a year for the next three years to your home area (the whole class must decide if this is a particular town, village, area of a city before you start).

The benefactor has said the money must be spent as follows:

- on a project which will benefit children up to 18 years of age
- the project must be sustainable and continuous
- the money may be spent on land, property, equipment, staff salaries, etc.
- the money will only become available when a firm project for development is presented to the benefactor's representatives and is accepted

Part 1

Work in a group of four to create a plan for how the money should be spent. Use the table below to make your notes; add any other areas for consideration at the bottom of the table.

Target group	
Overall aim	
Buildings needed	
Outdoor space needed	
Staff	
Equipment	

Part 2

Each group presents its project to the rest of the class, who are then the benefactor's representatives. The other groups should award points out of 20 for each project. Groups should not give points for their own projects. At the end the points should be added up to decide the winning project.

Unit 6 Communicative activity

Talking about holidays

Complete the information in the table about a holiday you went on once, and then ask your partner questions and complete the right-hand column of the table with their information.

	My holiday	My partner's holiday
Month / year		
Place, country		
Travel		
Accommodation		
Food and drink		
Activities		
Weather		
People		
Interesting attractions		
Entertainment		
Best thing about it		
Worst thing about it		
Other		

Unit 7 Communicative activity

A quiz about water

Student A

Ask your partner these questions about water. Keep a record of the number of correct answers they give.

1 Running a tap for five minutes uses the same energy as using a 60 watt light bulb for:
   a 4 hours.   b 14 hours.   c 40 hours.
   [answer b]

2 A six minute shower uses:
   a 15 litres of water.   b 25 litres of water.   c 55 litres of water.
   [answer c]

3 What is the name for a large sandy dry area?
   [answer: a desert]

4 Why is the delta of the Colorado River in Mexico like a salt flat now?
   [answer: because it has been dammed and diverted for agricultural purposes]

5 Cleaning ½ kilo of wool uses:
   a 850 litres of water.   b 8,500 litres of water.   c 85,000 litres of water.
   [answer: c]

6 What is desalination?
   [answer: the process of removing salt from sea-water]

7 Which uses more water to produce: a serving of goat meat or a serving of chicken?
   [Answer: a serving of chicken (580 litres compared to 42 for goat meat)]

- -

Student B

Ask your partner these questions about water. Keep a record of the number of correct answers they give.

1 What is the name for an underground water supply?
   [answer: an aquifer]

2 Making a hamburger uses:
   a 1,500 litres of water.   b 2,000 litres of water.   c 2,500 litres of water.
   [answer: c]

3 What is a lot of Las Vegas's water used for?
   [answer: watering golf courses]

4 How big is the Aral Sea in central Asia compared to what it was in 1960?
   a one tenth   b one fifth   c one half
   [answer: one tenth]

5 Making a 50g chocolate bar uses:
   a 141 litres of water.   b 1,410 litres of water.   c 14,100 litres of water.
   [answer: b]

6 What happens on many Greek islands each summer?
   [answer: the 16 million tourists cause water shortages]

7 Which uses more water to produce: a cup of coffee or a slice of bread?
   [answer: a cup of coffee (135 litres compared to 40)]

Unit 8 Communicative activity

Saying what's in the news

Think about a current or recent news story (local, national or international) which you know quite a lot about. Make some notes about it in the *My news story* column, under the various headings. Work with a partner who has dealt with a different story. Tell your partner the story while they make some notes as you speak. Then listen to your partner's news story and make brief notes about the fact. Afterwards compare ideas about the two stories.

	My news story	My partner's news story
Who?		
What?		
Where?		
When?		
Why?		
The outcome		
Other important information		

Unit 9 Communicative activity

Talents, skills and abilities

Use the table below to interview two people about their education, experience and talents. Make notes on their answers in the appropriate boxes.

	Student 1: _____	Student 2: _____
Education and qualifications		
Part-time jobs or voluntary work (how long for, responsibilities)		
Full-time jobs (how long for, responsibilities)		
Special skills and talents that help in current job or studies		
Future employment hopes		
Hobbies, sports, skills and abilities needed		
Other skills and abilities		
Other		

Unit 10 Communicative activity

Raising children

Until they reach the age of majority, children should always do what adults tell them.

✂ -

Children should never speak when adults are speaking.

✂ -

Children should never talk with their mouth full when they are eating.

✂ -

Children should not chew gum in public.

✂ -

Children should not stare or point at adults.

✂ -

Children should always be neatly and cleanly dressed in public.

✂ -

Children should always eat up all the food they are given.

✂ -

Children must expect punishment from adults if they misbehave.

✂ -

Children must always go to bed and get up at the correct time.

✂ -

Children must never be late.

✂ -

Until they reach the age of majority, children should always do what adults tell them.

✂ -

Children should never speak when adults are speaking.

✂ -

Children should never talk with their mouth full when they are eating.

✂ -

Children should not chew gum in public.

✂ -

Children should not stare or point at adults.

✂ -

Children should always be neatly and cleanly dressed in public.

✂ -

Children should always eat up all the food they are given.

✂ -

Children must expect punishment from adults if they misbehave.

✂ -

Children must always go to bed and get up at the correct time.

✂ -

Children must never be late.

✂ -

Unit 11 Communicative activity
The learning process

Read the text below and learn the information it gives you so that you can tell someone else. You may make notes if it helps you to learn the information, but you cannot use your notes when you pass on the information.

Woodpeckers in Britain

There are only three species of woodpecker in Britain. The largest of these is the green woodpecker, which is around 30–35 centimetres long. Green woodpeckers live in open forests, as well as farmland, parks and even large gardens. They feed mostly on ants, and frequently spend time catching them on the ground, unlike other woodpeckers. They are bright green birds with a red head, and have a loud 'laughing' call. The next largest species is the great spotted woodpecker, at around 24 centimetres long. They are noticeable black and white birds. The males also have red on the back of their head, and both males and females have red on the lower body and under the tail. They live in all kinds of woodland, parks and gardens. They call with a 'kick' sound, and also make a drumming noise on trees in spring. The smallest of the three is the lesser spotted woodpecker, which is only the size of a sparrow – 15 centimetres long. They live in parks and river valleys. Their small size makes them very difficult to see, however there has been a large decrease in numbers recently. Like the great spotted woodpecker it has a 'kick' call, and it also drums in spring.

✂ --

Read the text below and learn the information it gives you so that you can tell someone else. You may make notes if it helps you to learn the information, but you cannot use your notes when you pass on the information.

Thrushes in Britain

There are four members of the thrush family in Britain. The commonest and best-known of these is the blackbird, which lives in woodlands, but is very frequent in parks and gardens. Blackbirds are around 25 centimetres long, and males are all black with a bright yellow beak and eye-ring. They have a very beautiful song. Females are dark brown. The song thrush used to be a common garden bird, too, but over the last 50 years numbers have dropped seriously. It is about 20 cm long, with a light brown back and white chest covered in brown spots. As the name suggests, they sing beautifully, repeating each phrase twice. The mistle thrush is like a larger song thrush, with similar colour and markings, but around 27 centimetres long. They live in more open woodland, although they do come to parks and gardens. They do not sing so well as the first two. The fourth thrush is the ring ouzel, which lives in very different habitats – high rocky valleys and mountains. They are black like a blackbird, but have a white semicircle round their neck, which is very distinctive. They are also not great singers.

Unit 12 Communicative activity

The final quiz

How much information can you remember from the book? Answer the questions.

1 What is 'blood thicker than' in the proverb? _____

2 Which city does Bella (Zhou Jiyang) live in? _____

3 What racing driver was featured in Unit 2? _____

4 What is the *author* of a filmscript called? _____

5 What two endangered species live in the Kaziranga National Park? _____

6 What are Jacob and Wilhelm's surname? _____

7 What is *augmented reality*? _____

8 How is Melbourne different from Sydney? _____

9 What is *reverse graffiti*? _____

10 When and where did hip-hop begin? _____

11 Who is Anish Kapoor? _____

12 What and where is the Burj Khalifa? _____

13 Which organisation no longer finances hydroelectric projects? _____

14 What percentage of the world population lived in cities in 1800? _____

15 What and where is the Hotel de Glace? _____

16 What is a *staycation*? _____

17 In what country can you stay in a prison hotel and be treated badly? _____

18 Who had a garden at Giverny, France? _____

19 How much water do you need to flush the toilet? _____

20 Where did Britain find a lot of gas in the 1970s? _____

21 What is the world's fourth largest island? _____

22 Who is Sharbat Gula? _____

23 What did Peter Burkill do that made him a hero? _____

24 Where are they building supertrees? _____

25 What is a *mahout*? _____

26 When did Apollo 11 land on the moon? _____

27 Which woman became 'king of Egypt'? _____

28 What is *proxemics*? _____

29 What did Irene Pepperberg work with for many years? _____

30 What record does Norway hold? _____

Photocopiable communicative activities: Teacher's notes

Unit 1

AIM: To practise meeting people you know

MATERIALS: A copy of the worksheet for each pair of students

METHODOLOGY: Ask students to read through the information and think themselves into the role they are going to play. If necessary, ask them to look at the expressions in the box on page 16 of the Student's Book before they start. Stress that they are pleased to meet their old friend, and want to find out as much as they can about what they have been doing recently. They can change partners and roles when they have done it once.

Unit 2

AIM: To practise telling a story, using different past tenses

MATERIALS: A copy of the worksheet for each student

METHODOLOGY: Ask students to prepare for 10 minutes, completing the information in the *My story* side of the table. (You could give this as a homework task the previous lesson.) Ask them to tell their story, listen to their partner and make notes, then compare their notes when they have both told their stories.

Unit 3

AIM: To practise using future continuous and future perfect to talk about hypothetical situations in the future

MATERIALS: A copy of the worksheet for each student

METHODOLOGY: Remind students of the use of the future continuous and future perfect tenses by eliciting some examples of use (e.g. *will have invented, won't be using*). Ask them to get into groups of four and select an area for discussion. They should then make notes about what they think the situation will be in 2050, using the verbs suggested on the worksheet. Give them a fixed time limit to prepare, then ask them to take turns presenting their ideas to the rest of the group. The other students should comment on how likely the predictions are.

Unit 4

AIM: To talk about likes and dislikes related to the arts

MATERIALS: A copy of the worksheet for each student

METHODOLOGY: Once they have completed brief notes in their tables about their two areas, remind them of the appropriate language to talk about them using the expressions in the table on page 52. Ask them to get into threes to talk, listen and ask questions about and comment on each other's preferences.

Unit 5

AIM: To discuss and evaluate a development project

MATERIALS: A copy of the worksheet for each student

METHODOLOGY: First make a class decision about which place the project relates to – it is important to limit it to a small area, or the whole thing becomes too big and unmanageable. Ask students to work in teams of four to plan their project. They should use the language from the box on page 64 when doing this. Once planned, assign each group a letter (A, B, C etc.) and have them present their project to the other groups, who discuss the merits of the project and assign a score out of 20 for it. Collect all the marks after all the groups have presented and announce which project has won.

Unit 6

AIM: To ask and answer questions about a real holiday

MATERIALS: A copy of the worksheet for each student

METHODOLOGY: Give students a worksheet each, and ask them to choose one holiday which they remember well, and to complete the *My Holiday* column with brief notes about it. They should then tell their partner about it and answer questions about their holiday. Then they change roles, and listen to their partner and ask questions. They can make notes about their partner's holiday in the other column.

Unit 7

AIM: To have fun with the facts and figures about water given in the unit

MATERIALS: One copy of the worksheet for each pair of A and B students.

METHODOLOGY: You might want students to read through pages 82–83 again briefly before they do this quiz. Ask them to get into pairs, and give each student an A or B half of the worksheet. Tell them not to show them to each other, as they have the answers on them! They should take it in turns to ask all seven questions, and record the answers given by their partner, without saying whether they are right or wrong. Afterwards, they can discuss the answers given and see who got more correct answers. Remind them that it is for fun, and is not a test.

Unit 8

AIM: For students to practise organising their thoughts about a story (in this case a news story) in an ordered way, and then to present it

MATERIALS: A copy of the worksheet for each student

METHODOLOGY: Ask students to make notes about the key points of a current or relatively recent news story they know about (stress that it can be local, national or international); they should use the headings to organise their ideas and make sure they have good coverage of the events. Ask them to work with someone who has done a different story. They should tell each other their stories, and make notes as they listen. Finally they can compare and discuss the two stories.

Unit 9

AIM: To ask and answer questions about individual talents and skills

MATERIALS: A copy of the worksheet for each student

METHODOLOGY: Ask students to think about their own answers to the various elements, and how to ask the necessary questions correctly. They should then interview two students and be interviewed themselves. At the end, each student should find something positive to say about the people they interviewed in terms of their professional or private skills and abilities.

Unit 10

AIM: To get students to discuss what is right in the upbringing of children

MATERIALS: One copy of the worksheet for each pair of A and B students.

METHODOLOGY: Get students into groups of ten. Give each student a rule about childhood. Ask them to think about their rule, and how they feel about it (e.g. did it apply to them when they were growing up? Would they apply it to their own children?). They should then mingle with the other nine students in their group, and discuss their rule and feelings about it with others, and the other students' rules. If you wish, give them a set time – say two minutes with each person, then clap for them to change partner and start a new discussion. Afterwards, ask the groups of ten to sit in a circle and discuss the whole set of rules. Elicit ideas and opinions from the whole class.

Unit 11

AIM: To study and discuss the learning process

MATERIALS: One copy of the worksheet for each pair of A and B students.

METHODOLOGY: Ask students to work in pairs. A should read the A text and B the B text, and they should each memorise as much of the information in the text as they can. They should work individually to do this, and they can use any means they like. Give them a set amount of time – perhaps 15 minutes. After this, they should tell their partner their information, without looking at the text, or any notes, diagrams or other learning aids they

used. While one student talks, the other student can follow the text to check the information. They should then get together in groups of four (two pairs) and discuss how they learnt the information, what was difficult to remember, and so on. Elicit some comments from the whole class.

Unit 12

AIM: To have a fun test on the interesting content from the course

MATERIALS: A copy of the quiz questions for each student, pair of students, or group of four (see below)

METHODOLOGY: You could do this in several ways:

(a) Individuals answer as many as they can within a 20-minute time-limit. They exchange papers and mark each other's.

(b) Pairs work together and do the quiz.

(c) Teams of four do the quiz.

For (b) and (c) you can decide whether to limit time and make it competitive as for 1, or keep it more relaxed.

ANSWERS
1 water
2 Shanghai
3 Ayrton Senna
4 a screenwriter
5 tiger/single-horned rhino
6 Grimm
7 When we get extra information about things we see illustrated on a computer or mobile phone
8 Melbourne is the art, architectural and sports capital of Australia
9 Scraping dirt off walls to create pictures using the white surface underneath
10 New York Bronx in the mid-1970s
11 A British sculptor
12 the world's tallest building in Dubai
13 The World Bank
14 2%
15 An ice hotel in Quebec, Canada
16 A holiday where you stay at home
17 Latvia
18 Claude Monet (French Impressionist painter)
19 8 litres
20 The North Sea
21 Madagascar
22 An Afghan woman whose face featured on the cover of National Geographic
23 Prevented a British Airways plane from crashing
24 In Singapore
25 A person who trains a working elephant
26 July 1969
27 Hatshepsut
28 The study of standards of personal space
29 An African Grey Parrot called Alex
30 The highest quality of life in the world.

Workbook answer key

Unit 1

1a (pages 4 and 5)

1 b

2 1 b 2 b 3 b 4 c 5 a 6 a

3 1 truth 2 strength 3 warmth 4 length 5 depth

4
1 is dying out, you are trying, France is changing
2 we work with, we chat to, they reserve real intimacy
3 friendships have lost, you have ever visited
4 have been declining

5
1 have you spent *or* have you been spending
2 Do you consider
3 do you have
4 is increasing *or* has increased
5 Have you made
6 have you known
7 do you see
8 do you look for

6
1 intimate, close, strong   3 close, closest, true   5 casual
2 strong   4 complete

7
1 student   3 acquaintance   5 blood
2 companion   4 flat   6 passing

8
1 travel companion   4 fellow students
2 odd couple   5 close relative
3 mutual respect

9
1 out with   3 on   5 by   7 up
2 up with   4 round   6 up with   8 for

1b (pages 6 and 7)

1 1 T 2 F 3 T 4 F 5 T 6 F

2
1 rate   4 lifestyle
2 boom, retirement   5 expectancy
3 diet   6 vaccinations

3
1 are being forced   4 is being encouraged
2 has been raised   5 are reduced
3 isn't considered   6 hasn't been welcomed

4
1 is known
2 are obliged
3 have been educated
4 has been made
5 are also given *or* have also been given
6 is now outnumbered

5
1 is rising   4 have gone
2 is growing   5 are obliged
3 has not been received   6 are being encouraged

6a
1 are given   4 has not yet been found
2 have been made   5 is considered
3 is being discussed   6 are expected

6b 1 W 2 W 3 S 4 W 5 S 6 W

7
1 I think my parents' generation has been quite lucky.
2 My parents worked hard all their lives, but they both retired when they were 60 and they've been given good pensions. So now they can relax and enjoy themselves.
3 They've said that they don't want to be a burden on us, and that we children aren't expected to look after them when they get old.
4 Considering that my husband and I are now being asked to work until we are 68, I'm glad they said that.

1c (page 8)

1 c

2 1 F 2 T 3 T 4 T 5 F 6 T 7 F 8 F

3 1 a 2 a 3 c 4 b 5 b 6 c

4a
1 dynamic   3 economics   5 restriction
2 fantastic   4 generation   6 tradition
Rule: The penultimate syllable is always stressed.

4b specific italics terrific scientific characteristic impression relation interruption transformation comprehension

1d (page 9)

1
1 into   3 to   5 –   7 on   9 in
2 –   4 under   6 of   8 –   10 with

2 1 PPS 2 PPC 3 PPS 4 PPC

3
a present perfect continuous
b present perfect simple

4
1 been wondering   3 decided   5 finished
2 been working   4 been helping   6 lost

5
a Fancy bumping into you here
b What a nice surprise
c it obviously suits you
d how's it all going with you
e Do give her my best regards
f great to see you
g Good luck with the job

6 1 E 2 F 3 E 4 E 5 F 6 E

7 Students' own answers.

1e (page 10)

1 1 g 2 c 3 f 4 e 5 a 6 d 7 b

2
1 How are you **getting on**: doing
2 when you **get** a moment to write: have
3 you're able to **get by**: manage
4 I **got** a letter: received
5 I'm trying not to **get** too excited: become
6 to **get** a job: obtain
7 Sarah is going to **get** married: be

3
1 understand   4 arrive at *or* reach   7 won
2 put down   5 take *or* catch   8 find *or* bring
3 bought   6 recover from

4
1 received *or* got   11 don't think
2 am   12 have ever experienced
3 arrived *or* got   13 has happened
4 sounds   14 am trying *or* have tried
5 have had /*or* have been having   *or* have been trying
6 were *or* got   15 haven't been
7 hope   16 find *or* get
8 have recovered   17 helped *or* has helped
9 hasn't become *or* hasn't got /   *or* has been helping
   doesn't become *or* doesn't get   18 don't really understand
10 sounds   *or* don't really get

Wordbuilding / Learning skills (page 11)

1
-*ful*: respectful, helpful, playful
-*ish*: foolish, childish, selfish
-*ive*: sensitive, conservative, decisive
-*ous*: studious, humorous, industrious
-*ent/-ant*: dependent, different, dominant
-*al*: entrepreneurial, industrial, intellectual, practical
-*ing*: caring, controlling, dominating, loving

2 Possible answers:
1 dependent   6 intellectual/studious
2 caring/sensitive   7 humorous
3 conservative   8 entrepreunerial
4 dominant   9 industrious
5 practical

3 1 decisively   2 take   3 indecisive   4 conclusion

4 Students' own answers.

5 1 b   2 c   3 a   4 c   5 c

Unit 2

2a (pages 12 and 13)

1 1 They travel for hundreds of miles to breed.
2 The struggle between life and death.

2 1 have chicks   3 dramatic   5 in such hard conditions
2 their young   4 predictable

3 1 to shoot   4 to anticipate
2 inspired   5 struck (me)
3 documentary *or* drama

4 1 I have also worked as a cameraman.
2 I spent 14 months at the French scientific centre in Antarctica. *and* I helped to shoot another film in 1995.
3 They have never experienced any form of colonisation, so they're not scared of humans. *and* The penguins have learned to live where no other creature can.

5 1 have met   5 encountered   9 didn't run
2 have spent   6 adapted   10 did
3 have always felt   7 learned
4 got   8 has visited

6 1 director   5 cast   9 audience
2 sentimental   6 location   10 scenes
3 gripping   7 accurate
4 touching   8 storyline

7 There is a silent 'l' in the following words: talk, could, calf, folk, calm

8 1 setting for; thought-provoking book
2 characters are you and me and every other typical passenger
3 book is based on conversations that the author had
4 The idea behind it; can portray modern civilisation

2b (pages 14 and 15)

1 b

2 1 a   2 c   3 c   4 b   5 a

3 1 a   2 b   3 b   4 a   5 c   6 b

4 1 drove   7 were hanging
2 made   8 hadn't told
3 arrived   9 stood
4 had fallen   10 had crushed *or* was crusing
5 climbed   11 waited
6 had gone   12 had already decided

5 1 b   2 a   3 c

6 1 hadn't   3 isn't   5 weren't   7 had
2 are   4 was   6 was   8 haven't

7a The tenses used to describe the film are: present simple, present continuous and present perfect.

7b 1 gives   4 grow *or* are growing
2 begin   5 are getting
3 reaches *or* has reached

2c (page 16)

1 1 T   2 F   3 T   4 T   5 F   6 F

2 1 children; adults   4 moved
2 fairy tale   5 moral lessons
3 sadness

3 1 an elegant   5 people
2 watches closely   6 days
3 a little swallow stops off with him   7 catches cold
4 asks   8 destroy

4 1 c   2 b   3 d   4 a

5 1 kept you from *or* have kept you from   4 keep track of
2 kept an eye on   5 kept back
3 keep him company   6 keep a secret

2d (page 17)

1 1 tore   2 broke   3 stuck   4 made   5 froze   6 burst

2 a What a   f How
b That was   g Poor
c How *or* That was   h What *or* That must have been
d How *or* That was   i How *or* That must have been
e What   j What *or* That must have been
Possible answers:
1 a *or* c   2 a *or* j   3 a *or* c *or* i   4 c   5 a   6 a *or* j

3 1 Hannah's passport was out-of-date.
2 She went to the passport office in London to get a new passport.
3 Very stressed.

4 1 d   2 b   3 f   4 a   5 e   6 c

6 Students' own answers.

2e (page 18)

1a whispered, replied anxiously, moaned, muttered, cried

1b 1 c   2 b   3 g   4 d   5 e   6 a   7 f

2a a T   b T   c T   d T

2b 'I don't think this is going to work,' Christopher sighed. 'We've been trying to build this canoe for three days and it still looks like a lump of wood. The wood's too hard,' he added. 'Actually, Christopher,' said Jen encouragingly, 'we are making some progress. What we really need to do is find some better tools.' Just then Tom screamed, 'I've got it! Instead of using our penknives directly on the wood, why don't we make some better tools using our knives?'

3 Model answer:
'Look out,' screamed Fergus, 'I think he's angry now.' The two friends edged nervously backwards as the snake turned its head to face them. Josh had thrown a large rock at it, hoping that this would frighten it, but it seemed that it had had the opposite effect. Now Josh was looking around for something else to hit the snake with. 'Where's a stick when you need one?' he muttered. 'Too late for that,' said Fergus. 'Let's get out of here.' And with that, he leaped towards the trees and started running.

Wordbuilding / Learning skills (page 19)

1 an author – a novelist   a film – a movie
an audience – viewers   a hero – a heroine
a blockbuster – a best-seller   to publish – to release
a cinema – a multiplex   a remake – a re-release
to edit – to cut   a sequel – a follow-up

2 1 an author *or* a novelist   6 to cut
2 a heroine   7 a sequel *or* follow-up
3 viewers   8 a multiplex
4 a best-seller   9 a re-release
5 to release   10 a movie

3 1 b   2 a   3 a   4 b   5 b   6 a

4, 5 and 6 Students' own answers.

7 1 a a documentary
b a children's story *or* fairy tale
c a book-film adaptation
2 a film director *or* producer
b author *or* writer
c photographer
3 a shave   b stroke   c stretch

Unit 3

3a (pages 20 and 21)

1 c

2 1 standard of living
2 increase
3 more than *or* faster than
4 (two) children
5 one billion
6 three ways *or* three schools of thought *or* three alternatives

3 Greater: rise, boost, grow, increase, raise, peak
Smaller: dwindle, deplete, decrease, fall, lessen, reduce

4 1 reduce
2 rise *or* increase *or* grow
3 decrease *or* fall
4 reduce *or* lessen
5 increase *or* raise *or* boost
6 increase

5 1 will have; will be
2 are going to rely
3 I'll tell; I will be; doesn't start
4 won't solve; share
5 is going to save
6 I'm going; begins

6 1 Are you going *or* Are you going to go
2 are you getting *or* are you going to get
3 'll probably drive *or* am probably going to drive
4 'll go
5 'll give
6 are you leaving *or* are you going to leave
7 starts
8 will finish *or* will be finished

7 1 etcetera
2 contributed
3 lot
4 fifteen
5 years
6 powerful
7 motives
8 meet
9 secretly
10 Manhattan

3b Smart technology (pages 22 and 23)

1 Items mentioned: kitchen gadgets, water use, sound-proofing, visual media, lighting

2 1 a 2 b 3 c 4 c 5 c 6 b

3 1 b 2 g 3 a 4 f 5 h 6 c 7 e 8 d

4 1 will be hearing
2 will be making
3 will all be using
4 will have become
5 will be using
6 will be cleaning
7 will be installing
8 will have become
9 will be launching

5 1 will be doing
2 will be cleaning
3 will have developed
4 will be doing
5 will have been
6 won't have acquired

6 1 information age, information overload, information technology
2 data security, data storage
3 computer games, computer graphics, computer programmer

7 1 data security
2 information age
3 computer graphics
4 data storage
5 information overload

8 1 The weekday edition of *The New York Times* contains more information than the average person in 17th-century England learned in a lifetime.
2 Around a thousand books are published internationally every day and the total of all printed knowledge doubles every five years.
3 More information has been published in the last 30 years than in the previous 5,000.

3c (page 24)

1 1 b 2 c 3 c 4 b

2 1 2007; 6000 2 99.9% 3 15 4 700 5 30 6 2010

3 1 works
2 provides
3 contains
4 lasts
5 weighs
6 costs
7 run

4a 1 /ɪ/ 2 /ɪ/ 3 /aɪ/ 4 /ɪ/ 5 /aɪ/

5 1 neat
2 appropriate
3 consuming
4 handy
5 cutting
6 fix

3d (page 25)

1 1 sort
2 format
3 undo
4 copy
5 select
6 highlight
7 open
8 search
9 attach
10 paste
11 save
12 cut

2 1 He is having trouble sending the document. *or* He's trying to attach a document to an email, but he can't.
2 1 Compress the photos; 2 Divide the document into three or four separate documents.
3 It reduces the quality of the photos.

3 1 give
2 hand
3 trouble
4 exactly
5 trying
6 Let
7 look
8 trouble
9 can
10 involve
11 show
12 trick
13 see
14 else
15 tried
16 try
17 works
18 free

4 The two verbs which do not fit the stress pattern are: highlight and open

5 Students' own answers.

3e (page 26)

1 1 Please could I bring your memory stick back on my way home from work tonight?
2 Do you happen to know where I can find a battery charger for my old phone?
3 Could you please send me a brochure for your air conditioning units?
4 Do you know the phone number for Apricot Computers (please)?
5 Please (can/could you) advise me how to download photos from my X306 camera?
6 Would you be able to reduce the price?
7 Would you mind coming over and fixing my internet connection?
8 Please could you tell me what number I should call to get technical advice?

2 1 depth
2 question
3 business
4 date
5 order
6 way
7 interest
8 luck

3 1 f 2 d 3 g 4 c 5 h 6 b 7 a 8 e

4 Model answer:

Hi Jim

I hope all is well with you. I tried to call you earlier, but I couldn't get any answer. I wonder if you could do me a favour. My computer keeps crashing and I think it may have the same virus that yours had a few weeks ago. Would you mind emailing me the instructions about how to remove the virus to my work email? Then I can print them and try to see if it works. Alternatively, could you call me some time? I'll be at home most evenings this week.

Many thanks

Sam

Wordbuilding / Learning skills (page 27)

1 1 biodegradable, biodiversity
2 hypermarket, hypersensitive
3 megabyte, megastar
4 microchip, microwave
5 semi-conscious, semi-detached
6 ultrasonic, ultraviolet

2 1 hypermarket
2 microwave
3 megabyte
4 biodiversity
5 microchip
6 semi-detached
7 hypersensitive
8 ultraviolet
9 ultrasound
10 megastar
11 biodegradable
12 semi-conscious

3
address book	information technology
battery life	news story
credit card	repair manual
data protection	travel advice

4 Students' own answers.

5 1 gadget   3 overload   5 appropriate
2 lazy   4 breakthrough   6 luck
Word: global

Unit 4

4a (pages 28 and 29)

1 1 show, act   4 company, performance, theatre
2 gig, venue, band   5 play, musical
3 exhibition, gallery

2 1 Batman Live, This is Design
2 The Alternative Village Fete; Notting Hill Carnival
3 The Alternative Village Fete, Notting Hill Carnival
4 The Alternative Village Fete
5 The Floating Cinema
6 Notting Hill Carnival
7 Batman Live
8 The Alternative Village Fete

3 1 communal   3 eye candy   5 workshop
2 float   4 mundane

4 1 number   3 several/some   5 any
2 no   4 plenty/loads/lots   6 few

5 1 a little   5 a lack of
2 enough   6 many
3 a lot of; A large number of   7 hardly any
4 plenty of; no   8 a bit of

4b (pages 30 and 31)

1 1 portrait   3 installation   5 sculpture   7 still life
2 grafitti   4 sketch   6 landscape

2 1 In the first photo, the graffiti has been drawn on public walls. In the second photo, the graffiti is part of a piece of artwork.
2 Students' own answers.

3 1 A graffiti artist was convicted of vandalism.
2 Handy thought it was outrageous.
3 When the owner of a property doesn't like it or want it on their property. *or* When it's criminal damage.

4 1 c   2 b   3 c   4 c   5 a   6 a

5 1 person who was invited.
2 method works.
3 anyone came to the opening night.
4 our money.
5 countries have their own laws and rules.
6 world is waiting to see what will happen.

6 1 each; all   4 any   7 whole
2 no   5 Every   8 Either *or* Any
3 both   6 no

7 1 no   2 all the   3 the whole   4 each   5 Both

8 1 The message was clear: is this how far we have come since the Stone Age?
2 Often it carries a political or social message, but in an amusing way that ordinary people can relate to.
3 Despite not calling himself an artist, his work has been shown in galleries and has sold for thousands of dollars.
4 Banksy, who is based in the UK, is perhaps the world's best-known graffiti artist.
5 Banksy loves to surprise. In 2005, a picture showing a primitive human being pushing a shopping cart appeared in the British Museum.
The correct order is: 4, 3, 2, 5, 1

4c (page 32)

1 1 country music   2 dance music   3 (punk) rock   4 hip-hop

2 Possible answers:
a 3   b 1   c 1   d 4   e 2   f 2

3 1 Country; real   3 teenagers; rock
2 influences   4 sounds; technology

4 1 be connected to   4 discover
2 escape   5 think of
3 seem true   6 (not) be important

5 1 b   2 a   3 b   4 d   5 c   6 a

6 1 c   2 b   3 a   4 d

4d (page 33)

1 1 the Amazon River   2 He likes the presenter

2 1 X   2 X   3 X

3 1 kind of thing   4 got on my nerves
2 feel particularly inspired   5 listen to him
3 a big fan of   6 a bit tired of

4b 1 I can listen to Bach all day.
2 Documentaries don't really do anything for me.
3 I'm not really into TV.
4 I'm not particularly keen on the presenter.
5 I get a bit tired of reality TV shows.
6 I don't generally watch much TV.

5 1 documentary   5 separate
2 everywhere   6 restaurant
3 specifically   7 listener
4 interest   8 general

6 Students' own answers.

4e (page 34)

1 a I, we and you; it   e Avoid
b active; passive   f furthermore
c contracted; uncontracted   g Share
d formal

2 Possible answers:
¹ I've got to admit that ² I'm ³ not a big fan of stand-up comedy. ⁴ I always think that it's a rather unnatural thing. The comedian ⁵ stands up in front of an audience who stare at him or her as if to say, 'Come on, then, make me laugh.' The comedian then has a few minutes to make them laugh or the audience will start to get restless. It's all a bit too aggressive and combative for me. ⁶ So when ⁷ I went with an old school friend to see new British comedian Spencer Brown last Tuesday night at the Bristol Comedy Club, ⁸ I wasn't really looking forward to it.

1 contraction   5 active verb
2 contraction   6 conversational linking phrase
3 personal details   7 active verb
4 share your feelings   8 share your feelings

3 Possible answers:
1 But   5 you think at first
2 weren't   6 then *or* after that
3 the rest of the audience   7 that's
seemed to like his act   8 putting together
4 start   9 in fact *or* actually

4 Model answer:
The secret of the show's success is that Spencer Brown really understands his audience and what people find funny. Not only that, but he comes across as a nice guy too. If you are in Bristol, I'd definitely recommend going to see him. He'll be at the Bristol Comedy Club until Saturday 10th December. You'll be smiling for weeks afterwards!

Wordbuilding / Learning skills (page 35)

1
1 snowscape
2 metalworker
3 craftsmanship
4 politeness
5 saxophonist
6 romanticism

2
1 surrealism
2 guitarist
3 TV presenter
4 cityscape
5 calmness
6 modernism
7 moonscape
8 musicianship
9 trombonist
10 carpenter
11 directness
12 companionship

4
1 no, not really
2 /'kʌmftəbl/
3 You use *either* + singular noun, but *both* + plural noun.
4 Yes, 'it gets on my nerves'.
5 American
6 Yes, it's quite direct.

5
1 a Melbourne   b All   c American
2 a few   b folk   c fan
3 a an impersonal tone   b a lot of luck   c cool down
4 a gig; lyrics   b sketch; sculpture   c play; musical

Unit 5

5a (pages 36 and 37)

1   1 F   2 T   3 T   4 F

2
1 normal
2 floods; winds
3 love
4 co-ordinated
5 depressed
6 safe
7 imaginative *or* innovative
8 practical

3
1 to be
2 seeing
3 to hold
4 to return
5 to resettle
6 building
7 seeing
8 wondering

4
verb + *to* + infinitive: help, hope, want
verb + *someone* + to + infinitive: allow, ask, get, help, want
verb + *-ing*: carry on, enjoy, imagine
verb + *someone* + infinitive: help, imagine, make

5a
verb + *to* + infinitive: choose, learn
verb + *someone* + to + infinitive: force, teach
verb + *-ing*: avoid, finish, involve, (not) mind
verb + *someone* + infinitive: let

5b
1 to visit
2 rebuild
3 to participate
4 getting
5 to work
6 learning
7 to do
8 meeting

6
1 pedestrianised
2 mall
3 waterfront
4 luxury
5 housing
6 spaces
7 district
8 centre

7
1 modernise
2 transform
3 spoils
4 demolished
5 redeveloped
6 convert

8a
1 The fact that most people have returned says a lot about how special this city is. The people who live here can't imagine living anywhere else.
2 I'm a musician and making a living in New Orleans has always been a challenge. We hoped to see more investment in jobs and tourism after the hurricane.
3 But since Hurricane Katrina, life has definitely become harder. I love this city, but these days, I'm forced to go out of town to find work.
Answer: Yes, the resident is happy living in New Orleans.

8b   1 can't imagine living   2 hoped to see   3 I'm forced to go

5b (pages 38 and 39)

1   Sentences a and b are true of Monterey today.

2   1 T   2 N   3 F   4 T   5 T   6 T   7 F   8 T

3
1 in the intervening period
2 join (in) the party
3 just like that
4 old-timers
5 set up
6 sample

4
1 dynamic
2 industrial
3 attractive
4 preserved
5 regulated
6 essential

5   1 NC   2 NC   3 C   4 C   5 NC   6 NC   7 C   8 C

6
1 going
2 putting
3 catching
4 to say
5 fishing
6 to make
7 to go
8 eating

7
1 to visit
2 to see
3 to open
4 to do
5 having

8
China – minor
found – drowned
front – hunt
meant – sent
ocean – motion
placed – taste
rule – tool
way – weigh
whale – they'll
where – share

5c (page 40)

1   1 F   2 F   3 F   4 T   5 T

2
1 221
2 pollution
3 possible; easy
4 construction; business
5 materials
6 walk
7 electric *or* electric-powered
8 imported
9 UV
10 farms

3   1 b   2 c   3 c

4
1 pick on
2 pick up
3 pick (me) up
4 take your pick
5 pick holes in
6 pick your brains

5b
architect
architectural
electricity
energy generate
material
minimise
political
sustainable
sustainability

5d (page 41)

1   1 d   2 e   3 f   4 c   5 g   6 a   7 b

2
1 public
2 affordable
3 local
4 green
5 pedestrianised
6 leisure

3   1 d   2 b   3 a   4 c

4
1 I find it incredible that
I know what you mean.
2 Personally,
What's your view?
I agree,
We probably need
3 What do you think we should do?
The way I see it,
it really depends on
Exactly.
Are we all agreed on that?
4 If you ask me,
let's not be

5   Students' own answers.

5e (page 42)

1   1 B   2 D   3 A   4 C

2   c quoting what someone (often famous) has said about this problem

3   Possible answers:
(giving a dramatic example) You used to be able to drive from Washington to Boston, a distance of 450 miles, through rich, green landscape. Now the only green you see is the paint on people's houses!

(giving some statistics) In the United States, the area between Boston and Washington DC, a distance of 450 miles, is now a massive urban region with a population of about 50 million – that's almost 17% of the US population on 2% of the US land area.

4 1 In addition
2 Because of this; As a result
3 on the other hand

5b 1 … three acres of land, the house comes with a swimming pool. *or* … coming with three acres of land, the house has a swimming pool.
2 … rising crime, people have moved out of the centre.
3 … a good bus service, we have excellent roads into the city centre. *or* having a good bus service, we have excellent roads into the city centre.
4 … restrictions on building on green spaces, we are redeveloping city centres.

Wordbuilding / Learning skills (page 43)

1 1 long-term unemployed
2 politically correct
3 economically disadvantaged
4 upwardly mobile
5 ill prepared
6 ethnically mixed
7 highly cultured
8 cleverly designed

2 1 rebuild   3 retrain   5 redo
2 redecorate   4 readjust   6 reread

4 Possible answers:
- It doesn't say who wrote it, but it doesn't seem to be a travel article. The interest seems to be from a historical and urban development perspective.
- The main argument is that a fantastic city has grown up in a place you would not expect it, because of one person's dream and ambition.
- The writer doesn't say whether he/she likes what has happened to Dubai or not, but he/she seems uncertain that it will be a long-term success.
- I agree with the writer's argument. It seems an unsustainable development.

5 1 c   2 c   3 c   4 b   5 b

Unit 6

6a (pages 44 and 45)

1 b Speaker 4   c Speaker 1   e Speaker 2   f Speaker 3
The two extra items are a and d.

2 a Speaker 4   d Speaker 1
b Speaker 3   f Speaker 2
The two extra activities are c and e.

3 1 a   2 b   3 b   4 b   5 c

4 1 Let's not kid ourselves
2 Don't answer
3 You don't have to do
4 not to do
5 I don't think it's extravagant
6 I hope I didn't overdo it.
7 not to let the children know
8 you really mustn't let

5 1 I don't want a coffee now, thanks.
2 I don't think it's a great idea.
3 Let's not do anything to upset them.
4 I hope I didn't give her the wrong impression.
5 You don't have to give the book back to me immediately.
6 Try not to be late, please.
7 You mustn't take food into the library.
8 Have they decided not to stay?

6 1 off *or* holiday
2 catering
3 scenery
4 view
5 airlines
6 luggage *or* baggage
7 journey *or* drive *or* way
8 countryside
9 took
10 suitcase *or* bag

7 1 stay   2 drop   3 eating   4 stay   5 fill   6 join

8 1 In tough economic times, people will try not to spend so much on luxuries and that includes holidays.
2 However, they don't want to go without a holiday altogether, because holidays are an important break from the stresses of work and daily life.
3 You don't have to go abroad to go on holiday. You can have a staycation instead. These have increased in popularity in recent years.
4 I don't think it's a bad trend because it means that people discover more about their own country, and at the same time, they boost the local economy.

6b (pages 46 and 47)

1 1 consultancy-type roles
2 highly skilled professionals
3 four to six months
4 there isn't any flexibility
5 no costs

2 1 c   2 b   3 a   4 c   5 c   6 b

3 1 rewarding
2 tough
3 concentrated
4 fresh
5 set
6 one-off

4 1 Haven't you ever wondered
2 don't you translate
3 Wouldn't you like
4 Won't it harm
5 Aren't you going to lose out
6 Isn't it

5 1 do you
2 wouldn't it
3 is it
4 didn't you
5 mightn't there
6 wouldn't I

6 1 F   2 F   3 R   4 R   5 R   6 F   7 R   8 F

6c (page 48)

1 Items on *NG Endeavour*: a crane, a kayak, a microscope, an inflatable rubber boat, guides

2 1 educational
2 expensive
3 comfortable
4 well-equipped
5 exciting

3 1 fishing
2 $500
3 $1,000
4 video microscope
5 hydrophones
6 photographers
7 naturalists/guides
8 Mediterranean
9 Antarctica
11 dining

4 1 swanning around
2 set in stone
3 a healthy dose of
4 well-off
5 approachable
6 throughout

5 1 **If you had a cruise in mind**, try one of Lindblad's expeditions.
2 **If you don't mind a bit of danger and excitement**, Lindblad cruises are perfect.
3 The cruises are amazing. **Mind you**, they're not cheap.
4 **Bear in mind that** these are not typical cruises.
5 I used to think that cruises were for the old and retired, but **I've changed my mind** (now).
6 **I'm in two minds about** going on one of their cruises.

6b 1 Don't   2 No   3 It doesn't   4 No   5 Don't   6 It doesn't

6d (page 49)

1 1 in   2 up   3 to   4 on   5 out   6 on   7 up   8 out

2 1 He's working. *or* He's at work.
2 He'll get a bus, then walk.
3 At Steve's office.

3 1 The easiest thing is to take the bus.
2 Alternatively, I can take a taxi.
3 I can make my own way.
4 It's only a fifteen-minute bus ride.
5 I'm coming in by train.
6 If I get held up, I'll let you know.

4 1 drive   2 flight   3 ride   4 walk   5 ride   6 crossing

5a 1 d   2 b   3 a   4 e   5 c

6 Students' own answers.

6e (page 50)

1 1 She had to pay £30 to carry her coat onto the plane.
2 She wants a refund and she wants the airline to investigate the matter.

2 1 Oxford 2 customer – company 3 formal

3 1 register a complaint 6 attempted
2 unjust 7 wished
3 stated 8 opted
4 informed 9 the circumstances
5 placed 10 investigate

3b Model answer:

Dear Sir/Madam

I am writing to **register a complaint** about the meal we **were served** on our flight home last week – flight UZ332. On the booking confirmation, it **stated** that we **would be given** breakfast and lunch. **However**, breakfast **only consisted of** a cup of tea and lunch a tuna sandwich. By itself, this would not have been a problem, but **I regret to say that** my husband and I both **suffered** food poisoning from the sandwich.

4 Model answer:

Given the circumstances, I would ask you to do two things. Firstly, please ensure that in future communication with passengers you make it clear what kind of meal will be served. Secondly, please ensure that the food which you provide is fresh and has not been stored in the wrong conditions.

Yours faithfully

Thomas Garcia

Wordbuilding / Learning skills (page 51)

1 1 in 3 out 5 out 7 in 9 out or in
2 out 4 in 6 in 8 out 10 in

2 a fall out (with) e fall in (with) i drop out (of)
b take in f look out j give up
c drop in (on) g give in (to)
d look in (on) h take out

3 1 action wanted 3 examples
2 link the ideas 4 spelling

4 1 To complain about an extra charge; this point is made in the opening paragraph
2 Reason for writing; details or facts about the incident; action wanted
3 At the time; by this time; consequently; otherwise; Given these circumstances
4 formal
5 She didn't want to delay other passengers; it's not unreasonable to wear a coat onto a plane

5 1 She took a Japanese holiday in her own city.
2 The Great Continental Divide cycling and hiking trail.
3 In a prison hotel.
4 In an art hotel, e.g. Propeller Island City Lodge, in Berlin.
5 couch surfing

Unit 7

7a (pages 52 and 53)

1 Items which are mentioned: repairing broken water pipes, reusing rainwater, turning salt water into fresh water, making artificial rainclouds

2 1 c 2 b 3 b 4 b 5 c

3 a end-user e on the face of it
b hosepipe f ecological footprint
c water meter g sceptic
d water butt h every cloud has a silver lining

4 1 hadn't imposed; would be (mixed conditional)
2 had; would use (second conditional)
3 introduce; will buy (first conditional) or introduced; would buy (second conditional)
4 was; wouldn't need (second conditional)
5 weren't; would have been built (mixed conditional)
6 hadn't been; would feel (mixed conditional)
7 works; are (zero conditional)
8 had thought; would be (mixed conditional)

6 1 run out of 3 waste; conserve 5 protect
2 save 4 preserve 6 spend; consume

7b (pages 54 and 55)

1 1 oil tanker 3 oil slick 5 oil field 7 oil barrel
2 oil rig 4 oil refinery 6 oil well 8 oil pipeline

2 No, he doesn't.

3 1 c 2 a 3 b 4 a 5 c 6 b

4 1 would go 3 hadn't started 5 was
2 was able 4 have 6 ran

5 1 drove 4 had bought 7 had seen
2 had 5 not think 8 didn't speak
3 would stop 6 would become

7 The recent discovery of oil in the tar sands of Alberta has put Canada in third place in the world in oil reserves.
However, extracting this oil creates two to four times the quantity of greenhouse gases as conventional methods of extraction.

As a result, Canada has been under a lot of pressure to limit the environmental impact of its new oil industry.

7c (page 56)

1 1 forest, Cancún, no 2 giraffe, yes 3 tree, Britain, yes

2 1 F 2 T 3 T 4 N 5 N 6 F

3 1 rotting 3 sale 5 heroic 7 small
2 classic 4 victims 6 wonderful 8 rarest

The recent discovery of oil in the tar sands of Alberta has put Canada in third place in the world in oil reserves.
However, extracting this oil creates two to four times the quantity of greenhouse gases as conventional methods of extraction.

As a result, Canada has been under a lot of pressure to limit the environmental impact of its new oil industry.

4 1 classic 3 a victim 5 for sale
2 a decade 4 buried 6 rotting

5 Emotive words: back-breaking, deplore, desperate, majestic, obsessed with

6 1 rescue 4 exploit 7 plummeting
2 deprived 5 wonderful 8 overdeveloped
3 giant 6 most threatened

7d (page 57)

1 1 F 2 A 3 F 4 A

2 1 understand each other better
2 in rich countries to have cheaper goods and also goods out of season
3 natural economic phenomenon
4 the gap between the world's rich and poor

3 1 not, point 5 Imagine
2 just, accept 6 let, give
3 be honest 7 doubt
4 approaching, wrong

4 Speaker 1: c and e Speaker 3: a and d
Speaker 2: d Speaker 4: d

5a 1 Globalisation may have helped the <u>rich</u>, but it hasn't helped the <u>poor</u>.
2 Globalisation is not something that has been <u>invented</u>; it's a <u>natural</u> phenomenon.
3 I <u>like</u> having things that I can't buy locally, but I don't actually <u>need</u> them.
4 Globalisation doesn't <u>harm</u> poor countries; it <u>helps</u> them.
5 I <u>wish</u> you were <u>right</u>, but the <u>facts</u> show the <u>opposite</u>.

6 Students' own answers.

7e (page 58)

1 1 The writer feels that people waste resources such as food, energy and clothes.
2 There will be no more resources left.

2a 1 who live in more difficult circumstances than us
2 which is near its sell-by date
3 such as flat-screen TVs, computers or mobile phones
4 with only one driver in them
5 especially items of fashion clothing

2b Possible answers:
1 with over 70 apartments
2 such as the black poplar tree, which is not found anywhere else in the city
3 where old and young people can come and relax
4 like the old industrial estate in Meadow Leys
5 because they are ugly and in need of modernising

3 1 c 2 b 3 e 4 a 5 d

4 1 to wait 2 calling 3 do 4 to know

Wordbuilding / Learning skills (page 59)

1 1 wind instrument 4 wind chill 7 water jug
2 air bridge 5 water leak 8 air vent
3 wind farm 6 air force 9 water lily

2 sunrise and sunset

4 1 Globalisation <u>helps</u> <u>people</u> <u>in</u> <u>rich</u> <u>countries</u>.
2 They can have goods out <u>of</u> <u>season</u>.
3 But to be <u>honest</u>, I <u>don't</u> <u>need</u> <u>flowers</u> imported from <u>Africa</u> in <u>December</u>.

6 Across: 1 renewable 4 unique 5 ecosystem 7 salt
10 Colorado 12 save 13 well
Down: 1 reuse 2 loggers 3 extract 6 scarce 8 Aral
9 wool 11 oil

Unit 8

8a (pages 60 and 61)

1 Across: 1 hard 3 soft 7 editorial 8 news
Down: 2 article 4 feature 5 headline 6 column

2 1 cover; 1982 2 Nancy; Week

3 1 F 2 T 3 F 4 T 5 F 6 F 7 T 8 F

5 1 of manipulating reality.
2 altering the image *or* that they had altered the image.
3 doing anything wrong *or* that they had done anything wrong.
4 modern technology for making it easy to alter images.
5 their designers (that it is OK) to alter images for covers.
6 about being given a false impression. *or* that they had been given a false impression.
7 not to trust a photo if there's anything important riding on it.

6 1 for invading 4 to alter 7 for making
2 (for) taking 5 touching 8 to accept
3 for manipulating 6 to add

7 1 capture the moment 4 see through the lens
2 open the shutter 5 take a photo
3 record events 6 take a snapshot

8 1 recommends using an analogue camera
2 encourages you to look at the preview before you take a photo; keeps you in the moment
3 that with a digital camera, you need more time to edit the images after they've been taken
4 you can make them look like the image as you saw it

8b (pages 62 and 63)

1 1 b 2 d 3 a 4 c

2 a 3 b 2 c 3 d 4 e 1 f 1

3 1 wrecked 4 zimmer frame 7 plunged
2 donations 5 brainchild 8 speeding
3 longevity 6 brighten up

4 1 it is estimated that rioters 3 It is believed that
2 It was reported that 4 It is not thought that

5 1 It is said that 5 It has been estimated that
2 It is understood that 6 It is thought that
3 It was known that 7 It had been hoped that
4 It was believed that 8 It is supposed that

6 1 It is said that for every negative, there is always a positive.
2 It is expected that Mr Biber will carry on doing what he loves.
3 In the past, it was thought that a glass of red wine a day helped/would help you to live longer.
4 It is not recommended that you eat fast food if you want to live longer.
5 It was hoped that secret gifts would brighten up someone's day.
6 It was supposed that the tree prevented/had prevented the car falling further.
7 It was considered that the man had been/was lucky to survive the accident.
8 It has been reported that the idea was very successful.

7 amusing – serious quirky – ordinary
charming – dreary encouraging – depressing
inspiring – uninspiring optimistic – pessimistic

8c (page 64)

1 1 T 2 F 3 F

2 1 view 4 pipeline 7 dilemma
2 wonders 5 Strictly 8 the last word
3 beauty 6 jumped

3 1 strictly speaking 3 have the last word 5 dilemma
2 wonders 4 balanced view 6 jump the gun

4 1 b 2 b 3 a 4 a

5 1 word of mouth 5 gave his word
2 eat my words 6 From the word go
3 one person's word against another's 7 was lost for words
4 don't take my word for it 8 have the last word

8d (page 65)

1 1 take (B) 3 spread (D) 5 blown (D)
2 gets (B) 4 Take (D) 6 take (D)

2 1 Philip has been signed up by a theatrical agent.
2 Kate
3 Not to tell anyone. Patrick wants to keep quiet about it.

3 1 about; Guess 4 pinch 7 gossip
2 apparently 5 according to 8 seems; supposedly
3 reckons 6 heard

4 1 com<u>e</u>dy 4 reck<u>o</u>n 7 ag<u>e</u>ncy
2 festiv<u>a</u>l 5 <u>a</u>ccording 8 the<u>a</u>tric<u>a</u>l
3 <u>a</u>pp<u>a</u>r<u>e</u>ntly 6 diff<u>i</u>c<u>u</u>lt

5 Students' own answers.

8e (page 66)

1 1 attend, hold 3 make, reach 5 draft, write
2 make, put forward 4 discuss, weigh up

2
1 A meeting was held to discuss how to raise the money.
2 All the options were discussed.
3 One suggestion was to ask the local council for help.
4 Another idea was to have some fun events.
5 It was agreed that organising events would take too long.
6 No decision was reached/could be reached about funding the project.

3
1 Advantages: the incinerator will generate electricity and dispose of waste
Disadvantages: it will cause a lot of pollution
2 Everyone in the area would sign a petition. Harry would research another kind of plant.
3 To present some alternative locations.

4
1 a meeting was held to decide
2 It was suggested
3 It was agreed
4 It was thought that
5 The point was made
6 It was proposed that
7 This option would be researched and discussed

Wordbuilding / Learning skills (page 67)

1
| 1 worrying | 3 refreshing | 5 inspiring | 7 touching |
| 2 confusing | 4 charming | 6 depressing | 8 tiring |

2
| 1 inventive | 3 creative | 5 productive | 7 protective |
| 2 persuasive | 4 competitive | 6 talkative | 8 unresponsive |

3, 4 and 5 Students' own answers.

6
1 a words	b sell	c fast	
2 a zero	b iconic	c exinct	
3 a mouth	b feel-good	c spread	d feature

Unit 9

9a (pages 68 and 69)

1
1 small village in Illinois
2 radio broadcaster; (an) actor
3 the Soviet Union
4 was not very clever or read the lines given to him
5 listen to people or make people feel special
6 economic growth

2 1 b 2 a 3 a 4 b 5 b 6 a

3
| 1 graduated | 3 follow or pursue | 5 did |
| 2 worked | 4 joining | 6 become |

4
1 the United Arab Emirates, the Netherlands
2 the Amazon River, the countryside, the Moon
3 the weekend, the spring
4 the police, the poor

All the other nouns take zero article.

5
| 1 the; the; – | 3 the; the | 5 the | 7 –; – | 9 the |
| 2 the; – | 4 the; – | 6 the | 8 –; – | 10 the |

6
| 1 /r/ | 3 /j/ | 5 /r/ | 7 /j/ | 9 /w/ |
| 2 /j/ | 4 /j/ | 6 /r/ | 8 /w/ | |

7
1 I guess I was lucky to do a subject that not many other people at college did. I studied plant sciences and after my course, I got a job as a research assistant at the Institute of Botany.
2 It's not easy to be an artist and make a living from it. You are always wondering if it would be better just to get a job with a regular income.
3 I was always told that having good qualifications and the right degree opens doors, but actually it's good communication skills that help you advance in an organisation.

8
| 1 background | 3 qualifications | 5 knowledge |
| 2 experience | 4 qualities | 6 talents |

9b (pages 70 and 71)

1
1 My mission is to find simple, inexpensive ways to monitor health
2 these medicines can cause liver damage
3 The small piece of paper is a low-tech tool
4 to attend university
5 I want all women to believe in themselves and know they can transform society or to encourage young women who attend university abroad to bring their skills back to their homelands

2 1 c 2 b 3 c 4 a 5 b 6 b

3 1 a 2 b 3 c 4 b 5 c 6 c

4
1 … which detects disease by analysing bodily fluids.
2 … who attend university abroad
3 … which show up in less than a minute
4 … costing just a penny
5 … pioneered by a team at Harvard University

5
1 The piece of paper, **which** is the size of a postage stamp, could save thousands of lives. or The piece of paper, **which** could save thousands of lives, is the size of a postage stamp.
2 The charity 'Diagnostics for All', **which** was co-founded by Sindi, produces the tool. or The charity 'Diagnostics for All', **which** produces the tool, was co-founded by Sindi.
3 The tool will be used in developing countries **where** it is difficult to find clinics.
4 People take powerful drugs, **which** can cause liver damage, to combat diseases.
5 The results show up on the paper, **whose** colour changes if there is a problem.
6 Sindi went to England **when** she was a young woman.
7 Sindi, **who** was the first Saudi woman to study biotechnology at Cambridge, later went to Harvard. or Sindi, **who** later went to Harvard, was the first Saudi woman to study biotechnology at Cambridge.
8 Sindi has become a role model for other women **who** want to follow her example.

6
1 Sindi's low-tech tool helps people **suffering from the negative effects of the drugs**.
2 People **living far away from hospitals and clinics** will benefit from this technology.
3 The same medicines, **designed to fight disease**, can also harm people.
4 Sindi, **determined to succeed**, studied up to twenty hours a day.
5 Sindi uses her own experience to inspire other women **wishing to become scientists**.
6 A new foundation, **launched** recently by Sindi, offers help to young women **wanting to follow a career in science**.

7
| 1 determination | 3 inspiration |
| 2 accomplishment | 4 passion |

8
1 passionate	4 patient	7 daring
2 articulate	5 independent	8 easy-going
3 analytical	6 adaptable	

9c (page 72)

1 1 W 2 W 3 W 4 W 5 W 6 M 7 M and W 8 W

2 1 T 2 T 3 F 4 F 5 T 6 T

3
| 1 adventur**ous** | 3 sens**itive** | 5 assert**ive** | 7 autocr**atic** |
| 2 effect**ive** | 4 car**ing** | 6 persuas**ive** | 8 inclus**ive** |

4a
| 1 e<u>ffec</u>tive | 3 a<u>sser</u>tive | 5 in<u>clu</u>sive |
| 2 <u>sen</u>sitive | 4 per<u>sua</u>sive | |

The stress always falls on the second syllable. The exception is 'sensitive', where it falls on the first syllable.

4b
| 1 pro<u>tec</u>tive | 3 per<u>cep</u>tive | 5 re<u>spon</u>sive |
| 2 cre<u>a</u>tive | 4 i<u>ma</u>ginative | 6 im<u>pul</u>sive |

5 1 j 2 a 3 c 4 h 5 b 6 e 7 f 8 g 9 d 10 i

9d (page 73)

1 1 in 2 with 3 at 4 of 5 to 6 with 7 on 8 about

2 A job to lead outdoor activities and expeditions for young people.

3 1 Applicant 1: good at working with young children
Applicant 2: canoeing, water sports and outdoor activities; good organisational skills
Applicant 3: good at a number of different sports; experienced PE teacher
2 Applicant 1: hasn't got experience working with this age group
Applicant 2: hasn't got experience of mountaineering
Applicant 3: hasn't got experience of leading expeditions

4 1 participating   4 doing
2 to leave   5 to work/on working
3 travelling   6 to find out/in finding out

6 Students' own answers.

9e (page74)

1 1 b 2 d 3 a 4 f 5 c 6 e

2 1 marketing jobs   3 she's highly qualified
2 Japanese and English

3a 1 My job involves advising a British supermarket on their market plan for Japan.
2 I was responsible for the 'Winnie the Pooh' account.
3 I translated marketing documents for various British and US companies.
4 I'm currently doing a distance learning MBA.

3b 1 Specialist website designer
2 Designing interactive website for local sports and leisure centre
3 Computer programmer, British Telecom
Designer, patient communications website, local hospital
Set up company in 2010
4 Buckingham Grammar School;
Liverpool University

Wordbuilding / Learning skills (page 75)

1 The verbs which do not collocate are:
1 do   3 get   5 acquire   7 own   9 earn
2 make   4 make   6 win   8 work   10 take on

2 1 took   4 had   7 got or gained
2 follow   5 get   8 acquire or learn
3 get or do   6 joined or set up

3 1 d 2 f 3 b 4 h 5 e 6 a 7 c 8 g

4 1 felt   3 acquire or get   5 semi-formal
2 definite article   4 yes

5 1 a a mahout b an explorer
2 step, leap, mankind
3 a the Atlantic Ocean d the USA e the Moon
4 c

Unit 10

10a (pages 76 and 77)

1 Speaker 1: e   Speaker 3: a
Speaker 2: d   Speaker 4: c

2 a 2 b 4 c 2 d 1 e 3 f 4

3 1 b 2 a 3 a 4 c 5 b 6 a

4 Possible answers:
1 take   5 will design or design
2 think   6 are always fighting
3 teach   7 squabbling
4 will follow or follow   8 argue or will argue

9 say   13 will be
10 helps or will help   14 always follow or will always follow
11 tend   15 often get or will often get
12 generally follow or will generally follow

5 1 She's always talking   4 He's always talking
2 He's always asking if   5 He's always playing
3 She's always spending ages   6 She's always leaving

6 1 brought   4 discipline   7 rebelled   10 reward
2 spoil   5 disobey   8 pestering
3 punished   6 nagging   9 give

7 Everything depends on what you see as the future role of your children. In other words, what is it that you are raising them to do?

Do you want them to be good members of society? If so, you will teach them values such as obeying the law, co-operating with others and generally being good citizens.

Or do you want them to be successful individuals? If so, you will help them to be free thinkers and to be independent.

Or is it important that they are good family members? Then you will teach them to respect their elders and to follow family traditions.

10b (pages 78 and 79)

1 c

2 1 b 2 c 3 a 4 a 5 c

3 1 used to eat   5 usually eat out
2 used to use   6 are used to seeing
3 are used to eating   7 used to eat
4 have got used to eating or usually eat   8 usually eat

4 1 didn't use to cook
2 used to cook
3 wanted
4 used to hang or would hang
5 was
6 had
7 used to cook or would cook
8 were used to doing or used to do

5a /uː/: blue, fortune, lunar, rude, suit, truce
/juː/: consume, humanity, humour, menu, used, usually

6 1 D/S, P 2 F, F, P 3 S/F, P 4 P, D

10c (page 80)

1 1 F 2 F 3 T 4 T 5 F 6 T

2 1 d 2 b

3 1 rather 2 Unlike 3 little 4 such 5 At worst

5 a common good   b common interest

6 Across: 4 ground 5 sense
Down: 1 knowledge 2 mistakes 3 interest 4 good

10d (page 81)

1 1 honeymoon 3 stag 5 bells 7 proposal
2 vows 4 veil 6 groom

2 1 It's a sign of wealth and social status.
2 For the bride not working.
3 the bride's family
4 the groom's family
5 They bring gifts.
6 clothes and jewellery

3 1 symbolises 3 customary 5 occasion 7 traditional
2 rule 4 marks 6 place 8 On

4 1 /z/ 3 /z/ 5 /s/ 7 /s/ 9 /z/ 11 /z/
2 /s/ 4 /s/ 6 /z/ 8 /s/ 10 /s/ 12 /z/

5 Students' own answers.

10e (page 82)

1 Possible answer:

Hi Annabelle

<u>Very good</u> to see you the other day. <u>Hope</u> you <u>got back</u> to Leipzig safely. I forgot to mention that <u>I'm</u> travelling to Poland next month on business to visit a supplier. <u>I've really got no idea</u> about business customs in Poland and wondered if there was anything <u>I should know especially</u>. For example, should I take some gifts with me? Will they be <u>put out</u> that I <u>don't</u> speak any Polish? I certainly <u>don't</u> want to <u>put my foot in it</u> with my hosts in any way.

I <u>don't</u> want to <u>bother</u> you, but if <u>you've got</u> a moment to write me a few words of advice, <u>I'd be really</u> grateful.

<u>All the best</u>

2 Possible answers:
1 Hi	8 big	15 About
2 Good to see	9 be embarrassing	16 It's
3 thanks	10 You'll	17 Hope
4 helping	11 seem *or* are	18 let me know
5 Unfortunately	12 That's	19 when you get back
6 here's	13 I'm sure	20 All the best
7 don't	14 they'll	

Wordbuilding / Learning skills (page 83)

1
1 bride and groom	7 bits and pieces
2 husband and wife	8 time and trouble
3 friends and family	9 plans and arrangements
4 suit and tie	10 pomp and ceremony
5 food and drink	11 fun and games
6 singing and dancing	12 life and soul

2
1 pomp and ceremony	4 life and soul
2 time and trouble	5 friends and family
3 bits and pieces	6 suit and tie

5
1 in	3 back	5 sense	7 foot
2 out	4 in	6 ground	8 hen

Unit 11

11a (pages 84 and 85)

1 c

2 1 b   2 c   3 c   4 a   5 c   6 a

3
1 document	3 seeks out	5 store
2 trace; record	4 express	6 save

4
1 succeeded in discovering	4 was able to help
2 were able to help	5 could bring
3 managed to build	6 couldn't save

5 Possible answers:
1 managed to find *or* was able to find
2 could speak *or* was able to speak
3 never managed to convince *or* never succeeded in convincing *or* were never able to convince
4 couldn't understand *or* wasn't able to understand
5 could express *or* was able to express
6 could remember *or* was able to remember *or* managed to remember *or* succeeded in remembering

6 1 c   2 f   3 h   4 g   5 d   6 a   7 b   8 e

7
1 pick (it) up
2 inspire *or* motivate *or* engage with
3 ignorant
4 have a basic grasp
5 engage with *or* grasp *or* pick up
6 take in *or* grasp

8a
1 **a** Munichi   **b** Wappo
2 **a** Swarthmore   **b** Pennsylvania
3 **a** Arunchal   **b** Koro
4 Chary
5 Floccinaucinihilipilification

8b **a** 5   **b** 2a   **c** 4   **d** 1b   **e** 3b

11b (pages 86 and 87)

1 **a** 2   **b** 1   **c** 3

2 1 T   2 F   3 F   4 N   5 F   6 N   7 F   8 T   9 T

3
1 blank (something) out	4 turned out (that)
2 ran into	5 come across
3 came up (to)	6 get away with

4 Paragraph 1
1 My sister and I **were just about to go** to bed … *or* **were just going to go** to bed …
2 My sister **was going to say** goodnight … *or* **was about to say** goodnight …

Paragraph 2
3 I **would have asked** his name …
4 I **was supposed to know** …

Paragraph 3
5 who **was going to give** evidence in court … *or* **was supposed to give** evidence in court … *or* **was about to give evidence** in court …
6 her neighbour **wouldn't get away with** it … *or* **wasn't going to get away with** it …

5
1 was going to write *or* would have written
2 was just about to book; would be full
3 would speak
4 would have lasted *or* was supposed to last; were about to finish *or* were going to finish
5 was going to take *or* would have taken *or* was supposed to take
6 was just about to ask *or* was just going to ask

6a
1 I was <u>going</u> to <u>email</u> him, but I decided it would better to speak face to face.
2 He was <u>supposed</u> to get here <u>early</u>, but he's already ten minutes late.
3 I <u>would</u> have come by <u>train</u>, but there's a strike on at the moment.
4 She said she would be <u>pleased</u> if I talked to him, but she seemed <u>really</u> angry.
5 I was <u>about</u> to <u>buy</u> a flat, but Katie said I could rent hers for six months while she was away.
6 Liz was <u>going</u> to be in charge of the project, but now she's just acting as an advisor.

6b
1 I was going to email him, but I decided it would better to speak <u>face to face.</u>
2 He was supposed to get here early, but he's already <u>ten minutes late.</u>
3 I would have come by train, but there's a <u>strike</u> on at the moment.
4 She said she would be pleased if I talked to him, but she seemed <u>really angry.</u>
5 I was about to buy a flat, but Katie said I could <u>rent hers</u> for six months while she was away.
6 Liz was going to be in charge of the project, but now she's just acting as an <u>advisor.</u>

7 1 c   2 d   3 a   4 e   5 b

11c (page 88)

1
1 border collie	3 dolphin	5 scrub-jay
2 crow	4 Bonobo monkey	

2 **a** 3   **b** 4   **c** 1   **d** 5   **e** 2

3 **a** 2   **b** 3   **c** 5   **d** 1   **e** 4

4
1 smart	3 playful	5 mischevious
2 inventive	4 expressive	

5
1 walk	3 mistakes	5 lesson	7 way
2 late	4 tricks	6 live	8 heart

11d (page 89)

1
1 mean	3 explain	5 saying	7 take
2 speak	4 'm	6 give	8 catch *or* hear

2
1 Greek and Roman history
2 He doesn't have as much background knowledge as the other students.
3 Reading some history *or* a book by Herodotus.

3
1 what the course is going to be about
2 no previous knowledge of ancient history is needed
4 stories like the war at Troy and so on
5 a book I could read now, outside class
6 Herodotus

4 1 me 5 me 6 me
The other sentences don't need an indirect personal object.

6 Students' own answers.

11e (page 90)

1 1 c 2 e 3 d 4 b 5 a
The writer's application for a course has been rejected even though he/she applied before the deadline.

2
1 While we sympathise with your situation, it is too late to do anything about it now.
2 Although you sent your form in before the deadline, we had already received too many applications.
3 You say in your letter that we have no right to do this, but in actual fact, the college has the right to close the application process early.
4 We don't 'make up the rules as we go along' as you suggest. On the contrary, we are very careful to follow the rules.
5 Whereas most colleges would keep your application fee, we are refunding it to you.

3 Model answer:

Dear Sir/Madam

I am writing to inform you that I will be unable to attend the accountancy course (B102) this term owing to a misunderstanding.

When I enrolled for the course, I had assumed it was an evening class. In actual fact it turns out to be on Tuesdays between 10 a.m. and 12.30 p.m. I have asked my employer if it would be possible to release me for this period each Tuesday. Although they would like to do this, they say that the timing makes it impossible.

While I realise that this is probably my fault for not reading the timetable carefully enough, I hope you will be sympathetic. I hope to enrol on a future course, but for the moment I would be grateful if you could refund the course fees I have paid.

I look forward to hearing from you.

Yours faithfully

Mark Riley

Wordbuilding / Learning skills / (page 91)

1 1 e *or* d 2 a 3 d *or* e 4 c 5 b 6 f
2, 3, 4 and 5 Students' own answers.
6 Across: 1 engage 5 selective 7 tip 8 external 10 catch
Down: 2 grasp 3 succeed 4 botanist 6 ignorant
8 error 9 late

Unit 12

12a (pages 92 and 93)

1
1 savers and spenders
2 No, these stereotypes are too simplistic.

2 1 b 2 a 3 c 4 a 5 b 6 c

3
fund – finance	wages – salaries
prudent – careful	wasteful – extravagant
transaction – deal	

4
1 hard up	3 reasonable; cheap	5 earnings	7 loaded
2 afford	4 pricey	6 well off	

R	H	P	I	M	O	I	N
E	A	R	N	I	N	G	S
A	R	I	C	C	F	O	T
S	D	C	H	E	A	P	O
O	U	E	S	O	F	U	L
N	P	Y	B	A	F	L	E
A	W	E	L	L	O	F	F
B	I	L	E	F	R	A	T
L	O	A	D	E	D	E	S
E	S	T	O	N	R	I	A

5
1 just / also	3 even / also	5 only
2 as well / too; only	4 also	

6
1 Some people believe that if you go through life ONLY saving money, you will never have any fun. *or* Some people believe that if you ONLY go through life saving money, you will never have any fun.
2 Some people carry on spending money EVEN when they can't afford to.
3 You can guard against bad times by putting aside JUST a small amount of money each week.
4 If ONLY a few people save money, the banks won't have any to lend.
5 I'm not the only person who has debts. Other people ALSO have them. / Other people have them ALSO.
6 Attitude to money is partly a cultural thing, but it has something to do with your upbringing AS WELL.
7 Some people are careful with money in hard times and in good times TOO.
8 Borrowers admit that EVEN they sometimes borrow money irresponsibly. EVEN borrowers admit that they sometimes borrow money irresponsibly.

7
1 payments	3 investment	5 grant	7 debts
2 spending	4 loan	6 borrowing	8 earnings

8a I think that people often get into debt because they want a lifestyle that they can't really afford.
It's a lifestyle which is sold to them constantly through advertisements, for example on TV and in magazines.
This desire to have a better lifestyle can affect some governments too. They want to improve their citizens' standard of living so that people will vote for them again.

12b (pages 94 and 95)

1 a

2 1 F 2 T 3 T 4 T 5 N 6 T 7 N 8 T

3
1 track	3 sufficient	5 of choice	7 blacksmith
2 striking	4 competent	6 infirm	8 trade

4
1 have people work	5 got the slaves to work
2 get their work done	6 had their slaves work
3 get your labourers to work	7 got them to learn
4 had 10,000 slaves a year sent	8 had cheap cotton shipped

5a
/ʃ/: abolished, sugar	/ʒ/: decision, usually
/tʃ/: cheap, riches	/dʒ/: carriage, wages

6
1 fit	3 decorate	5 fixed	7 plaster
2 put	4 assemble	6 tiled	8 hang

7 1 b 2 f 3 a 4 d 5 c 6 e

12c (page 96)

1 b

2 1 c 2 b 3 b 4 c 5 a

3 1 hard up   3 hard bargain   5 hard done by
   2 hard-headed   4 hard feelings

4 1 **a** is running hard   3 **a** hardly know
   1 **b** is hardly running   4 **a** thought hard
   2 **a** hardly works *or* is hardly   4 **b** hardly thought
      working   5 **a** hardly tried
   2 **b** works hard *or* is working hard   5 **b** tried hard

12d (page 97)

1 1 d 2 b 3 f 4 a 5 c 6 e

2 1 a leaving party for a colleague   2 a reduction in the price

3 1 honest   3 hoping   5 face   7 appreciate
   2 mind   4 would   6 shoes   8 key

4 1 Can I just <u>explain</u> our <u>position</u>?
   2 To tell you the <u>truth</u>, …
   3 If you look at it from <u>our side</u>, …
   4 That's going to be a <u>bit</u> of a <u>sticking point</u>.
   5 To be <u>perfectly honest</u>, …
   6 What you have to <u>bear</u> in <u>mind</u> is …

5 1 I'm afraid that would be difficult for me.
   2 Would you move a bit on the price?
   3 Would you be willing to negotiate?
   4 I would need to have some kind of guarantee.
   5 When would you need to know?
   6 I wouldn't want to put you to any trouble.

12e (page 98)

1 The report is about the catering for the Annual General Meeting.

2 1 • How much food do we need to provide?
      • Cost?
      • Any special dietary needs?
   2 • Hot food: about £10 per person
      • Cold food: about £7 per person
   3 I propose that we go with Angel Foods. They seemed to understand better what we want, and I think they will do it all for a better price.

3 **Summary**
I visited our caterer to discuss the arrangements for our office party on 12th December.

Food
  • Sandwiches: £6 per person
  • Sandwiches and cold canapés: £8 per person
  • Sandwiches and hot canapés: £10 per person

Drinks
  • The caterer can provide drinks or we can buy our own.
  • Charge: £1 per person.

Recommendation
I propose we go for the mixture of sandwiches and cold canapés, and provide our own drinks.

Wordbuilding / Learning skills (page 99)

1 1 the rich   5 the elderly   8 the deaf
   2 the unemployed   6 the famous   9 the illiterate
   3 the poor   7 the blind   10 the sick
   4 the homeless

2 1 P 2 N 3 N 4 N 5 X 6 P 7 X 8 X 9 N 10 N

3 and 4 Students' own answers.

5 1 relative   3 cleaner   5 end
   2 investing   4 hunter   6 spending
   Word: RICHES

IELTS practice test

Listening Test answer key

1 C   so my flatmate was saying

2 B   Just the morning or the afternoon would suit me fine

3 A   you'd have to sign up like anyone else – and there's a monthly fee

4 A   tips on how to put a CV together

5 D   a seminar led by one of the big recruitment agencies

6 JAYNES   J.A.Y.N.E.S

7 Business studies   M: Which faculty's that? Economics? F: Business Studies actually

8 technical translations   This time she's doing technical translations

9 construction industry   He's going to be talking about openings in the construction industry

10 Geology   He's working in the Geology department

11 C   visitors can walk along a pathway not far from the base

12 B   an adult single ticket would cost £6.50 in the summer months and £5.50 at other times of year, whereas a family ticket would cost either £24.00 or £20.00.

13 C/D   explore the universe using hands-on activities

14 D/C   the glass-walled café with outside terrace

15 Botany   it wasn't the Astrophysics department that bought it though, but the Botany department.

16 meteor shower   installed just in time to observe a meteor shower

17 1947   in 1947 the 218-foot Transit Telescope

18 Mark 1 / one / I   This was named the Mark One Telescope

19 solar system   a scale model of the solar system

20 World Heritage   to place Jodrell Bank on the UK shortlist for consideration as a site with World Heritage status

21 A   how you balance these two aspects is up to you

22 C   I hadn't even chosen a speciality – that made it tough.

23 B   I'd have done better with a straight four-week split.

24 A   talk to people ... that's how I found the one I went with

25 emergency   I went for emergency

26 beach   photos ... of the beach that drew me to Belize

27 300,000   with 300,000 people

28 (the) North   up north where I was

29 Cuban   a lot of the doctors working there were actually Cuban

30 teaching (the staff)   I'd rather think of teaching the staff

31 One/1 metre/meter   that grows to around one metre

32 Dark brown   the male ... is a dark brown

33 Silver(-)grey/grey   the female is distinguishable by its silver-grey skin

34 (dense) undergrowth   has a preference for dense undergrowth

35 Lizard(s)   tends to rely on lizards as its main source of food

36 Bird   Bird island, the place where one was eventually spotted

37 (six-week) survey   They commissioned a six-week survey

38 100   supporting a racer population of around 100 individuals

39 B/C   The right kind of habitat is not found over a wide area

40 C/B   although the snake's habitat does remain vulnerable to hurricane damage

Reading Test answer key

1 TRUE   Start by identifying the appropriate granting body to contact
2 TRUE   check ... the deadline for the submission of proposals
3 FALSE   Your proposal should be written out in the format stipulated
4 FALSE   It's a good idea to propose only those objectives that you feel confident of achieving within the grant period
5 NOT GIVEN   (there is no mention of whether this is advisable or not)
6 TRUE   cover what is already known about the problem in scientific literature
7 FALSE   In addition, many forms now have a section ... required to describe how the research is likely to contribute to economic development
8 NOT GIVEN   (there is no mention of whether they do this or not)
9 TRUE   state clearly that you're aware of the limitations of your approach
10 FALSE   describe briefly any particular strengths of your laboratory
11 iii   like to see a concise description of the results of any work you have already carried out
12 v   your application should include latitude, longitude, elevation, vegetation ...
13 vii   Describe how you plan to identify people to take part in experiments
14 ii   lab procedures ... a brief description of the various analytical techniques that you will carry out
15 vi   how it will be entered on a computerised database and what software will be used
16 viii   the partners with whom you intend to work
17 C   evidence for at least 15 separate occasions when it acted as a home
18 B   predate other known examples of plant matting by approximately 50,000 years
19 A   a tree whose foliage contains chemicals that kill biting insects. Dr Wadley thus thinks ... mattresses on which the inhabitants slept.
20 A   a range of hitherto unknown artefacts ... pictograms
21 C   a range of hitherto unknown artefacts ... arrows
22 D   a range of hitherto unknown artefacts ... needles
23 (a/the) tree(s)   They probably settled in trees at night
24 climbing   they still retained features useful for climbing, such as curved fingers and long arms
25 chimpanzees   just as chimpanzees do today
26 fire   once hominids learned how to control fire they discovered they could sleep on the ground
27 grass   Neanderthals were also building grass beds
28 cellulose   *Macrotermes* species live on cellulose
29 gardens   by cultivating gardens for fungi
30 (digestible) nutrients   which can turn it into digestible nutrients
31 heat   heat from the fungi's metabolism and termites' bodies
32 (central) chimney   causes stagnant air ... to rise up a central chimney
33 base   air is sucked in at the base
34 humidity   their temperature and humidity closely controlled
35 TRUE   This simple ... idea spawned at least one artificial imitation
36 TRUE   rules out any kind of buoyant flow ... showed little evidence of steady, convective air circulation
37 NOT GIVEN   (there is no mention of their methodology)
38 TRUE   the mound functions as a giant lung
39 FALSE   Turner thinks there's something to be gleaned from the termites' approach.
40 FALSE   idea among the biologists that architects could learn much from us. I think the opposite is also true

How to mark the Writing Test

Task 1

There are four criteria for marking the Part One tasks, which are equally weighted.

Task achievement

This is an assessment of how well the student has fulfilled the task.

A successful task will:
■ include at least the minimum number of words
■ have a text structure appropriate to a letter
■ be relevant to the context established in the input material
■ achieve the writer's intended purpose
■ cover the functions indicated in the bullet points

Coherence and cohesion

This is an assessment of how clear and fluent the writing is.

A successful task will:
■ be appropriately organised
■ successfully link information and ideas
■ contain logical sequencing
■ make effective use of cohesive devices

Lexical resource

This is an assessment of the use of vocabulary.

A successful task will:
■ include a range of relevant vocabulary
■ use vocabulary accurately
■ use vocabulary in an appropriate way

Grammatical resource

This is an assessment of the use of grammar.

A successful task will:
■ use an appropriate range of grammatical forms at sentence level
■ use grammatical forms accurately

Task 2

There are four criteria for marking the Part Two tasks, which are equally weighted.

Task response

This is an assessment of how well the student has responded to the task.

A successful task will:
■ make clear the writer's position on the issues raised in a question or statement
■ develop arguments to support that position

- support the arguments with evidence and examples
- include at least the minimum number of words

Coherence and cohesion

This is an assessment of how clear and fluent the writing is.

A successful task will:
- be appropriately organised
- successfully link information and ideas
- contain logical sequencing
- make effective use of cohesive devices

Lexical resource

This is an assessment of the use of vocabulary.

A successful task will:
- include a range of relevant vocabulary
- use vocabulary accurately
- use vocabulary in an appropriate way

Grammatical resource

This is an assessment of the use of grammar.

A successful task will:
- use an appropriate range of grammatical forms at sentence level
- use grammatical forms accurately

How to mark the Speaking Test

The speaking test is an assessment of how effectively students can communicate in English.

There are four criteria for marking the Speaking Test, which are equally weighted.

Fluency and coherence

This is the ability to:
- talk at a consistently normal speed
- link ideas and language together in logical sequences
- use the language features which create coherent, connected speech

Lexical resource

This is the ability to:
- use a range of relevant vocabulary
- use words appropriately to convey meaning
- use paraphrase strategies when required

Grammatical range and accuracy

This is the ability to:

use a range of grammatical forms appropriately

use grammatical forms accurately

Pronunciation

This is the ability to:
- use a range of phonological features to convey meaning
- produce intelligible individual sounds
- use stress, rhythm and intonation effectively

Listening Test audioscript

 [2.53]

PRESENTER: In this test you'll hear a number of different recordings and you'll have to answer questions on what you hear. There will be time for you to read the instructions and questions and you will have a chance to check your answers. The recording will be played once only. The test is in four sections.

Now turn to section one on page 100 of your book. You will hear a student called Martin telling his friend about a careers day which is being held in the city where they are studying. First you have some time to look at questions 1 to 5. You will see that there is also an example which has been done for you.

Now we shall begin. You should answer the questions as you listen, because you will not hear the recording a second time. Listen carefully and answer questions 1 to 5.

WOMAN: Hi, Martin. Did you hear about the careers day that the college is holding? My tutor was just talking about it.

MARTIN: Yeah, apparently there's something on the notice board about it, or so my flatmate was saying.

WOMAN: Well, it's probably this leaflet he saw pinned up there. Look, it's got all the details.

MARTIN: Great. Is it being held in the college then? I heard they were going to hire space in the Town Hall.

WOMAN: Really? I think you must be thinking of some other event. Our college is actually sharing the day with the technical university, and they're putting the day on at their campus. It's going to be outside in the grounds if the weather's nice.

MARTIN: Look, it goes on all day from ten till five. I wouldn't want to hang around that long though, just the morning or the afternoon would suit me fine. I start getting bored after a couple of hours at these things.

WOMAN: Well, look at the programme of talks – it'll help you decide which.

MARTIN: Anyway, there's a website with all the talks on, so it doesn't matter if you miss some of them.

WOMAN: Well, the event is free to students enrolled at the college, but the website isn't: you'd have to sign up like anybody else, and there's a monthly fee. But then you do see stuff from other similar events around the country too.

MARTIN: Sounds good. There are some sessions on in the lunchtime too. Look. And it's not the usual talks by old students or videos about voluntary work in other countries either. You can get tips on how to put a CV together or go to a seminar led by one of the big recruitment agencies.

WOMAN: Right. My careers advisor was recommending those when I met her for my one-to-one advice session the other day.

MARTIN: Should be good then.

PRESENTER: Before you listen to the rest of the conversation, you have some time to read questions 6 to 10.

Now listen and answer questions 6 to 10.

MARTIN: So what are the main talks on the programme, then?

WOMAN: Well, each faculty's put up one speaker. Our college in the morning and the technical university in the afternoon. But the speakers aren't only talking about stuff relevant to those subjects.

MARTIN: Sure. So let's see. It starts at ten and the Law faculty is putting up Professor Jaynes.

WOMAN: The famous judge?

MARTIN: No, you're thinking of James. This is Jaynes, J . A . Y . N . E . S. And he's talking about contracts of employment.

WOMAN: Oh right. Could be interesting though.

MARTIN: Maybe. But eleven o'clock you've got Professor Smith talking about internships – that should be more interesting. She lectures in accountancy, apparently. So which faculty's that? Economics?

WOMAN: Business Studies actually.

MARTIN: Oh yes, of course. Then Dr Wentworth is representing the Languages faculty at eleven. I heard her give a really good talk on cross-cultural misunderstandings last term – you know gestures and stuff you can get wrong – it was brilliant. But this time, she's doing technical translations.

WOMAN: Oh right. Yeah, she's a good speaker.

MARTIN: Then after lunch, there's Dr Shah from the Engineering faculty. It says here he's an expert in computer modelling, but he's going to be talking about openings in the construction industry.

WOMAN: Shame, I'd rather hear about the models.

MARTIN: Me too. Then there's Dr Bellucci from Sports Science – she's doing something on the Olympic Games which should be interesting – all the different jobs from different disciplines that are involved.

WOMAN: Right. And then it's our old friend Dr Fulton doing interview techniques. He's working in the Geology department at the technical university now, and they've put him up for this. Though when he was here, he was in the faculty of Geography.

MARTIN: Still he's a great speaker – always gets a laugh.

WOMAN: So what do you think ...

PRESENTER: Now turn to Section 2 on page 102 of your book. You will hear some information about Jodrell Bank, a famous radio telescope which is part of the University of Manchester. First you have some time to look at questions 11 to 14.

Now listen and answer questions 11 to 14.

MAN: Good evening. I'm here to tell you about the Jodrell Bank Observatory, which has been a world leader in radio astronomy since the second half of the twentieth century. The site is part of the University of Manchester and there's also an arboretum with over 2,500 rare trees. A visitor centre provides information about both the famous radio telescope and the trees.

The giant Lovell Telescope that stands on the site is an internationally renowned and awe-inspiring landmark. This is a radio telescope so visitors cannot look through it directly. The observatory buildings are also still in use for operating the telescope so are not usually open to the public. But the visitor centre provides a good view of the telescope and visitors can walk along a pathway not far from the base, where they will find plenty of notices providing information about the history of the telescope and how it works. The centre also provides opportunities to meet the scientists who work at the Observatory.

The visitor centre also provides activities for visitors of all ages. Admission prices at the centre vary according to the type of ticket and the season in which the visit is made. For example, an adult single ticket would cost £6.50 in the summer months and £5.50 at other times of year, whereas a family ticket would cost either £24 or £20. An annual ticket is available for individuals at £19.50 and for families at £60. Concessionary tickets are available at all times for children, students and retired people.

In terms of facilities available at the visitor centre, these are divided between two buildings: the Planet Pavilion, where you'll find the entrance as well as the glass-walled café with outside terrace – you get amazing views of the telescope from there. There's also a gift shop and a small exhibition space where visitors can learn about the planets. The second building is the Space Pavilion, which is the main exhibition area. Here visitors can find answers to the wonders of the universe, listen to the sound of the Big Bang and explore the universe using hands-on activities. As many returning visitors are aware, our planetarium was demolished in 2003, along with the old visitor centre. But we are looking to secure funding to restore this feature in the not-too-distant future.

Presenter: Before you hear the rest of the presentation, you have some time to look at questions 15 to 20.

Now listen and answer questions 15 to 20.

MAN: Next, a bit about the history of the telescope. It's named after Sir Bernard Lovell, who was a pioneer in the study of astrophysics in the twentieth century. The site itself, which is about fifteen miles south of the other university buildings in Manchester, first came into the university's possession in 1939. It wasn't the Astrophysics department that bought it, though, but the Botany department who were looking for a place to cultivate wild plants. In 1945, Bernard Lovell was given some equipment to use in his work, including a radar. But because of electrical interference from trams passing the university buildings, it didn't work properly in central Manchester, so he asked to move it to Jodrell Bank instead. It was installed just in time to observe a meteor shower that was visible that year.

Over the next few years, Lovell installed other equipment on the site, including an aerial on a searchlight mount in 1946, and in 1947, the 218-foot Transit Telescope – at the time the largest in the world. This telescope was superseded by a larger and more up-to-date model in 1957. This was named the Mark One Telescope, later upgraded and eventually renamed the Lovell Telescope in honour of Sir Bernard. This telescope became famous in the 1960s for tracking manned and unmanned space missions, as well as providing information about astronomy itself. And the telescope remains a world leader in this field.

Further developments followed in the 1960s and 1970s, including a teaching telescope for use by undergraduates, and the creation of the arboretum in 1972. This features national collections of various rare trees and other plants as well as a scale model of the solar system.

More recent developments at the site have included the opening of a new Discovery Centre in 2011, an event which coincided with a decision to place Jodrell Bank on the UK shortlist for consideration as a site with World Heritage status. In July that year the site also hosted a rock concert called 'Live from Jodrell Bank'. These are excellent examples of how the scientists at Jodrell Bank have always worked hard to engage with the wider community and increase the impact of their science.

PRESENTER: Now turn to Section 3 on page 103 of your book. You will hear an interview with a medical student called Damian, who is talking about his elective, a period of work experience he did overseas as part of his degree course. First you have some time to look at questions 21 to 24.

Now listen and answer questions 21 to 24.

WOMAN: Hi, Damian.

DAMIAN: Hi.

WOMAN: Thanks for coming to talk to college radio about your elective. Now that's a period of work experience in a hospital you do in your final year as a medical student, isn't it?

DAMIAN: That's right. The idea is that being a doctor is about understanding the psycho-social factors involved in each patient, as well as the medical ones. You do an elective in a speciality, to explore it in greater breadth and depth, and that's especially interesting when the placement's abroad.

WOMAN: So is it a sort of working holiday really?

DAMIAN: No. I wouldn't say that. But electives do also give you the opportunity to travel and have fun. How you balance these two aspects is up to you. Whilst in Belize, I learnt to scuba dive, climbed Mayan ruins and explored the jungle, not something you can say about every medical placement!

WOMAN: And it's up to you to organise the whole thing, isn't it?

DAMIAN: That's right. Many students have problems when it comes to organising an elective. For some it's the first time they've travelled alone or the first experience of being exposed to different cultures. I was cool with all that, but it's important to choose your speciality well. I had no idea where I wanted to go because I hadn't even chosen a speciality, so that made it tough.

WOMAN: Do you have to spend the whole period in one place, or can you split it up?

DAMIAN: You can choose. I chose to divide mine into a six-week placement abroad and a two-week placement at home in the UK. Many people would argue that a two-week placement doesn't give you enough time to fit into a team and gain relevant experience, and I'd go along with that. With the benefit of hindsight, I'd have done better with a straight four-week split.

WOMAN: And where can you go for help with these decisions?

DAMIAN: Well, many companies will organise elective placements for you, as well as providing cover and support ... at a price! But there are lots of companies out there, and I've heard that if you're willing to hunt around, you can find some reasonably priced deals. It's always worth asking round though. If you can talk to people about companies they've used, you can check whether those companies are any good or not. That's how I found the one I went with and I've no complaints.

PRESENTER: Before you hear the rest of the conversation, you have some time to look at questions 25 to 30.

Now listen and answer questions 25 to 30.

WOMAN: So Damian, tell us about your placement in Belize.

DAMIAN: Well, having been undecided for a long time between specialising in surgery or emergency medicine, I went for emergency, because I thought it would give me a broader experience than surgery would. My first choice of country would've been Jamaica, but they only had places for dermatology and obstetrics, so that's how Belize came up. I'd never really heard of the country before.

WOMAN: And was it a company that helped you?

DAMIAN: Yes, they provided photos of medical and non-medical facilities in a couple of different countries in the Caribbean and Central America. In the end, it wasn't the photos of the hospital, but those of the beach that drew me to Belize – perhaps I shouldn't admit to that!

WOMAN: So tell us a bit about working there.

DAMIAN: The health system in Belize is a mixed one of both public and private. The government subsidises a significant proportion of health care for the average Belizean, although there's a limited number of hospitals with in-patient facilities. Belize has an area of 22,000 square kilometres with only 300,000 people spread sparsely around it, and a big town is one with about 20,000 inhabitants. It means that a significant percentage of the population is rural based and nowhere near a free national hospital.

WOMAN: Right.

DAMIAN: I was one of three British students placed by the company; the two others were in the south of the country and I think they had a different experience, but up in the north where I was, the biggest frustration was that despite Belize being an English-speaking country, the default language was Spanish, because a lot of the doctors working there are actually Cuban. I speak French, but not Spanish, so when consultations weren't in English, I needed the doctor to explain what had been said.

WOMAN: Would you go to Belize again?

DAMIAN: Yes. And people do sometimes get jobs in the places they've been to on electives. But, next time I wouldn't go with the idea of being a hospital doctor, I'd rather think of teaching the staff. But I think I could've made better use of my clinical experience if I'd learned basic Spanish – so that would be a priority before I went back.

WOMAN: Damian. Thanks.

PRESENTER: Now turn to Section 4 on page 104 of your book. You will hear a student giving a presentation about the Antiguan Racer Snake, a rare species living on a Caribbean island. First you have some time to look at questions 31 to 35.

Now listen and answer questions 31 to 35.

WOMAN: In my presentation today I want to talk about the rarest snake in the world – the Antiguan Racer Snake – an animal that has been rescued from the brink of extinction by the efforts of conservationists.

The snake is one of the racer snake family that is found in various regions across the Americas. It's a small harmless snake that grows to around one metre, with the female being slightly longer than the male.

Many of the racer snakes found in the Caribbean region, and especially those in the southern states of the USA, are black in colour, whereas the Antiguan racer is lighter. The male is closer in colouring to the black racers, being a dark brown, whilst the female is distinguishable by its silver-grey skin.

The Antiguan racer is found in various habitats, including sandy beaches and rocky ridges, but has a preference for dense undergrowth, which is one of the reasons why it's relatively rarely seen.

In terms of diet, the Antiguan racer is very choosy. Other racer snakes feed on small mammals, and amphibians such as frogs, but the Antiguan sub-species tends to rely on lizards as its main source of food. Maybe this is one of the reasons why it's an endangered species, although there is little evidence that its prey has ever been in short supply.

PRESENTER: Before you hear the rest of the presentation, you have some time to look at questions 36 to 40.

Now listen and answer questions 36 to 40.

WOMAN: By the end of the twentieth century, it was feared that the Antiguan racer, which was once common on the large island of Antigua after which it's named, had indeed become extinct. And this was probably the case. The snake had once been common on the neighbouring island of Barbuda too, but hadn't survived the human development of these large islands. But the local inhabitants were convinced that the snakes might be surviving on one of the smaller islands off the Antiguan coast, such as Rabbit Island or Crump Island, or on Bird Island – the place where one was eventually spotted in 1995.

The tiny island was uninhabited and looked after by the Antiguan Forestry Unit, which was keen for scientists to establish how many snakes might be living there. They commissioned a six-week survey, to be carried out by one of the conservationists who had made the discovery, Mark Day, who later went on to work for the conservation body, Fauna and Flora International.

What was established by his work was that the small island, only measuring some 18,000 square metres, was supporting a racer population of around 100 individuals. The rarest snake in the world was alive and well, but seriously endangered. In 1996, a conservation project was set up to ensure its survival.

And with the current population standing at around 500 snakes, this project has been hailed a success. A captive breeding programme has been effective in increasing numbers, even though it was adversely affected by disease at first. Reintroduction to other nearby islands, and to the mainland of Antigua, has meant eradicating the rats that had decimated the snake population in the twentieth century – a programme that has worked, although the snake's habitat does remain vulnerable to hurricane damage. Now that the species is officially protected, there are unlikely to be further incursions of tourist development into its natural habitat, another cause of its earlier decline. The right kind of habitat is not found over a wide area, though, and this will eventually limit the extent of the snake population. So before I go on to ...